The Invincible Twelfth

The 12th South Carolina Infantry of the Gregg-McGowan Brigade, Army of Northern Virginia

Benjamin L. Cwayna

SB
Savas Beatie
California

First edition, first printing

Library of Congress Cataloging-in-Publication Data

Names: Cwayna, Benjamin L., 1980- author.
Title: The Invincible Twelfth: The 12th South Carolina Infantry of the Gregg-McGowan Brigade, Army of Northern Virginia / Benjamin L Cwayna.
Description: El Dorado Hills, CA : Savas Beatie, [2025] | Includes bibliographical references. | Summary: "Dixon Barnes instilled discipline and strong leadership in the unit and began a transformational process that turned the raw recruits into some of the Confederacy's most reliable soldiers. Through the words of its soldiers and officers, the stories of long and arduous marches, lack of food, horrendous and unimaginable carnage in battle, and a singular focus on continuing the struggle to gain independence at any cost and under innumerable odds takes shape. Former Confederate Brigadier General Samuel McGowan lauded the 12th South Carolina Infantry as "The finest of that immortal army," "foremost in the charge," and "the invincible Twelfth." This is the story of a remarkable regiment which has long deserved to have its story told"-- Provided by publisher.
Identifiers: LCCN 2024061014 | ISBN 9781611217360 (hardcover) | ISBN 9781611217377 (ebook)
Subjects: LCSH: Confederate States of America. Army. South Carolina Infantry Regiment, 12th. | Confederate States of America. Army. Gregg's Brigade. | Confederate States of America. Army. McGowan's Brigade. | Confederate States of America. Army of Northern Virginia. | Confederate States of America--History, Military. | United States--History--Civil War, 1861-1865.
Classification: LCC E577.5 12th .C93 2025 | DDC 973.7/4757--dc23/eng/20250220
LC record available at https://lccn.loc.gov/2024061014

SB
Savas Beatie
989 Governor Drive, Suite 101
El Dorado Hills, CA 95762
916-941-6896 / sales@savasbeatie.com / www.savasbeatie.com

All of our titles are available at special discount rates for bulk purchases in the United States. Contact us for information.

Printed and bound in the United Kingdom

For my parents, Daniel and Patsy Cwayna, whose unending support for my passion for history is appreciated more than they could possibly know.

For my grandparents, Bud and Vera Apple, who fostered in me a way of life that harkened back to a simpler, more honorable time.

For Robert "Cap'n Bob" Helsel, whose zeal and knowledge of history inspired a young, impressionable mind.

And for my son, Grant Benjamin Cwayna, who is the greatest joy in my life.

Table of Contents

List of Maps

Photos have been placed throughout the text for the convenience of the reader.

Foreword

IT WAS WITH a heavy heart that Robert E. Lee exited the McLean House on April 9, 1865, after agreeing to surrender the Army of Northern Virginia. The men in Lee's celebrated army were no less dejected by the moment, although after nearly a year of having their ranks relentlessly truncated by Ulysses S. Grant's forces, finally watching the Confederate capital of Richmond fall, and finding a last-gasp escape route to North Carolina blocked, only the specific timing and circumstances of their defeat were much of a surprise. On April 10, Lee sought to salve his men's wounded pride with assurances that the enemy's "overwhelming numbers and resources" had precipitated this grievous outcome and not any shortcomings on their part in soldierly skill, courage, or commitment to southern independence.

Lee needed only to look at the thinned ranks of the 12th South Carolina to buttress the conviction he long held that his army "would be invincible if it could be properly organized and officered" and there "never were such men in an army before." Roughly 1,400 men total would serve in the 12th South Carolina during the Civil War. Yet, as Benjamin L. Cwayna notes in *The Invincible Twelfth*, the regiment counted only ten officers and 145 men in its ranks at the time of Lee's final Appomattox Court House surrender. In all, 414 men in the 12th South Carolina gave their lives in the pursuit of southern independence, its record as a hard-fighting unit notable by the higher number of casualties incurred in combat rather than disease, including three commanders.

Few Confederate regiments could say they had found themselves in more hot places on some of the hottest battlefields of the war than the 12th South Carolina.

After seeing action in minor operations along the Atlantic Coast, the regiment was called to Virginia and assigned to a unit that would secure ultimate fame as the Gregg–McGowan brigade, fighting alongside four other Palmetto State units in a new division led by Maj. Gen. Ambrose Powell Hill. Being part of Hill's so-called "Light Division"—steered as such by some of the most aggressive, and able, members of the command team Lee forged in 1862—ensured that the 12th South Carolina would find its eagerness for the fray gratified.

Under the command of Col. Dixon Barnes, the 12th began earning recognition as a fighting powerhouse during Lee's first Army of Northern Virginia victory at Gaines's Mill on June 27, 1862. At Second Manassas later that summer, the regiment lost more than half its number fighting off Union assaults near Sudley Church on August 29. After participating in Maryland campaign operations at Harpers Ferry that produced the greatest surrender of United States forces until 1942, the Light Division rushed to Sharpsburg, where the 12th South Carolina helped stave off an outright Confederate defeat by delivering a timely attack on the Union left, though it regrettably lost Colonel Barnes in the process. At Fredericksburg in December 1862, the courage and tactical skill of the regiment and its new commander, Col. Cadwallader Jones, were critical to the containment of a possibly catastrophic Union breakthrough near Prospect Hill.

With Brig. Gen. Maxcy Gregg's mortal wounding at Fredericksburg, the brigade passed into the capable hands of Brig. Gen. Samuel McGowan. After McGowan's wounding at Chancellorsville the following May, Brig. Gen. Abner Perrin took his place as, with Hill's elevation to corps command, the Light Division came under the direction of Maj. Gen. William Dorsey Pender. As a consequence, the 12th South Carolina, now under the reins of Col. John Miller, would find itself crossing Willoughby Run at Gettysburg on July 1, 1863, to spearhead the assault that would produce the collapse of Union defenses on Seminary Ridge.

The opening of the 1864 campaign season found McGowan back in brigade command, but with the division now under Maj. Gen. Cadmus Wilcox's aegis. What had not changed was the 12th South Carolina's talent for finding tough fighting. At the Wilderness, the South Carolinians lost Miller in brutal combat along the Orange Plank Road. At Spotsylvania, they participated in the counterattack that contained the Federal breakthrough at the Mule Shoe Salient on May 12, then found themselves locked in brutal combat for 18 hours at the Bloody Angle. After being roughly handled in fighting at Jericho Mill on May 23, the toll the operations had taken on the regiment were evident, as it would be led by a captain, Robert M. Kerr, until Lt. Col. Edwin F. Bookter returned from serious wounds suffered in the Wilderness to assume command. Bookter's tenure did not last long, though, as his name was among those added to the regiment's list of fallen as a consequence of fighting south and west of Petersburg at the Jones Farm in September. In addition to further lengthening this list at Deep Bottom, Fussell's Mill, and the Jones Farm, the second half of 1864 saw the South Carolinians come face to face with African-American troops north of the James River—and respond in the spirit of Confederate comrades at Fort Pillow and the Crater in their treatment of black troops.

The final campaigns of 1865 began with the regiment once again under Captain Kerr. Although the end of the struggle for Virginia was clearly in view, the South Carolinians once again acquitted themselves well in final operations at Gravelly Run and Sutherland's Station before surrendering at Appomattox.

Given the regiment's outstanding and conspicuous history, it is remarkable that it took so long for it to be fully told. Undoubtedly, some of the explanation can be found in the declaration of one South Carolinian in 1862 that: "We do not object to giving praise where it is due, and there is no doubt [that] Virginians fought as bravely as any other State troops, but then, they did not do all the work themselves." As Cwayna's contribution to the impressive body of literature on the Army of Northern Virginia makes clear, they certainly did not. Readers will find in *The Invincible Twelfth* not only a provocative and engaging story, but also a comprehensive study that gives them a fuller understanding of the war that the great historian Charles P. Roland proclaimed the "American Iliad."

Ethan S. Rafuse
author of *From the Mountains to the Bay: The War in Virginia, January–May 1862* and *Robert E. Lee and the Fall of the Confederacy, 1863–1865*

Preface

GROWING UP IN the Midwest during the 1980s and 1990s, the Civil War was constantly on my mind yet physically so far away. With the help of two very supportive parents (and a reluctant little sister) who fostered and nurtured my interest in history, however, I vividly recall our family's first trip "out east" in 1991 on the heels of both Ken Burns's Civil War documentary success and the movie *Glory*. Visiting Washington, D.C., Gettysburg National Military Park, and Appomattox Court House near Lynchburg, Virginia, in the span of a week was a dream come true for an 11-year-old interested in my nation's seminal fraternal struggle. As I explored the rocks of Devil's Den and took in the view from Little Round Top at Gettysburg, the story of the war became much more real and important. That trip, more than anything, cemented my lifelong passion for studying the conflict—a passion that continues to this day.

Later that summer, my parents learned of a large Civil War reenactment pending in Jackson, Michigan. I was anxious to attend, of course, and the family loaded up in the van and drove two-plus hours to an extravaganza the likes of which I had never seen. Military encampments, artillery, horses, and hundreds of soldiers re-creating the July 20, 1864, Atlanta campaign battle at Peach Tree Creek, Georgia, brought the war to me in even more realistic terms. I immediately decided that I had to join, and within a year I was the youngest member of the 12th South Carolina/4th Michigan Volunteer Infantry, Inc.—a Civil War reenacting company that portrayed both sides of the conflict.

Our commanding officer at the time was named Bob Helsel. In his mid-50's, Bob looked and acted every inch a Civil War officer. Marine training gave him the bearing and presence of a commander, and his gray beard and steel gray eyes reminded one of "Marse" Robert E. Lee himself. With three direct ancestors who fought in the 12th South Carolina, he was a founding member of the reenacting organization bearing its name. As a result, the regiment's history in battle and beyond was the focus of many of our campfire discussions. Listening to the zeal and passion Bob had for the regiment and those exploits gave me an appreciation for reading and learning more; before long, I had purchased and read every Civil War book I could find that touched on the 12th's activities, always checking the index of each to ensure that it contained some reference to the regiment.

Bob's death in 1995 left a void in our organization. Picking up his mantle, I determined to continue my studies, intending one day to honor the regiment for which his ancestors fought with a full-length history. In 2012–13, Ken Oberholtzer, a former member of our group and co-author of the excellent book, *The 4th Michigan at Gettysburg—The Battle for the Wheatfield*, greatly assisted me in securing manuscript material from the United Daughters of the Confederacy and the South Carolina Relic Room in Columbia, South Carolina, as well as providing me with electronic versions of the *Official Records* relating to the 12th South Carolina. A marriage, the birth of my son, a divorce, a successful bout with cancer, and an unsuccessful run for judge delayed but did not stop my research and writing; through all those life-changing events, capturing the story of the 12th South Carolina remained a constant draw—something to look forward to after a long day in the courtroom arguing cases. Never a night owl, I nevertheless looked forward to pouring a glass of wine or bourbon in the evening after my son went to bed, devoting the remainder of the night and sometimes well into the morning in my home library, and spending time with the men of the 12th by poring over their recollections, official records, and other primary source material.

Throughout the process, I enjoyed reading the reminiscences of officers such as Lieutenant J. R. Boyles, a prolific and descriptive writer who lost a leg at Gettysburg; Captain William S. Dunlop, who fought in every major battle of the regiment; and Captain Cadwallader Jones Jr., the young son of the 12th's lieutenant colonel who left the famed Hampton Legion to join this rough-and-tumble regiment of volunteers of which his father was second in command. The accounts of lesser-known enlisted men such as William H. Miller, D. J. Carter, and Joseph and William Templeton were equally fascinating, and I began to feel a real connection with each of them as I mined every possible piece of information from their writings, newspaper accounts, and other sources to create as full and complete a story as possible. I felt their wartime losses and failures as much as their victories and successes. The loss of the brave, sensitive, and conscientious Lieutenant Boyles after his wound and the devastation he felt was particularly saddening after having spent so much time getting to know him through his memoir.

Writing this history brought me immense joy and satisfaction but also some frustration, based mostly on the desire to find more detailed primary sources from the regiment's officers and enlisted men. Squeezing every ounce I could out of the primary source material (much of it incomplete and not as thorough as I would have hoped), the story of the 12th took on a life of its own. From the bare-bones letters of the Templeton brothers of Company B, to the direct and rough prose of William Miller of Company H, to the polished writings of J. R. Boyles of Company C and Captain Dunlop of Company B; along with other sources, the story of this brave and courageous group of men began to assemble itself from these fragments. I shared in their triumphs and tragedies and learned a great deal about life, logistics, and protocols in one of the best and most consistent brigades in the illustrious Army of Northern Virginia.

This work is the result of more than a decade's worth of research and writing and chronicles the formation of the 12th South Carolina Infantry from its muster in August 1861 through its surrender at Appomattox and beyond, to its postwar reunions. It is a strictly military history in its purest form and delves into the tactical minutiae of the regiment's actions in camp, in battles, and on the march. It chronicles both the regiment's soldiers and commanders, and sprinkles in vignettes of the legendary leaders who interacted with the regiment throughout the war: A. P. Hill, Thomas J. "Stonewall" Jackson, Cadmus Wilcox, Maxcy Gregg, and of course Robert E. Lee. Chief among the units represented in the book are the 12th's brother regiments who served together for the majority of the war: The 1st, 13th, and 14th South Carolina; Orr's Rifles Regiment; and the other component brigades in what became famously known as the "Light Division."

In an army filled with outstanding regiments and colonels, the 12th South Carolina was second to none in the Army of Northern Virginia. Drilled incessantly by its second colonel, Dixon Barnes, and those who followed, the regiment garnered a hard-earned reputation for aggressive maneuvers and unforgiving attacks. Impetuous almost to a fault during some engagements, the regiment caused panic and fear in the enemy and invariably drove it from point to point on a number of bloody battlefields. In doing so, the 12th epitomized the hard-hitting and daring tactics of Robert E. Lee and the qualities he attempted to instill throughout his army. Often leaving its supports behind, the regiment was at the forefront of major turning points in battles conducted by Lee's army: defending the left flank of Jackson's line at Second Manassas, turning the tide in the 40-acre cornfield at Sharpsburg, buying time and saving Gregg's brigade at Fredericksburg, driving the Union I Corps troops off Seminary Ridge at Gettysburg, and plugging the most dangerous of gaps in the "Mule Shoe" at Spotsylvania Court House. This penchant for offensive-minded tactics, however, came at a price. Of just more than 1,400 men who served during the four-year conflict, about 150 men remained at Appomattox.

Equally interesting as the regiment's record in battle is the continued connection the soldiers felt to their home localities and the unqualified support the regiment received from the citizenry back home. For the duration of the conflict, the regiment was the beneficiary of a strong mail system, regular care packages, and a wealth of support from private relief societies and the South Carolina Central Association. Consistent communication both to and from the home front strengthened the regiment both morally and physically and contributed to its success. Regular updates written by soldiers to local newspapers kept the folks back home informed as to the casualties, news, and political feelings of the regiment and fed the citizenry with much needed information about their loved ones. This reciprocal exchange of information on the part of the soldiers and material items on the part of civilians benefited the regiment in ways that cannot be quantified and continued to the end of the war.

When that end came, the men went home, carrying great pride in their service. While it took several years to formulate and organize, the survivors of the regiment met annually for festive reunions. The war certainly occupied the minds and memories of the soldiers of the 12th long after the last guns were fired, and their collective desire to remember their service was one of the most interesting and enjoyable parts to chronicle in this work. In this, the regiment never truly demobilized but rather transformed itself from a military organization into a mechanism for remembrance of their service. Despite calls by its survivors to draft a regimental history then, a full accounting of the regiment was never authored. Until now.

It is my hope that this history will serve as an educational tool for military historians and aficionados interested in learning about one of the storied but underrepresented regiments in the Army of Northern Virginia.

Acknowledgments

AS A PRACTICING attorney in the state of Michigan, research is a well-established and accepted concept in my profession. As an amateur historian taking on the task of chronicling a regiment from South Carolina, however, archival research can be daunting. I would like to thank my longtime friend, Ken Oberholtzer, co-author of *The 4th Michigan at Gettysburg—The Battle for the Wheatfield*, for inspiring me to write the history of the 12th South Carolina and for his great assistance in getting me started on the project. While my Civil War library is vast, when I started the work, I had yet to obtain the *Official Records of the War of the Rebellion*. Ken took the time not only to type up every reference to the regiment from the *OR*s but also assisted me in locating primary source material at various repositories in South Carolina. I am indebted to Ken for not only his moral support, but for his assistance, without which, this book could not have been written.

Besides Ken, there are numerous individuals who assisted me in procuring sources and visual aids for the work. Michelle Sellars, the cataloging historian at the South Carolina Historical Society in Charleston, provided great assistance in locating outstanding manuscript material with regard to William H. Miller and J. R. Boyles; two sources which were indispensable in writing this history. Betty Luck, the research librarian, and Jamie Likins, the President General, at the United Daughters of the Confederacy in Richmond, provided nearly a dozen excerpts from soldiers in the 12th South Carolina to add color and context to the manuscript as well. All of the folks at the South Carolina Confederate Relic Room and Military Museum in Columbia are appreciated as well, but I want to specifically thank Chelsea

Sigourney for assistance in procuring photographs of Colonel Barnes and the 12th's battle flag. Finally, McKenzie Lemhouse, library specialist, and Beth Bilderback, Visual Materials Archivist, at the South Caroliniana Library at the University of South Carolina were invaluable in helping me locate the letters and an ambrotype of William and Joseph Templeton. The various library assistants at the University of North Carolina's Southern Historical Collection assisted me in obtaining the wonderful letters of Cadwallader Jones Jr. and are likewise greatly appreciated.

Just like A. P. Hill arriving in the nick of time at Sharpsburg, I am very thankful to Robert K. Krick, who, at the eleventh hour, was introduced to me by Ted Savas. Mr. Krick, along with his son Robert E. L. Krick, provided me with some excellent additional source material via his wonderfully detailed ledgers on the regiment. Mr. Krick also took time to correspond with me regularly and send certain sources from his personal collection that I did not have and could not retrieve with the publishing date drawing near. As Chris Snyder, my excellent editor, and Veronica Kane, the formatter of this book well know, adding what became known as the "Krick material" posed some challenges at the last minute, but its addition has made this book all the more rich in detail and a more complete story of the regiment for the reader.

Understanding and visualizing troop movements and marches can sometimes be difficult when reading from text. Creating maps which focus on a specific regiment in an action is much more challenging than creating one for a brigade, division, or corps and takes a skilled and detailed cartographer. I would like to express a special thank you to Hal Jespersen for his magnificent and accurate battle maps for this book. Hal is a consummate professional and the best in the business when it comes to creating inviting and understandable visual aids of troop movements. The maps Hal created, some of which bore down to the company level, are simply amazing and add much interest and visual comprehension to this work.

As a first-time author, I had no idea how to go about getting a book published and reached out to many houses that published Civil War literature. Throughout the course of this process, one man, Theodore P. Savas of Savas Beatie, LLC stood out among the rest. Ted and I clicked instantly as we discussed our passion for the war and he was gracious enough to put my manuscript at the top of his list to review one weekend in March 2021. To be honest, I was simply honored that someone of Ted's stature would even consider my work and was completely at a loss for words when he offered me a publishing contract. I would also like to thank Chris Howland, the editor Ted assigned to help me develop the manuscript. Chris, who edited *Civil War Times* magazine, is a pro at every level and helped me in too many ways to count. I cannot thank him enough for his insightful suggestions and for his assistance in recruiting Ethan S. Rafuse, to whom I am also indebted, to write the Foreword.. I would also like to thank David Snyder for the final copy edit. The long wait due to circumstances beyond Ted's control, a bottleneck caused by COVID, was worth it.

I would be remiss if I did not mention one of my dearest friends in reenacting and otherwise, Jim Haywood, who took time to read the numerous drafts of various chapters of the book and provided suggestions and comments to me; usually over bourbons and gas lit lamps in his Civil War themed tavern with portraits of Lee, Longstreet, Cleburne, and John B. Gordon presiding over us. Jim and his lovely wife, Amie, hosted me on many evenings over the past several years and together we commiserated over the 12th's role in the war and how we could make the story more accurate and entertaining. They are truly wonderful friends and I am deeply thankful for them.

As a Civil War reenactor, I have spent many weekends touring battlefields and sitting around the campfire discussing battles and tactics. While space prohibits mentioning all of my fellow reenactors in the 12th South Carolina/4th Michigan Volunteer Infantry, Inc., several stand out as frequent listeners, contributors, and supporters of my work: Bob Helsel, Al Coe, Dan Hall, Ben Flowerday, Ernie Greer, Jack Swartzinski, Matt Lindeman, Wally Coots, Scott Farver, Neil Farver, Ed Escher, and Ben Bever.

Lastly, I want to thank my family for their unending support of my passion for history. My parents, Daniel and Patsy Cwayna, helped spark my youthful interest in the time period through numerous trips, purchasing books, taking me to reenactments, and supporting my historical endeavors. My late grandparents, Cloyce "Bud" and Vera Apple, facilitated my interest through their rural roots, old-fashioned living, and constant listening to my stories about the Civil War. My wonderful sister, Katie, who I am so very proud of, has always supported my interest in the war and has been a rock to me as both a friend, confidante, and sibling. Despite not completely understanding my zeal for the past, she has always been the rock on which I lean in times of difficulty.

Finally, I want to acknowledge the true miracle and light of my life—my wonderful, tender-hearted, funny, and intelligent son, Grant. I started my research for this book before he was born; today he is nearly a teenager and a magnificent specimen of a human being. Most of my writing was done while burning the midnight oil after his bedtime. His innocent interruptions—needing a drink, a bad dream or curiosity why his father was up so late in the office—often forced me to stop and go to bed; hence, the length of time it took me to complete the manuscript. But I am so thankful for every one of them. They don't come any better than Grant. He makes every day a blessing to be alive, and I am so very thankful that God gave him to me.

I am truly indebted to Ted and his Savas Beatie team for having me on board as one of their authors. It has been a pleasure to work with every one of them; from Sarah Keeney and Ian Hughes designing a first rate cover to Veronica Kane for transforming the rough manuscript into a beautiful polished piece in final form to Ryan Quint for indexing and Sarah Closson for providing exceptional marketing for the final product. Being a part of this exclusive group of dedicated individuals and witnessing the excitement and professionalism they bring to the table has made this entire experience enjoyable and worthwhile.

And with that, I present the long-awaited history of the 12th South Carolina Volunteer Infantry—160 years in the making.

Benjamin L. Cwayna
Grand Ledge, Michigan
February 13, 2025

Chapter One

Palmetto State Provenance

John Logan Black was a busy man in late August 1861. A captain in the newly formed Provisional Army of the Confederate States of America, Black was the chief mustering officer at South Carolina's Lightwood Knot Springs, a Confederate military encampment four miles northeast of the state capital of Columbia. Since early July, throngs of fervent volunteers from across the Palmetto State, answering Confederate President Jefferson Davis's latest call for troops, had descended on the grounds of a popular antebellum recreational resort. In a war projected to be short but now in its fifth month, having troops ready to fight was no luxury. It was time to transition the 20 or so loosely assembled companies at Lightwood Knot Springs into formal regiments, a novel endeavor for which no one in the region had first-hand experience.

One can only wonder the patience the West Point-trained Black showed these raw recruits, particularly those from the state's more rural Piedmont region known as the Upcountry. A native of York, South Carolina, he was a stern man accustomed to being obeyed, and described by his biographer as "decided in his opinion, egotistical and determined." Black was eventually commissioned lieutenant colonel of the 1st South Carolina Cavalry, becoming its commanding officer in 1862 and serving until the end of the war. Now, however, he was the first official liaison between these novice soldiers and the burgeoning Confederate army. He needed to handle them with both a firm and delicate touch.

The first regiment Black mustered into service would eventually be designated the 12th South Carolina Volunteer Infantry. Until it was formally assigned that designation in late September, however, the soldiers at the encampment referred to it simply as "the first Regiment."[1] "First" would have been an appropriate alias, as by the end of the war the 12th had earned its place among the elite fighting units ever to represent the Palmetto State, beyond merely the Civil War.

The regiment's 10 companies had mustered that summer in the wake of the April attack on Fort Sumter by South Carolina troops and US President Abraham Lincoln's subsequent call for 75,000 volunteers to suppress the budding rebellion. The men hailed primarily from the Upcountry counties of York, Fairfield, Richland, Lancaster, and Pickens. One of the 12th's first companies to organize in May called itself the "Campbell Rifles." Electing local attorney John L. Miller as its captain and William S. Dunlop as first lieutenant, the 86 men from York County encamped in Yorkville and began a regimen of drill and other military exercises.[2]

Other companies in the region followed the Campbell Rifles's lead. With more men in the county anxious to join the Confederate cause, a second York company—the "Palmer Guards"—was recruited in July and officially organized on August 7, electing William H. McCorkle as captain, Lewis M. Grist as first lieutenant, and John Parker and I. D. Witherspoon second and third lieutenants, respectively. Named in honor of Lt. Richard Palmer, a York County man killed at the first battle of Manassas that July, the Palmer Guards fielded approximately 96 men when formed. A third company from the county's Rock Hill area formed, calling itself the "Indian Land Guards." Commanded by Cadwallader Jones, it had 81 men.[3]

Pickens County, in the northwestern corner of the state, contributed two companies. The first, with 76 men, identified itself as the "Bonham Rifles." Organized in the town of Pickens on July 11, the company elected A. D. Gaillard

1 Eleanor McSwain, ed., *Crumbling Defenses or Memoirs and Reminiscences of John Logan Black, Colonel C.S.A* (Macon, GA, 1960), 9, 37; L. M. G., "From Lightwood Knot," *The Yorkville Enquirer*, Sept. 5, 1861, 1. (All newspaper references are to South Carolina unless otherwise noted.) Although John Logan Black served primarily in the Carolinas during the conflict, he was with the Army of Northern Virginia during the Gettysburg campaign. Leading an ad hoc detachment of 200–300 cavalrymen (whom Black referred to as "game-legged cusses and wagon rats") and a battery of artillery, Black reported to none other than Robert E. Lee the morning of July 2, 1863, and was assigned to Lt. Gen. James Longstreet to assist Longstreet's Corps in reconnoitering the area southwest of Gettysburg. In an ironic crossing of paths, when Black reported that morning to Lee he witnessed a meeting between the commanding general, Longstreet, and Lt. Gen. A. P. Hill and was likely within earshot and eyesight of the bivouac of the 12th South Carolina on Seminary Ridge, featuring some of the same men he mustered into service two years earlier at Lightwood Knot Springs.

2 "The Campbell Rifles," *Yorkville Enquirer*, June 5, 1861, 2; L. M. G., "From Lightwood Knot," *Yorkville Enquirer*, Aug. 19, 1861, 1.

3 "The Palmer Guards," *Yorkville Enquirer*, Aug. 8, 1861, 1; "The Campbell Rifles"; L. M. G., "From Lightwood Knot."

as captain, John Moody as first lieutenant, and J. A. Ballinger and P. J. Dryman second and third lieutenants, respectively. The second Pickens County company, with reportedly up to 90 men, was known as the "Grisham Rifles," commanded by Capt. L. B. Johnson.[4]

Men primarily from Fairfield County, just north of Columbia, constituted two companies. One organized as the "Cedar Creek Rifles" with 78 men, electing Henry C. Davis as captain. The second, commanded by Hayne McMeekin and fielding approximately as many soldiers as the Cedar Creek Rifles, was known as the "Means Light Infantry." Richland County, in the middle of the state, contributed a company known as the "Richland Guards." Its 77 men, under Capt. Edwin F. Bookter, came mostly from Columbia, with a spattering from surrounding Fairfield, Chester, Lexington, and Charleston counties.[5]

Later in the summer, Lancaster County, bordering North Carolina, produced three companies in short succession. The 84-man "Blair Guards" from the eastern portion of the county formed on August 14, electing C. F. Hinson as captain, T. F. Clyburn as first lieutenant, C. C. Welsh as second lieutenant, and Ransom Gardner as third lieutenant. J. T. Brasington, a local preacher, served as first sergeant.

Two smaller units consolidated in mid-August to form the county's second company, the "Lancaster Hornets." The 87 men of that command elected a well-known state legislator and planter, Dixon Barnes, as captain, and N. B. Valandingham, W. J. Stover, and J. C. Rollins as first, second, and third lieutenant, respectively. The third Lancaster company, 80 men under Capt. John Q. McManus, had a checkered beginning in August, though, and disbanded between September 4 and September 11 because of chronic absenteeism and "dissatisfaction" among the volunteers. Accordingly, it never mustered into the regiment. Consisting of Lancaster County men, it is likely, however, that some of the men in McManus's company joined the Blair Guards or Lancaster Hornets.[6]

Black was methodical in preparing the muster rolls of all 10 companies, mobilizing companies from the same region on the same dates. The process would take three days, but August 28, 1861, was cited as the regiment's official muster date. On the first day, the Palmer Guards became Company A, the Campbell Rifles Company B, and the Indian Land Guards Company H. William McCorkle

4 "The Bonham Rifles," *Keowee Courier,* July 13, 1861, 2.

5 L. M. G., "From Lightwood Knot, *Yorkville Enquirer,* Aug. 19, 1861, 1.

6 "The Lancaster Guards," *Lancaster Ledger,* Aug. 14, 1861, 2; L. M. G., "From Lightwood Knot"; "Another Company," *Lancaster Ledger*, Aug. 21, 1861, 2; "Still Another," *Lancaster Ledger*, Sept. 11, 1861, 2; "Our Volunteers in Camp," *Lancaster Ledger*, Sept. 11, 1861, 2; "We regret . . .," *The Lancaster Ledger*, Sept 4, 1861, 2.

of the Palmer Guards became the regiment's senior captain, as determined by a random drawing of lots preceding the muster.

On August 29, Black assigned Bookter's Richland Guards as Company D, Gaillard's Bonham Rifles as Company G, and Johnson's Grisham Rifles as Company K. Black completed the muster on August 30, with Davis's Cedar Creek Rifles as Company C, Hinson's Blair Guards as Company E, and Barnes's Lancaster Hornets as Company I. McMeekin's Company F (the Means Light Infantry) mustered in after September 6, presumably as a replacement for McManus's disbanding company. Available records, however, do not indicate when it formally joined the regiment.

* * *

The regiment's initial muster listed more than 900 enlisted men and officers.[7] Most of the companies had been at the camp for a few weeks, although Barnes's and Hinson's commands arrived just before the muster. Company I's journey south to Lightwood Knot Springs typified the patriotic fervor sweeping the Confederacy that summer: "All along the way . . . the company was enthusiastically cheered by the people," wrote one soldier. While marching through Chester en route to the rail line that would take them to Columbia, Barnes and his men enjoyed a picnic prepared by the locals. "The dinner was excellent and so pronounced by the Company and their friends the Company subsequently passed a resolution of thanks, showing their grateful appreciation of the kindness extended them," the soldier recalled. Nevertheless, the following evening was not so pleasant, as a rainstorm pelted the men while they attempted to sleep without tents in a field.

The companies that formed the 12th South Carolina arrived at Lightwood Knot Springs with at least a loosely elected organization and command staff, although that did not stop those seeking military rank from swarming the encampment from across the state. "You would be pleased (or perhaps disgusted) to see the great number of office seekers in camp," wrote a soldier from another regiment. "They seem almost as numerous as the privates. Some little men want very high offices, and some big men would be satisfied with any office whatever, just so they can serve their country and undergo no hardships."

While widespread in similar training camps both north and south that summer and fall, the practice of popular election for company officers at the encampment was, in hindsight, a mistake to at least one 12th South Carolina private: William J. Miller of Company H, who observed, "[W]e always vote for some favorite, having

7 *Supplement to OR,* part II, vol. 65:10–25.

no regard to the merits of the man as a tactician. Our officers were brave men but very often deficient of other qualifications."[8]

On August 30, Richard Gill Mills Dunovant was elected the regiment's colonel—his bona fides commendable, at least on paper. Born May 18, 1821, to a wealthy and established South Carolina family, Dunovant was married to the sister of South Carolina representative Preston Brooks, the cane-beating assailant of Charles Sumner in the U.S. Senate during the politically charged 1850s. A graduate of South Carolina College in Columbia, Dunovant practiced medicine in Texas prior to the Mexican War. When that war began in 1846, he returned to Chester, South Carolina, and raised a company of volunteers, eventually becoming colonel of the famed Palmetto Regiment. After the war Dunovant became a planter, and the state legislature eventually appointed him adjutant and inspector of the South Carolina State Militia, a post he held from 1855 to 1861.

Dunovant, an ardent secessionist, owned 47 slaves and was a delegate to the state's secession convention in Charleston, at which he proudly signed the ordinance withdrawing South Carolina from the Union on December 20, 1860. Assigned command of troops in Charleston Harbor in January 1861, he was soon promoted to brigadier general of South Carolina state troops. Stationed at Fort Moultrie, Dunovant commanded two regiments on Sullivan's Island during the April 12–14 bombardment of Fort Sumter. When the troops under his command mustered into formal Confederate service, however, Dunovant resigned his commission and waited for another opportunity to serve. A favorite of South Carolina Governor Francis Pickens, who praised Dunovant's "noble self-abnegation" (unusual modesty in those times), his star was on the rise when "the first Regiment" was organized at Lightwood Knot Springs. Given that it was one of the first volunteer regiments raised in the state's Provisional Confederate Army, it is not surprising Dunovant became its first colonel.[9]

Dixon Barnes, Company I's 45-year-old captain, was elected the regiment's lieutenant colonel. Born of Scotch-Irish ancestry in the Kershaw District outside Columbia in 1816, Barnes intermittently attended South Carolina College, finally graduating in 1838. He then studied law and was admitted to the state bar. Accounts vary, but in 1839 or 1840, he married Charlotte Rebecca Brown, three years

8 William Joseph Miller, "My Experience as a Soldier in the Confederate Army," UDC *Recollections and Reminiscences* (Columbia, SC, 1992) 216. L. K., "Camp Correspondence," *Carolina Spartan*, Sept. 5, 1861, 1; William S. Dunlop, "The Confederate War: Company B, Twelfth S.C.V. in Bivouac and Battles," *Yorkville Enquirer*, Oct. 23, 1889, 1. Hereafter cited as *Bivouac and Battles (Part I)*; LOCAL, "Our Volunteers in Camp," *Lancaster Ledger*, 1st ed., Sept. 4, 1861, 2.

9 Dunlop, *Bivouac and Battles (Part I)*, 2; Bruce Allardice, *More Generals in Gray* (Baton Rouge, LA, 1995), 83.

Richard Gill Mills Dunovant served as the first colonel of the 12th South Carolina Volunteer Infantry. *South Caroliniana Library at the University of South Carolina*

younger, and established a plantation in Lancaster County. Charlotte passed in 1846 or 1847, leaving a young daughter, Mary, whom Barnes sent to live with his in-laws.

Before the war, Mary returned to live with her father and accompanied him to sessions while he served in the state legislature in Columbia. Barnes lived and breathed politics, becoming a dominating political force in the region. In 1844, just 28, he was elected a state representative and was easily reelected in 1846 before becoming a state senator in 1848. In 1860, two years after Barnes declined to run for reelection, voters urged him to run again, which he did unopposed.

Even as he led Lancaster County's husbands, sons, and brothers in uniform, Barnes continued to represent Lancaster in the state senate. With Abraham Lincoln's election, Barnes became an ardent proponent of secession and, like Dunovant, served as a delegate to the secession convention in which he was "prominently forward in the measure which resulted in the Secession of South Carolina from the Federal Union."

At the outbreak of war, Barnes was, as expected, at the forefront. "No man among us has a larger hold upon the confidence of our people," wrote one admirer. He was unanimously elected captain of the first volunteer company raised in the Lancaster district and was then elected major of the 2nd South Carolina Regiment of state troops early in the conflict. Like Dunovant, when the transfer of state troops into Confederate service left him without a command, Barnes returned to Lancaster and raised the Hornets. Again, he was unanimously elected captain, and then again elected unanimously lieutenant colonel during elections for field officers of the regiment.

As one would expect of a politician and southern gentleman, Barnes was, in the words of a contemporary, a man whose "manners were full of courtesy and refinement and through the whole ran a most pleasant vein of cheerfulness and humor." One soldier described him as "a quiet gentlemen, with a long white beard," which no doubt made him look older than his 45 years, and another soldier called him the epitome of a true "Carolina gentleman." Despite his lack of formal military training, Barnes proved entirely capable of leading men in battle. Within a year, he was regarded among the best colonels in the entire Confederate army.[10]

The regiment's major would be 48-year-old Cadwallader Jones, a native North Carolinian who had enjoyed a lengthy career in law and public service before relocating to South Carolina in 1857. Jones graduated from the University of North Carolina at the age of 19 and married Annie Isabella Iredell Jones in 1836. His family roots were steeped in American military tradition. His father (and namesake) was a naval officer in the War of 1812, and his grandfather, Maj. Cadwallader Jones, served as an aide-de-camp to Marquis de Lafayette during the Revolutionary War. Lafayette held the elder Jones in such high esteem that he presented him an ornate sword that remained in the family and, ironically, was now carried by his grandson attempting to break apart the nation his ancestors earnestly fought to create.

The impending war would be another family affair for the Jones clan. Jones's son, Cadwallader Jones Jr., served in Company H, eventually promoted to first lieutenant and given command of the company at Gettysburg, just 16 years old. Major Jones's brother, Capt. Robin Jones, organized and commanded Company H of the 1st South Carolina Cavalry.[11]

* * *

The men whom Dunovant, Barnes, and Jones commanded came from all walks of life. Their rebellious bloodlines established well before 1776, they were used

10 *Lancaster Ledger*, Oct. 15, 1862, 1; "Personal," *Lancaster Ledger*, July 31, 1861, 1; Caldwell, *The History of a Brigade of South Carolinians*, 79–80; Louise H. Daly, *Alexander Cheves Haskell: The Portrait of a Man* (Norwood, MA, 1934), 77; "Death of Col. Dixon Barnes," *Yorkville Enquirer*, Oct. 8, 1862, 2.

11 "Colonel Cad Jones," *Yorkville Enquirer*, Dec. 6, 1899, 2; Willie Jones, "Roll of Company H, 12th South Carolina Regiment," in *Recollections and Reminiscences*, 11 vols. (Columbia, SC, 1916), 6:456.

to fending for themselves with little reliance on government. Coming primarily from the northern and western tier counties in South Carolina that lined the North Carolina border, their ancestors were primarily English and Scotch-Irish. Most of the men raised in and around Columbia were descendants of the English who landed on the coast in the early 17th century and moved west, following the region's rivers to establish settlements.

Most in the regiment were Upcountry boys, also of primarily Scotch-Irish lineage, the descendants of migrants from Pennsylvania and Virginia in the second half of the 18th century. According to one officer, they had settled the area with "the rifle, the axe and the Bible." Godfearing and tough, many of them were loyal to the crown of England prior to the Revolutionary War, yet their religious tenets stipulated that man-made laws should be consistent with the will of the Almighty. As such, as time progressed, these rough and hardscrabble frontiersmen came to believe firmly in many of the doctrines of republican government while remaining loyal British subjects. It is not surprising that when the founders finally decreed independence from England in 1776, many in the region were suspicious of the sentiment of "independence," initially resisting the call. Indeed, the region's yeomen were blissfully ignorant of or indifferent to many egregious acts by King George III that did not affect them directly, such as the 1765 Stamp Act and rigid restrictions on commerce—issues of the day that seriously impacted their fellow colonists in New England.

This mindset changed when British troops instituted brutal tactics in the Carolinas during the war, specifically the 1780 Waxhaws Massacre and subsequent demands by British commander Francis Lord Rawdon that citizens in the war's southern theater formally pledge not to participate in the fighting. Moreover, despite the loyalty of the Upcountry Carolinians to the monarchy, in many instances British authorities treated Upcountry citizens the same as the colonial rebels, burning their meeting houses and destroying bibles in churches that contained Scotch psalms. By the end of the Revolutionary War, an increasing number of Carolinians favored the bid for independence and proudly fought and spilled blood on behalf of the colonies. These were the ancestors of the men who enlisted in the 12th South Carolina, men who were later described as "the very best troops which marched under the leaves of the Palmetto." They were rebels again, only this time it was against the country their ancestors had created.[12]

12 Edward McCrady Jr., "Heroes of the Old Camden District, South Carolina, 1776–1861," in Robert Alonzo Brock, ed., *Southern Historical Society Papers,* 52 vols. (Richmond, 1888), 16:3–14. Hereafter cited as *SHSP*.

Not all who served the Confederacy were Anglo-Saxon, however. Inhabiting the area around Rock Hill near the North Carolina border was a small but proud population of Catawba Indians, a tribe that at one point represented the largest and most powerful native American population in the Piedmont region. Reduced to a population of about 100 or so by 1861, only a handful of Catawba males were of military age at the start of the war. Eleven would enlist in the 5th, 17th and 12th South Carolina, with five serving in Cadwallader Jones's original command, Company H (the Indian Land Guards): William Cantey, Nelson George, James Harris, John Harris, and Alexander Tims. James Harris may have been with the Army of Northern Virginia at its final surrender at Appomattox.[13]

No matter their ethnic roots, the men in the 12th South Carolina enjoyed varied backgrounds, education levels, and social status. Among the first to answer the call was William Miller, a 15-year-old from York who in June 1861 had recessed for summer break from his parochial school. "The entire class of which I was a member, and the youngest in the class, was going to volunteer," he would recall. Later that month, Miller and several neighbors and classmates joined a group of enthusiastic volunteers assembling in Yorkville under John Miller (no confirmed relation) and William Dunlop.

Within a few days, the volunteers headed to Lightwood Knot Springs where, the younger Miller noted, "we found several other Companies drilling." That July, instructors from the state's military school had arrived to take charge of the training. Although Miller initially joined Company B, he subsequently transferred to Company H for reasons never made clear. A straightforward and blunt storyteller, Miller would leave one of the richest reminiscences of his time in the regiment, titled "My Experience as a Soldier in the Confederate Army."[14]

Andrew Kohath Smith was another of the zealous young men who joined the Confederate ranks. He was a northerner by birth, from Abraham Lincoln's own state of Illinois, but his parents' roots were in South Carolina, and in 1844 they returned

13 Thomas Blummer, "Record of Catawba Indians' Confederate Service," *The South Carolina Historical Magazine* 96, no. 3 (July 1995): 222, 224–30. According to Catawba tradition, Franklyn Cantey—the brother of William Cantey—was killed in the war. He quite possibly was the sixth Catawba to serve in the regiment, although no available service records confirm this; Ibid., 225. Blummer's article implies James Harris surrendered with the 12th at Appomattox; however, his name does not appear on the list of parolees for the 12th nor does it appear on the National Park Service's list of Appomattox parolees with the 12th. Three men named James Harris, however, are listed as being paroled from South Carolina regiments at Appomattox—two from the 2nd South Carolina Rifles and one from the 18th South Carolina. If James Harris, the Catawba Indian, did in fact surrender at Appomattox, perhaps he transferred to one of those regiments prior to the surrender or joined one during the chaotic retreat. Cf., *SHSP* 15:371–73 and https://www.nps.gov/apco/learn/historyculture/upload/parolelist-h1.pdf.

14 Miller, "My Experience," 226.

there to raise their son, now 7. Smith became a farmer near Rock Hill and after South Carolina seceded in 1860, he and others from the surrounding area began to drill in nearby Ebenezer. With war declared, Smith and his compatriots were asked to volunteer in Company H for the duration of the conflict. Their commanding officer, Cadwallader Jones, drew a line in the dirt with his heirloom Revolutionary War sword and, according to Company H lore, Smith was the first to cross that line, therefore making him the first York County man to volunteer officially for the Confederate army. Smith would serve as a sergeant in Company H as a comrade of William Miller and survived some of the war's most horrific fighting.[15]

Among notables to serve in Henry Davis's Company C were J. R. Boyles and Orastin D. Rawl. After the war, Boyles penned a thorough narrative of his time in the regiment titled *Reminiscences of the Civil War*, published in 1890. Seriously wounded twice, Boyles served as a sergeant and in 1863 was promoted to lieutenant. Rawl volunteered on August 10, 1861, and officially mustered into Company C on September 18. Serving under Boyle, he was one of the few men in the regiment to survive the war and surrender at Appomattox. Unfortunately, Rawl left no known account of his experiences in the regiment.[16]

Like Rawl, William R. Sims was there when the last of the guns were fired at Appomattox. Notably, he also experienced the first at Fort Sumter in 1861. A 20-year-old, born in Union County, South Carolina, Sims resided in Charleston that first April of the war, volunteering in a local militia company and serving on Morris Island during the bombardment of Fort Sumter. Following the fort's surrender, the company in which he was serving disbanded. On a trip to Yorkville that summer to visit his mother, Sims joined Company A under Captain McCorkle and served all four years "without a scratch or furlough," missing only the battle of Antietam in September 1862.[17]

York County product Thomas Jefferson Roach began the war with a volunteer company from Rock Hill that eventually joined the 5th South Carolina. When that unit disbanded, Roach enlisted in Company H of the 12th. Captured while with the Army of Northern Virginia in September 1862, Roach was paroled immediately and sent to Richmond, directed not to serve again until exchanged. Learning he had been exchanged when he arrived in Richmond, he returned to his regiment and would fight with it for the remainder of the war in the Eastern Theater.[18]

15 UDC *Recollections*, 9:542–43.

16 J. R. Boyles, *Reminiscences of The Civil War* (Columbia, SC, 1892), 3; UDC *Recollections*, 2:552.

17 UDC *Recollections*, 6:226.

18 Ibid., 221–222; UDC *Recollections*, 8:275–76.

Lancaster County native Benjamin M. Powell became perhaps the most celebrated of the regiment's enlisted men. Like many, Powell enlisted in the Lancaster Grays with the portent of civil war and served in Charleston during the bombardment of Fort Sumter. His company was later mustered into the 5th South Carolina and served on the Virginia Peninsula during the Seven Days' Campaign in June–July 1862, fighting at Gaines's Mill and Glendale/Frayser's Farm. That summer, however, Powell secured a transfer to Company I of the 12th South Carolina, with whom he served until the end of the war.

As a scout and sharpshooter, he was soon celebrated as one of the best shots in the Army of Northern Virginia and eventually received one of two Whitfield rifles distributed to his brigade. Though it has never been corroborated officially, Powell's prowess with the rifle purportedly wreaked havoc in the Federal high command at Spotsylvania Court House, credited by some for the long-range sniper shot that killed Union VI Corps commander Maj. Gen. John Sedgwick on May 9, 1864. Despite two offers of promotion to lieutenant in Company I, Powell chose to remain an enlisted man, joining a special battalion of sharpshooters featuring the army's top marksmen. In that role, he became one of only a handful of truly independent, roving sharpshooters and scouts to serve at the pleasure of the high command, generally allowed to operate at will to scout the enemy, gain information, and inflict damage.[19]

Near Powell's name in the regiment's roll book was another Lancaster County native, Jonas Plyler, a 20-year-old who enlisted with Barnes at Lancaster Court House in August 1861. Eventually he was joined by his brother, Ellison, who enlisted on May 15, 1862, just after the regiment arrived in Virginia. A third brother, Ransom, joined the regiment in 1864. By war's end, the three brothers had been wounded in combat, but all survived.[20]

James Harris, the Catawba in Company H, survived some of the war's most horrific fighting and was wounded at least once in combat. Initially enlisting as a cook, Harris eventually served as an enlisted man in the ranks and fought at Antietam, Gettysburg, and in the 1863 Mine Run and 1864 Overland campaigns. Records are incomplete, but, as referenced above, it is possible he was among the 32 Company H men who surrendered at Appomattox. Described as a "brave soldier," James was wounded in the 40-acre cornfield at Antietam, as was his brother John, who would be captured. Exchanged at some point in 1863, John was eventually transferred to the Southern Invalid Corps, crippled for life. Contemporaries

19 Benjamin Powell to Wife, Nov. 21, 1907, in "The Westchester Civil War Round Table Newsletter," Croton Falls, NY, 1980.

20 Bob Helsel, personal interview, Aug. 27, 1994.

described both men as "good soldiers" with "great courage and fidelity"—proud members of the Indian Land Guards. Both James and John survived the war, though James died in 1874 at the age of 40. In 1869–71, John became chief of the Catawba Tribe.[21]

The Rev. J. Monroe Anderson served as the 12th South Carolina's dedicated chaplain. Described as "pious, energetic, and kind," he was a pillar of the regiment from the beginning of the war until he resigned because of health issues in November 1863. Anderson ministered to the men both spiritually and physically. When supplies such as shoes, socks, and blankets became scarce, he routinely returned home to make patriotic pleas to citizens to donate to the troops, making the rounds in person if necessary. Anderson seemed everywhere the first two years of the war and even witnessed the mortal wounding of Brig. Gen. Maxcy Gregg at the battle of Fredericksburg in December 1862, caring for the Columbia native on the field and accompanying him to his death bed (he would die December 15).

Anderson's compassion, faith, service, and philanthropy cannot be understated. His presence on the field and his actions off the field made him perhaps the regiment's most indispensable and important individual. He almost single-handedly kept the regiment's spirits high during difficult times when faith in a higher power seemed to be all that the men had to sustain themselves. Religion became a recurring theme the soldiers embraced when they were not on campaign, and Anderson's influence in making religious services accessible and understandable to the veterans was indispensable.[22]

A world away from Anderson's quiet piety was the hard-fighting William Dunlop, a dependable, aggressive fighter who became an influential historian and proponent of the regiment after the war. Elected first lieutenant of Company B in 1861, Dunlop became its captain, fought in most of the regiment's battles, and eventually was promoted to major, commanding an elite battalion of sharpshooters in 1864–65. Dunlop authored a book on his experiences as the commander of that unit, *Lee's Sharpshooters*, and kept readers of the *Yorkville Enquirer* informed with his "Bivouac and Battles" series during the 1880s. A riveting and descriptive writer, Dunlop's descriptions of the 12th's camps, marches, and battles offer fascinating and detailed glimpses into not only the horror of war but also its tranquil side.

D. J. Carter was in his early 20s when he enlisted in Company I several months after the initial muster. A musician, he survived the war and kept a detailed diary of his service focusing on the minutiae of the soldier's life. Carter's

21 Blummer, "Record of Catawba Indians' Service," 225–26, 228–29.

22 LOCAL, "For the Lancaster Ledger," *Lancaster Ledger*, Nov. 25, 1863, 2.

recollections on nearly a weekly basis provided an excellent and informative road map of the regiment's endeavors in 1862–63. He also routinely kept readers of the *Lancaster Ledger* newspaper updated through editorials and updates, using the pseudonym, "LOCAL." After the war, Carter became an influential surrogate for the survivor's association of the regiment and was instrumental in organizing many of its reunions.

Brothers Joseph and William Templeton, privates in Company B, were among those to survive the conflict. The elder Joseph joined the company in 1861, William a year later. Despite specifically enlisting in the 12th at Lightwood Knot Springs in August 1862, William was assigned duty in the 5th South Carolina when he and other new recruits slated to join the 12th arrived too late to catch the regiment in Richmond as it headed north with Maj. Gen. A. P. Hill's "Light Division" during the Second Manassas campaign. Together, the Templeton brothers wrote 115 letters home during the conflict and posed together proudly for one of the only known photographs of enlisted men in the regiment wearing standard-issue Confederate uniforms. The Templetons were simple, yeomen Upcountry farmers, classic representatives of the rank-and-file not only of the 12th South Carolina but also the Army of Northern Virginia as a whole. Barely literate, they could read and write but only in rough rudimentary terms. Their letters to family members show more concern about news from home, the state of the crops, and mundane routines in camp rather than describe in any detail the momentous campaigns and battles in which they were engaged. Despite the letters' lack of detail regarding the fighting, the Templeton letters ably filled gaps with their consistent reports on rations, camp duties, and the regiment's overall health.[23]

* * *

The regiment's training at Lightwood Knot Springs would prove a rite of passage for the raw volunteers in those early months of the conflict. The facility, described by one soldier as a "beautiful sandy plain," was a popular resort area prior to the war for those seeking a respite from poor health, heat, and mosquitoes, blessed with both boiling mineral hot springs and reliable railroad access. On July 18, 1861, South Carolina Governor Francis Pickens designated Lightwood Knot Springs and Aiken as the state's instruction sites. Companies then being raised were instructed to "repair to the camp nearest to it."

23 "Introduction" to "The Civil War Letters of Joseph and William Templeton," transcribed by The South Caroliniana Library, 1994, 1.

Although it was known as a resort, the area was anything but "resortish," according to one ill visitor, who wrote: "On my arrival there I was as much astonished as surprised at the appearance of the place. Instead of finding from the fashionable resort to the Springs, some romantic spot, selected by some romantic genius decorated with all the art man's ingenuity is capable of displaying—Lo & behold I was at the consecrated spot when I inquired of the driver how far before we reached it. Just think reader how awful you would feel to be hurried from a bed of sickness with the expectations of soon being translated to some such place as before described, when to your horror was presented to your view a square of ground enclosed in the midst of the woods by a rough plank fence in the center of which stood 3 or 4 log cabins intended for the accommodations of visitors."[24]

If the "resort" did not meet the expectations of that visitor, the area at Lightwood Knot Springs proved an ideal military camp for the recruits. The "square of ground" provided a fitting encampment and drill field, and its proximity to Columbia and the nearby railroad ensured the camp could be stocked full of enthusiastic troops as well as supplies. Soon, other regiments mustered there, including the 13th and 14th South Carolina. The encampment became known as "Camp Johnson" in honor of William Johnson, then-president of the Charlotte and Columbia Railroad, which ran near the camp. As August turned to September, Camp Johnson looked more and more like a military encampment. "All the Companies at Lightwood Knot Springs seem to be comfortably situated," recalled a soldier in early September. "It is a good location for the purpose—high, health, dry, level and good water abundant. About thirty companies are in camp. In all, forty-two Infantry, three cavalry, and two Artillery companies have been accepted under the late call."[25]

In early September, Dunovant appointed Lt. W. H. Talley of Company C (Cedar Creek Rifles) as the regimental adjutant, and men within the various companies began to organize messes of between seven and twelve men each. Messes fulfilled assorted functions both in camp and on campaign. The soldiers would share the load carrying cooking utensils and tentage on the march, cooking, and completing camp chores such as filling canteens. Although the 12th South Carolina's initial messes were numbered within each company, it was common for soldiers in other units to christen their messes with interesting and thematic names. Messes invariably changed throughout the war as new men joined the

24 *Lightwood Knot Herald and Daily Expositor*, June 15, 1837; Miller, "My Experience," 216; Boyles, *Reminiscences,* 4–5; L. K., "Camp Correspondence," 1; Francis Pickens, "By the Governor of South Carolina, A Proclamation," *Keowee Courier*, July 27, 1861, 3.

25 Helen King, "Lightwood Knot Springs," *The State*, May 5, 1959 (the page number is missing in the copy in author's possession); Caldwell, *The History of a Brigade of South Carolinians*, 33; LOCAL, "Our Volunteers in Camp," 2.

ranks or departed as casualties. Inviting a man into one's mess was akin to asking someone to join a family unit.[26]

Because many officers had no prior military experience, molding the raw recruits into soldiers could take time and effort. At least some of the men had antebellum military experience either in local militia companies or by enlisting in companies that disbanded after Fort Sumter. Lieutenant Dunlop recalled that Company B "was at once put upon drill in the squad, platoon and school of the company, as well as brought under the restraints of army regulations." William Miller of Company H noted that he arrived at Lightwood Knot Springs about July 1 and was there for nearly three months, "drilling every day, for both the officers and men had to be instructed."

To rectify the lack of military training, cadets arrived from the South Carolina Military Academy in Charleston (today's Citadel) to train both enlisted men and officers in the art of war. As many of the volunteers cut their teeth in the prewar militia using "heavy" infantry manuals by the likes of William Gilham and William McComb, adopting the famed "Hardee's Rifle and Light Infantry Tactics" (authored by U.S. Army colonel-turned-Confederate general William Hardee) was a radical change and awkward to many, according to one officer. As time progressed, however, the men became accustomed to the change and were initiated into the mundane duties of camp life, including such things as fatigue duty and guard mount. To prevent mischief, guards were placed around the camp and at quartermasters' and company stores. Despite the occasional misdeed, "the discipline was fairly good," recalled one soldier. Writing from the camp, regimental chaplain Anderson observed that, "remarkably good order prevails here. I have only heard one profane expression since I have been in camp, and that was from a negro."[27]

Writing to a local paper and describing his day as the "dull routine," one soldier from York County recounted each day's itinerary:

5:00 a.m. Reveille

5:30–6:30 Drill

7:00 Breakfast

8:00 Surgeon's Call

26 L. M. G., "From Lightwood Knot," Sept. 5, 1861, 1.

27 James Hoyt, "Recollections and Reminiscences," *The State*, May 9, 1901; Dunlop, *Bivouac and Battles (Part I)*, 1; J. Monroe Anderson, "For the Yorkville Enquirer," *Yorkville Enquirer*, Oct. 10, 1861, 2.

8:00–9:00 Officer's Drill

10:00–11:00 Drill

11:00 Orderly call

1:00 p.m. Dinner

2:00–3:00 Drill

4:30–5:30 Drill

7:00 Supper

9:00 Tattoo [Bugle call to signal the imminence of "Taps."]

9:30 Taps[28]

Away from their homes for the first time in their lives, hundreds of the young soldiers readily welcomed the more innocent perks of soldiering, however. This included devouring the boxes of delicacies sent from home or volunteering to carry supplies from the train to the camp commissary (although it is evident some of those supplies never made it that far). "[I have] seen the men of the camp break up the large sheets of baker's bread or 'wasp's nest' as they called it, and play snow ball game with the loaves, chunking one another until there would be no baker's bread left to carry over to the commissary," wrote one man. "These were great times for the officers and men and how anxious they were for hostilities to commence! Dress parades were held every afternoon, and hundreds of men, ladies and children—mostly ladies—would come up to the camp each afternoon from Columbia to see the drills and parades of the soldiers."

When time permitted, the men also took trips into Columbia, whether they had permission or not. Watching the train thunder down the track also broke the monotony of camp life, and regular church services took place throughout the day. The men's daily rations consisted of bacon, beef, rice, sugar, coffee, flour, and crackers, and the water was described by some as "good."[29]

"Considerable sickness," however, inevitably impacted the newly formed companies—with the men from rural areas, in close contact with many others for the first time and thus especially susceptible, their immune systems had yet to build sufficient resistance to various diseases. The regiment, in fact, suffered a significant outbreak of measles in the latter half of September. On October 2,

28 L. M. G., "From Lightwood Knot," *Yorkville Enquirer*, Sept. 19, 1861, 2.

29 King, "Lightwood Knot Springs"; Hoyt, "Recollections and Reminiscences"; Boyles, *Reminiscences*, 4; L. K., *Camp Correspondence*.

Anderson reported that the outbreak claimed several lives and that 136 men in the regiment were on the sick list. Joseph Templeton wrote home to his brother William about this time that out of the roughly 900 troops in the regiment, only about 300 were present for roll call on any given morning. Fortunately, favorable weather and proactive measures by the regimental surgeons, led by chief surgeon E. B. Turnipseed, helped contain the outbreak.

Lack of ambition and laziness played a role as well in the reduction of troop numbers. J. R. Boyles of Company C wrote sarcastically that a "new" company was soon formed: Company O. "It embraced members from all the other companies," he wrote. "It consisted of those that were really sick and of a goodly number who were not sick, but too lazy to drill. Every morning, Joe Taylor and his kettle drum and fife man would beat surgeon's call. The boys had a tune and words for it:

Come along sick, and get your ipecac;
Come along sick, and get your ipecac;
If you don't come soon, you needn't come at all;
Come along sick and get your ipecac; etc."

Boyles recalled in detail the process every morning as dozens of men would fall out of ranks for the surgeon's call. "Co. O, which was invariably the largest company in the regiment, would fall in and march in solemn procession, with long faces and despondent looks, to the tent of Dr. E. B. Turnipseed, surgeon of the regiment, whose first command to each one in turn was, 'Let me see your tongue.' He would then prescribe for them. . . . Co. O was always full. It seemed the more members of the regiment died and were killed, the larger it got."[30]

To combat the growing problems of sickness at Camp Johnson, and to help separate those in need of care from the camp, a hospital was established at the fairgrounds in nearby Columbia. A steady stream of wagons and ambulances transported the sick there, and female volunteers assisted the regimental surgeons to comfort the sick men and attend to their needs. "There liberality knows no bounds short of the comfort of every soldier committed to their care," Anderson recalled. "It is truly wonderful to see what they have done, and are doing for the relief of our suffering soldiers."

30 Boyles, *Reminiscences*, 4; J. Monroe Anderson, "Fair Grounds Hospital," *Yorkville Enquirer*, Oct. 17, 1861; Joseph Templeton to William Templeton, Sept. 26, 1861, in "The Civil War Letters of Joseph and William Templeton," transcribed by The South Caroliniana Library, 1994; L. M. G., "From Lightwood Knot."

Private J. P. Robertson of Company I in a homemade uniform at the outset of the war. *Library of Congress*

By mid-October, the surgeons of the 12th and 13th South Carolina were treating more than 200 men for ailments. In addition to his duties as chaplain, Anderson routinely penned updates about the regiment for newspapers in the region, also documenting how individual soldiers were faring—welcome missives to the families and others back home.[31]

Throughout September, the troops were issued homemade uniforms, primarily cut and sewn by women in the towns where individual companies originated. Uniforms for Company I's "Lancaster Hornets" were prepared in that manner at the Odd-Fellows Hall in Lancaster Court House. William Miller attested that the uniform he received in camp that fall "was the only clothing I ever got from the government for the entire four years. What I got after that time was sent by my parents from home, and these were often badly needed before getting there, owing to their not being able to get them to me." Miller came to understand the economics of rebellion through his uniforms: "Why I got no more clothes was for the reason that so many of the soldiers had no one at home that could furnish them clothes, and the clothing issued to companies only two or three suits at a time. The most needy got them if possible to get them on, so you can see, I spent the next four years of my life working for one suit of clothes and for $11.00 per month, and the rations when they had them for us. The $11.00 soon depreciated in value at the last to about what would buy stamps, paper and envelopes for writing letters home."[32]

Miller's experience sheds light on uniform distribution for the regiment in the later years of the war, as uniforms apparently were issued in limited quantities and given exclusively to those in most need. Those from families with means were

31 J. Monroe Anderson, "Ladies Retreat for Sick Soldiers," *Yorkville Enquirer*, Oct. 10, 1861, 2; J. Monroe Anderson, "Fair Grounds Hospital," *Yorkville Enquirer*, Oct. 17, 1861, 1.

32 Miller, "My Experience," 216; "To the Ladies," *Lancaster Ledger*, Sept. 25, 1861, 2.

outfitted in clothing originating from home and not through any formal military disbursement system. As one can imagine, these garments varied among the soldiers, meaning a consistent appearance in the ranks was unlikely, particularly this early in the war. Period photographs show that the South Carolina regiments eventually were issued a basic frock coat with black taped worsted wool outlining the edges of the collar and in some circumstances an upside-down chevron pattern near the wrist to the forearm. These uniforms were invariably constructed of jean cloth (wool and cotton fabric woven with a twill pattern) in a variety of colors and dyes. South Carolina supplied its state troops this type of uniform through late 1862.[33]

Like most regiments in the Confederate army, troops in individual companies of the 12th were from the same region (and in many cases the same county or town). Military age males of entire families typically enlisted in the same unit. Lieutenant Colonel Edward McCrady of the 1st South Carolina, speaking at the October 21, 1886, reunion of the Association Army of Northern Virginia in Richmond, perhaps best described this phenomenon:

> The assembling of our armies was really the gathering of clans. . . . The young men of a neighborhood formed themselves together into a company at the call of some one who had been a leader in the community; the company was in fact but a representative part of the community from which it came. A letter from home to any individual member was of interest to all. The neighborhood news was of equal concern to the captain as to the humblest private, and the box from home was sure to be shared in common. The casualties of battle affected the whole community. No one could afford to shirk, for news of his conduct was sure to go home with the news of the battle. Every private, as well as every officer, fought every engagement in the presence, as it were, of his home people, and he could not afford to disgrace them. This was the great incentive, no doubt, to the extraordinary perseverance and patience of our soldiers amidst the greatest privation as well as of the individual valor of men who could hope for no particular notice in orders or reports.[34]

The 12th South Carolina was considered "the first Regiment" when it mustered in at Lightwood Knot Springs, and it took nearly a month to receive its designation. Not until September 25, 1861, would the regiment receive its formal designation as "the 12th." According to a short blurb in the *Lancaster Ledger*: "The

33 Ron Field, "Clothing the Confederate Soldiers of South Carolina, 1861–1865," *The Military Collector & Historian*, 70:1, 4–5.

34 *SHSP* 14:202.

correspondent of the *Yorkville Enquirer*, writing from Camp Johnson, Lightwood Knot Springs, says: 'By an order read out at dress parade yesterday evening, we learn that Colonel Dunovant's Regiment is designated as the 12th.'"[35]

With that, the die was cast. The "first Regiment" at Lightwood Knot Springs became, in an instant, the 12th South Carolina Volunteer Infantry. As summer turned to fall at Camp Johnson, the winds of change were in store not only for the men of the newly minted regiment but also the others stationed there. They would soon leave the idyllic and peaceful confines of their "square of ground" campsite, drill field, and the innocent forays into Columbia, for their first campaign of the war. Union naval and ground forces were knocking on the door of their beloved Palmetto State. The perseverance and patience of the soldiers would be severely tested as the regiment set forth for South Carolina's Lowcountry. The privations, hardships, and sacrifices of warfare soon became a persistent reality. Many would not make it home, and all were forever changed by their experience in the coming conflict.

35 "The correspondent . . ." *Lancaster Ledger*, Sept. 25, 1861, 2.

Chapter Two

Lowcountry Blues

CHARLESTON WASN'T MERELY the Confederacy's most vital harbor along its Atlantic coastline. As the home of Fort Sumter, it was now the very symbol of the Southern rebellion. When Federal naval activity accelerated off the coast of North Carolina in the late summer and early fall of 1861, Confederate officials grew increasingly alarmed about the security of both Charleston and the entire Atlantic seaboard and, on August 21, handed command of the Department of South Carolina to Brig. Gen. Roswell S. Ripley. A Charleston transplant born in Ohio, Ripley began immediate work on defense of the state's vulnerable 187-mile-long coastline by erecting fortifications and batteries at several strategic points. To the men of the 12th and their comrades in fellow regiments, the haste behind Ripley's enterprise was no mystery.

Ripley had reputable military roots. He graduated from West Point in 1843—alongside future Union notables Ulysses Grant, William Franklin, and Rufus Ingalls—and served with distinction in both the Mexican War and the Second Seminole War in Florida. The commander's urgent need for troops of all stripes was why the 12th South Carolina—already encamped at Lightwood Knots Springs since early July—figured in his early plans.[1]

In mid-October, Union Brig. Gen. Thomas W. Sherman and a 12,000-man expeditionary force were en route by water from Hampton Roads, Virginia, to

1 Ellison Capers, "South Carolina," in Clement Evans, ed., *Confederate Military History,* 12 vols. (Atlanta, 1899), 5:29, 418. Hereafter cited as *CMH*. All references are to volume 5 unless otherwise noted.

join Flag Officer Samuel Francis Du Pont's fleet off the South Carolina coast. The Federal objective was straight-forward: take Port Royal Sound and the surrounding islands of Hilton Head, Beaufort, and Edisto to establish a base of operations and gain a foothold from which future operations in the region could be conducted. Holding onto Port Royal Harbor would be crucial to the Confederates' defense of the southern Atlantic coast. To buttress the effort, Ripley ordered the 12th and other South Carolina troops to the new fortified positions he had established along the water.[2]

One wing—approximately half the 12th's strength—was among the first wave of troops involved, departing Camp Johnson at stages in late September and early October. (The other wing would follow in mid- to late-October and consolidate at Beaufort.)

The regiment's precise breakdown was never certified, but Companies C and H were the first to leave Lightwood Knot Springs. "Early in October (I think the 2nd), we boarded the cars for Charleston," Boyles wrote. "Arriving there, we were not permitted to stop, but were hurried down to the wharf and hustled . . . onto an old cotton steamboat and started for we know not where, although [fellow soldiers] Rolling Moss and Jim Farmer kept things lively by singing."

In an October 1 report, Ripley detailed the strength of his force in the state:

> Orr's First Rifles, on Sullivan's island, 1,5121; Hagood's First, Cole's island and stone forts, 1,115; Dunovant's Twelfth, north and south of Edisto, 367; Maginault's Tenth, Georgetown and defenses, 538; Jones's Fourteenth, camp near Aiken, 739; Heyward's Eleventh, Beaufort and defenses, 758; cavalry, camp near Columbia, 173; cavalry, camp near Aiken, 62; arsenal, Charleston (artillery), 68; Edwards' Thirteenth, De Saussure's Fifteenth, and remainder of Dunovant's Twelfth, 2,372.

The venture from Camp Johnson to the coast—at least for Companies C and H—was not without incident. At Charleston, inadequate room had the men separated on two vessels rather than one. Then, Hastings Reynolds of Company C drowned after falling overboard, the efforts to retrieve his body unsuccessful. "His body was seen by another boat the next day floating among the sea-weeds," Boyles

2 United States War Department, *The War of the Rebellion: A Compilation of the Official Records of the Union and Confederate Armies*, 128 vols. (Harrisburg, PA, 1971), Series I, 16:3–4. Hereafter cited as *OR*. All references are to Series 1 unless otherwise noted; *SHSP* 1:104.

A view of the earthen Fort Beauregard located at Bay Point on Port Royal Sound in November 1861 after the Confederate evacuation. *Library of Congress*

recalled, "but was left there—food for the fish and vultures. This was the first man we lost from our company, and it made us all feel quite sad."[3]

* * *

In late October, with the entire regiment finally consolidated in and around Beaufort, the 12th was ordered to divide again, assigned with guarding the opposing entry points to Port Royal Sound at Bay Point and Hilton Head Island, which were defended respectively by Fort Beauregard and Fort Walker, about three miles apart. Spirits were high. Boyles, for one, remembered believing naively that the men were in for "a nice time" on the coast.

Roughly 640 men in six companies (A, C, D, E, F, and I) garrisoned Fort Beauregard under the command of Colonel Dunovant and Lt. Col. Barnes. Major Cadwallader Jones commanded the other four companies, approximately 260 men, at Fort Walker—joined by about 622 men in three companies of the 11th South Carolina and assorted cavalry. At Hilton Head, the regiment encamped behind the fort in tents, using a small nearby cottage for its headquarters.

At Fort Beauregard the men faced true hardships for the first time. "Here we began to experience a little of what a soldier's life was," Boyles wrote. "The

3 Boyles, *Reminiscences*, 5.

water that we drank and used for cooking was obtained by sinking a flour barrel about two feet into the sand; it was miserable water." Despite the water quality, the men passed the remainder of the month and early November in relatively leisurely fashion. Free time involved card-playing, fishing for crabs, and walks along the beach gathering seashells. The men also enjoyed welcome additions to their rations—typically consisting of hard tack and salt pork, which they mocked as "salt horse or mule"—with sweet potatoes, oranges, limes, figs, and pomegranates plentiful in the area. Some adventurous souls ventured into wild areas not only to pick fruit but also to hunt alligators, as many of the men had never before seen one. Even the infamous "Co. O," the company designated for the regiment's "sick and lazy," was nearly disbanded, "as there was very little to do," according to a Company C soldier.[4]

The officers enjoyed their comforts, too. "The major commanding had everything in the line of furniture and camp equipage that a soldier could reasonably desire," recalled Lieutenant Dunlop, who served as the battalion's adjutant. "The adjutant also set up in good style," Dunlop fondly recalled, referring to himself in the third person. "He had a nice camp cot and mattress with nice pillows, sheets, heavy white double blankets, campstools with Brussels seats, books, papers and periodicals, and eleven nice new linen shirts, which he considered would last him through the war."

By early November, the men watched with trepidation as Federal warships anchored off the coast in ever-increasing numbers, evidently preparing for an attack on Port Royal Sound. Nevertheless, their spirits and confidence remained high. "We felt pretty secure, thinking our heavy guns and those at Hilton Head would be able to knock their fleet to atoms," Boyles boasted naively, a sentiment to which one Company B officer concurred: "[A]ll Yankeedom could not drive the Confederates from the island."[5]

Despite the troops' pluck, the distance between the two forts and their relative positions to the harbor created problems for the South Carolinians and their comrades in the artillery. Only the heaviest guns were capable of reaching the Union vessels as they hovered in their current positions outside the forts. Hilton Head's Fort Walker had 20 guns and Bay Point's Fort Beauregard 19. Of these, however, Walker could use only 13 against an attacking fleet, Beauregard just seven. The remaining guns could be used only against a land attack, which could not be discounted. Armistead L. Long, Robert E. Lee's chief of artillery at the time,

4 Ibid.; Miller, "My Experience," 217; *CMH*, 31–32; *OR* 6: 7, 24–29; Dunlop, *Bivouac and Battles (Part I)*, 1; Boyles, *Reminiscences*, 6; "From the 12th Regiment," *Yorkville Enquirer*, Oct. 31, 1861, 1.

5 Boyles, *Reminiscences*, 5–6; Dunlop, *Bivouac and Battles (Part I)*, 1.

described the inadequacy of coastal defenses such as Beauregard and Walker after the war. "Many of the defences, being injudiciously located and hastily erected, offered but little resistance to the enemy when attacked," he wrote. "These defects were not surprising when we take into consideration the inexperience of the engineers and the long line of seacoast to be defended." Needless to say, infantry in such a fight was essentially useless.[6]

On November 5, with more Federal vessels anchored outside Port Royal Sound, Dunovant prepared for an imminent attack on Fort Beauregard. To address a possible infantry assault, he covered the main land approaches with the 12th South Carolina companies on hand. According to the colonel's after-action report, he sent A and D to a "a range of sand hills, about 200 yards distant from Fort Beauregard, for the purpose of protecting that work in case of an attempt of the enemy to land." Companies C and E took position at a site known as "The Narrows" to the north, and F and I remained in reserve near the regiment's camp. Meanwhile, Dunlop reported that at Fort Walker, "All was life and activity in camp. The boys polished their rusty rifles, replenished their cartridge boxes and donned their long bowie-knives, with which all were armed, and made general preparations for the impending collision."

In the sound, however, Federal vessels summarily handled Confederate steamers sent to engage them, forcing those ships to retreat above the forts and up the Broad River. When the Federal ships followed the steamers into the sound, they came within range of Fort Beauregard's guns, which promptly launched repeated rounds in their direction. That in turn drew a heavy Federal response on the fort and the other infantry-occupied areas of the island. After two hours of bombardment by both sides, the Federal fleet withdrew to the Atlantic, remaining there for the remainder of the day. From all accounts, this was the first time the men of the 12th South Carolina came under enemy fire. To its fortune, no casualties were reported.

With no action from the Union fleet on the 6th, Dunovant recalled several companies to the camp. That evening, the six companies of the 12th slept on their arms near the fort, anticipating another attack but ready to move at a moment's notice.[7]

Although November 7 dawned still and clear, events would develop quickly. As Dunovant recalled in his after-action report: "[A]t 8:30 a.m. the fleet of war vessels, headed by what is supposed to have been the Minnesota, bore towards the northwest till reaching the main channel, they moved directly towards our

6 *CMH*, 31–32; Armistead Long, *Memoirs of Robert E. Lee* (Secaucus, NJ, 1983), 137.

7 *OR* 6: 24–29; Dunlop, *Bivouac and Battles (Part I)*, 1.

A view of the rear of Fort Walker located at Hilton Head on Port Royal Sound in November 1861 after the Confederate evacuation. *Library of Congress*

batteries. As soon as they came within range[,] Fort Beauregard opened upon the vessel in advance, which, being seconded by Fort Walker and replied to by the enemy, the action became general."

Still anticipating a land assault, Dunovant sent Companies C and E back to the Narrows, a strip of land just 50 yards wide and 1,000 yards long, keeping the remaining four companies in camp to await developments. As the men in C and E double-quicked through the sand, Dunovant changed his mind and sent the remaining four companies (A, E, F, and I) to the sand hills behind Fort Beauregard. Provided excellent cover from the shelling, they remained there the rest of the day. Soon, Dunovant ordered C and E to fall back to supporting distance on the sand hills to operate as a reserve.

Moving into the heart of the sound, the Union fleet rained shot and shell not only on Fort Beauregard but also over the surrounding terrain, then reversed course and continued the devastating barrage. Despite the terrible conditions and the inability of the infantry to counter the fire, Dunovant recalled that the men of the 12th "exhibited great coolness and promptness in obedience to orders. Notwithstanding the protection afforded by the sand hills many shot and shell fell around them, but fortunately without inflicting injury of any kind. The batteries at Fort Beauregard were worked with great gallantry, skill, and energy." Even though the barrage did little damage to the fort, the howling and whistling of the shells through the trees had the men hugging the sand throughout.

At 2:00 p.m., the Federal ships diverted their attention to the south, intent on reducing Fort Walker, where four companies of the 12th were stationed under Maj. Cadwallader Jones. The missiles, Private Miller recalled, destroyed the potato patches the men had enjoyed raiding days before: "They shot bombs at us that fell in the potato patches and dug enough potatoes for several messes, but that was one time our appetites were not the trouble." About 3:00 p.m., Walker's guns fell silent, creating anxiety for the men at Beauregard that the fort had been taken and a renewed threat to their bastion was inevitable. From the precarious position of his six companies in the sand hills, Dunovant rushed into the fort on foot and implored Capt. Stephen Elliott Jr. of the Beaufort Artillery his opinion on Walker's status. Having observed the action across the sound from his battery's position, Elliott replied that Walker, its guns now silenced, was likely abandoned. "Well sir," Dunovant replied as the missiles shrieked over Beauregard, "it having been proved that these works cannot accomplish the end for which they were designed—that of protecting the harbor—you will prepare to retire."

With the writing on the wall for the security of his own command, Dunovant ordered an evacuation of Beauregard, although he formed his infantry along the beach in full view of the Federal fleet as the sun set. Dunovant's bravado notwithstanding, the six companies of the 12th and the rest of the command (the 11th South Carolina [9th Volunteers]; Elliott's artillery; the Colleton [SC] Rifles; and an independent company of infantry) were soon in full retreat from the area, unaware of the fate of their comrades at Fort Walker. The regiment's baggage and heavy guns were left behind. Dunovant explained these orders to his superiors, judging that the "impracticability of transportation" in the swampy ground justified his decision.[8] Dunovant, however, could hardly be blamed for doing what he could to save his command. The Narrows was the only reliable retreat route, taking the column first to Eddings Island and then toward Beaufort.

Dunovant described the terrain as "an extensive swamp, entirely impenetrable save by a trail known to few, and of such extreme difficulty as to preclude the possibility of transporting baggage of any kind beyond what could be borne on the shoulders of the men." The experience was miserable for the men in the ranks and constituted their first real trying march. As darkness fell, they struggled to keep pace in knee- to waist-deep water for several miles, undoubtedly wondering whether they would be cut off and captured.

About 11:00 p.m., Boyles would recall, the ragged troops halted for about an hour to cross Station Creek while waiting for flats "rowed or pulled by Gullahs, down-the-country-negroes, whose language we could not understand a word of."

8 *OR* 6: 25; Boyles, *Reminiscences*, 6–9; Miller, "My Experience," 217.

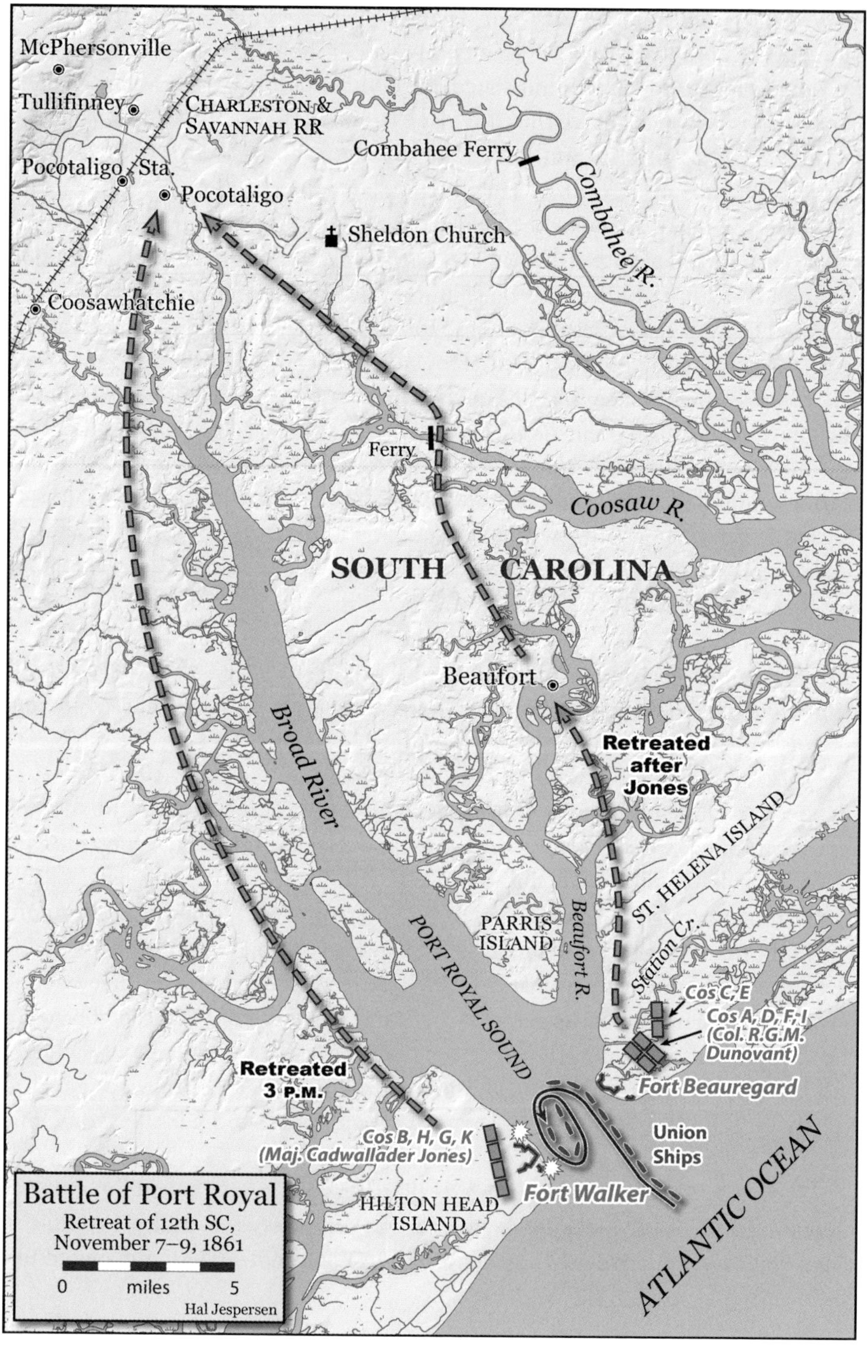
McPhersonville
Tullifinney
Charleston & Savannah RR
Combahee Ferry
Pocotaligo Sta.
Pocotaligo
Combahee R.
Sheldon Church
Coosawhatchie
Ferry
Coosaw R.
SOUTH CAROLINA
Beaufort
Broad River
Retreated after Jones
St. Helena Island
Parris Island
Beaufort R.
Port Royal Sound
Station Cr.
Cos C, E
Cos A, D, F, I (Col. R.G.M. Dunovant)
Retreated 3 P.M.
Fort Beauregard
Cos B, H, G, K (Maj. Cadwallader Jones)
Union Ships
Fort Walker
Hilton Head Island
Atlantic Ocean
Battle of Port Royal
Retreat of 12th SC, November 7–9, 1861
0 miles 5
Hal Jespersen

After crossing, the men eventually made their way to the residence of a Dr. Jenkins, who generously offered the troops any subsistence they could find, even though previous commands retreating through the area had already scoured the area and commandeered all of the cooked provender. During a brief halt at the Jenkins home, some of the troops were able to locate and cook some sweet potatoes and grist. The drawn-out column of 500 or so then continued toward Beaufort, aided by one of Dr. Jenkins's slaves as a guide, but only after Orderly Sgt. S. W. Broom threatened the man with a loaded musket. The march on the sandy trails was tiresome, the men sinking several inches with each step. On November 8, after an all-night march, Dunovant's command arrived near Beaufort to find the town deserted by its White population.[9]

There was another problem. The Beaufort River stood between the men and the town, with no apparent means of transportation across. Luckily, a steamboat was docked on the other side. With tensions and emotions running high and fearing capture by the Federals, Sergeant Brown and two other men from Company C found a rowboat and crossed the river. Threatening to "blow out his brains" if he resisted, they directed the captain of the steamboat to carry the men over. He readily complied. As Boyles recalled:

> We marched up into the little town, but how changed from what it was a few short weeks before. There were a few of the citizens still remaining [all the loyal citizens had gone], but they seemed perfectly contented and even glad. Capt. Davis ordered myself and two others to sally forth and see if we could find some whiskey to strengthen and encourage us before taking up our line of march to the ferry. We went into the store where an old fellow was brushing up his goods, arranging his bottles on the shelves, apparently happy in anticipation of a lively run from the Yankee soldiers—dreaming of greenbacks instead of graybacks. I told him our situation, and that we wanted some whiskey. He politely told us he could not sell for graybacks any more. We politely walked behind the counter, pressed what we wanted, marched out and up to where we had left our comrades. After all had taken a good stout drink, we took up our line of march to Port Royal ferry—tired, sleepy and hungry as wolves.

Once across, Dunovant and his men prudently slogged toward Port Royal Ferry and Pocataligo on South Carolina's mainland, where he hoped to prepare a defense and open a line of communication with his superiors. The final stretch to the crossing at Port Royal Ferry was an arduous and difficult nine miles, and by

9 *OR* 6: 23–27.

now many of the men were in terrible shape, having not eaten in two days. Many marched in bare feet and expected to be captured at every turn. From late Saturday to early Sunday, November 9–10, the anxious and worn-out command reached Pocataligo. There, they were reunited with their comrades in Companies B, H, G, and K who had suffered significantly as well during their own harrowing retreat from Fort Walker. Those companies received the worst of the attack on the 7th, withstanding the brunt of close-range shelling for several hours before being forced from the fort. Their retreat was just as distressing as that of Dunovant's command, if not worse. Panic set in during their evacuation, and in their haste some of the men tossed away their haversacks, canteens, knapsacks, cartridge boxes, and even rifles. They, too, filed through dirty swamps and rough terrain to reach the mainland, fearing capture the entire way.

The men, still not yet seasoned veterans, often had trouble with wounds that normally could be easily treated but became infected without proper attention. That was the case for one soldier, John B. Whitesides of York County. By the time Whitesides made it to Pocataligo, a now-infected wound compelled his transfer to a facility offering better care. Within several months, Whitesides's deteriorating health meant a discharge, and what was originally a minor injury would plague him the rest of his life. His story was commonplace in a war in which disease and infection claimed more men than enemy fire.[10]

* * *

The defense of Port Royal Sound and subsequent retreat debilitated the 12th, so much that the Confederate high command took notice. On November 5, just two days before the attack, Robert E. Lee assumed command of the Department of South Carolina, Georgia, and Florida after a disappointing series of engagements against Gens. George B. McClellan and William S. Rosecrans in western Virginia. In one of his first letters to then–Secretary of War Judah P. Benjamin, Lee mentioned the size and condition of Dunovant's command: "General [Thomas] Drayton reports he has but 955 men with him, and no field battery, the troops from Georgia that were on the island having returned to Savannah without orders. Colonel Dunovant's regiment is in as destitute a condition as General Drayton's command, as they were obliged to leave everything behind, and number between 600 and 700 men."

Observing the 12th on November 10 while the regiment was camped near Pocataligo, a captain in the neighboring 14th South Carolina also described the

10 Boyles, *Reminiscences*, 10; *OR* 6: 23–27, 31; *Recollections and Reminiscences*, 6:222.

12th as in "destitute" condition. "We passed the poor fellows . . . and they were rejoiced to see us coming to their relief," he recalled. "They barely escaped from being taken prisoners and had to leave all their baggage, tents and provisions and in fact brought nothing but their muskets with them. The poor fellows will be supplied again. . . . They were muddy up to their waists by wading through the marsh in their hasty retreat."[11]

Despite the regiment's poor physical shape and the misfortune that the panicked, disorganized retreat had stamped on its record, morale remained high, likely because all 10 companies were reunited. The men gave positive reviews to their new camp at Pocataligo, called "Camp Lee" in honor of the new department commander. "It was a beautiful place to camp, with plenty of potatoes, fish and oysters to eat," William Miller recalled, and Boyles fondly remembered: "We were once more a reunited command; and although sorry, indeed, that the enemy had obtained a foothold on our soil, we felt we were in much better condition for resistance than we had been at Bay Point and Hilton Head. We slept soundly and contentedly that night, dreaming of wives, sweethearts and those dear to us—they little dreaming of the many hardships we had endured during the past forty-eight hours. The next day we drilled a little and cleaned up our guns. I do not remember who was in command of Co. O; but whoever it was, recruiting began, and soon it became a very large company," he recalled.[12]

For the Confederacy, Port Royal was an unmitigated disaster. Evacuation of the forts allowed the Federals to transport men, munitions, and materiel into the region without much hassle, and seizing a beachhead on the coast transformed the area into a military Gibraltar the Union could use as a base for operations against the mainland. Port Royal Sound's deep harbor also provided safe anchorage for the Union navy, and the length of the channel brought Federal ships to within a few miles of the Charleston and Savannah Railroad, a major supply route. The loss of Hilton Head Island also jeopardized Savannah, only about 25 miles south.

Dunovant did not hesitate to submit his report on the affair. While the outcome of the mostly naval engagement was certainly not the regiment's fault, the portion of the report describing his troops' retreat indicates he anticipated criticism for not planning ahead in the event retreat became necessary. He would write:

> No soldier threw away his arms. In regard to the manner in which the retreat was arranged and effected, justice to myself and others requires that I should add a

11 *OR* 6: 309, 312; Varina Brown, *A Colonel at Gettysburg and Spotsylvania* (Columbia, SC, 1931), 39.

12 Boyles, *Reminiscences*, 10–11.

> word of explanation. Having received no instructions as to the mode in which the island of Bay Point should be defended, nor of the contingencies upon which it should be abandoned, with no arrangement for receiving orders, by means of signals or otherwise, from headquarters, and totally without information of any plan devised or facilities provided for the retreat of my command in case of disaster, I felt these circumstances imposed upon me the obligation of endeavoring to secure some means of evacuating the island in the event such a step should become necessary.
>
> Accordingly, the state of facts above referred to continuing, on Tuesday [November 5] I went in person to Captain Elliott, who perhaps was more familiar with the localities than any other person, and after learning from him, in answer to my inquiries, that a retreat was practicable through Eddings' Island, if boats and flats could be secured to take the forces across Station Creek, I instructed him to select some prudent and trusty person to superintend the collection of the necessary means of transportation at the landing on Eddings' Island. The Rev. Stephen Elliott was chosen to discharge this important duty, and left on Thursday morning for that purpose. Fortunately Capt. Thomas Hanckel, Mr. Henry Stuart, and Mr. W. H. Cuthbert, of Beaufort, had already secured a large number of flats at Dr. Jenkins' Landing, for the purpose of taking them to some point on Eddings' Island for our relief. Mr. Elliott informed them of the plan agreed upon, and thus, through the co-operation of these gentlemen and the valuable assistance of Captain Tripp and his command, the evacuation of the island was effected. I communicated the plan of retreat to none save Captain Elliott, the adjutant, and the quartermaster.[13]

In the wake of the Port Royal disaster, Lee—already highly regarded as a military engineer—went to work with his engineers in fortifying the areas, placing heavy guns, and withdrawing his infantry to the mainland. Establishing his headquarters at Coosawhatchie, Lee reinforced important positions along his new interior line by placing troops at Georgetown, Charleston, Pocataligo, Coosawhatchie, and Savannah, using the railroad to shift troops to and from the various positions in the event of attack. Port Royal Ferry, the crucial and strategic crossing of the Coosaw and Broad Rivers, was the gateway to Lee's mainland defenses. Four miles north of the ferry, Col. James Jones and the 14th South Carolina were positioned as an advanced guard, supported by cavalry and a single battery.

13 *OR* 6: 24–29; *SHSP* 1:105.

For the next few months, Lee's troops held this secure and interior line. According to Armistead Long, "there was thus a defensive relation throughout the entire line." With his calm and reassuring temperament and efficiency, Lee stabilized the region and the troops under his command—as he famously would do with the Army of Northern Virginia. In a letter home, Lt. Lewis Grist of Company A echoed Long's sentiment, writing: "In regard to our forces, suffice it to say that a sufficient number of men can be concentrated, at any point where our enemies can harm us, to drive them back to the cover of their gun boats. We have no fear that they will accomplish much towards subjugation in South Carolina."[14]

As the regiment rested and recuperated at Pocataligo, the men's behavior ran afoul of the few locals left in the area, particularly with respect to foraging, which they attempted for the first time. "The boys . . . began to learn the art of foraging for grub," Boyles wrote, "and the sweet potato patches near camp soon looked as if a drove of hogs had been turned in upon them, and those old low country gentlemen began to complain." After an incident in which two men "appropriated" a duck owned by a local resident named Mr. Heyward, the victim complained directly to Dunovant, who promptly had the offenders arrested, placed under guard, and provided a diet of only bread and water. "I have no doubt Mr. Heyward soon bitterly regretted having reported the matter," Boyles noted. "[H]e passed camp every day going to the railroad, and from time to time he came in sight until he disappeared, he was greeted with: 'Quack! Quack!', 'Here's your ducks' @&c. He looked as if he felt very mean, and have no doubt he did, because he knew we were guarding and trying to keep the enemy back from his door—he knew not how soon his ducks and all he had might fall into the hands of the Yankees." As for the treatment the regiment received by the local population at large, Boyles was even more decided in his observations: "I am bound to express what is an undeniable fact, and that is that he [Heyward] and many of like caliber in the country on the coast treated us with no respect."[15]

The men's mischievous behavior was not limited to the civilian population but extended also to their comrades. Privates Wylie Wyrick, Bill Smith, and Henry Rains were members of the same mess. Rains was an avid pipe smoker, and on one occasion, Wyrick and Smith made off with his pipe and filled it with gunpowder and tobacco. When they lit it and offered it to Rains, Boyles recalled, "he was soon

14 *SHSP* 1: 106; Brown, *A Colonel at Gettysburg and Spotsylvania*, 39; L. M. G., "From the 12th Regiment," *Yorkville Enquirer*, Jan. 9, 1862, 2.

15 Boyles, *Reminiscences*, 11–12.

minus hat, eye-brows, eye lashes and came very near losing his eyes." For their antics, Wyrick and Smith were arrested.[16]

* * *

The regiment remained encamped at Pocataligo through December, attending to fatigue duties and drilling and continuing to forage. It was also frequently called into action by the long roll; invariably false alarms that caused the men great consternation. Writing to the *Yorkville Enquirer* from "Camp Pemberton" on December 29, Grist described the annoying phenomenon. "Rumors abound in our camp nearly everyday, startling enough to satisfy the most inveterate newsmonger, but on investigation, the mountain is generally found to have been in labor, and the product, a mouse," he scoffed. Within one week in December alone, the 12th responded to at least four false alarms, one emanating from Lee himself, who ordered the regiment to double quick to Gardens Corner (seven miles east of Pocataligo) to respond to an alleged crossing by the enemy at Port Royal Ferry; the other three were by jittery pickets claiming imminent attacks. Every time, the regiment quickly assembled and marched to the alleged point of danger only to find out that it was, in Grist's words, just another "wolf story."[17]

As the Christmas season approached, Dunovant began to grant furloughs, allowing one or two men from each company 10-days' leave—and evidently the regiment, as a whole, soon recovered physically and mentally from the Forts Walker and Beauregard debacle. In late December, the regiment marched south to Pagis Point, closer to Port Royal Ferry, where it spent its first Christmas dining on turkeys, chickens, "fat pigs," and delicacies from home. There, it continued picket duty "up and down the river" and was subjected to regular false alarms by inexperienced pickets. The regiment also gained a few noncombatant recruits. On December 20, James and John Harris, the Catawba brothers from Rock Hill, joined Company H as cooks.

For some, the stay at Pagis Point was brief. Between Christmas and New Year's Eve, seven companies of the 12th moved north to Gardens Corner and established a permanent camp under Dixon Barnes's command, with Companies D, C, and F under Captain Bookter remaining at Pagis Point. The 12th's new camp at Gardens Corner stood at the crucial intersection of the Port Royal Ferry Road, running south to the ferry, and the Sheldon/Gardens Corner Road, which followed roughly

16 Ibid.

17 L. M. G., "From the 12th Regiment."

an east-west course. From Gardens Corner, the regiment could be deployed in various directions toward the 14th South Carolina, then encamped closer to the ferry, in case of a Federal attack. In this alignment, Port Royal Ferry was essentially the "front door" of any potential attack, which also meant the three companies stationed at Pagis Point now covered the "back door."[18]

The peace of the holiday revelries did not last. On January 1, Union Brig. Gen. Isaac Stevens moved an infantry force of 2,500 men north from Beaufort toward the Coosaw River, the main waterway between the coastal regions and the mainland. Five gunboats accompanied Stevens's column. The Federal plan, described as a "dash," revolved around quickly and efficiently capturing and/or destroying the Confederate heavy guns positioned at Port Royal Ferry. Disembarking on the north bank of the Coosaw from Beaufort Island, the Federal strike force would move west to the ferry from Chisholm Point, guided by the river as the gunboats moved alongside in support. Stevens's plan was a surgical raid into enemy territory, not a full-scale assault or invasion into the South Carolina interior. Once the guns were out of action, the men were to disengage.[19]

On New Year's Eve, the Federals moved to staging positions on the south bank of the Coosaw, crossing the river at several points along a two-mile front, from Pagis Point to Chisholm Landing, as 1862 dawned. Port Royal Ferry, their destination, was about seven miles south of Gardens Corner and "Camp Pemberton," the bivouac of a portion of the 12th South Carolina, whose men were enjoying a lazy first day of 1862. Dunovant was in Columbia at the time, attending the state's political convention. About 10 a.m., ominous gunfire, including fire from Federal gunboats on the Coosaw, was heard to the south and east. Unlike the desultory gunboat and artillery fire that proved to be false alarms in December, the noise this day was described by one officer in the 12th as "heavy" and increased and moved closer to the regiment's camp as the morning progressed. Something was clearly different.[20]

The overall commander in the area, Brig. Gen. John C. Pemberton—of future Vicksburg notoriety—paced nervously at his headquarters near Pocataligo Station, seven miles northwest of the 12th's camp bearing his name at Gardens Corner. Hearing the same approaching gunfire as the men of the 12th up the road, Pemberton mounted his horse and galloped rapidly down the Sheldon/Gardens Corner Road toward the sound. Drawing rein at the 12th's camp in the thicket,

18 Ibid., 12–13; *CMH*, 38; Blummer, "Catawba Indians' Service," 225.

19 *OR* 6: 44–46.

20 *OR* 6: 48–49, 67, 72, 74; L. M. G., "Dear Enquirer," *Yorkville Enquirer*, Jan. 9, 1862, 2.

Federal sentries stand guard on the south bank of the Coosaw River across from Port Royal Ferry near the scene of the fighting by the 12th South Carolina on New Year's Day, 1862. *Library of Congress*

Pemberton sought out Barnes, and the two assessed the situation as the gunfire increased. Barnes surmised essentially what Pemberton was thinking: that the Yankees must be attacking toward Port Royal Ferry from the east and had likely run headlong into Confederate skirmishers of the 14th South Carolina, encamped at the intersection of the Kean's Neck Road and Port Royal Ferry Road. It was about 10:30 a.m.[21]

Barnes was correct. At that moment, troops in James Jones's 14th South Carolina were in fact contesting a strong and determined Union advance up the Kean's Neck Road, a couple miles east of the 14th's camp. Jones prudently threw out his Companies B and H as skirmishers, and they engaged Stevens's attack force consisting of the 8th Michigan, 47th New York, 48th New York, 79th New York Highlanders, and 50th Pennsylvania. Concerned, Pemberton established his field headquarters at the 12th's Gardens Corner camp and communicated with Jones via a courier, who advised him at about 11:30 a.m. that Federals were on the mainland and approaching the ferry. Pemberton ordered Jones to double his defenses on the Kean's Neck Road by pushing forward with the rest of the 14th South Carolina. Most important, though, he ordered the removal of the heavy guns from the ferry.

21 *OR* 6: 67.

As Pemberton decided what to do with the 12th South Carolina, the men instinctively prepared for action—quickly packing their knapsacks, filling their canteens from nearby Stoney Creek, throwing whatever rations they had in their haversacks, and filling their cartridge boxes. There was an unmistakable buzz in camp; something was up. After an hour or so of indecision, Pemberton turned to Barnes and ordered him to take four companies of the 12th South Carolina to reinforce Jones's effort on the Kean's Neck Road.[22]

With Colonel Dunovant away, the always-ambitious Barnes recognized the moment at hand. He wasted no time and ordered the men into line. "The battalion was formed in a few minutes and moved off at once, for the scene of action," wrote one soldier. A mounted Barnes, accompanied by the regiment's adjutant, Lt. W. H. Talley, led Companies A (Captain McCorkle), B (Captain Miller), G (Lieutenant Moody) and I (Lieutenant Campbell) from their camp south along the Port Royal Ferry Road to reinforce the 14th South Carolina. Before departing, Barnes dispatched Major Jones to Pagis Point to relieve Bookter and take direct command of Companies D, C, and F and watch for a Federal advance from that sector. As the battalion of approximately 200–300 men stepped off, a courier arrived from the front with news that enemy forces had neared the 14th's position on the Kean's Neck Road. Fearing the 14th's vulnerability without support, Barnes ordered his men to double-quick, and with "admirable celerity" the four companies hurried down the road at right-shoulder-shift. In their wake followed portions of Brig. Gen. Daniel S. Donelson's Tennessee brigade and a field battery. Barnes reported that he left Gardens Corner between 1:00 and 2:00 p.m.

Pushing forward "vigorously," according to one officer, Barnes and the four companies marched four miles to reach the 14th South Carolina's camp in less than two hours. Other than a small detachment of men and a howitzer, however, the camp was deserted. After talking to some of the soldiers, Barnes ascertained that the earthworks at the ferry to the south were abandoned, with most of the guns already carried off, and that the 14th faced a heavy attack to the east. Barnes turned the head of his column left onto the Kean's Neck Road, and as they proceeded, the men received fire on their right flank from enemy gunboats on the Coosaw River.

Luckily, nobody was hit. "The Yankees saluted our arrival with a number of shells, which fell uncomfortably close to us," an officer remembered. About a half mile from the 14th's camp, Barnes encountered Colonel Jones and his men. As Barnes rode up, Jones's regiment began filing right of the road into a partially wooded area to deploy in battle line. Its left flank would be anchored next to a battery on the Kean's Neck Road, extending south toward the river. Directly behind

22 *OR* 6: 47, 49, 67.

Barnes and the 12th were an additional 42 cavalrymen, whom Jones dispatched to guard his far-left flank.[23]

The aid pleased Jones. Through open-order skirmishing, the 14th had done its best to contest Stevens's deliberate advance, but reinforcements were needed to stem the tide and prevent this main force from gaining additional ground, especially between Jones's right flank and the river. Jones directed Barnes to countermarch the 12th behind the 14th, then move off the road and form on the 14th's right and rear near "Chaplin's house" and occupy the vulnerable ground there. On renewing their advance, the Federals would now be opposed by two regiments.

Barnes moved without delay. Pine woods prohibited a direct link of the lines, but Barnes was satisfied his left had made sufficient contact with the 14th's right flank, although his own right did not extend to the river; rather, it was stationed on a ridge overlooking the water. As his four companies deployed, Barnes summoned Captain Miller and ordered him to send three Company A soldiers forward as scouts. The patrol quickly returned with information that the Federals intended to flank the 14th on its right and were likely unaware of the 12th's arrival. To their front was an open expanse. Taking cover behind a split rail fence, the detachment of the 12th hunkered down and waited, unseen by the enemy but enduring shelling from the nearby Yankee gunboats on the Coosaw. From his position, Barnes had an unobstructed view of the Federal advance, preceded by skirmishers from the 8th Michigan, 50th Pennsylvania, and 79th New York Highlanders. Instead of advancing directly down the Kean's Neck Road, where they could count on artillery support, the Federals left their guns to the rear and attacked through the woods and cotton fields merely with infantry.[24]

"We had just taken the position assigned to us, when bang! went one of the field pieces," recalled a soldier. Another man exclaimed, "They are coming!" Reported Barnes: "Through this open area we soon saw the enemy advancing as skirmishers upon the right of the Fourteenth Regiment, apparently in ignorance of our position. That regiment opened fire, and immediately afterward I ordered my detachment to advance. They responded promptly, with a cheer, and, leaping the fence, we advanced at the run, firing upon the enemy."

"When they had approached within some two hundred and fifty yards of our position, the order was given to charge them," reported Lieutenant Grist. "Our boys immediately jumped the fence and the Yankees scampered off again." Two

23 *OR* 6: 70, 72.

24 *OR* 6: 49–50, 65–68, 70, 72–74; L. M. G., "Footsteps of the Fathers," *Yorkville Enquirer*, Feb. 2, 1915, 1; M. A. Moore, "War Correspondence," *Yorkville Enquirer*, Jan. 16, 1862, 2; L. M. G., "Dear Enquirer."

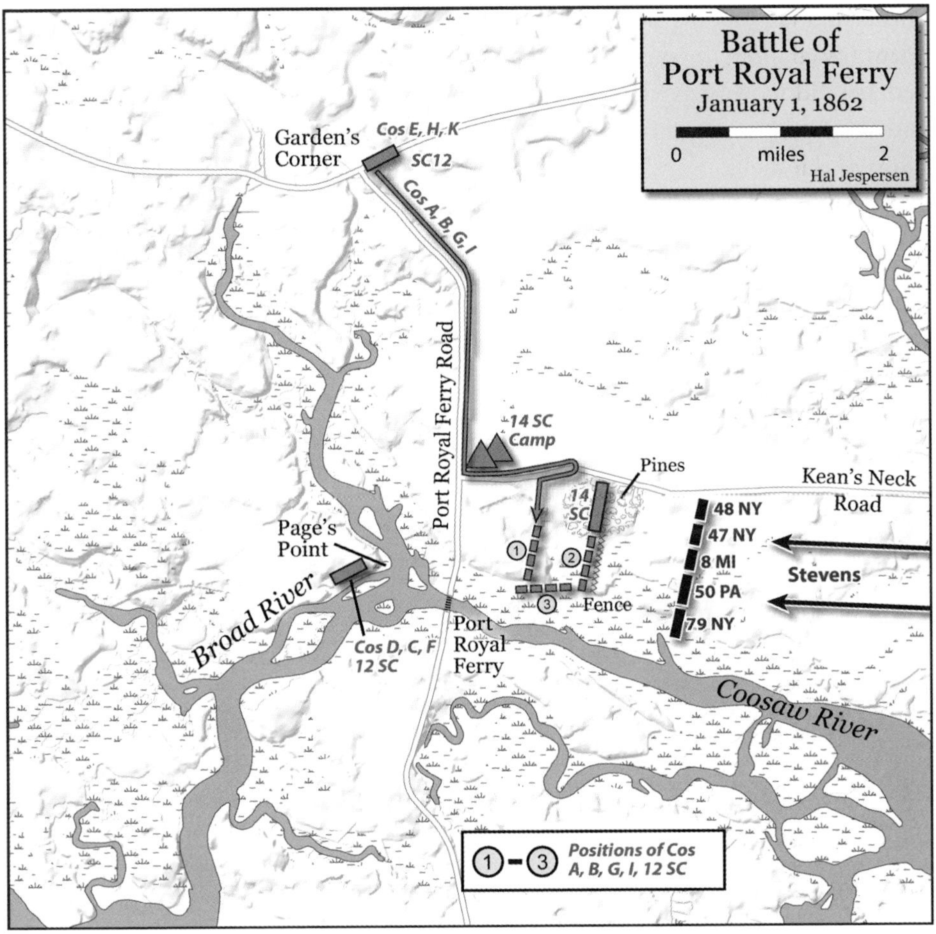

men were wounded during the advance. As elements of the Highlanders fled to the right and took cover in some woods, Barnes received reports from Company B that additional enemy troops were sliding to their right to gain the 12th's flank and interpose between the regiment and the ferry. Quickly reacting to this threat, Barnes redeployed his four companies, changing their front to the undulating ridge on his right at a right angle to the line originally established, generally facing the Coosaw. The Federals advanced on this line, directly striking both the right and left flanks of the detachment. Barnes had the superior position, however, and soon the Federals "gave way and ran precipitately" to a thick growth of pine woods after a few shots, though not before Sgt. David Jackson of Company A had the crown of his kepi blown off.

It was all for show, however. The Federal attack by this point had accomplished its objective by driving the Confederates from Port Royal Ferry, and Federal gunboats were making life miserable for the South Carolinians at close range. As Barnes was about to push the 12th forward in a vain attempt to scatter more Federals, support arrived from the rear in the form of the 14th South Carolina and 8th Tennessee, and Colonel Jones ordered the three regiments to retire out of range of the shells.

Barnes commended his regiment's effort. "The conduct of the whole command was good," he wrote. "They obeyed orders promptly, and exhibited enthusiasm when the prospect was presented of meeting the foe face to face upon a fair field of battle." The minor affair buoyed the men's confidence, especially after the harrowing retreat from the coast in November. "This was our first time to be shot at and to shoot at men with our rifles," recalled one soldier. "I cannot say that we enjoyed it, but after driving them back to their gun boats, we felt important." That evening, the battalion withdrew about two miles and bivouacked; the next morning, Barnes led it back to the regiment's encampment at Gardens Corner. While this was the first time he had successfully maneuvered the regiment under fire, it would not be his last. Nor would it be the last time the 12th and 14th South Carolina supported each other in battle.[25]

In his after-action report, Pemberton specifically recognized 12th South Carolina surgeon E. B. Turnipseed "for his untiring professional zeal, as well in the field as in the camp." Turnipseed ably administered care to the soldiers injured during the skirmish and complained afterward about the "inhumane conduct of the enemy in firing upon he and his Surgeons while dressing the wounds upon the battlefield." Casualties were light: four wounded and one killed. Company G's William Duke was grazed by a musket ball on the left side of the head. W. M. Barton of Company I was wounded by a musket ball in the left chest, and his comrade A. A. Caskey was wounded by a shell fragment in the buttocks. The one death in the regiment also came from Company I: J. T. C. Valandingham, killed by an artillery shell. In Company A, an artillery shell explosion concussed H. M. Gwinn. There were no casualties in Company B.[26]

On their return to Gardens Corner, those engaged in the skirmish wasted little time boasting to their comrades, but the entire regiment would be honored. "Our troops acted gallantly," Grist wrote. "When all done well, it is invidious to make distinctions. The greatest difficulty was to restrain the men without due bounds.

25 *OR* 6: 72–73; Miller, "My Experience," 217; L. M. G., "Footsteps of the Fathers"; Moore, "War Correspondence"; L. M. G., "Dear Enquirer."

26 *OR* 6: 68; E. B. Turnipseed to William H. Talley, Jan. 5, 1862, copy in author's possession. This correspondence appears in a digitalized version of the *Official Records* from Duke University; however, it does not appear in the hardcover edition of the *Official Records* used by the author in this work.

Of one thing our people may rest assured, that the 12th and 14th Regiments of South Carolina Volunteers will never do any act calculated to bring reproach upon the fair fame of our beloved state."[27]

The next day, after reports by skittish pickets that a large enemy force had landed to their rear near Combahee Ferry, the 12th repositioned and formed a line of battle. Amid continued Federal shelling, fearing their communications and line of retreat could be cut, commanders sent scouts to ascertain the enemy's location, only to learn upon their return that the morning's reports were false and the Yankees had abandoned the area. In response, the troops were redirected toward Stoney Creek, making camp near their original November encampment at Pocataligo, about three miles from the Charleston & Savannah.[28]

Following the skirmish at Port Royal Ferry, the regiment's records show no real military activity other than an occasional scouting mission. In early January, flank companies A and B were issued new British Enfield rifles brought through the Union blockade by the steamship *Bermuda*. Boyles would recall an unpleasant incident in which a patrol to corral contraband slaves on an island backfired when a careless guard was overpowered and "left for dead by the negroes, who made their escape." During this period, a portion of the regiment was moved farther inland to Colleton, where the men continued their regimen of drill and picket duty.

* * *

A few days after the New Year's Day skirmish at Port Royal Ferry, Major Jones's son, Cadwallader Jones Jr., joined his father's Company H as an enlisted man. The younger Jones was a transfer from the famed Hampton Legion serving in Virginia and had seen action at First Manassas in July 1861. In a letter home, Jones immediately drew contrasts between the men serving in the legion and those in the 12th: "I was very reluctant in leaving our old company; especially after I had gone through a battle and so many severe hardships for seven months with them; and then there is such a difference between the men composing that company, and these, this company; there they were mostly educated men—nearly all gentlemen, here they are a set of men that can scarcely read." He continued, however: "I ought not to be complaining for they are a straight-forward people, clever in their way."

In February, those troops sent to Colleton were moved back to the Pocataligo area, with picket duty again the norm. Another portion of the regiment apparently

27 L. M. G., "Dear Enquirer."

28 L. M. G., "Footsteps of the Fathers."

moved to Greenpond about this time. Wherever their camp was located, however, the men contended with poor living conditions and filth, as well as a new enemy: mosquitos ("the largest and hungriest, I ever saw," Boyles observed). There were also outbreaks of mumps in late February, and the men's uniforms—now approximately six months old—began to disintegrate, leaving them looking ragged. Nevertheless, the overall health of the command was reportedly stable. One visitor to the camp of Captain Valandingham's Lancaster Hornets (Company I) in April recorded that the men were in "excellent health."[29]

In March, assorted companies conducted extensive recruiting efforts in their home counties, hoping to bolster the ranks. Although battle casualties were limited during the engagements at Fort Walker, Fort Beauregard, and Port Royal Ferry, several men had been discharged because of sickness or ill health, dating to the measles outbreak at Camp Johnson the previous September. The acute shortage of men in the camps throughout the winter necessitated these recruiting efforts, and officers and noncommissioned officers returned home with offers of a $50 bounty for any enlistee. One young man, David J. Carter of Lancaster Court House, enlisted with Company I on March 9 and by April 13 had arrived at the Pocataligo encampment with two other recruits. Evidently, the recruiting efforts were quite successful, as the regiment boasted nearly 1,000 men by mid-April, with several companies increasing their numbers by 20 or more.[30]

Despite the recruiting uptick, February defeats in Tennessee (Forts Henry and Donelson, then Nashville), tempered the men's spirits. Writing from "Camp Blake" near Greenpond on March 12, Cadwallader Jones Jr. described his comrades in Company H as dejected and humiliated. (He would note, however, the delightful reception of the men at a perceived Confederate naval victory off Hampton Roads,

29 Many of the inhabitants of the Lowcountry, panic-stricken over the Federal invasion, left their plantations and their slaves without oversight during this period. As a result, runaway slaves populated the swamps and thickets near the camps, a problem that soon became an issue requiring military intervention such as the one young Boyles described: "You cannot imagine the dreadful state of things existing here. Plantations are deserted and negroes by the hundreds wandering through the country without a master or anyone to tell them what to do or where to go." See Joseph N. Brown to Mother, in *Brown, A Colonel at Gettysburg and Spotsylvania*, 39; Boyles, *Reminiscences*, 14; Miller, "My Experience," 217; Courier, "Dunovant's Regiment," *Yorkville Enquirer,* March 6, 1862, 2; L. M. G., "Footsteps of the Fathers"; "The 12th S.C. Regiment," *Lancaster Ledger,* April 23, 1862, 2; L. M. G., "From the 12th Regiment," *Yorkville Enquirer*, Jan. 9, 1862, 2; Cadwallader Jones Jr. to My Dear Sister, Jan. 11, 1862, Cadwallader Jones Papers, #2487, Southern Historical Collection, The Wilson Library, University of North Carolina–Chapel Hill; Cadwallader Jones Jr. to Brother, July 19, 1922, UNC.

30 "Recruiting," *Lancaster Ledger*, March 19, 1862, 2; John Miller, "Recruits Wanted for Capt. Miller's Company," *Yorkville Enquirer*, March 13, 1862, 2; D. J. Carter, "Campaign of 1862," *Lancaster Ledger*, Dec. 11, 1889, 1; "The 12th S.C. Regiment," *Lancaster Ledger,* April 23, 1862, 2.

Virginia—the historic March 9 engagement between USS *Monitor* and CSS *Virginia* that ended essentially as a deadlock.)

In taking a long-term view of the conflict, Jones wrote that, "we should look to the ultimate result; and not mind the few reverses we are bound to have. The more dearly bought our independence is, the more appreciated will it be, when we gain it, so I am willing to fight no matter how long the war may last—till every detestable and haralling yankee is driven off our soil." Despite this sentiment, Jones believed it was already too late in the season for the Federals to attempt any form of campaign into South Carolina's interior, assured the weather was far too warm already and the thick woods would prevent such an endeavor.[31]

In the winter/spring of 1861–62, critical changes in the 12th South Carolina's command structure would affect the regiment for the rest of the war. On December 14, 1861, Col. Maxcy Gregg, a Columbia native, was promoted to brigadier general after serving as colonel of the 1st South Carolina early in the war. The 48-year-old Gregg soon proved a force with which to be reckoned. A graduate of South Carolina College, he was a distinguished lawyer and committed secessionist, voting to withdraw South Carolina from the union in 1860 as a delegate to the state's secession convention. When the 1st South Carolina's enlistment term expired after six months, Gregg reorganized it under its former numerical designation in the summer and fall of 1861. On January 5, 1862, Gregg was assigned command of the 4th Military District's 2nd Brigade—consisting of the 12th, 13th, 14th South Carolina Infantry, the South Carolina Rangers (Robert Josiah Jeffords's 5th South Carolina Cavalry), and two artillery companies. Gregg's 1st South Carolina would eventually join the brigade as well.

Another major change was Colonel Dunovant's resignation on April 2, 1862. Purportedly, Dunovant was upset when Jefferson Davis passed on promoting him to brigadier general in favor of another officer whom Dunovant insisted did not "possess the same right to the position, either through military knowledge or experience." With this slight to his honor, Dunovant resigned "under feelings of deep mortifications and disgust, as every military man would have done under similar circumstances."

Although that rationale may well have played a role in Dunovant's decision to resign, the more likely scenario is that the colonel conceded to himself he was not up to training and leading men into battle and did not necessarily desire to do so after eight months of underwhelming service. Spending the foreseeable future living out of a tent in South Carolina's Lowcountry, leading a regiment

31 Cadwallader Jones Jr. to My Dear Sister, March 12, 1862, UNC.

of Upcountry volunteers, or serving on a distant battlefield in Virginia, were not attractive prospects to a man accustomed to comfort.

Dunovant's uninspiring performance at Port Royal in November 1861, his failure to be with the troops during their first fight at Port Royal Ferry in January 1862 as he attended a political convention, and his apparent lack of presence as a leader since the regiment's muster cannot be understated. Virtually no soldier accounts mention, let alone praise, him. In an era when soldiers were proud of their leaders and wrote glowingly about them to their loved ones back home, the absence of such testimony is striking. Richard Gill Mills Dunovant was simply not the man to lead the 12th into the next phase of the war and he probably knew it. Being passed over for promotion was an honorable reason to resign, giving him a perfect out as spring approached. His resignation was a net positive for the regiment.

Taking his place was Dixon Barnes, a man with a similar, privileged background but who was nevertheless dissimilar to Dunovant in zeal, dedication, bravery, charisma, and persona. Upon Dunovant's resignation, Barnes was promoted to colonel, Major Jones to lieutenant colonel, and Captain McCorkle to major. Wholly dedicated to the cause, Barnes itched to relieve the dour, uninspiring, and often-absent Dunovant. Writing about the new colonel, a visitor to the camp that spring remarked: "Col. Barnes well deserves the position. The 12th Regiment has the reputation of being the best drilled regiment on the coast, and this proficiency is attributed to his superior qualities as a drill officer. As a commander, his merits have been tested both in camp and in the field, and his Regiment—both officers and privates have unbounded confidence in him."

A newspaper correspondent, writing about the skirmish at Port Royal Ferry, described him as having a "gallant bearing . . . conspicuous throughout the entire engagement—His coolness and utter disregard of personal danger, elicited the highest and merited encomiums from the soldiers under his command." A more prescient description of Dixon Barnes as a military leader could not be rendered.[32]

McCorkle was a native of York County, born near Rock Hill in 1821. In 1840, he settled in Yorkville and worked as a store clerk before becoming a successful antebellum businessman in the county, returning to those pursuits after the war and, in 1888, beginning an extended stint as a local probate judge. With the war's outbreak, McCorkle raised the Palmer Guards, which became Company A, and served reputably as its commander during its early existence. In 1863, however,

32 *CMH*, 399; Carnot, "General R. G. M. Dunovant," *Edgefield Advertiser*, Aug. 19, 1863, 2; Caldwell, *The History of a Brigade of South Carolinians*, 29–32, 35; *OR* 6: 108; "The 12th S.C. Regiment"; Allardice, *More Generals in Gray*, 83; "A correspondent," *Lancaster Ledger*, Jan. 22, 1862, 2.

health issues forced McCorkle to resign after he was promoted to lieutenant colonel. He would become a quartermaster, serving in that capacity until the end of the war.

The trio of older gentlemen that assumed command in the wake of Dunovant's resignation—Barnes, Jones, and McCorkle—brought the regiment needed stability and discipline, which would go far in cementing its remarkable wartime legacy.[33] And, against the backdrop of these command changes, Gregg's new brigade was ordered to Virginia at the behest of Robert E. Lee, who had been transferred to Richmond to serve as a special military adviser to Jefferson Davis. Lee and Davis needed more men to defend Richmond, and South Carolina's loss was Richmond's gain. On April 21, Lee wired Pemberton, the new commander of the Department of South Carolina, Georgia, and Florida, requesting the transfer of "a good brigade" to the Confederate capital "as soon as possible." Pemberton wasted no time, and in what turned out to be a momentous decision for the 12th South Carolina, chose Maxcy Gregg and his three South Carolina regiments for the task. The men received the news with great enthusiasm. They had spent six months in the Lowcountry coastal areas, enduring the doldrums of living in the wilderness. The desire for new scenery was more than welcome. Ordered to pack up their things, strike their tents, and cook rations, the men diligently obeyed—"which we did in a hurry, so glad to get away from the coast," Boyles proclaimed.[34]

33 "York's County Officers," *Yorkville Enquirer*, Feb. 13, 1895, 1; "Promotion," *Yorkville Enquirer*, Aug. 7, 1862, 2.

34 Boyles, *Reminiscences*, 15; Carter, "Campaign of 1862"; *OR* 11(3):455.

Chapter Three

Baptism of Fire in Virginia

THE WAR WAS but a year old when the 12th South Carolina, with roughly 1,000 men now in the ranks, headed north by train from Pocataligo on April 23, 1862. Arriving about sunset in Charleston, 80 miles away, the regiment disembarked and marched through the city to the South Carolina Railroad depot, where another train, yet to arrive, was to carry the men to Columbia. At the depot, newly minted Colonel Dixon Barnes granted that a break was in order and permitted his troops time to enjoy themselves as they waited, a proposition they readily welcomed after several months in the Lowcountry wilderness and swamps. "Before leaving Charleston," recalled J. R. Boyles, "every man in the regiment who had ever taken a drink of whiskey, and many who had never taken any, supplied himself with one or more long-necked 'Black Betties'; the result was very soon a lively, noisy, fussy crowd, and some few knock-down and drag-out fights."

Their train arrived about 10:00 that evening and, Boyles added, what the men had not already consumed on their empty stomachs, they carried onto the boxcars bound for Columbia. The 115-mile trek to the state capital would take about 12 hours, but the men reportedly enjoyed the ride in their intoxicated state. From Columbia, the regiment continued north on a third train, with many of the individual companies soon passing the communities they called home. Without permission, several jumped off the train as it passed their respective home stations to visit their families and then jumped aboard a regular passenger train running about three hours behind, eventually catching up to their comrades in Charlotte.

From there, they continued their journey first to Weldon, North Carolina, and then on to Richmond via Petersburg.

Quartered in the heart of Richmond, the 12th "had a jubilee of a time for a few days," noted one soldier, adding that they also had an opportunity to enjoy the company of the "fairer sex," who regarded them all as heroes. A few days later, the regiment boarded a train to join Brig. Gen. Joseph R. Anderson's independent command near Fredericksburg, which was keeping an eye on Union Maj. Gen. Irvin McDowell's Department of the Rappahannock. Purportedly, McDowell was moving through Virginia from the Shenandoah Valley to threaten Richmond from the north.

After a few days at Milford Station, the regiment marched closer to Fredericksburg, establishing a strong picket line unencumbered by the tentage and baggage the men were accustomed to in the static camps in South Carolina. Here, the various regiments in Anderson's command alternated positions every few days, an effort designed to familiarize them in being able to march at a moment's notice. Routine picket duty often meant long-range skirmishing with the enemy (typically positioned 300–1,000 yards away), but the time spent in camp was relatively uneventful, although on May 10, Lieutenant J. B. Fellows and 13 soldiers from the 13th South Carolina were captured near Fredericksburg. "Firing is kept up constantly during the day," wrote a Company I soldier, "but whether any good is effected, or any advantage gained by this system of warfare, between ours and the enemy's pickets, I am unable to judge."

The transition to active campaigning in Virginia allowed the regiment to demonstrate immediately its prowess and experience as a military organization in the field, as it had significantly improved in all facets from the one mired in the ragged retreat from Port Royal Sound the previous November. The men did not hesitate, however, to size up the other units in their command, drawing their own distinctions, comparisons, and critical assessments. "The 12th Regiment compares favorably with any I have seen in Virginia, both in numbers and looks," one soldier proudly wrote to the *Lancaster Ledger* in late May. "In point of discipline and efficiency in drill, no Regt. has yet presented itself to our view, that can equal it. Colonel Barnes has no superior as a drill officer in the Confederacy. He is kind and obliging to his command, and has the entire confidence of every one. All are willing to trust their lives, their honor and the welfare of the country to his keeping. Rest assured, wherever he strikes, he will leave his mark."[1]

Amid looming Union threats against Richmond, Anderson's "army" was recalled on May 24. Marching on substandard, muddy roads, the troops completed

1 Boyles, *Reminiscences*, 16–19; LOCAL, "Army Correspondence," *Yorkville Enquirer*, June 4, 1862.

a 40-mile forced march on May 29–30 and bivouacked at Smith's Farm on the Nine Mile Road, just south of the Chickahominy River and within sight of the threatened capital. It was here that the 1st South Carolina Infantry and the 1st South Carolina Rifles (better known as Orr's Rifles after its founder, James Lawrence Orr, but now commanded by Col. John F. Marshall) joined what became known as Gregg's Brigade, roughly 5,000 men in five regiments. To bolster the capital's defenses against Maj. Gen. George McClellan's colossal Army of the Potomac then snaking its way up the Virginia Peninsula, Brig. Gen. Maxcy Gregg's South Carolinians joined five other brigades—J. R. Anderson's Georgians and North Carolinians; Lawrence O'Bryan Branch's North Carolinians; Charles W. Fields's Alabamians and Virginians; James Archer's Alabamians, Georgians, and Tennesseans; and Dorsey Pender's North Carolinians—and Lt. Col. Lewis M. Coleman's Artillery to form Maj. Gen. Ambrose Powell Hill's soon-to-be- legendary "Light Division."[2]

McClellan's strategic plan in the Peninsula Campaign was a sound one. As his troops advanced up the peninsula toward Richmond, he used Federal gunboats on the York and James rivers to protect the army's flanks. General Joseph E. Johnston commanded the Confederate forces defending Richmond and began concentrating his forces in eastern Virginia to contest McClellan's approach. For the better part of April, Maj. Gen. John B. Magruder's Army of the Peninsula—only about 13,000 men—boldly stalled McClellan, resorting at times to military theatrics to foil the Federals. Johnston used the delay to hurry troops south from the Rapidan and Rappahannock rivers, principally as protection for Richmond but also to put them within supporting distance of Magruder. The troops in Gregg's Brigade, including the 12th South Carolina, were among the last to leave the Rappahannock River line near Fredericksburg. By late May, Magruder had evacuated Yorktown, Williamsburg had fallen to the Yankees, and Johnston's army was in a defensive posture to the east and northeast of Richmond.

Although the proverbial wolf was at Richmond's door, McClellan's sluggish advance up the peninsula had helped Johnston immensely.[3] As June beckoned, the Federals were partially encamped on the Chickahominy River in the shape of a "V"—the point at Bottom's Bridge and the left arm, roughly 40,000 men, aligned along the York River Railroad and Williamsburg Road, extending toward Richmond as far as a crossroads known as "Seven Pines." McClellan's right, the

2 Boyles, *Reminiscences*, 16–19; Caldwell, *The History of a Brigade of South Carolinians*, 34–35; Spencer Welch, *A Confederate Surgeon's Letters to His Wife* (New York, 1911), 9, 11; *OR* 11(2):487; *SHSP* 16:19; Daly, *Alexander Cheves Haskell*, 69.

3 William Allan, *Stonewall Jackson, Robert E. Lee, and the Army of Northern Virginia, 1862* (New York, 1995), 2–16.

Brigadier General Maxcy Gregg commanded the brigade consisting of the 1st, 12th, 13th, 14th South Carolina and Orr's Rifles Regiment. *Savas Beatie*

General Robert E. Lee, commander of the Army of Northern Virginia. *Library of Congress*

longer of the two arms with 60,000 men, stretched along the north bank of the Chickahominy, extending to Meadow Bridge. The two wings, however, were separated by the river, swollen by a recent round of fierce storms.

As of May 21, Joe Johnston's command totaled approximately 53,688. Detecting an opportunity to attack the Federals' isolated left wing, Johnston concentrated his army and attacked on May 31 at Seven Pines/Fair Oaks. Gregg's Brigade saw no action in the two-day battle, a tactical draw that proved monumental for the command shakeup it produced. Seriously wounded during the first-day of fighting, Johnston would be replaced on June 1 by Robert E. Lee, then serving as Jefferson Davis's adviser in Richmond. On June 1, Lee referred to his new command as the Army of Northern Virginia. The name stuck.[4]

For most of the month, little fighting occurred on this front. Gregg's Brigade remained encamped on the Nine Mile Road along the marshy Chickahominy River, the action usually little more than rounds of artillery fire between the lines. With the bulk of the Federal force more than a mile away, picket duty was the 12th South Carolina's primary focus. The men's daily ration consisted of crackers and bacon, which according to one soldier was plentiful, but Pvt. Joseph Templeton of Company B wrote home to his brother William in early June that the troops were suffering. "We have a great deal of sickness in the regiment, mostly the flu," he wrote, further complaining that the troops had no tentage to protect them from the torrential rains. Knee-deep mud hampered the men in camp, and sickness increased as the month progressed. With suitable accommodations to house the sick nonexistent, four members of the regiment would die. Twenty-seven men

4 Ibid., 36–49, 51, 59, 70; *OR* 11(3):569.

from Company B alone were sick and out of the ranks, and in a subsequent letter to William in June, Joseph pled with his brother not to enlist because of the conditions. "I do not want you to leave home," he implored. "[W]ee never knew what hard times was before." The regiment had only about 540 men in the ranks during this period, roughly half the number brought from South Carolina.

During the lull that followed his assumption of command, Lee prepared for an attack on McClellan, bringing in troops from other areas to augment his force. McClellan would cooperate by remaining dormant along the Chickahominy, opting to build bridges, fortifications, and roads in the thick woods and marshes to improve his communications and allowing troops to be shifted from one wing to the other. There was another reason for McClellan's idleness: He was also planning on a reunion with McDowell's command, which had been diverted from the Fredericksburg area to contend with Stonewall Jackson's spectacular success in the spring Shenandoah Valley campaign. Also contributing to inactivity was the sustained rain that flooded the Richmond area in late May and early June.

Despite the miserable conditions, Gregg's men were anxious for movement that June, according to the brigade's historian, J. F. J. Caldwell:

> The brigade was now large, well drilled, thoroughly disciplined, and in the highest spirits. The unwholesome atmosphere of the Chickahominy swamps, and the exposure to rain and sun, to which we were not yet accustomed, had made deep inroads into our numbers, so that, out of the five thousand and upwards who stood upon our rolls, only about three thousand were fit for duty. But these viewed with satisfaction the approach of battle, in which they counted on securing for themselves the sage experience and the laurels of victory, which seemed to be the peculiar possession of war beaten Confederate soldiers. Their desire was soon granted.[5]

By late June, Lee had consolidated a formidable force in Richmond, but he would wait for the arrival of Jackson's Valley army, then moving through Ashland, before he attacked McClellan. The Federal army stretched around Richmond from north to east, its component wings still separated by the Chickahominy. McClellan's center and left flank were positioned south of the river, his right flank to the north. Lee's defenses were more compact, but only two divisions blocked

5 Boyles, *Reminiscences*, 21; Joseph Templeton to William Templeton, June 4, 1862, and June 9, 1862; Joseph Templeton to Catherine Templeton, June 15, 1862; D. J Carter, "Army Correspondence," *Lancaster Ledger*, June 28, 1862, 1. Allan, *The Army of Northern Virginia*, 59–61, 65; Caldwell, *The History of a Brigade of South Carolinians*, 36; Welch, *A Confederate Surgeon's Letters to His Wife*, 11.

the main approaches to Richmond and the majority of McClellan's army. Major General Benjamin Huger's division held the right flank from the Charles City Road north across the Williamsburg Road to the York River Railroad; Magruder's troops extended from Huger's left flank to the Chickahominy; and Longstreet's and D. H. Hill's divisions were within supporting distance of Magruder and Huger, closer to Richmond. A. P. Hill's Light Division, featuring Gregg's Brigade and the 12th South Carolina, extended along the south bank of the Chickahominy from Magruder's left to Meadow Bridge—directly across from Maj. Gen. Fitz John Porter's Federal V Corps, strongly entrenched near Beaver Dam Creek.[6]

Lee's plan, scheduled for June 26, called for a strike on Porter's position by the divisions of A. P. Hill, D. H. Hill, and Longstreet, which would cross the Chickahominy at Mechanicsville, near Meadow Bridge. Hill's division would open the fight from the left, supported by D. H. Hill's and Longstreet's commands. The plan also called for Jackson to arrive in Porter's rear near Beaver Dam Creek and assist in the attack. D. H. Hill's troops were to support Jackson while Longstreet assisted the Light Division. In theory the four divisions, acting in concert, would drive in Porter and collapse McClellan's right flank. More than three weeks since the conclusion of Seven Pines/Fair Oaks, the fighting would resume. The Seven Days' Battles were about to begin.[7]

June 26: Mechanicsville/Beaver Creek Dam

On Wednesday, June 25, the 12th South Carolina and the rest of Gregg's Brigade (other than the 14th South Carolina, consigned to picket duty) began preparations to march. The men received rations and ammunition, and pickets were recalled from the riverbank. After dark, the brigade moved out, following the contours of the Chickahominy. The division moved left (north), with Gregg's men on the division's extreme right, holding the rear. That position in the column, especially at night, meant repeated halts while navigating already challenging roads becoming increasingly congested by men, wagons, and horses—frustrating Gregg's officers and soldiers alike. After several tedious hours, the command halted on the Meadow Bridge Road for much-needed rest out of sight of the enemy's skirmishers across the river.

The brigade stayed in this position until 3:00 p.m. the next day, when an impatient A. P. Hill—still waiting for confirmation that Jackson and his troops

6 Allan, *The Army of Northern Virginia*, 70–73; *CMH*, 57.

7 Allan, *The Army of Northern Virginia*, 75–76; *CMH*, 57–58.

were finally in Porter's rear—decided preemptively to launch the attack. Advancing across the bridge, Fields's Brigade opened the engagement. Gregg's Brigade eventually followed, aligned in a column of fours, as Fields's men drove Federal skirmishers from Mechanicsville and toward Beaver Dam Creek. Federal batteries "saluted" the brigade with a barrage as it advanced, one soldier recalled.

As Fields's command pushed ahead, Gregg's men positioned themselves in reserve behind some hills, compelled by the intensity of fire from the evolving battle, both artillery and small-arms, to "hug the ground." They would stay there the remainder of the night, sleeping on their arms, Colonel Barnes reporting only one man wounded by a bursting shell.[8]

June 27: Gaines's Mill

After a difficult night, the men rose early on the 27th and formed ranks on the Mechanicsville Road. While waiting in line, they were greeted by none other than their new division commander, A. P. Hill, who walked along the regiment with entreaties of encouragement. Unlike the previous day, it was apparent Gregg's men were in store for action. Their orders were simple and clear. Essentially, Gregg would resume the work of June 26, leading the Light Division toward Ellison's Mill (on Beaver Dam Creek) and dislodge the enemy from its position there. Halted short of the creek after a march of about a half-mile, the brigade formed a stacked battle line: the 1st South Carolina on the right ahead of the 13th South Carolina, and the 12th on the left ahead of Orr's Rifles. The regiments in front threw out skirmishers—Barnes handed Captain John Miller's Company B that assignment—and resumed the advance to Beaver Dam Creek.

About 8:00 a.m., the brigade crossed the waist-high creek without much enemy resistance to secure the position the Federals held the day before, but not before encountering scores of Confederate bodies from the previous assaults that needed to be moved from the road for artillery to be brought forward. On the other side of the creek were the deserted Federal camps, full of abandoned equipment (e.g., knapsacks, quartermaster stores, arms, accoutrements), some of it smoldering from fire. The array of equipment strewn along the roadside gave evidence of the hasty retreat by the Yankees. J. R. Boyles spotted a full Federal knapsack. "I snatched one up, ripped it open and appropriated some fine cigars, writing paper and a bunch of envelopes," he recalled. "[T]hey were the only things I felt I could carry," he recalled.

8 Allan, *The Army of Northern Virginia*, 79; Caldwell, *The History of a Brigade of South Carolinians*, 38–39; *OR* 11(3):852–858; Boyles, *Reminiscences*, 20.

Halting near a clearing about a half-mile beyond the deserted camps, Gregg ordered the 12th South Carolina (still on the left) to form in a "column of companies," which entailed each of the regiment's 10 companies to advance aligned in a narrow column, one behind the other. Enough space was left between the companies to allow the regiment to redeploy quickly into a battle line if necessary. As the regiment executed the maneuver, Barnes received word of Federal forces approaching from the left and sought instructions from Gregg, who ordered the rear two companies (B under Captain Miller and K under Captain Neville) to peel left to conduct a reconnaissance under Lt. Col. Cadwallader Jones's command. Were the main line to move forward, those two companies were ordered to conform by adjusting their own movements accordingly.

As the reconnaissance force moved left cautiously, Miller had a Company B platoon, commanded by Lt. William Dunlop, fan out and scout for a potential attack or ambush. Deploying into a patch of woods, the contingent ran headlong into about 100 men of the 8th Pennsylvania Reserves near a swamp. "We expected a lively tilt with the Pennsylvanians," Dunlop recalled, "but at the command, a well-directed volley was delivered with such deadly effect that, to our great relief, with increased celerity, the [enemy] bounded into the woods in our front and disappeared, leaving their killed and wounded on the ground, with seventeen prisoners in our hands, who declined to run the gauntlet of a second volley, and laid down their arms on demand."[9]

This was the first time in the war that the regiment encountered enemy soldiers in such close proximity. As the smoke lifted, in the heat of the moment, one of Dunlop's impassioned soldiers threatened to shoot a surrendering Federal, alarming Union Sgt. D. B. Anderson, who pleaded with a Company B sergeant for permission to speak to a commissioned officer. That was Dunlop, who made his way across the swamp from the other end of the line and assured Sergeant Anderson that his Pennsylvanians would be treated kindly as prisoners. Convinced that Dunlop was a "pretty good fellow," Anderson disclosed privately to the lieutenant the threat made by one of Dunlop's soldiers and his concern for his men's safety. Confirming the story's accuracy, Dunlop ordered the wrongdoer not to accompany the prisoners back to the regiment.[10]

Years later, Dunlop recalled, tongue in cheek, that he and his small force felt as though they had achieved a great military conquest in driving back the Pennsylvanians and capturing 17 prisoners:

9 William Dunlop, "A Reminiscence of the War," *Yorkville Enquirer*, Aug. 8, 1888, 1.

10 Ibid., 1.

> This, in our estimation, was a grand achievement for Company B, the ultimate result of which would be the capitulation of Gen. McClellan with what forces were left of the Federal army; the triumphant return of Gen. Lee at the head of the Army of Northern Virginia to the Confederate capital; a grand military ovation to the second platoon of Company B and its illustrious commander; the declaration of peace; the establishment of the independence of the Southern Confederacy; the dispersion of the government in the South, the like of which the world had never seen. But we were slightly disappointed; for when we marched the seventeen Bucktails triumphantly to the rear and met the Confederate commander, he refused to pull off his hat and cheer, or in any manner whatever to recognize the eminent service rendered by Company B, but continued to push McClellan upon his base, as if nothing of importance occurred, and McClellan declining to surrender, the struggle continued.

While Companies B and K were off to the left "winning the war" with their capture of the Pennsylvanians, Barnes advanced with the remaining eight companies, still aligned in a column. Reaching Walnut Grove Church, they encountered troops in Stonewall Jackson's command, seeing the renowned general in person for the first time. Lee was there, too, as well as other officers discussing the army's next move.

Meanwhile, the detachment from Companies B and K arrived with their prisoners. Much to Dunlop's chagrin, neither Lee nor Jackson—nor anyone else in the high command present that day—complimented or praised his company's role in capturing the Yankees, which it achieved without a single reported casualty.[11]

After a brief conference with his regimental commanders and members of the high command, Gregg resumed the brigade's advance in the same order: skirmishers followed by the 1st South Carolina on the right and the 12th South Carolina on the left, followed by the 13th and Orr's Rifles, respectively. The 12th remained deployed in a column of companies, but it is unknown whether the 1st was in the same formation.

Gregg would meet with Lee again during the advance before continuing to Powhite Creek, again passing through deserted camps strewn with abandoned Federal equipment that was no doubt too tempting for the passing troops to leave untouched.

11 *OR* 11(2):852–858, 862–866; Caldwell, *The History of a Brigade of South Carolinians*, 39; Boyles, *Reminiscences*, 20; Miller, "My Experience," 218; Dunlop, "A Reminiscence of War"; Dunlop, *Bivouac and Battles (Part I)*, 1.

Arriving in the vicinity of Gaines's Mill on Powhite Creek, the Confederates were met with Federal fire. Barnes ordered the regiment into a battle line. Once deployed, Boyles recalled, "the entire regiment, as if by magic, blazed away in one simultaneous volley at about a dozen Yankees; no aim being taken, many balls ploughed up the ground not twenty feet ahead of us, while others clipped the limbs from the trees thirty feet from the ground." It is not surprising that both Barnes and Gregg omitted this somewhat embarrassing episode from their official reports.

With Federals on his front, Barnes ordered Miller's Company B to advance as skirmishers, and Gregg ordered Colonel Hamilton of the 1st South Carolina, still positioned to the 12th's right, to deploy two companies of skirmishers as well. After a brisk firefight, Gregg ordered a charge, his skirmishers succeeding in driving the Federals back across the creek to a pine thicket in what Barnes termed a "spirited attack."

The remaining companies of both the 12th and 1st followed the skirmishers to the bank of the creek, finally crossing once their engineers repaired the bridge, which had fallen into disrepair. Reforming their ranks on the other side, the South Carolinians charged the pine thicket, arraying Companies A and I as skirmishers to drive away the Federal defenders. It was about 2:00 p.m., and the men halted briefly, finding a cache of Yankee whiskey in a sutler's tent, which was consumed and no doubt poured into more than a few canteens.[12]

From there, the brigade continued at the double quick, under heavy fire, toward Cold Harbor, with the 12th and 1st still in the lead. Maintaining alignment in the marshy, wooded terrain was a challenge, but Gregg's men enjoyed repeated success in dislodging the enemy troops they encountered. Reaching Cold Harbor about 2:30 p.m., Hill ordered a halt and called for reinforcements, which certainly made the winded, footsore South Carolinians grateful after several long hours marching under fire. As the men caught their breath, filled canteens, and tended to the wounded, Hill ordered Barnes to send Captain McMeekin's Company F and Captain Erwin's Company H forward to ascertain the position and movements of the enemy on the ridge to their front. They eventually were relieved by Captain Bookter's Company D and Lieutenant Garvin's Company G.[13]

Companies D and G learned that the topography they were navigating featured a slope leading to thick pine woods and then opened into a field that descended into a creek-filled ravine before rising steeply on the other side. On top of that steep hill was a strong line of Federal infantry and artillery, men from Porter's V

12 Dunlop, "A Reminiscence of War"; Dunlop, *Bivouac and Battles (Part I)*, 1; Boyles, *Reminiscence*, 21.

13 Dunlop, *Bivouac and Battles (Part I)*, 1.

Lieutenant J. W. Delleny of Company C.
Wade Hampton Sons of Confederate Veterans

Corps. Greeted with shelling from the Federal big guns, the Confederates hugged the ground, with some of the men reportedly falling asleep somehow amid the chaos. About 4:00 p.m., however, the brigade was back on its feet and in line of battle.[14]

As before, the 12th and 1st South Carolina went first, advancing as General Gregg bellowed: "1st and 12th South Carolina Volunteers, forward!" Scrambling through the pine trees and brush, the two regiments struggled to maintain order. After clearing the thicket and advancing another 100 yards, they would be met by renewed Federal shelling on their right as well as small-arms fire from the ridge beyond the gully they hoped to cross. Several members of the 12th were wounded or killed, including Lt. J. W. Delleny, a promising young officer in Company C who was killed, and the artillery fire checked the 1st's advance completely, leaving the 12th in an exposed position on the open plain with no support on its right.

Barnes faced a critical choice. He could change his front to the right, sweep past the 1st South Carolina, and attack the batteries enfilading his line, or he could move his regiment to the left, toward the ravine and away from the guns. Under immense fire, Barnes opted for the latter. After moving the regiment by the left flank and reaching the creek at the base of the hill, Barnes moved the 12th back to the right and formed in the ravine opposite the pine thicket—out of artillery range for now. At this point, Companies D and G rejoined the regiment from their reconnaissance, and Gregg ordered Orr's Rifles into the combat.[15]

By now, the 1st South Carolina had joined the 12th in the ravine, and the two regiments resumed the advance in tandem, although their assault up the hill—conducted on particularly difficult terrain—quickly became intermingled and

14 Caldwell, *The History of a Brigade of South Carolinians*, 41–42.

15 Boyles, *Reminiscences*, 23; *OR* 11(2):852–858, 862–866.

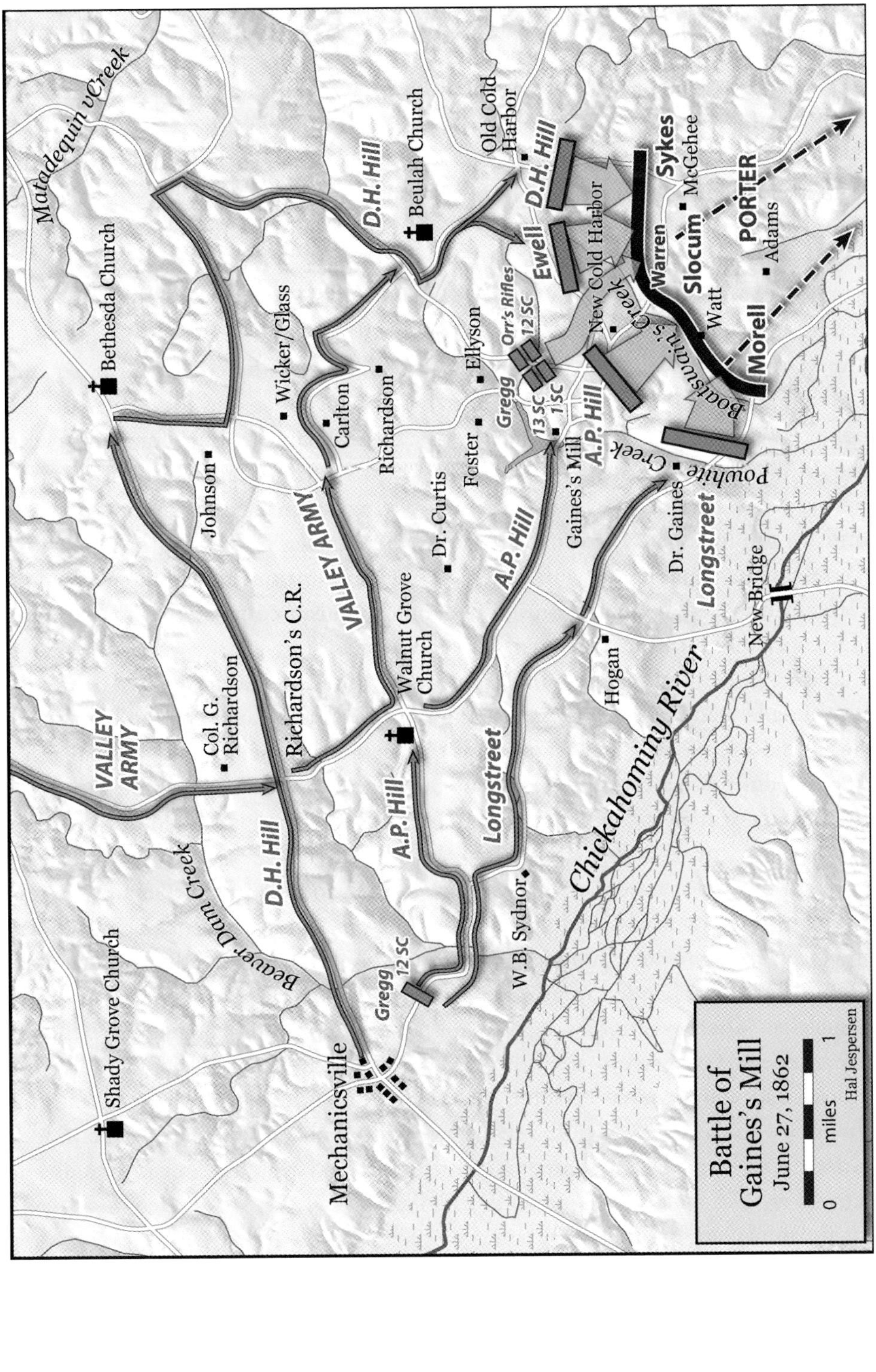
Battle of
Gaines's Mill
June 27, 1862
0 miles 1
Hal Jespersen
Mechanicsville
Shady Grove Church
Beaver Dam Creek
Bethesda Church
Matadequin Creek
Beulah Church
Old Cold Harbor
New Cold Harbor
Boatswain's Creek
Powhite Creek
Chickahominy River
New Bridge
Gaines's Mill
Walnut Grove Church
Richardson's C.R.
Col. G. Richardson
Johnson
Wicker/Glass
Carlton
Richardson
Ellyson
Foster
Dr. Curtis
Dr. Gaines
Hogan
W.B. Sydnor
McGehee
Watt
Adams
VALLEY ARMY
D.H. Hill
A.P. Hill
Longstreet
Gregg
12 SC
13 SC
1 SC
Orr's Rifles
Ewell
PORTER
Sykes
Warren
Slocum
Morell

disorganized. When their flanks overlapped, in fact, the danger of friendly fire became a matter of concern for both regiments.

After a brief halt, Barnes and Hamilton got their commands in order and resumed the advance. Even then, the Federal fire proved too severe. Unable to hold their ground, Barnes recalled that they were forced back in some confusion, "suffering seriously in killed and wounded." Barnes, however, rallied the broken remnants of the regiment. The men stood firm, holding their original position, and poured steady fire into the Yankees until compelled to fall back.

The Confederates' determined stand would be costly. A thigh wound sidelined Barnes, and Captain Vanlandingham of Company I and Captain McMeekin of Company F also went down with wounds. The mounting command losses and the rough terrain cost the regiment all semblance of order, and the 12th soon lost contact with the rest of the brigade. In the ensuing melee, some companies even fought in other regiments. "In the progress of the battle, after the wound received by Colonel Barnes, the Twelfth Regiment having suffered heavy loss and being in difficult grounds, became somewhat separated," Gregg reported. "[B]ut portions of the regiment, falling in with other commands, continued the fight to the end. Captain Bookter's company thus joined and fought in company with Col. James Cantey's regiment from Alabama [15th Infantry]."[16]

The desperate firefight would continue into the evening, as the South Carolinians made little progress dislodging the stubborn foe from the high ridge. About 8:30 p.m., a frontal assault by Brig. Gen. John Bell Hood's Texas Brigade finally helped drive the Federals from the field. The men slept on the field that night, some still trying to find and organize their commands and doing what they could to care for wounded comrades.

During the chaotic evening, an aide to the wounded Barnes made his way through the dark woods and located the 12th's acting adjutant, Lt. Lewis Grist, then sleeping with his comrades in Company A. Arising from the blood-soaked ground, Grist was handed an order from A. P. Hill requesting a list of the regiment's casualties. "There was not a scrap of paper to be found in my belongings or about my clothes," Grist wrote after the war, "but after searching about among the officers and men, I procured some old memorandum leaves on which to transmit the orders to the captains of the respective companies." After drafting the orders, Grist left to locate all 10 company commanders. "Within an hour or two all the reports were in, and before morning I had the casualty list of the regiment ready for the office of Gen. Hill's adjutant general," he recalled.

16 *OR* 11(2):852-58, 862-866.

In his after-action report, Barnes noted the regiment's strength at 430 the morning of June 27 and the loss of about 30 during the day from straggling and falling out. Reporting 148 total casualties (17 killed, 131 wounded or missing), Barnes described the 12th's performance as "gallant and commendable."[17]

Gaines's Mill was the 12th's first large-scale infantry fight featuring the entire regiment, which by all accounts performed admirably. The men marched well both in a column of companies and in line of battle, kept the pressure on the enemy while advancing, and conducted complicated maneuvers under fire for a telling 6–7 miles. They also demonstrated they could conduct skirmish and reconnaissance operations effectively. If anything, the 12th's breakdown at the end of the day was the result of fatigue, mental exhaustion, and the loss of several officers, most critically Colonel Barnes.

But even without those officers, the 12th showed it was ready to fight until the end, a trait further demonstrated when some men even chose to fight in other commands rather than retire. "That was our first real fighting," William Miller recalled. "We had the opportunity to show what was in us as soldiers. We did fine as long as we met the enemy in the open, but late in the evening, we came on the enemy in breastworks with plenty of cannon. Then we were checked. . . . By the time night came on we had a pretty good idea of the duties of a soldier, viz; To obey orders, and that about sums up the whole if it."[18]

"The next morning we were a pitiable multitude to behold—haggard, hungry, sleepy, and a field in front covered with blood, dead and dying, guns, knapsacks, canteens, &c.," Boyles noted. "A small ration was issued to us and a little whiskey, and we were detailed [on June 28] to perform the mournful task of burying our own and the enemy's dead." Among those they buried was Lieutenant Delleny, and two empty barrels were used to bury another comrade. Federals, meanwhile, were buried in shallow mass graves in the areas where they lay the thickest. Some of the men walked to the scene of the fighting to their right, where Boyles noted that the ground "was literally blue with the corpses of bloated Yankees."

Writing a hasty note home, Pvt. D. J. Carter described the fighting on the 26th and offered a bold assessment of where things stood. "We flanked the enemy and drove them for six miles before they made a decided stand," he penned. "We now have possession of the battle ground and have been resting all day. 'Stonewall Jackson' is in their rear and we have the enemy nearly surrounded . . . as I write this the battle is not decided, but the Confederates are in pursuit. We are confident of

17 "Gaines Mill Casualty List," *Yorkville Enquirer,* March 23, 1901: 3; *OR* 11(2):852–858.

18 Miller, "My Experience," 218.

Unburied dead on the Gaines's Mill battlefield. *Library of Congress*

victory." Carter's optimistic note was fairly accurate. While the Union army was not surrounded, McClellan was falling back.

On June 29, in extreme heat, Gregg's Brigade joined the pursuit of McClellan's army, crossing the Chickahominy and heading toward the James River. Little did the South Carolinians know that as they moved fighting had broken out at Savage's Station. Headed toward Richmond via the Charles City Road and then the Quaker Road, the tired troops finally camped about 15 miles from the capital. The next morning, the brigade continued its chase, arriving at Frayser's Farm about 5:00 p.m., where it joined Longstreet's Division already in line of battle.[19]

June 30–July 1: Glendale/Frayser's Farm and Malvern Hill

Halting right of the Long Road, the 12th stacked arms in woods near Longstreet's position. Fighting at what the Federals would label the battle of Glendale, and the Confederates Frayser's Farm, began about 6:30 p.m., as Federal artillery began shelling the waiting Confederates, hoping to deter them from intercepting their retreat along the Quaker Road. When Longstreet's subsequent attack stalled, "Old

19 Boyles, *Reminiscences*, 25; Caldwell, *The History of a Brigade of South Carolinians*, 46; D. J. Carter, "Mr. Editor," *Lancaster Ledger*, July 9, 1862, 2.

Pete" was quickly reinforced by Hill's Light Division. Gregg's Brigade advanced to Longstreet's left to bolster the "checked" brigades of Brig. Gens. Roger Pryor and Winfield Featherston, with the 14th South Carolina bearing the brunt of the fighting. Attacking with portions of 12 brigades, Hill and Longstreet pushed back the Union troops and held fast against several counterattacks. The Federal forces finally retreated under cover of darkness. Although the 12th was involved only as support, the regiment likely experienced enemy fire, as Boyles reported being wounded in the left elbow.

The wounded Boyles's experience sheds some light on the operations of field hospitals in the Army of Northern Virginia. Because hospitals were set up by division, brigade, and regiment, wounded men seeking attention were encouraged to be seen at their designated unit hospital. As he headed to the rear, Boyles passed a house converted into a hospital and overheard someone calling out for a Dr. Sykes. Because Boyles had known a Dr. Sikes in South Carolina, he figured it was the same individual and weaved his way through a number of other surgeons hoping a familiar face could be the one to dress his wound. Boyles, however, soon learned this was not the doctor he knew from home but rather one who served in an Alabama regiment. Nevertheless, when Boyles requested the surgeon treat his wound, Sykes declined, already tasked with caring for too many of his own men.

Sykes directed Boyles to find his own regimental hospital, which Boyles did the following day. His wound finally treated, Boyles was placed on a wagon bound for Richmond, where he was transferred to a receiving hospital to recuperate. Boyles received a 30-day furlough to recover at home, but he would need longer to heal properly and did not return to his regiment until much later in the year.

At the end of the fighting at Frayser's Farm, Gregg's Brigade countermarched and bivouacked at its original position on the Long Bridge Road. The bivouac ended at 6:00 a.m. July 1, when Gregg's men marched forward about two miles, passing over the previous day's battlefield. July 1 marked another Confederate attack, this time at Malvern Hill near the James River. The results were disastrous, as the Federals were dug in with artillery covering all approaches. The Light Division would be barely engaged, and Gregg's Brigade remained mostly in reserve throughout the battle. Malvern Hill would be the Seven Days' final battle, as the Army of the Potomac disengaged and retreated down the peninsula—McClellan's ambitious quest to capture Richmond rudely foiled.[20]

Assessing the 12th South Carolina's performance during the week-long series of marches and battles, the regiment responded well to the pressure of the

20 *CMH*, 70–71; OR 11(2):852–858; Caldwell, *The History of a Brigade of South Carolinians*, 49; Boyles, *Reminiscences*, 26–27.

moment, particularly at Gaines's Mill. As William Miller pointed out, that action constituted the regiment's real "baptism of fire," overshadowing the relatively minor engagements in South Carolina. Colonel Barnes's leadership, especially at that critical juncture at Gaines's Mill when Federal artillery had the isolated regiment on the verge of destruction, was composed and competent. His rally of the regiment later in the day, when he was wounded in the thigh, only served to heighten his status, so much that he was one of three Light Division colonels A. P. Hill recognized for conspicuous gallantry during the campaign.[21]

Surprisingly, over the next few weeks, harsh criticism and gossip regarding the regiment's performance at Gaines's Mill began to mount back home in South Carolina. The whispers in York County were so serious, in fact, that an anonymous writer known only as "Y" felt compelled to write into the *Yorkville Enquirer* and offer a full-throated defense of the regiment. "Y" apparently was a civilian who either received or had access to letters from soldiers at the front, which he used in his defense. The letter to the editor by "Y" appeared nearly six weeks after the campaign's conclusion, in the *Enquirer*'s August 13, 1862, edition. "Y" staunchly defended the troops fighting hundreds of miles away and castigated those at home who dared criticize them from the safety of the home front:

> Mr. Editor—It is the habit of many who are careful to remain at home, and have none to represent in camp, except such as utterly worthless, to decry the services of our brave soldiers, and rest from their hard, well-earned laurels.
>
> This is exemplified in numerous instances, but perhaps in no case more glaringly than in the 12th South Carolina regiment, in the late series of battles before Richmond. Envy and Malice have no stopping place, and the consciousness and degradation prompts to the endeavor to reduce others to the same level. Hence it has been represented that cowardice pervaded the whole regiment, and that particular companies were wanting in bravery. What a pity these home men had not been there, to infuse courage and impart a portion of their own bravery!
>
> But we have a right to require that men who will not battle for their own rights, and who contribute grudgingly for the support of the cause, at least bridle their tongues, and refrain from aspersing our brave soldiers.
>
> The casualties occurring ought to be a sufficient refutation of these home slanders, and the undivided testimony of those who were present, and in a situation to know, should settle the matter. In addition to this, permit me to hand you the

21 Caldwell, *The History of a Brigade of South Carolinians*, 49.

following extracts from a private letter, written by one who gallantly performed his part in the severe struggle:

"The campaign of the Chickahominy was a severe trial. Our men bore up quite as well as could be expected, and when the day of trial came the 12th fought as well as any in the army, though it may not get much credit. One point as regards the 12th has not been understood by the country. It is this: The 12th and 1st were in the advance in the entire march down the Chickahominy, made three charges, driving the enemy before them during the march and on arriving on the field of battle were the first to engage, after driving back their heavy skirmishers. At one time the 12th stood alone, without any support in the face of the enemy—this after having been subjected to a cross fire of artillery—a fire so terrible that the colonel had to take his men out by a flank movement; and, forming again, marched in another direction, where we were met by the great odds I have mentioned. The regiment was finally thrown into some confusion by the forces of overwhelming numbers.—Those, therefore who came in last will most likely have most of the glory. All fought well or we should all have been whipped."

Extract from another, by one who ought to know:

"Some malicious person has spread a report in the country that the 12th regiment behaved badly. It is utterly false. It is true it became disorganized in the latter part of the fight, but it was in the face of overwhelming numbers, without support, having been thrown forward fully one hour before the main action commenced, and had been compelled to fall back by reason of the terrible cross fires of artillery and infantry. Besides this regiment, with the 1st, was broken down in the long marches of that day, together with the heavy skirmishes and repeated charges which they had made."

Both field and company officers, as well as men, did their whole duty, carping, canting non-combatants at home; with home-bred and home-brewed braved to the contrary notwithstanding. It's the nature of the serpent to hiss and of the adder to sting; but if some of our slandered soldiers are permitted to reach home; it will be their business; as it will be their duty, to call to reckoning these home braves, the soldier's defamers.

August 13, 1862. Y[22]

Anyone who decried the regiment's performance at Gaines's Mill needed to wait only 60 days to be proved wrong. By the end of August, Barnes and the

22 "Y," "Mr. Editor," *Yorkville Enquirer*, Aug. 27, 1862, 1.

12th South Carolina would silence the naysayers with their exploits and gallantry near what became known to history as the "Unfinished Railroad Cut" during the Second Battle of Manassas. There, facing overwhelming odds, the 12th established itself as one of the hardest-hitting regiments in the entire Confederate army and greatly assisted the Army of Northern Virginia in winning one of its most memorable victories.

Chapter Four

Glory and Redemption at Manassas

WHAT TO DO with one's accoutrements in battle or on the march was a familiar dilemma for soldiers during the war, particularly for regiments with limited experience like the 12th South Carolina. Essentials such as knapsacks or blankets were sometimes tossed aside to lighten one's load—and just as often never recovered, it seemed—and the loss of those essentials impacted the 12th South Carolina as the regiment recovered from the Seven Days' fighting. Few men were left with a change of clothes and had to continue wearing uniforms that were beyond filthy. Lice infestations were rampant.

"Prior to the battles I had seen one of these loathsome vermin and grown sick over it, recalled J. F. J. Caldwell, the brigade's historian. "Now scarcely an hour passed but I saw some soldier killing or scratching them."

Caldwell noted, however, that unhealthy living conditions or a lack of clothing were not the only culprits, as long-engrained personal habits contributed greatly to the regiment's collective poor health during this transitional period from garrison troops to front line soldiers. "The men failed to wash what clothing they had nor bathed regularly and did not take care to prevent against germs when cooking their rations," he wrote, adding that a "soldier, of all men in the world must be practical and careful, and this we had not yet even begun to be."[1]

1 Caldwell, *The History of a Brigade of South Carolinians*, 51–52. Because infrastructure deficiencies made it difficult for the early Confederate government to fully supply its armies, a so-called "commutation system" was instituted in which troops would provide for their own uniforms or clothing and receive compensation from their respective state governments, which in turn were to

The Seven Days' Battles and the preceding month's buildup around Richmond weighed heavily on the regiment, both physically and emotionally. To some extent, a malaise set in as the 12th attempted to rest and regroup, camped in the lowlands around Richmond until the end of July, primarily at Laurel Church. As Colonel Barnes recovered from his wound, drill was suspended and military exercises, even at the brigade level, were limited mainly to guard duty and the occasional dress parade. "Thoroughly exhausted" was one soldier's banal assessment of the regiment's mindset, and Caldwell disparaged the stay at Laurel Church, located about 12 miles southeast of Richmond on the James River Road. "The location was not a healthy one," he wrote. "Crowds of men were huddled together, sweltering with heat and wasting with idleness."

Private Joseph Templeton also ridiculed the conditions at "Camp Laurel," writing in a letter home that "the 12 Rigment is badly beet up." Tents were scarce, he noted, and the exposure to the hot and humid Virginia summer—exacerbated by pouring summer rains that brought out mosquitos, combined with the exertions of the men as well as increasing anxiety—made the troops susceptible to various diseases and illnesses. Chief among them were typhoid fever and dysentery, which soon filled the hospitals with numbers roughly equal to those still on duty. Although few deaths were attributed to those ailments, the number of absences was staggering. By July 7, for example, Templeton's company had only 34 men present for duty "oubt of 98," and Company I's aggregate was even worse. At one point, it fielded merely 18 effectives and was without its commanding officer, Captain Valandingham, who was wounded at Gaines's Mill and had a leg amputated.

Despite the pitiful conditions, there were positives. Distribution of rations increased marginally in July as Lee prioritized supply—the daily serving now three-fourths a pound of bacon or one pound of beef, one and one-eighth pound of flour, salt or occasionally molasses, and beans. One soldier was unimpressed, though, lamenting: "But the bacon was almost invariably fried, and the bread was half cooked—two things which are certain to derange any stomach and bowels."

In addition, camp visitors usually arrived bearing tidings from loved ones back home, compelling one soldier to urge in a letter to the *Lancaster Ledger* that anyone planning future visits give advance notice so that delivery of care packages could be arranged. And the mid-July return of Barnes to the regiment, praised by

be reimbursed by the national government. The unreliable system was in place as late as December 1862, when government quartermasters officially assumed the responsibility for the remainder of the war. Caldwell commented on the clothing shortage the 12th faced, writing that the stipend to purchase uniforms was "hardly enough to cover one's nakedness for prices were at least treble the peace standard."

one soldier as "our brave and gallant colonel," after a brief stint in a Richmond hospital, significantly raised the men's morale.

Another satisfying distraction for those at Camp Laurel was the "capture" of several Yankees, who, as Templeton recalled, were, "penned up in the swamps of the James River" and who "come oubt every day or to and gives up." "They seem to be in good spirits," wrote another soldier, "perfectly well satisfied, always ready for a joke." A captured Yankee of Irish descent, conversing with men in Company I, indicated that he had once thought the North would conquer the South but now believed otherwise. The man, it seemed, was "satisfactorily convinced that before McClellan reaches Richmond, he has a deep Branch to cross, a Longstreet to travel, two tremendous big Hills to climb, and a solid Stonewall to batter down"—playful deference to a legion of prominent Confederate generals that included Brig. Gen. Lawrence O'Bryan Branch of North Carolina. The wordplay aside, minor demonstrations continued well into the month, as 12th South Carolina pickets and their Federal counterparts repeatedly tested each other along the river.

* * *

On July 25, whether it was to relieve their plight or simply give the South Carolinians a beneficial military exercise, Gregg's Brigade formed ranks and marched several miles to a new "beautiful" and "picturesque" camp on the New Market Road, about 10 miles from Richmond. It remained there a few days before countermarching back to its original bivouac on the James River Road.

Describing the scene at the temporary new bivouac, one Company I soldier wrote home that "the camps are dull—nothing to excite or interest. Some while [*sic*] away their time at reading and writing, others endeavor to hunt up some innocent amusement, while a large number 'lounge it out.'" Refuting common misconception that illnesses in the camp resulted from too much exposure, the soldier in turn argued, "The life of a soldier is a lazy one, and it requires determination in a man, such are the temptations set before him, to keep the body properly exercised. Exercise of the body is the mainspring to health." Evidently, many in the regiment were not active during this period.[2]

Military developments soon had the brigade in action. Outgeneraled during the Seven Days' fighting, George McClellan withdrew the Army of the Potomac to

2 Caldwell, *The History of a Brigade of South Carolinians*, 51–52; Joseph Templeton to William Templeton, July 7, 1862; Joseph Templeton to Sarah Templeton, July 27, 1862; LOCAL, "Army Correspondence," *Lancaster Ledger*, July 23, 1862, 1; D. J. Carter, "Casualties in the Lancaster Companies," *Lancaster Ledger*, July 9, 1862, 2; LOCAL, "Army Correspondence," *Lancaster Ledger*, Aug. 6, 1862, 1.

safer confines at Harrison's Landing on the Virginia Peninsula, where the Federal naval presence, as well as heavy artillery, would make a Confederate attack quite risky. There, McClellan and his large army dug in and waited for an assault Lee and the Army of Northern Virginia did not intend to make.

Meanwhile, in central Virginia, Federal commands that operated against Stonewall Jackson earlier in the year in the Shenandoah Valley were united under Maj. Gen. John Pope, transferred to the Eastern Theater after notable success in the West. Consisting of corps commanded by Maj. Gens. Irvin McDowell, Nathaniel Banks, and Franz Sigel, this force would be named the Army of Virginia. As McClellan could not be coerced to lead another attack on Richmond from the Peninsula, in early August Lincoln directed the Army of the Potomac to return to Washington, unite with Pope's army, and then move on Richmond overland from the north. The army's transfer by water to Alexandria, Virginia, began August 14.[3]

Lee faced a strategic conundrum. With McClellan's army at Harrison's Landing and still within striking distance of Richmond, Lee had to maintain a defensive stronghold around the capital. Pope's united army, however, was in position to move on Richmond with fresh troops from the north. A pincer movement involving Pope's and McClellan's commands would have Lee, fielding an army smaller than each of his opponents, facing attacks from two sides.

Lee's decision to divide his army despite this threat and carry the war north was a calculated risk few commanders might make. Predicting McClellan would stand fast at Harrison's Landing and, if anything, ship his army north to Washington to face the threat Lee had begun to implement, he ordered Jackson and the Army of Northern Virginia's Left Wing to march north and check Pope near the railroad junction of Gordonsville, Virginia, in late July. A. P. Hill's Light Division, assigned to Longstreet's wing, was not initially slated to join Jackson's march north; however, a developing feud between Longstreet and Hill began to fracture the two commanders' relationship and would change the trajectory of the Light Division's future within Lee's army.

The feud began after John Daniel, the over-the-top editor of the *Richmond Examiner*, served as a volunteer aide to Hill during the Seven Days'. When Daniel suffered an arm wound at Gaines's Mill, he returned to his cozy office in Richmond and began writing exaggerated, glowing columns about Hill's service in the recent battles. Hill, Daniel wrote, was responsible for the "investment at Mechanicsville" and singlehandedly fought the battle of Glendale/Frayser's Farm, excluding mention of Longstreet's contributions in those fights.

3 *CMH*, 120.

Daniel embellished the number of men in Hill's Division and his total casualties, and in a subsequent editorial, claimed that Hill's Light Division and "one of Longstreet's two divisions" completely annihilated the enemy and "completed the circuit of our victories," which elevated Hill's role at Longstreet's expense. Daniel also inferred that Longstreet was inexcusably absent for a period from the field at Frayser's Farm. Although these claims were not necessarily false, the articles could be construed as misleading and exaggerated; especially for those in Longstreet's command.

Because the *Examiner* was widely read in all the camps, Daniel's gleaming articles about Hill and the Light Division incensed Longstreet, who felt slighted. In this politically charged atmosphere, "Old Pete" prepared a rebuttal and requested that Moxley Sorrel, his assistant adjutant general, have it published under his name and not Longstreet's. The young and loyal Sorrel, "ever too willing" to defend the honor of the commander he served, agreed to the request and submitted the rebuttal, signed, to the rival *Richmond Whig*, which published it on July 11. Longstreet's position through his surrogate was clear: No one begrudged Hill receiving accolades for his service in the recent battles, but the suggestion that his division did the fighting alone and sustained the majority of the casualties, and that officers were improperly absent from their commands, harmed the army's reputation.

Hill, who had nothing to do with Daniel's articles, was now irate, too. He and Longstreet had worked well together during the recent campaign, but on July 12 Hill asked Lee to be relieved from Longstreet's command, though the request had to go through Longstreet's headquarters first. Longstreet would concur, stating to Lee in the correspondence: "Respectfully forwarded. If it is convenient to exchange the troops, or to exchange the commanders, I see no particular reason why Maj. Gen. A. P. Hill should not be gratified."[4]

With tensions simmering between the two proud officers, Longstreet played a new card in the drama. Requesting a routine report from Hill through Sorrel, Longstreet was probably not surprised by the abrupt response written across the paperwork when it arrived on his field desk: "Maj. Gen. Hill declines to hold further communication with Major Sorrel." Unmoved by Hill's bluster, Longstreet ordered Sorrel to request the report again from Hill, and Hill again demurred. Hill refused several other attempts by Longstreet, who finally decided it had gone too far. Longstreet was, according to his staff, "on fire" at the disobedience and

4 Douglas S. Freeman, *Lee's Lieutenants: A Study in Command*, 3 vols. (New York, 1942–1944), 1:664–666; Gilbert Moxley Sorrel, *Recollections of a Confederate Staff Officer* (New York, 1905), 85–86; *OR* 11(3):639–640.

dispatched Sorrel to inform the Light Division commander that he was under arrest. Hill complied with the arrest order, confining himself to his camp.

When further missives between the two produced little more than hurt egos, they apparently agreed to a duel. Lee, however, quenched that extreme remedy and agreed to transfer Hill and his division north to join Jackson. Although some historians and battlefield guides maintain the claim that the Longstreet–Hill relationship was irrevocably strained and affected their compatibility in future campaigns—most notably at Gettysburg—there is evidence the matter was quickly forgotten and that the commanders' partnership turned amicable again.[5]

With the transfer, the 12th South Carolina and Gregg's Brigade had been given an unexpected opportunity to share in the legendary Stonewall's triumphs, glories, and controversies heading forward. On August 1, the Light Division departed to join its new command, traveling from Richmond to Gordonsville on the Central Railroad.

Just missing the regiment in Richmond were fresh recruits from South Carolina, including William Templeton, who had been training at Lightwood Knot Springs. While in training, William volunteered to serve with his brother in the 12th, a privilege granted to the first 300 men at the camp who made their wishes known. "I thot I had better go when I had the chance," he wrote of the opportunity to serve with Joseph. When they arrived in Richmond, however, he and the others were disappointed to learn that the 12th had already "gone to the [Shenandoah] valley." As a result, William was assigned to the 5th South Carolina.

Gregg's Brigade remained in Gordonsville until August 6, then marched 10 miles toward Orange Court House. The march was strenuous, given the mountains around Gordonsville, but a treat awaited the 12th when it bivouacked about midnight: the men were able to cook fresh beef and were issued flour to bake biscuits. Late on August 7, the column snaked its way through Orange Court House. Accounts from the brigade indicate that the heat was unbearable and resulted in considerable straggling.[6]

5 Freeman, *Lee's Lieutenants*, 1:666–667; Sorrel, *Recollections*, 87–88; "Confederate" (Thomas J. Goree) to *Houston Daily Post*, Jan. 31, 1888, in Thomas W. Cutrer, ed., *Longstreet's Aide: The Civil War Letters of Major Thomas J. Goree* (Charlottesville, VA, 1995), 168. In Goree's letter, he denied that Hill ever offered a duel that was likewise rejected by Longstreet; instead, he suggested that any talk of a duel was between Sorrel and Hill. Sorrel, however, confirmed that the discussion of a duel was between "the principals" Longstreet and Hill and that D. H. Hill and Robert Toombs were asked to interfere and possibly act as intermediaries to arrange the "hostile meeting" on Longstreet's behalf. Sorrel, *Recollections*, 87.

6 Caldwell, *The History of a Brigade of* South *Carolinians*, 52–53; William A. Templeton to Mother, Aug. 5, 1862; William Templeton to Catherine Templeton, Sept. 22, 1862.

In August 1862, the 12th South Carolina and A. P. Hill's Light Division joined Thomas J. "Stonewall" Jackson's Wing of the army. *Library of Congress*

On August 9, the entire Light Division joined Maj. Gen. Richard S. Ewell's Division and the Stonewall Brigade, commanded by Col. Charles A. Ronald, and marched in the direction of Culpeper Court House, where elements of Pope's army were assembled. After crossing the Rapidan River at Barnett's Ford, Gregg was ordered to guard the wing's baggage trains against enemy cavalry during the battle of Cedar Mountain on August 9, an eventual Confederate victory. Waiting within earshot as the fighting raged displeased the South Carolinians, anxious to engage. "I am credibly informed that Gen. Gregg twice applied to Gen. Hill to be relieved from the wagon guard and sent to the front," Caldwell wrote, "but the latter replied that Gen. Gregg was in the very place where he was most needed, and therefore refused his consent."

* * *

Cedar Mountain had important repercussions. Jackson's swift attack on the Army of Virginia's vanguard—Banks's II Corps—blindsided Pope as he prepared to move on Gordonsville and then toward Richmond. Although the Federals, outnumbered roughly 2-to-1, had success during the morning fighting, a Confederate counterattack famously inspired by Jackson proved decisive, chasing Banks from the field. That night, the 12th South Carolina and the rest of Gregg's Brigade moved toward Culpeper Court House in support but eventually fell back toward Orange Court House and bivouacked.[7]

In his brigade history, Caldwell recounted a notable development that occurred shortly after the fighting at Cedar Mountain:

7 Caldwell, *The History of a Brigade of South Carolinians*, 53.

> On the night of Monday (11th) Jackson commenced retiring toward Orange Court House. During the night, the first and greatest panic I ever saw occurred. Our brigade was bivouacked in the woods, on both sides of the road from Orange to Culpepper, and in the rear of the rest of the army. Soon after dark the retrograde movement was commenced by the troops at the front retiring past us. The men of our brigade lay down and slept, most of them taking off their shoes, and some of them even their outer clothing. I remember waking during the night and seeing dense bodies of troops marching along the narrow defile below us. About midnight, or a little after, we were aroused by a loud, confused sound of voices, the tramp of feet, and the rattle of canteens and accoutrements. At the same moment a line of men rushed over us, crying out loud "O Lord!" and similar exclamations, stamping upon us in the dark, and in many instances, beating us down with their guns (which men in a panic always carry at a trail), as we rose out of sleep.
>
> The effect upon us is not so difficult to conjecture. Men started so rudely naturally took fright, especially as the cry of "Yankee cavalry!" began to circulate freely. It became really a frightful scene for a few minutes—crowds of men dashing hither and thither, barely visible in the deep fog, running against trees, stumbling over the sleepers, and crying out everything dreadful and unreasonable. Some of the brigade, as a matter of course, joined in with the fugitives. One man, I remember, only returned to us at noon the next day, and then without hat or jacket. But nearly the whole of the brigade soon learned its mistake and got under arms. The alarm originated with a brigade marching past us, and was caused, some say, by the rattling of an ambulance; others, by the coming of two small dogs![8]

Unimpressed, William Miller of Company H opined in a letter home that cavalry kindled the affair: "At a late hour of the night cavalry troops coming back from the front, some of them riding through the woods to get around some artillery standing in the road, rode over men sleeping. They woke up under the impression it was the enemy, and it was very dark and there was much confusion. I heard that some men ran off for safety for a short time and came back after daylight to be made fun of. Steve Johnson and myself had lain down under a cedar tree with low limbs. We thought in the darkness it was a good place so kept quiet." Regardless of the cause of the panic, the situation remained a prominent memory for both men when they recorded their reminiscences years later.[9]

8 Caldwell, *The History of a Brigade of South Carolinians*, 53–54.

9 Miller, "My Experience," 219.

The next morning, August 12, the South Carolinians followed their comrades who had passed through them the evening before. After recrossing the Rapidan, they were allowed to rest. The march resumed in the afternoon until the column halted for the night somewhere between Gordonsville and Orange Court House, where they remained until August 16. The men felt fortunate to have time to catch their breath and write loved ones. "We have been marching through the mountains & valley for the last eight days," a tired Joseph Templeton wrote to his sister, Sarah.

On the 16th, the regiment returned to the main thoroughfare, heading north toward Orange Court House. Passing through the village, the brigade halted at "Crenshaw's Farm," where it remained for another two days. Despite the heat, the lengthy marches, and a lack of shelter, the regiment's overall health continued improving. On the morning of August 20, the brigade recrossed the Rapidan at Somerville Ford and marched through Stevensburg, camping just outside the town that evening. When Longstreet's Right Wing moved to unite with Jackson, Pope pulled his army back to the Rappahannock River.

With Lee's two wings now within supporting distance of each other, Jackson accelerated his movements, sweeping around Pope's flank as Longstreet remained temporarily in place on the Army of Virginia's front. On the night of August 21, Gregg's command camped near the Rappahannock; the next day, the brigade headed west up the river and crossed Hazel River. Despite the oppressively humid weather, well into the 90s, the South Carolinians plowed ahead, at times crossing dried-out waterways, and many unwisely tossed aside their blankets—"hundreds . . . were thrown away by the troops," one man would recall.

A two-hour rainstorm that afternoon, which the troops deemed refreshing, did not stymie the advance, although the heat, exposure, and grueling march would take its toll. Straggling was inevitable, but Gregg's men pressed on until after dark to reach the home of a Dr. Scott on hills overlooking the Rappahannock and Warrenton Springs Ford.[10]

It was here, in the yard of a country residence, where the seeds were sown for another troubling feud between high-ranking officers in the Army of Northern Virginia, with A. P. Hill again in the mix. This quarrel would pit the stern and generally undiplomatic Stonewall Jackson and his staff on one side and Hill, Maxcy Gregg, and Dixon Barnes on the other, and it made the Hill/Longstreet showdown in July seem like a small skirmish. It also would carry over to future campaigns and eventually required intervention by Lee.

10 Caldwell, *The History of a Brigade of South Carolinians*, 54–56; Welch, *A Confederate Surgeon's Letters to His Wife*, 19–20; Joseph Templeton to Sarah Templeton, Aug. 14, 1862.

It started because of an ornamental fence. As luck (or fate) would have it, the five regiments of Gregg's Brigade were instructed to camp for the night around Dr. Scott's home. Jackson set up his headquarters inside the residence. The home's abundant yard contained what one veteran described as "a very nice paling fence," and as the footsore regiments filed off the road and broke ranks into the areas around the home to make camp, start their fires, and cook rations, Jackson sent orders that the fence was not to be used as firewood. That evening, another severe rainstorm soaked the troops, some of whom defied orders and used palings for firewood. When Jackson awoke the next morning to see portions of the fence down and burning in the fires of the South Carolinians, he immediately placed Barnes and the four other regimental commanders under arrest.

With all five of his regimental commanders in military custody, Gregg needed a quick resolution. Only the promise of the five colonels to compensate Scott for the fence's destruction secured their release. Years after the war, one of the arrested commanders, Col. Edward McCrady of the 1st South Carolina, remained vexed about the mass arrest: "Five regimental commanders . . . all arrested for a few palings of an ornamental fence taken under such circumstances!" The incident was merely the first in a series of disagreements, differences, and unnecessary drama in the coming weeks between the uncompromising Jackson and the Light Division's high command.[11]

On August 23, with the five colonels now free, Gregg moved his command into the nearby woods, about a half-mile from the scene of the crime and encamped. Although it was never confirmed that the relocation was a punitive measure by Jackson, that was likely the case. The next morning, members of the brigade attended church services, and that evening they moved out, following the Rappahannock through Jeffersonton and camping on the hamlet's outskirts.

At dawn on the 25th, the men in each company in each regiment were ordered to drop their knapsacks, containing all of their extra clothing, in a pile to be picked up by the wagon train and then "hurried upstream" to the crossing at Henson's Mill. That would be a grueling, 28-mile forced march, and the knapsacks unsurprisingly were never seen again. While the men marched, Wade H. Rives of Company D recalled them nibbling on their hard tack and raw bacon as they did not have sufficient time to cook it that morning.[12]

In what was known as "Salem Valley," the hungry and footsore South Carolinians wreaked havoc on the lush cornfields in an area yet to be touched by

11 *SHSP* 14:209–10.

12 Wade H. Rives, "Incidents Recalled of Second Manassas," *The State* [Columbia, SC], Feb. 20, 1910, 24; Miller, "My Experience," 219.

war, sending out details to gather as many ears as possible and rashly feasting on them raw. On the 26th, the march continued at first light. The brigade filed through Thoroughfare Gap in the Bull Run Mountains, traversing another punishing 29 miles with some straggling and with blood from men's bare feet staining the road. Bivouacking that night at Bristoe Station on the Orange and Alexandria Railroad, the 12th sent out more details to gather "roasting ears"—again eating "them on the cob raw," according to William Miller.[13]

The two-day, 57-mile excursion had paid off. As one officer wrote, "We were now in rear of Pope's army," and very close to Pope's base of supplies at Manassas Junction. But they were also in terrible condition. Many of the troops were barefoot and their clothes in tatters. The knapsacks collected two days earlier were gone forever, and many were suffering from dysentery and corn-induced diarrhea, and, as one soldier noted, all were "half-famished." As the dusty column trudged past Thoroughfare Gap, a mounted courier from Maj. Gen. J. E. B. Stuart's headquarters rode by. When they called out asking whether there was anything ahead to eat, the courier yelled back: "Yes you are almost in sight of Manassas Junction and Gen. Stuart had surrounded and captured the whole garrison." At the news, a soldier recalled, "the boys gave the old rebel yell and marched on," hopeful they would soon have their hands on the spoils of war.[14]

Realizing the aggressive forced marches meant Jackson was threatening his right flank, an agitated Pope hesitated and began to fall back. On August 27, Gregg's Brigade arrived at Manassas Junction anxious to enjoy the supply splendor Stuart's courier had promised. Other units in the Light Division were engaged in driving away Federal infantry on their front, and the South Carolinians moved to nearby Bull Run to support the effort before countermarching to Manassas Junction. There, courtesy of the US government, they were issued hardtack, bacon, coffee, sugar, and an essential they sorely needed: soap. "[T]here was a general jubilee," Caldwell would write.[15]

In only a few days, Jackson's aggressive sweep around Pope's flank had forced the Union army to fall back while relinquishing its principal supply depot, now in the hands of famished Confederate troops. After the toils of the past two weeks, the spoils captured at Manassas Junction seemed heaven-sent. As Rives recalled:

13 Miller, "My Experience," 219.

14 Caldwell, *The History of a Brigade of South Carolinians*, 56–57; *SHSP* 13:9–11

15 Ibid.

> We loafed around the junction and . . . feasted on Yankee grub for several days. The depot was a very large frame building and there were two or three out houses all filled with everything that was good to eat. Barrels of flour, barrels of rice, coffee, Irish potatoes, onions, molasses, barrels of pickle pork, corn beef, bacon, hams, and in addition there were three or four large sutlers stores filled with lots of good things, small sugar cured hams, canned goods, condensed milk and some of the boys got some brandied peaches, pinders, etc. There were several long side tracks on both sides of the depot, and the cars being heavily ladened with rations, hospital stores, sabres, new uniforms, haversacks, canteens, etc.[16]

The booty was no doubt foremost in the men's minds as they feasted, but from a strategic assessment of the situation, Jackson's hard marching and the troops' perseverance and sacrifice meant that roughly half of Lee's army was now squarely behind Pope, his position very much in jeopardy.

The capture of Manassas Junction kept the 12th South Carolina and the other regiments supplied for several days. Before moving out, the 12th's wagons were loaded with all the plunder they could hold. The men stuffed haversacks to the brim with rations, and some even reported wrapping food-filled sacks around their necks. Each man was also issued 60 rounds of ammunition. That evening about sunset, the brigade moved about a half-mile south of Manassas Junction and deployed at the edge of a woodlot facing Bristoe Station. As the regiment waited anxiously, a horseman bounded out of the woods in front of the 12th's position and into the lines. One of Jackson's spies, he had just come from Pope's headquarters. Questioned by men in Company D, the excited spy indicated that the loss of Manassas Junction had Pope's army down to three-days' rations and the Union general planned to move soon against Jackson. A battle was imminent.

One gruff, older enlisted man in Company D was not impressed, declaring, "All right let him come and we will lick him before his rations are out. We've got his grub and grannys, we hain't gwinter give 'em up." As twilight approached, the spy rode off to find Jackson and report the information. Relying on the information and expecting an attack at any moment, the 12th sent a heavy picket line to the front for the evening. Prudently, Barnes also sent out videttes well in advance of the picket line to ensure they were not surprised by Pope's advancing army. That accomplished, Barnes opened his ranks (creating intervals of 3–5 feet between the front rank and the rear), ordered the regiment to fix bayonets, and put the men to rest under arms in battle formation.[17]

16 Rives, "Incidents Recalled of Second Manassas," 24.

17 Ibid.

Awakened at 2:00 a.m. on the 28th, the brigade crossed Bull Run at Blackburn's Ford and marched to Centreville before halting for breakfast. Behind them, they heard explosions and saw red flames from the commissary stores at Manassas Junction, burned by their fellow Confederates to ensure they would not fall back into Yankee hands. As the ammunition boxcars exploded, one by one, one soldier labeled it a "pyrotechnic display."

The foray to Centreville was essentially pointless, insisted Caldwell and Rives, who recalled that they simply loitered for two or three hours and that some of the men explored earthworks that had been built the previous year. Excited couriers and scouts brought claims that McClellan, commanding 20,000 Union troops, was moving to reinforce Pope and surround Jackson's command. The brigade re-formed and headed west on the Warrenton Turnpike, crossing Bull Run near the Stone Bridge that had figured prominently during the July 1861 battle. As they moved, the men had a chance to see a "good deal" of the First Manassas battlefield, with one soldier pointing out the position held by Brig. Gen. Milledge L. Bonham's primarily South Carolinian First Brigade during the previous engagement. Jackson personally led the column, turning it right off the turnpike near Sudley Ford and establishing a position near the cuts and fills of an unfinished railroad cut paralleling the Warrenton Turnpike—what had been an ambitious but recently abandoned project to build the Independent Line of the Manassas Gap Railroad between Gainesville and Alexandria.[18]

The area in which the South Carolinians were posted was an expanse of land between two bodies of woods. To the right was an open field; to the front and rear were dense woods and underbrush; and a cornfield occupied the ground to the left. The men were confident a great battle was at hand, or "boding," as one soldier framed it. To the right, General Ewell's Division engaged Federals probing his lines as they advanced east on the turnpike. As a precaution, skirmishers from Gregg's command were sent forward about 100 yards into the woods, and the brigade was shelled briefly, with no reported injuries.

As the sun went down, and just as the men began to relax along the railroad cut, they were ordered to fall in and march to the right to support Ewell. According to Caldwell, the brigade formed "in a column of regiments," meaning that each regiment was arrayed in a battle line, two ranks deep behind one another. It is

18 Ibid.; Caldwell, *The History of a Brigade of South Carolinians*, 58–59; *OR* 12(2):678; Wade E. [H]. Revis [Rives], "Second Battle of Manassas," *The State* [Columbia, SC], March 27, 1910, 21. (This was evidently a continuation of Rives's "Incidents Recalled of Second Manassas" narrative that first appeared in the February 20, 1910, edition of *The State* and is cited above. Rives's name was misspelled as Revis in this updated account. This source will hereafter be cited as Rives, "Second Battle of Manassas.")

likely that the 12th South Carolina was the third regiment in this formation. The men, Rives recalled, slept on their arms with strict orders to keep silent, "with one eye open . . . [expecting] an attack at any moment." To their front, they reported hearing exulted cheers of the enemy as darkness enveloped the field.[19]

* * *

Barnes had the men up early on August 29. Using the captured rations, "[t]he boys commenced cooking breakfast by the crack of day," Rives recalled, noting: "Our menu for breakfast was fried ham, rice, can goods, oysters, sardines, corn beef, etc., coffee with sugar and condensed milk." Whether it was the smoke from the South Carolinians' breakfast fires or an attempt to develop Jackson's lines, Federal artillery soon shelled their position, disrupting the men's carefree morning.

Those who had not finished their breakfast by 7:00 a.m. were sorely disappointed as Gregg was ordered back to his original position along the unfinished railroad cut, not far from the Sudley Church. Marching in a column of fours, Barnes and the 12th South Carolina were in the center of Gregg's column. Per the morning reports, the regiment numbered approximately 320 men. During the circuitous march, which took them first toward Thoroughfare Gap, each regiment threw out skirmishers to guard their flanks as the column moved cautiously through the woods and fields.

At one point, according to Rives, Jackson and his staff "came dashing across the old field and struck the column at the head of the 12th South Carolina Regiment." Jackson, who had arrested Barnes after the "paling fence" incident only a few weeks earlier, demanded of the colonel the troops' identity, to which Barnes responded: "This is the Twelfth South Carolina Volunteers, Gen. Gregg's brigade." When Jackson inquired about Gregg's location, Barnes replied bluntly that the general was at the head of the column and that two other regiments were marching ahead of the 12th. After directing a staff officer to ride forward and inform Gregg he was needed, Jackson ordered Barnes to lead his regiment to the right and follow him at the double-quick. Barnes complied, doing his best to keep pace as Jackson and his staff jumped a rail fence 20 yards ahead of the 12th. Jackson's orders called for the rest of Gregg's command to divert into the woods that lined the unfinished railroad, approximately where they had deployed the day before.

Shortly after the 12th reached the position with Jackson, Gregg arrived with his remaining regiments and deployed the brigade, about 1,500 men, on a rocky knoll overlooking the railroad cut. It was about 8:00 a.m. On the brigade's right,

19 Caldwell, *The History of a Brigade of South Carolinians*, 60; *SHSP* 13:14–15; Rives, "Second Battle of Manassas."

the knoll descended into thick underbrush; on the left was a vast open field surrounded by a fence. Gregg personally posted each of his regiments. The 1st South Carolina, under Major McCrady, formed as the right flank. Extending to the left were the 13th under the command of Col. Oliver Edwards, the 12th under Barnes, and the 14th under Colonel McGowan. Orr's Rifles, under Colonel Marshall, were placed in reserve at the center of the line.

Given the contours of the knoll, the position resembled an obtuse angle with its "point" facing the cut. The men looked anxiously toward the woods for any sight or sound of the enemy. As Gregg posted the brigade, a soldier in the 12th overheard a tense exchange between the brigadier and Jackson. "General Gregg, you must hold this position at all hazards," Jackson stipulated, to which Gregg asserted: "I will hold it, sir." As Jackson galloped off, Gregg and his staff dismounted. They established a post about 50 yards in the rear of the brigade's lines.[20]

The men in the ranks might not have realized it, but Gregg's Brigade was the extreme left flank of Hill's Division and, as such, the extreme left flank of Jackson's entire wing, which was anchored on Stony Ridge running roughly parallel to the unfinished railroad. Given the ground's jagged nature, calling it a battle line was generous; in fact, various units along the two-mile front were not close to standing shoulder to shoulder, and significant gaps existed not only between regiments but also the adjoining brigades in the Light Division. On the rocky knoll, the South Carolinians were isolated from the rest of the line. McCrady's 1st South Carolina found itself separated 100–200 yards from the left flank of Colonel Edward L. Thomas's Brigade, consisting of the 14th, 35th, 45th, and 49th Georgia. On Thomas's right was Charlie Field's Virginia Brigade, which constituted the division's extreme right.

The division's other three brigades were deployed in reasonable supporting distance to the rear. Branch's North Carolinians were to Gregg's left rear; nevertheless, Gregg was somewhat "in the air"—on his own to repel any threat from that direction unless the Tar Heels moved forward to support. Dorsey Pender's North Carolinians, meanwhile, were posted at a slight angle in rear of Thomas's Georgians and Field's Virginians, and James Archer's Tennessee and Alabama troops were posted well behind the gap that had opened between Thomas and Gregg.

As the regiments hunkered down, Barnes ordered Company C (Captain Clyburn) and Company E (Captain Davis) forward as skirmishers, a move McCrady mirrored with his regiment. Deployed in open order, the skirmishers streamed down and across the gradual slope of the railroad cut and disappeared into

20 Caldwell, *The History of a Brigade of South* Carolinians, 62; *SHSP* 13:15–16; *OR* 12(2): 693; Rives, "Second Battle of Manassas."

the thick woods and underbrush on their front. According to Lt. Col. Cadwallader Jones, 50 members of the 12th were among the skirmishers, leaving approximately 270 men on the knoll.[21]

In 1884, as a guest speaker at a 12th South Carolina regimental reunion, McCrady recalled: "The skirmishers crossed the railroad cut, and pushed into the woods opposite. We had been posted in our position but a few moments, I think, when the crack of the rifles in the woods in our front informed us that our skirmishers had come upon the enemy." That enemy was the 54th and 58th New York in Col. Wlodzimierz Krzyzanowski's 2nd Brigade in Brig. Gen. Carl Schurz's 3rd Division in Maj. Gen. Franz Sigel's I Corps.

As the skirmish fire intensified in the woods, Gregg deduced that the Federal skirmishers were harbingers of a concerted attack on his position and sought McCrady for confirmation. Although he reiterated to McCrady that Jackson did not wish to bring on a general engagement, Gregg nevertheless ordered the colonel to advance with the rest of his regiment into the woods, and "give them two or three volleys, and then charge them with the bayonet."

Though perplexed, McCrady followed Gregg's orders. After crossing the railroad cut into the woods, McCrady came upon Lieutenant Fellows of the 13th South Carolina, who guided the 1st South Carolina forward, obliquing the regiment to the left into the dark woods. As the 1st advanced, Krzyzanowski's New York regiments unleashed rounds of sharp, direct fire that stopped the 1st in its tracks. The 1st traded volleys with the enemy but were outnumbered, and the New Yorkers soon overlapped McCrady's right and left flanks, "threatening to envelop the small command."

Facing flank fire and the possibility of being cut off from the rest of the brigade, McCrady initially requested support from the rear before pulling his men back on his own and barely avoiding outright disaster. According to Caldwell's postwar history, as the 1st fell back to the railroad cut, four men from the 12th's Companies C and E who had been wounded in the skirmish in the woods safely made it back to the knoll. Those from Companies C and E remaining in the woods did all they could to harass Krzyzanowski's determined Yankees.[22]

Despite Jackson's orders not to bring on a general engagement that morning and his own desire to hold the position by defensive measures, Gregg was not one to back down from a fight. Seeing his old 1st South Carolina scrambling back through the smoke-filled woods in disorder after the brief firefight, he doubled

21 *OR* 12(2):693; *SHSP* 13:15–16.

22 *SHSP* 13:16–17; Caldwell, *The History of a Brigade of South Carolinians*, 62; *OR* 12(2):693, 685–686.

down and ordered Barnes and the 12th off the knoll to assist their beleaguered comrades. Gregg's orders were clear: drive back the enemy. As historian James I. Robertson Jr. noted in his renowned 1992 biography of A. P. Hill, Gregg "responded with the best defense he could make: he attacked."[23]

If Gregg's best defense was indeed a good offense, his choice of Dixon Barnes and the 12th South Carolina to support McCrady proved propitious. With his white beard flowing, Barnes drew his sword and led the remaining 270 men forward. He had been itching for a fight like this: a chance to showcase the men's discipline and fighting qualities, completely confident they would not be outdone in close-range combat. After nearly a year serving under the indolent and uninspiring R. G. M. Dunovant, followed by the mostly indecisive Seven Days' Battles, Barnes's seminal moment as commander was at hand. "I recollect," McCrady recalled, "just before the battle, Colonel Barnes saying to me that he intended to use the bayonet on every opportunity. He said he thought long-taw firing [was] a mistake on our part, that it wasted ammunition, which was a matter of great consequence to us, and more than that, lost to us the advantages of the 'elan' of our troops, which he thought greater than that of the enemy, and he was determined, therefore, to close with him whenever the occasion offered."[24]

Barnes and the 12th advanced swiftly. The colonel angled the regiment obliquely to the 1st South Carolina's left, then re-formed in the railroad cut. Taking Barnes's lead, McCrady ordered the 1st to advance in tandem; together, they slammed headlong into the Empire State regiments, driving them back. Krzyzanowski's brigade contained one other regiment, the 75th Pennsylvania, which soon came forward to support the retreating New Yorkers. Also moving into the fray was Schurz's other brigade, Col. Alexander Schimmelfenning's 1st, containing the 61st Ohio, 74th Pennsylvania, and 8th West Virginia. This situation had the understrength 12th and 1st South Carolina tangling with two relatively fresh brigades of infantry (five regiments in all).[25]

Although the 12th South Carolina's arrival pushed the 54th and 58th back, the New Yorkers quickly re-formed and counterattacked, focusing principally on the 12th. The 54th pressured the regiment's left flank while the 58th occupied its front. The South Carolinians fired away at the blue mass in the woods, with one volley killing the 54th's color-bearer. To the right, the 75th Pennsylvania poured deadly fire into McCrady's right flank, forcing the 1st to halt as well.

23 James Robertson, *General A. P. Hill: The Story of a Confederate Warrior* (New York, 1987), 119; Caldwell, *The History of a Brigade of South Carolinians*, 62; *OR* 12(2):693.

24 *SHSP* 13:16.

25 Ibid., 18–20; *OR* 12(2):311–312, 314.

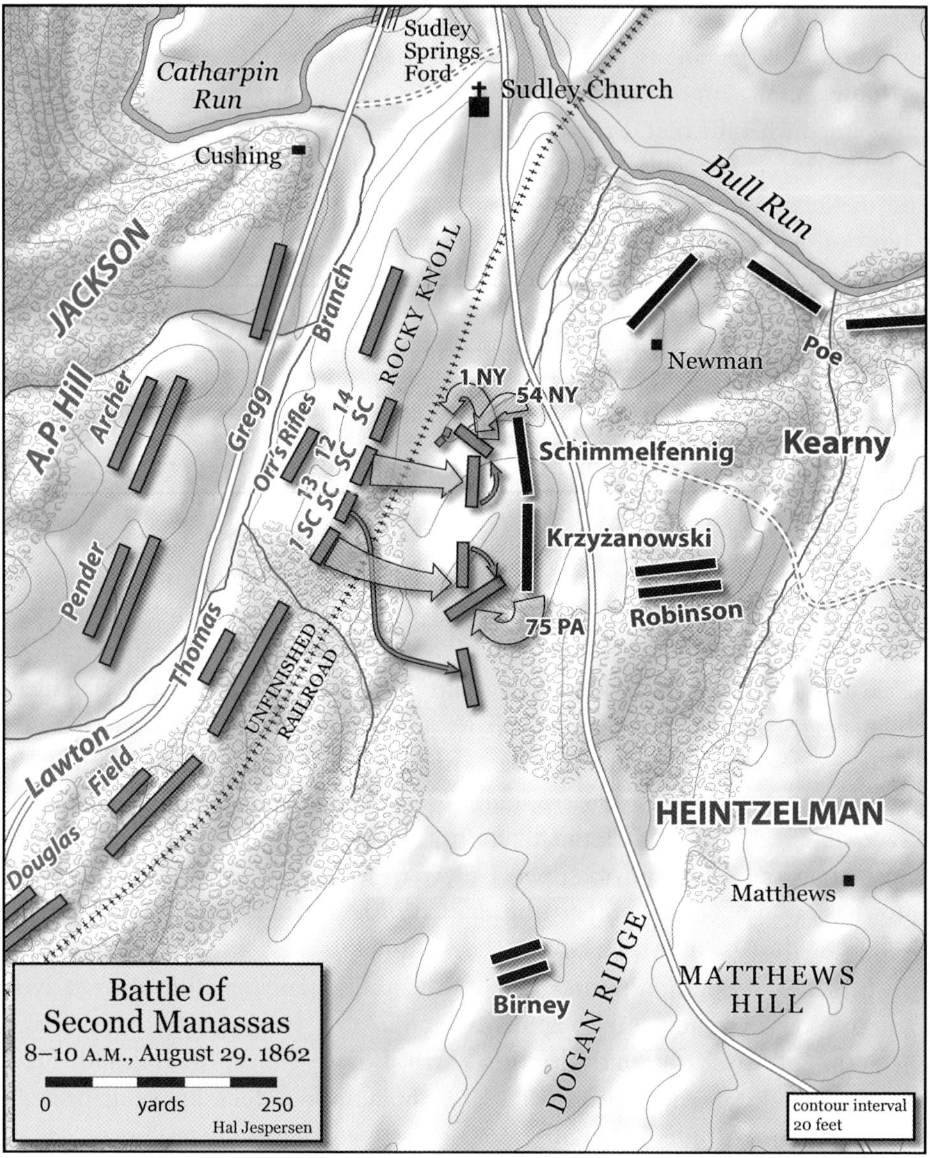

As the fire intensified in the woods and the smoke hung low, McCrady and Barnes were forced to separate their regiments by changing their respective fronts outward, hoping to provide better fighting angles—the 1st changing front to the right, the 12th to the left. The maneuvers, however, also created a gap between their regiments. The 12th checked the 54th New York's flank attack as it handled the 58th on its front, but the 1st bore the brunt of the 75th Pennsylvania's aggressive flank fire, and McCrady again requested support from the rear.

The resolute Gregg ordered in Edwards's 13th South Carolina, but the smoke enveloping the woods made it impossible to see more than a few yards in any direction. In its vain attempt to find McCrady's right flank, the 13th came upon the 75th Pennsylvania and turned quickly to face this threat. Eventually, the 1st and 13th connected and pushed the 75th through the thick underbrush, leaving heavy casualties, but they would lose contact with each other.[26]

While the 1st, 12th and 13th South Carolina continued to fight doggedly on independent fronts in the woods, little was being accomplished other than a bloody impasse. Federal reinforcements from Schimmelfenning's brigade began descending on the 12th's left flank, beyond the 54th New York. To make matters worse, the 1st New York in Brig. Gen. David Birney's 2nd Brigade, part of Phil Kearny's division in Heintzelman's III Corps, entered the fray, bolstering the 58th. Peering through the smoke, Barnes realized three regiments were attempting to flank him on the left and wheeled his two leftmost companies to re-fuse his flank, continuing to fire.

Barnes did not shy away from this critical moment. His choices were limited: stand his ground, retreat, or charge. He could not sit still, as it would invite more withering volleys to which his reduced regiment could not stand, and retreat was never really an option for Barnes. He did what was most natural and made a split-second decision to go on the offensive. Earlier in the day, Barnes promised McCrady he would close on the enemy at every opportunity. Honoring that vow, the colonel rushed to the front of his regiment, drew his sword, and yelled, "Twelfth, right half wheel, forward, charge" and led his men through the smoke with—in the words of one observer—"characteristic impetuosity." The woods and timber filled with electric shrieks and howls that echoed off the trees, as a section of the 12th swarmed ahead, tearing into the 1st New York's left flank. Stunned by the wild dash, the Empire State boys fell back in disorder for 300 yards.

Simultaneously, the 12th's left-flank companies wheeled right and tore into the 54th New York's exposed right flank as well as the left of the surprised 8th West Virginia in Schimmelfenning's brigade, which had just arrived. Smelling blood in the water, Barnes was not content to simply rout one regiment. He directed close-range fire into the exposed wings of the two Yankee regiments, which soon fled "in wild disorder." Almost singlehandedly, Barnes and the 12th South Carolina had cracked the center of the Federal line in the woods, overwhelming three regiments from three Union brigades.[27]

26 *SHSP* 13:20; Caldwell, *The History of a Brigade of South Carolinians*, 62; *OR* 12(2):311–312.

27 *OR* 12(2):298, 310–312, 428; Caldwell, *The History of a Brigade of South* Carolinians, 62; "The 12th South Carolina Regiment," *Yorkville Enquirer*, Feb. 4, 1863, 1; Rives, "Second Battle of Manassas."

Barnes and his men followed the broken Federals several hundred yards to the edge of the wood, but approaching the woods they ran into the 29th New York, part of Brig. Gen. Adolph von Steinwehr's 2nd Division in the I Corps. The New Yorkers fired a volley at close range, generating prompt return fire from Barnes's men. Although the 29th fell back across the field, Barnes could not follow. He needed reinforcements to advance into the open field and sent Lt. Col. Cadwallader Jones sprinting back into the woods to find help. "About this time I received a message from Lieutenant-Colonel Jones of the Twelfth, requesting me to move the First forward to support of the Twelfth," McCrady told the veterans at the 1884 reunion. "Colonel Barnes had pushed you upon the enemy to some distance in advance, and you were then being pressed by them in superior numbers. The enemy, however, upon our right rendered it impossible for the First to advance; indeed, it was all we could do to hold our own position."

Barnes continued to slug it out at the tree line, trading fire at long range with the 29th New York. To his delight, he was soon joined by Colonel Marshall and his Orr's Rifles, and the two regiments overran a second line of Federals making a move against them from the field. As the Federals retreated in confusion, Barnes and Marshall received an order to return to the rocky knoll. It was now between 10:00 and 11:00 a.m.[28]

Falling back through the woods, the winded regiments likely rounded up wounded comrades and stragglers, and according to one soldier, "a good many prisoners." Gregg met Barnes at the railroad cut. "Your regiment, Colonel Barnes, has covered itself with glory," Gregg beamed. "Let the men rest until further orders." Back on the knoll, the regiments were directed into new positions as Gregg reconfigured the brigade. The 13th would now be on the right flank, and the 1st was placed in its rear in support. Gregg sent the 12th well in reserve of the 1st to recuperate and placed the 14th and Orr's Rifles on the left flank facing the field. He then sent four companies of the 1st South Carolina into the woods as skirmishers to scout for a possible new attack before walking back to the resting 12th's position.

As details gathered to fill canteens, Gregg sought Barnes, then resting by a tree. Seeing the general approach, Barnes called the regiment to attention, but Gregg shook him off. "No, do not disturb your men, I ordered them back here to rest," he said. "I came to congratulate them for their gallantry. Say to the Twelfth that they have repulsed every charge today and held the line. Say to the Twelfth, Colonel Barnes, that I will not put them in the fight today as their ammunition is exhausted unless the enemy should break the line. In case they do, say to the

28 *SHSP* 13:20; Caldwell, *The History of a Brigade of South Carolinians*, 62–63; *OR* 12(2):693.

Twelfth that I will depend on the Twelfth to drive them back at the point of the bayonet. Say to the Twelfth that they have covered themselves in glory today."

Gregg had barely finished speaking when the popping of muskets in the woods indicated another assault. As Gregg's skirmishers fell back to the main line, the men on the knoll distinctly heard breaking branches and the orders of Federal officers echoing through the woods as the enemy approached.[29]

"And now began the really terrific work of the day," recalled McCrady. "From the dense growth which shielded the enemy from our view, they poured upon us a deadly fire. Our men had seldom better direction for their aim then the bushes from which the fire came from." Failing to dislodge the stubborn South Carolinians, the Federal troops soon fell back. As they listened to cheers from other advancing Yankees, Gregg's men braced for another attack. These were more of Birney's troops.[30]

The renewed attack, launched about 1:00 p.m., hit the South Carolinians across their entire front. According to McCrady, the Yankees swarmed over the railroad cut "in force," his 1st positioned directly ahead of the 13th and 12th on the right, respectively. Krzyzanowski's and Birney's brigades struck the roughly 150-yard-wide gap between Thomas's Georgia Brigade and Gregg's command with ferocity, compelling the Georgians to fall back. In possession of the gap and with Thomas's men running, the Federals turned their attention to the South Carolinians to the east. Gregg had been cut off from the rest of the Light Division, his brigade fighting for its life. To the left, Schimmelfenning's brigade was over the cut, trading fire with the 14th South Carolina. The knoll was being enveloped.

With Yankees on three sides, and in a desperate measure to prevent the brigade's right flank from collapsing after the Georgians' retreat, McCrady wheeled several companies of the 1st South Carolina to the right to engage the Federals, as did Edwards's 13th. "We had no time to form a regular line to meet them," McCrady wrote of the maneuver. A desperate, close-quarters firefight erupted. Using the railroad cut for their own protection now, Federal troops came within 10 paces at

29 Wade Rives reported the conversation between Gregg and Barnes in his wonderfully rich narrative of the battle in 1910. While Rives's recollections of the battle are fairly consistent with other accounts, it seems unlikely he would have recalled this conversation verbatim. That said, what Rives quoted in his account is used here. It conveys the spirit of the interaction between Gregg and Barnes, as it is clear the commander was impressed with the regiment's performance that morning. See Rives, "Second Battle of Manassas." More contemporary accounts indicate that Gregg was pleased with the 12th's actions and give similar but more truncated praise to Barnes. See, "The 12th South Carolina Regiment" and "Resignation of Col. C. Jones," *Yorkville Enquirer*, March 18, 1863, 1; *SHSP* 13:23–24.

30 *SHSP* 13:23–24.

certain points. "The work of death was terrific, but as each man fell, his place was filled by another," McCrady recalled.

Gregg's command, on Jackson's extreme left, faced being cut off and caught in a deadly cross fire, which potentially required him to abandon the position altogether. That scenario could allow the Federals to roll up the rest of the line from that flank. The 1st and 13th began to give way on the right, as did Orr's Rifles on the left. The Federal noose around the rocky knoll had tightened. McCrady looked "anxiously" to the rear for the 12th South Carolina. Where were they?

"We were not in line of battle but somewhat scattered about, lying down resting with coats unbuttoned and cartridge belts loosened, and our guns in stack," Rives recalled of the attack's opening moments. In an instant, though, Barnes ordered the men of the 12th to grab their rifles from the stacks just as all seemed lost. With the Rebel yell echoing among the trees, Barnes led his men in another brash charge that slammed into the Yankees surging against the brigade's right flank. The charge even stiffened some of the Georgians falling back and lagging in the rear, rallying at least one regiment that assisted in the charge (likely the 49th, as there are accounts of 12th South Carolina soldiers fighting within the 49th Georgia's ranks). For a moment, blue and gray collided in a bloody hand-to-hand clash. Stunned by the 12th's frenzied attack, the Federals on this part of the hill started to give ground.

About now, McGowan's 14th South Carolina, having assisted on the left flank in repulsing Schimmelfenning's 61st Ohio and 74th Pennsylvania, rushed to the scene. Together, and at great cost, the 12th and 14th South Carolina and the 49th Georgia pushed the Federals off the knoll and stabilized the position. In the confusion, elements of the 12th pursued the retreating Federals across the railroad cut and into the woods.[31]

With the Yankees on their heels, Barnes returned the regiment to its previous position in the rear. He then placed one of the more dependable soldiers from his old company, Pvt. Ben Powell of the Lancaster Hornets (Company I), in command of the regiment's infirmary corps. Powell wasted no time. He set up a makeshift field hospital, with large numbers of wounded "lying on the ground as thick as a drove of hogs in a lot," according to one surgeon. There, amid stray bullets and the further clamor of battle, Surgeon J. F. Prioleau and assistant surgeon W. W. Keith vigorously administered care to the dozens of wounded making their way back from the lines. As the South Carolinians and Georgians reorganized and shuttled their wounded to the rear, the dense smoke began to rise, revealing the carnage. William Miller had been detailed to the rear to fill canteens prior to the Federals'

31 Ibid., 28–31; *OR* 12(2):693; Rives, "Second Battle of Manassas."

mid-morning counterattack. On his return to the regiment, he witnessed the dead and wounded of both sides. Some of the wounded begged him for water. "One was a Yankee, badly hurt," he recalled. "I gave him a drink then dragged his gun away and next delivered the canteens to their respective owners."[32]

During the lull, the 12th's ammunition wagon arrived and the regiment received an additional 60 rounds. Canteens were filled, and men were gathered and organized. The South Carolinians, however, enjoyed little time to rest and regroup. At 3:00 p.m., a massive Federal assault by Krzyzanowski's, Schimmelfenning's, and Birney's brigades commenced again along the railroad cut and against Gregg's worn line. Like hornets ejected from their hive, "the woods swarmed with them," Caldwell recalled. Masses of blue troops were everywhere, coming through the woods in all directions, he wrote, "pressing up with an energy never before witnessed by us, and certainly never surpassed since." The desperate defenders somehow held on as the blue wave stormed the railroad cut—"[a] perfect death storm all around," recalled one soldier.

There would be no semblance of order, as men of the 12th no doubt fought alongside men of other regiments. "We fought them, so close that men picked out their marks, and on some occasions, saved their lives by anticipating the fire of someone on the other side," Caldwell recalled. "Officers used their pistols with effect." Barnes went down with a wound at the height of the action, leaving Jones in command. All officers in Company B were either killed or wounded, forcing Sgt. Jasper McKnight to assume the reins. Despite at least nine wounds from Yankee bullets that day, McKnight somehow survived. As Gregg's command drew back tighter on the knoll to face yet another attack, the Yankees delivered several devasting volleys. The "fire now formed a semicircle of flame and smoke, extending at least half round the devoted hill," McGown recalled.[33]

As the Federals rushed the hill from three sides, the brigade was compelled to fall back, its line contracting with the onset of more wounded streaming to the rear. Just as the regiments started to give way, however, Gen. Branch sent forward one of his North Carolina regiments, temporarily checking the advance. Stiffened by the Tar Heels' support, the 1st, 12th, and 13th stubbornly maintained their tenuous foothold on the position, fighting hand-to-hand and even counterattacking in

32 Miller, "My Experience," 219.

33 Caldwell, *The History of a Brigade of South Carolinians*, 63–64; *OR* 12(2):681; Benjamin Powell to Wife, Nov. 21, 1907; Welch, *A Confederate Surgeon's Letters to His Wife*, 26; *OR* 12(2):695; William S. Dunlop, "The Confederate War. Company B, Twelfth S. C. V. in Bivouac and Battles," *Yorkville Enquirer*, Oct. 30, 1889, 1 [hereafter cited as *Bivouac and Battles (Part II)*]; Rives, "Second Battle of Manassas."

small groups. For the third time that day, the brigade sent the bluecoats streaming back across the railroad cut in confusion.[34]

With the Federals regrouping in the woods, Gregg was in a bind. Other than Jones, McCrady, and Lt. Col. William Simpson of the 14th, all his regimental field officers had gone down killed or wounded, with company-level officers now in command. In addition to the horrific casualties, the brigade's ammunition was almost exhausted. The situation was so bad that, before he could be treated by the infirmary corps, one wounded soldier was stripped of his accoutrements and his ammunition divided among those nearby. For hours, the men had fought with ammunition and weapons procured from the dead and wounded of both sides, but even that source had run dry. The cheers of Federals re-forming in the woods signaled another looming assault.

As the South Carolinians braced, a staff officer sent by A. P. Hill rode up to the rocky knoll and asked Gregg whether the brigade could continue to hold the position "Tell General Hill that my ammunition is exhausted," the general responded, "but that I will hold my position with the bayonet." The officer galloped off to report that to Hill, and Gregg quickly re-formed his shattered regiments in yet another defensive configuration. From left to right, the front line consisted respectively of the 12th, 13th, and 14th, all reduced in strength. Gregg placed Simpson in command of this formation and McCrady the 1st and Orr's Rifles manning the rear line. Drawing his Revolutionary War heirloom sword from its scabbard, Gregg entreated his men as he walked up and down the line: "Let us die here, my men, let us die here!"

Gregg and his gallant band of survivors grimly waited in silence with bayonets fixed as the Federals began their advance across the railroad cut. As the enemy troops came into view, however, the South Carolinians heard a sudden commotion to their rear. Turning in fear, expecting to be cut off and surrounded by another Yankee force, they were elated to realize these were friendly reinforcements: Branch's Tar Heels and Brig. Gen. Jubal Early's Virginians. Advancing on both sides of Gregg, the Confederates slammed into the advancing enemy troops with a "wild Confederate yell," chasing them through the woods beyond the railroad cut. With that devastating counterattack, the fight was over. Jackson's all-important left flank held.[35]

34 *SHSP* 13:33.

35 Ibid., 33–35; *OR* 12(2):681–682. Although McCrady recalled that Dorsey Pender's North Carolinians and Charles Field's Virginians had come to their rescue, McGowan's brigade report—penned after General Gregg's death—cites Branch and Early. His version is generally accepted as accurate.

As darkness fell, the survivors slept where they were on the rocky knoll. "We were worn and lay down on the battlefield and slept soundly, expecting to wake in the morning and renew the contest," William Miller recalled. The next day, the regiment and brigade held its position but was not engaged while the fierce fighting continued and the battle decided. When a 3:00 p.m. attack on the right of Jackson's Stony Ridge position by Fitz John Porter's V Corps was stopped, an assault on the Union left by Longstreet's Wing completed a Confederate rout—perhaps Lee's most complete and impressive triumph of the war.[36]

* * *

August 29 had been the 12th South Carolina's most intense day since its formation a year earlier; indeed, few others came close to equaling it. The regiment started the day with reportedly 320 men and suffered 145 casualties (24 killed, 121 wounded)—the highest total of any of Gregg's five units. Several top officers were also lost. Lieutenants May and Hunnicut were killed and Colonel Barnes, Maj. W. H. McCorkle, Capt. Lewis Grist, and Lieutenants J. Burdock and David L. Glenn were wounded. One account showed 613 total casualties in the brigade, another 619.

In holding the rocky knoll, the brigade had almost singlehandedly staved off disaster for Jackson's entire line against four assaults in nine hours.[37] "Friday, the 29th, was the glorious but bloody day for the brigade," McGowan would write. "It may be allowed for us to claim that by holding the left steady on Friday we contributed something to the success of the great battle on Saturday." McGowan was correct. Each regiment in the brigade fought well amid overwhelming numbers, followed orders explicitly, and took action and displayed initiative when needed. Maxcy Gregg, ever the gambler, had played his cards right from the outset. Cautioned that morning not to bring on a general engagement, his decision to send in regiments piecemeal during the early fighting certainly caught the attacking Federals off-balance as Gregg developed their intentions. His actions had brought on a general engagement, but it was on his terms.[38]

36 Miller, "My Experience," 220.

37 Caldwell, *The History of a Brigade of South Carolinians*, 65; Miller, "My Experience," 220; *SHSP* 13:40. In his address to the survivors of the regiment in 1884, McCrady cites Caldwell's figures but cautions that official reports contradict the 613 number in favor of 619 total brigade casualties. For a detailed list of casualties in the August 29 fighting, see "Casualties in the 12th Regiment South Carolina Volunteers," *Richmond Enquirer*, Sept. 23, 1862, 1.

38 *OR* 12(2):681.

The 12th South Carolina's action in the battle deserves particular commendation, from Barnes to the men in the ranks. It was no accident Gregg turned to Barnes for help when the 1st South Carolina was heavily pressed in the early-morning fight in the woods. The subsequent firefight in those woods lining the knoll firmly established Barnes as an elite combat officer in an army famous for them. The maneuvers and charges the 12th executed that day were the result of long hours of drill and training for which Barnes must receive proper credit. "The rare perfection to which this Regiment has attained, in drill and discipline, is attributable to the brave and heroic Barnes," wrote one admiring soldier. Although the reputation of Barnes and the regiment was questioned by some at home after Gaines's Mill, it was cemented as positive at Second Manassas.

Others took notice. As proof of the 12th's rising prominence in Lee's army, Col. Edward Porter Alexander stated in his memoirs that the "12th Regiment was particularly distinguished for conduct both on the march & in battle." It is notable that Alexander was an artillery commander in another section of the army, and given his eventual status in the pantheon of Confederate leaders to pen renowned recollections after the war, his affirmation of the 12th's ability and reputation is high praise indeed.[39]

39 "The 12th South Carolina Regiment"; Gary W. Gallagher, ed., *Fighting for the Confederacy* (Chapel Hill, NC, 1989), 157.

Chapter Five

Slaughter Along a Stone Wall

Rain and cooler temperatures greeted the exuberant but exhausted Army of Northern Virginia on August 31. For the survivors on the rocky knoll, though, the scene was somewhat subdued. Wounded comrades needing care in a makeshift hospital and the struggle to stay dry with only a few tents available tempered the gratification Gregg's men felt after their success on August 29, which had paved the way for the spectacular victory the following day. Any hopes that an extended recovery period might be in store, however, were quickly dashed. In less than three weeks, these battle-tested, victorious, and confident veterans would clash with a familiar but reenergized enemy army at Sharpsburg, Maryland, in what would be the war's single bloodiest day.

In Centreville, a few miles to the east, the rattled Federals took stock, contemplating what was next. "Do not be uneasy," John Pope had attempted to placate General-in-Chief Henry Halleck the previous evening. "We will hold our own here. We have delayed the enemy as long as possible without losing the army. We have damaged him heavily, and I think the army entitled to the gratitude of the country. Be easy; everything will go well." But as historian John J. Hennessy notes in the seminal work on the Second Manassas campaign, *Return to Bull Run*, "reduced confidence, spirit and energy" clearly framed the once-haughty Union commander's façade on August 31. Despite insisting that "I shall fight as long as a man will stand up to the work," Pope also wanted guidance from Halleck.

Should he stay in Centreville, renew the fight, or rush back toward Washington to protect the capital?[1]

Lee would force Pope's hand. By midday August 31, he had Jackson's Wing—led by the Light Division—trudging with undeniable misery over mud-caked roads around the Union right flank. After crossing nearby Bull Run, Jackson and his men headed north toward Gum Springs and then to the Little River Turnpike, where they turned east and bivouacked before moving toward Fairfax Court House on September 1.

Jackson's advance caught Pope off-guard, the Union commander deterred both by his army's underperforming cavalry and Lee's directive for Longstreet to remain in place and demonstrate before the Union position at Centreville. Nevertheless, once Pope grasped the magnitude of the Confederate threat against Fairfax Court House, he ordered a prompt response, sending troops from his army and two Army of the Potomac brigades toward the community of Germantown, where the Warrenton and Little River Turnpikes intersected near a 500-foot rise known as Ox Hill. Furious fighting would break out around this crossroads that afternoon, with the 12th South Carolina and Gregg's Brigade again involved.

* * *

Robert E. Lee developed his plan to maneuver around Pope's right flank during a respite in the Second Manassas fighting the morning of August 30. Although forced to postpone such a move when hostilities resumed that afternoon, leading to the attack by Longstreet's troops that chased the Federals from the field, Lee was not about to remain idle on August 31. For Jackson's 20,000 men, the 12-mile slog to the Little River Turnpike would take about eight hours, and their progress the following morning, despite a brief end to the rain, was not much better. By 9:30 a.m. September 1, Jackson's command had reached the Chantilly mansion only a few miles away, breaking until noon before resuming the march toward Ox Hill.

The delay helped Federal forces consolidate troops between Ox Hill and the Germantown crossroads. At 2:30 p.m., unsure of the size of the Federal force that lay ahead, Jackson prepared an attack down the turnpike. J. E. B. Stuart's cavalry led the way, accompanied by two infantry columns and several batteries. The fighting opened with a cavalry clash between the 1st Rhode Island Cavalry and one of Stuart's units, the 5th Virginia, which was soon followed by a skirmish

1 Peter Cozzens, *General John Pope: A Life for the Nation* (Urbana, IL, 2000), 182; *OR* 12(2):78–79; John J. Hennessy, *Return to Bull Run: The Campaign and Battle of Second Manassas* (Norman, OK, 1999), 442–443.

between two of General Hooker's New York regiments and the Stonewall Brigade. As 4:00 p.m. approached, Jackson realized the enemy presence was bigger than he had expected. He ordered a pause, deciding to wait for the arrival of Longstreet's Wing, which was marching about two hours behind him.

Major General Jesse Reno's IX Corps waylaid those hopes quickly. That afternoon, Pope ordered the corps, positioned at Centreville, to reinforce the Federals at Germantown. With Reno ill, Brig. Gen. Isaac Stevens assumed command of the march, and at 2:00 p.m. he led the men down the Warrenton Turnpike, diverting onto Ox Hill after about two hours.

Having learned of Stevens's advance shortly after it began, Jackson had aligned his three infantry divisions in a wide arc at the base of Ox Hill, hidden behind a heavy concentration of trees. On the left was Jackson's Old Division, under Brig. Gen. William E. Starke; in the center was Ewell's Division, now commanded by Alexander Lawton; and on the right was Hill's Light Division, including Gregg's entire brigade.[2]

The caution the typically aggressive Jackson displayed was new for many of the troops. Nevertheless, what would become a two-hour battle—contested during an unrelenting thunderstorm—soon erupted after Stevens and his men stumbled into Jackson's lines. Stevens was killed during the engagement, as was Maj. Gen. Phil Kearny while leading reinforcements. The battle would end in a tactical draw, but the Federals could claim a strategic victory, having foiled Lee's move on Fairfax Court House and possibly even the capital city itself.

Just before the fighting broke out, Gregg deployed his South Carolinians in two lines on the right during the Light Division's advance. He placed the 13th and 14th right-to-left on the front line, followed respectively by the 12th and Orr's Rifles, with McCrady's 1st in reserve. Ahead of the South Carolinians were Gen. Charles Field's Virginia Brigade (with Col. John Brockenbrough commanding) and Gen. Lawrence O'Bryan Branch's North Carolinians. Gregg ordered his men to fix bayonets and soon had them moving across the field to the Virginians' left. When the South Carolinians suddenly encountered small-arms fire, they rushed toward a split rail fence and hunkered down.

Gregg ordered the 12th to the left of the front line. Under fire, the 12th marched by the left flank, which left the 14th South Carolina uncovered, and then changed front to extend the brigade line to the left as it advanced to the fence. The right portion of the line became heavily engaged, the left to a lesser extent. When

2 William Allan, *Stonewall Jackson, Robert E. Lee, and the Army of Northern* Virginia, *1862* (New York, 1995), 311–314; *OR* 12:2, 695; Welch, *A Confederate Surgeon's Letters to His Wife*, 27; William Templeton to Catherine Templeton, Sept. 22, 1862.

the fighting concluded about 7:00 p.m., the Federals withdrew and the brigade slept on the field that night. Casualties were light. The 12th had only one killed (W. C. Buchanan, the regimental adjutant) and 10 wounded.[3]

Informed on September 2 that the enemy had withdrawn toward Washington, Lee shelved a further pursuit of Pope. The Union commander was no doubt headed for the safety of Alexandria and Washington, where his army would be protected by the city's massive fortifications and heavy artillery. Chasing Pope to the doorsteps of Washington was pointless given the advantages offered there for defense. Instead, Lee opted to keep the Army of Northern Virginia in place on the bloodied field at Chantilly for at least another day. That same September 2, Lincoln moved to place George McClellan in command of all the troops around Washington, including Pope's badly mauled army. News that "Little Mac" was back in charge was celebrated by many in Washington and among Pope's former troops.[4]

In three months, Robert E. Lee had completely altered the trajectory of the Confederate war effort in Virginia. Since replacing the wounded Joe Johnston in early June, Lee had driven McClellan's Army of the Potomac from the gates of Richmond, swiftly marched north to confront and soundly defeat the Army of Virginia at Second Manassas, and—before McClellan could transport his full army from the Peninsula to be of much help—finally forced Pope back to the gates of the US capital. Not only was his army now perched on the outskirts of the enemy capital, but Lee had also ridden Virginia of a significant Federal military presence.

Pope, relieved of his command on September 6, was reassigned to Minnesota and the Department of the Northwest, his Army of Virginia troops amalgamated into McClellan's Army of the Potomac. Despite misgivings about McClellan's command attributes among many in Washington, including the President himself, he was again at the head of the Union quest to defeat Lee and the vaunted Army of Northern Virginia.[5]

* * *

With the enemy sheltered around Washington, Lee favored a northwest pivot over the Potomac River and into Maryland—and ideally Pennsylvania from there. The army, with more than 9,000 casualties suffered at Second Manassas and Chantilly, was in terrible condition, however. The men were poorly clothed and

3 Allan, *The Army of Northern Virginia*, 315, 318; *OR* 12(2):677–683, 693–694.

4 Allan, *The Army of Northern Virginia*, 319–320.

5 Ibid., 321.

armed, and the summer marches had substantially reduced the quantity and health of the horses. In addition, subsistence for both men and animals were not at levels required to mount a sustained campaign. Despite those concerns, Lee wasted no time ruminating. Because falling back on ground won through the exertions of his army in the recent campaigns was not acceptable, he issued orders the evening of September 2 for a march toward Leesburg, Virginia, and then Frederick, Maryland, about 20–25 miles from the banks of the Potomac.[6]

The next day, the men of Gregg's Brigade drew two-days' rations of crackers and bacon, threw them in their haversacks, and accompanied the Light Division's march, encamping that evening near Dranesville, Virginia. At Dranesville, another flare-up occurred in the saga between Jackson and Hill's command, directly involving the South Carolinians. It had been only a little more than two weeks since the "paling fence" incident, but this time the dispute did not involve the regimental colonels but Hill himself.

With the Light Division encamped at Dranesville, Jackson delivered his orders for September 4. The march toward Leesburg was to continue before dawn, and Jackson summoned his three division commanders to ensure that the troops moved on time. As was his custom, Jackson made it a personal mission to check on his troops' status, that they were on the road and ready to march as directed. Hill's command had been assigned as the vanguard, but Jackson would find only half the Light Division ready to march, the other half still in camp.

Unable to locate Hill, Jackson sought a subordinate on whom he could vent his rising anger. He came across Gregg and grilled him harshly on why his South Carolinians were not on the road yet. Caught off-guard but unsurprised by Jackson's aggressiveness, Gregg responded that the men were still filling their canteens from a nearby creek. Jackson was not satisfied with the explanation. Within earshot of Barnes and the 12th South Carolina, Jackson turned his horse and shouted as he rode off in a tantrum: "There are but few commanders who properly appreciate the value of celerity!" One can only surmise what the proud Gregg was thinking after the scolding in front of his men.[7]

Fuming from his encounter with Gregg and no doubt looking to lash out at another for the delay, Jackson rode to the head of Hill's column, led by Col. Edward Thomas's Georgia Brigade. Jackson dismounted and walked alongside the troops, but when Thomas failed to allow his men a pre-established hourly 10-minute rest, the general—without consulting Hill—ordered Thomas to halt. After the break,

6 Ibid., 323.

7 James Robertson, *Stonewall Jackson* (New York, 1997), 585; Welch, *A Confederate Surgeon's Letters to His Wife*, 30.

Jackson also ordered Thomas to resume the march, which drew Hill's attention. Thomas was standing between Jackson and Hill when the latter confronted him about the brief delay. He sheepishly informed Hill that Jackson mandated the halt. Incredulous at the interference in his command, Hill unsheathed his sword and handed it to Jackson, stating emphatically: "If you take command of my troops in my presence, take my sword also."

Unmoved by Hill's bluster in the presence of the Georgians, Jackson told him to sheath his sword and had him immediately arrested, handing command of the Light Division to Branch. That evening, a portion of the 12th South Carolina was assigned picket duty for the division. Assigned to post the pickets, Lt. Col. Cadwallader Jones reported in person to Hill's headquarters. "I called on General Hill's tent for instructions," Jones recounted. "He and General Branch were seated together. I addressed my remarks to General Hill and he promptly, but good naturedly, said, 'I refer you for instructions to General Branch; that inspired fool, Jackson, has me under arrest. I couldn't please him on the march this morning.'"[8]

With arguably the best of Lee's division commanders under arrest and marching on foot in humiliation at the rear of his column, Gregg's Brigade crossed the Potomac on September 5 at White's Ford. The 12th was in jubilant spirits, as the men waded the waste-high water chanting "Maryland, My Maryland"—a poem composed by a Southern sympathizer in April 1861. Once across, the men maintained their ranks in a column of fours as they marched, averaging a disciplined 3-4 miles per hour despite their "wretched" condition. Indeed, many of the men were without shoes, and many were without blankets. By September 7, they reached Frederick, about 25 miles from where they had crossed the Potomac, and camped south of town.

As Alexander Rossino notes in his 2023 book *Calamity at Frederick*, Lee's objectives for his expedition into Maryland were "feeding his army, pulling Maryland out of the old Union, entering Pennsylvania, and, at some point, winning a war-ending victory north of the Potomac." After Second Manassas, however, Lee assumed he had weeks, if not months, to achieve his goals. News that McClellan was again in charge of Union fortunes and was in pursuit of his army altered such contentment. Lee also could not overlook the Federal-occupied towns

8 Robertson, *Stonewall Jackson*, 585; Robertson, *A.P. Hill*, 131–132; *SHSP* 20:385; "Colonel Cad. Jones." Jones's description of this event, recounted more than 35 years after the war, mistakenly placed this conversation after the Maryland campaign. Branch, however, was killed at Sharpsburg and commanded the Light Division only briefly before the battle.

of Martinsburg and Harpers Ferry in Virginia, which posed a significant threat to his army's supply line in a march north.[9]

Lee's response was Special Orders No. 191, which would become one of the war's most important and consequential documents. In it, Lee ordered a risky division of the army. From Frederick, the army would march north, but at Boonsboro, Jackson would head back across the Potomac to capture Martinsburg and Harpers Ferry. With control of Harpers Ferry, Jackson would return to Maryland and reunite forces with Lee in Hagerstown, a crossroads town that would provide the Confederates a solid base from which they could continue moving north.

What Lee could not have expected was the discovery of a copy of those orders by two Union soldiers on September 13. With knowledge that the Confederate army was divided and vulnerable, McClellan realized he could catch and defeat part of that army before it could reconsolidate. Heavy fighting would break out the next day at South Mountain, a Union victory that cost Lee nearly 3,000 hard-to-replace casualties. Lee managed to withdraw from South Mountain toward Boonsboro that evening, and his still-divided army would clash with McClellan again three days later at Sharpsburg.

* * *

At daylight on September 10, the Light Division began marching toward Boonsboro, roughly 15 miles away. During the march, yet another incident in the Jackson-Light Division drama would play out, this time with Colonel Barnes at center stage. Jackson had ordered his men not to pillage in any manner while on the march. When Barnes at one point allowed his regiment to stop and rest alongside a ripe apple orchard, the men sought shade wherever they could. Major Frank Paxton, one of Jackson's staff officers, happened to be riding nearby and spotted some soldiers in the orchard picking apples. Eager to please his commander, the young Paxton reined in his horse and asked the soldiers to which regiment they belonged. When the apple-picking soldiers yelled back, "12th South Carolina," Paxton thundered down the road in search of Barnes. Finding the genteel colonel resting by the road with the regiment, Paxton, without inquiry or explanation, ordered him to surrender his sword and placed him under arrest. Though surprised,

9 Alexander B. Rossino, *Calamity at Frederick: Robert E. Lee, Special Orders No. 191, and Confederate Misfortune on the Road to Antietam* (El Dorado Hills, CA, 2023), x.

Barnes complied without complaint and was placed at the rear of the regiment with the provost guard.[10]

For Barnes, it was the second arrest in three weeks by either Jackson or one of his subordinates. (Ironically, the culprits who had plundered the orchard were not from the 12th but Jackson's esteemed former unit, the Stonewall Brigade.) Barnes's latest arrest was the last straw for Gregg. Barnes was not an impetuous or incompetent young colonel disobeying orders; he was one of the Light Division's most respected regimental commanders. Describing Jackson as "tyrannical and unjust," Gregg fumed over the continued harassment not only of his troops and his regimental commanders but also A. P. Hill, deciding that he would prefer military charges against Jackson once the campaign closed.[11]

As this drama played out, the Federal garrisons at Martinsburg and Harpers Ferry across the Potomac had General Lee unsettled. He intended with the pivot into Maryland to draw McClellan away from heavily defended Washington, hoping to capitalize on the fertile Shenandoah Valley as a supply route for his army. The Federal garrisons at Martinsburg and Harpers Ferry, however, were menacing obstacles to keeping that supply line open. Lee expected the Federals to abandon both strongholds once his army reached Frederick, but that had not happened, which threatened to seriously derail his invasion plans. Jackson's march to Boonsboro would be the first step in eliminating these threats.[12]

On September 11, without Barnes in command, the 12th was on the road at daylight, headed with the Light Division for Williamsport, Maryland. From there, the brigade was to recross the Potomac into Virginia and then turn southeast toward Martinsburg. The following day, Gregg's Brigade, now leading the column, would march directly on the important regional railroad hub the Federals occupied. The Yankees, however, departed without risking a fight. When the Confederates

10 Caldwell, *The History of a Brigade of South Carolinians*, 69; Allan, *The Army of Northern Virginia*, 326; Robertson, *Stonewall Jackson*, 588; Welch, *A Confederate Surgeon's Letters to His Wife*, 23.

11 Daly, *Alexander Cheves Haskell*, 77; Gallagher, ed., *Fighting for the Confederacy*, 157. In his memoir, Edward Porter Alexander recalled that Colonel Hamilton of the 1st South Carolina was also arrested during this march. See "Colonel Cad. Jones." Jones indicated in his account, written long after the war, that the perpetrators were indeed men from the regiment who had stopped at a well to fill their canteens during the march, in violation of orders from Jackson that no straggling occur. Jones, however, made no reference to an orchard but confirmed the arrest of Barnes for this minor infraction. It is likely that Jones mistook this incident for the incident on Sept. 4 at Dranesville when the men were filling their canteens and Jackson scolded Gregg for not having his men on the road to march.

12 *CMH*, 141–142; Allan, *The Army of Northern Virginia*, 331.

entered the town about 10:00 a.m., they received an enthusiastic welcome and were treated to bread and meat for the first time in several days.[13]

Later that day, the column headed toward Harpers Ferry, about 20 miles away, arriving near the Federal camps on Bolivar Heights overlooking Harpers Ferry on September 13. Jackson spent the next two days enveloping the Federal presence in and around the town with his three divisions, preparing an attack. Three elevated positions surrounded the town—Bolivar Heights, Maryland Heights, and Loudoun Heights—and Union commander Col. Dixon Miles had only left a force of any substantial size on Bolivar Heights, which Jackson secured with relative ease.[14]

The assault on Harpers Ferry would be September 15. In addition to the meticulously placed infantry, Jackson also had the Union garrison encircled by artillery. Those big guns would open early that morning to precede the infantry attacks. The 12th South Carolina, positioned on Bolivar Heights, was to be in the thick of the fighting. It was an emotional moment for Barnes, still under arrest. He wanted in on the action and found it excruciating to watch from the sideline as his beloved regiment entered the fray. Swallowing his pride, he sought Gregg to plea for permission to go into the fight. Words, however, somehow failed the long-time lawyer and legislator, who became emotional. Gregg was a stern and taciturn aristocrat, but he clearly sensed something in Barnes's demeanor and gently took his hand. The touching gesture worked. Barnes finally found his voice and, given the noise of the bombardment and because Gregg was partially deaf, probably did so in an elevated tone: "General, I came up to ask leave to go with my regiment as a private in the fight."

The plea had Gregg conflicted. Probably more than anyone in the Light Division, save A. P. Hill, the brigadier was aware of how difficult Jackson could be, and also knew that Barnes's recent arrest was pure folly. Indeed, Gregg had been subject to Jackson's abusive, verbal tirades and unbending ways. On the other hand, he also reckoned that exercising any discretion and allowing Barnes to join the regiment, even as a private, while under arrest as an officer all but guaranteed Jackson would punish Gregg, likely with an arrest and a court martial. Conceding that outcome should he stray from Jackson's unbending edicts, Gregg reluctantly, and almost guiltily, denied the request. "No, Colonel Barnes," he replied gently. "You are under arrest by the General commanding, and orders must be obeyed."

13 Caldwell, *The History of a Brigade of South Carolinians*, 70.

14 Caldwell, *The History of a Brigade of South Carolinians*, 70–71; Allan, *The Army of Northern Virginia*, 337–339.

As that drama played out amid the pre-attack artillery barrage, Hill fortunately was riding among the lines. Hill, of course, had no love for Jackson with the recent flurry of arrests and command micro-management. Despite his own arrest at the beginning of the march to Maryland, Hill requested reassignment to command of the Light Division a few days earlier. As battle loomed, Jackson reluctantly assented to the request, with a provision that Hill would be placed back under arrest after the current campaign. Witnessing the gravity of the moment between Barnes and Gregg, Hill reined in his horse and inquired. According to an eyewitness, Hill's countenance was "pale and stern" as he listened to Gregg explain the dilemma he faced. Concurring it was ludicrous for one of his top colonels to sit by while his regiment went into battle, and knowing well what the autocratic Jackson had put him through personally, Hill made a decision that endeared him to the men of the 12th South Carolina forever. "General Gregg," Hill stated in a clear voice while stiffening in the saddle, "I order you to give Colonel Barnes his sword and put him in command of his regiment."[15]

The dramatic council lasted only minutes, but it provides remarkable insights into the working relationship of these Confederate chieftains and the dynamics at play in their complicated and adversarial connection to Stonewall Jackson—a connection Hill was willing to cross to ensure that Barnes was appropriately leading his command. Never known for his affectionate or gentle personality, Gregg demonstrated remarkable tenderness at this critical moment, moving Barnes almost to tears in grasping his hand. And Hill recognized that Barnes's honor and the army's effectiveness during a critical campaign superseded Jackson's autocratic ways, even at the risk of his own military career. That Hill directly disobeyed Jackson's orders while already facing a possible court-martial clearly demonstrated the respect and confidence Hill had in Barnes, not to mention his opinion of Jackson's arrest protocols. "Of course he was wrong to do this," a staff officer granted of Hill's decision, "but the case would stir the heart of a rock."[16]

As Barnes secured his sword and prepared to lead the regiment in the attack, though, the Federal garrison in Harpers Ferry raised a white flag, surrendering without a fight. To deal with a sudden influx of 14,000 captured Federals, Jackson directed the Light Division to remain behind to parole prisoners while he hurried his other two divisions the 17 or so miles to Sharpsburg, where fighting was about to break out between the rest of Lee's army and the Army of the Potomac. Purportedly the decision was a personal afront against A. P. Hill; nevertheless,

15 Daly, *Alexander Cheves Haskell*, 77–78.

16 Ibid., 78.

General A. P. Hill, commander of the Light Division and future commander of the Third Corps, Army of Northern Virginia. *Library of Congress*

the South Carolinians in Gregg's Brigade were more than happy to oblige, as it allowed them a chance to partake in the spoils of war. "We fared sumptuously," wrote one officer. "In addition to meat, crackers, sugar, coffee, shoes, blankets, underclothing, etc., many of us captured horses roaming at large, on whom to transport our plunder."[17]

With control of Harpers Ferry, the men of the 12th made sure to rest but also reveled in the victory. Gregg's Brigade was tasked with the formal surrender ceremony, which allowed the men to exchange their worn-out rifles for new ones the Yankees had carried.[18]

"Next morning [September 17] we got orders to press for Sharpsburg, where every man was needed, and that sorely," recalled one soldier. Shortly after dawn, the brigade was on the road toward Shepherdstown, Virginia, as the division's vanguard. Only Thomas's Georgia Brigade remained in Harpers Ferry to keep order.

* * *

Unwarranted concerns that the Confederate army he faced was substantially larger than it was had stymied George McClellan's decision-making throughout the Peninsula and Seven Days' campaigns. As he lumbered toward Richmond from Yorktown in April and May, an indecisive Little Mac missed repeated opportunities where alacrity might well have been the difference between victory and stalemate. McClellan's inability to capture the Confederate capital and likely end the war would stain his legacy irreversibly.

Now in early September, with Union hopes against Lee back on his shoulders, McClellan pursued the Army of Northern Virginia into Maryland with commendable speed. When his forces reached Frederick on September 11–12, he chased away a contingent of Confederates that Lee had left behind and encamped. Until discovery of the copy of Special Orders No. 191, McClellan remained uncertain of Lee's intentions, but he felt his army was well-positioned depending on the response needed and, indeed, already had troops in motion.

The battle of South Mountain, Rossino writes, had three major effects: "[I]t ruined Lee's plan for the campaign after the capture of Harpers Ferry; it forced Lee to take a less than favorable *ad hoc* position at Sharpsburg; and it weakened the Army of Northern Virginia's combat strength in the days leading up to the clash there on September 16–17." By the morning of September 15, Jackson knew he

17 Caldwell, *The History of a Brigade of South Carolinians*, 72.

18 Daly, *Alexander Cheves Haskell*, 79.

likely would be needed in Sharpsburg immediately, receiving an official order to that effect from Lee that afternoon after Colonel Miles's surrender.

The bulk of Jackson's command, with Lawton's Division in front, began marching that evening and reached Shepherdstown in stages overnight, completing the trek on the 16th. Jackson established a position north of Sharpsburg around a soon-to-be-famous building known as the Dunker Church. Much of the morning fighting on September 17 would be across Jackson's front there.[19]

The order from Lee for the Light Division to rush to Sharpsburg reached A. P. Hill about 6:30 a.m., and he had five of his brigades en route within an hour. Gregg's Brigade led what would be an unrelenting 17-mile march, followed by the brigades of Branch, Archer, Pender, and Field (Brockenbrough). The heat and fine dust of the road suffocated, choked, covered, and played havoc on the immense gray-clad column. As the division pushed closer to the Potomac, the men could hear the cannon fire ahead, and the column would be directed onward by couriers on horseback.

An order to double-quick soon arrived. Dispensing with the directive to have the men rest 10 minutes for every 50 minutes of marching, Hill furiously pressed the column onward. There would be only two short breaks allowing the men simply a chance to catch their breath. Straggling increased as the day progressed, with hundreds dropping to the side of the road in exhaustion. The need for haste, though, outweighed the loss of men. At Sharpsburg, Lee had committed all his available troops thus far, and the Army of Northern Virginia's resolute fighting had kept the battle essentially a bloody stalemate. Federal momentum, however, had Lee at the breaking point—a likely overwhelming defeat was in the making without reinforcements.

About 2:00 p.m., Gregg's Brigade, leading the Light Division, reached Boteler's Ford south of Shepherdstown and quickly crossed the Potomac. "Our feet fizzed in the cool water," one officer jokingly remembered. Lee met with Hill on the other side and, within earshot of the 12th, reportedly told him matter-of-factly: "General Hill, this is the last force we have. You must hold half in reserve and send in the other half." Taking a route along roughly what is now the Miller Sawmill Road, the dusty column pushed ahead toward the sound of the guns raging from the southern end of Sharpsburg.

At the Rohrbach (Lower) Bridge on Lee's right flank, Union Maj. Gen. Ambrose Burnside's IX Corps had paid heavily in blood (500 total casualties) against a determined Confederate defense before finally forcing its way across

19 Rossino, *Calamity at Frederick*, 103; Bradley M. Gottfried, *The* Maps *of Antietam* (El Dorado Hills, CA, 2013), 116.

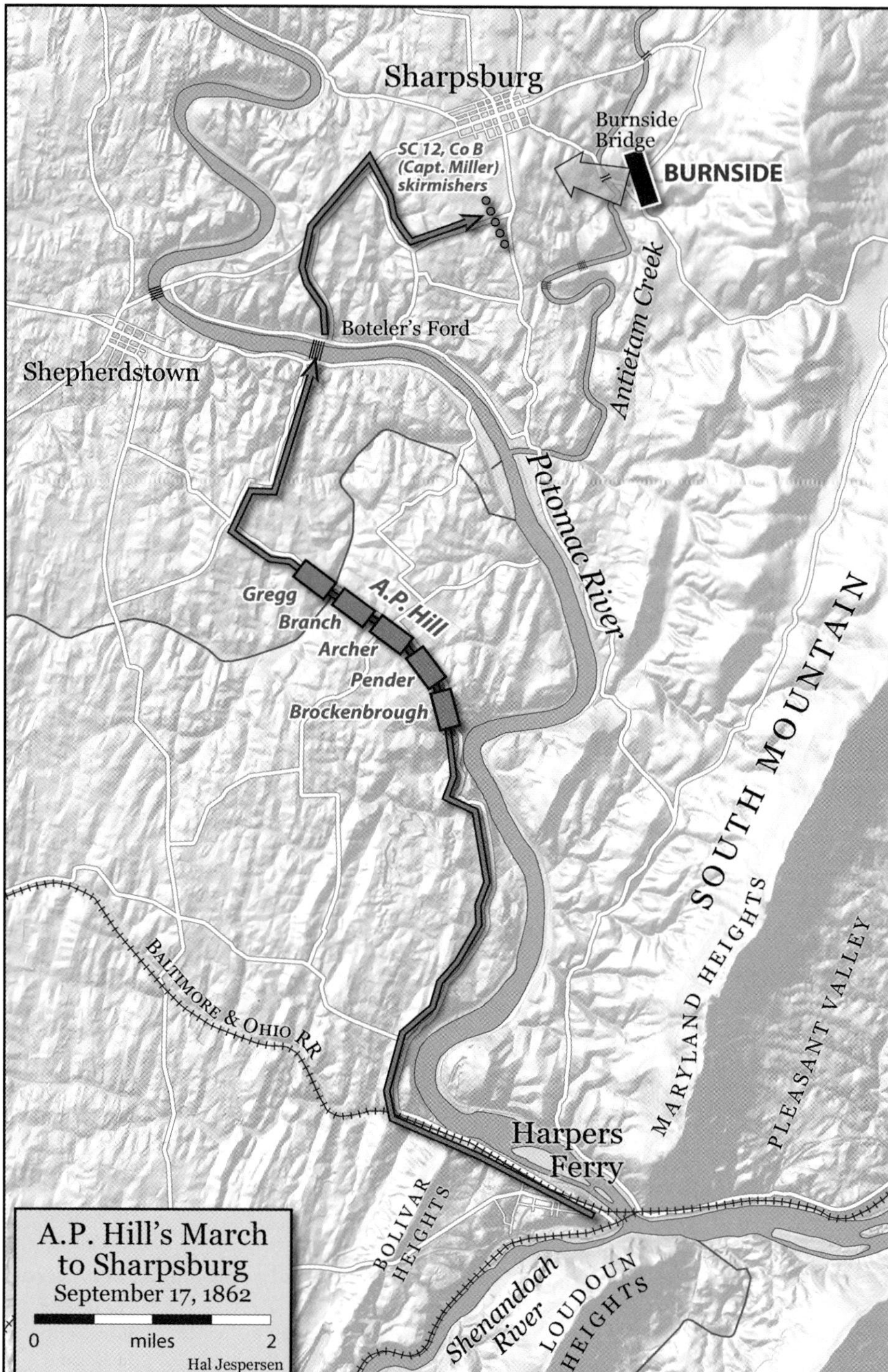

Sharpsburg
Burnside Bridge
SC 12, Co B (Capt. Miller) skirmishers
BURNSIDE
Antietam Creek
Boteler's Ford
Shepherdstown
Potomac River
A.P. Hill
Gregg
Branch
Archer
Pender
Brockenbrough
SOUTH MOUNTAIN
MARYLAND HEIGHTS
PLEASANT VALLEY
BALTIMORE & OHIO RR
Harpers Ferry
BOLIVAR HEIGHTS
Shenandoah River
LOUDOUN HEIGHTS
A.P. Hill's March to Sharpsburg
September 17, 1862
0 miles 2
Hal Jespersen

Antietam Creek about 1:00 p.m., threatening to cut off Lee's escape route across the Potomac. Had Burnside continued moving after crossing the bridge that now bears his name, the battle might well have ended before elements of the Light Division, now fielding about 3,400 men, could engage. Burnside, however, called a halt until roughly 3:30 p.m. to consolidate his position at the bridgehead. The delay would be costly.[20]

* * *

After climbing the banks of the Potomac into Maryland, the 12th hustled alongside the column's other regiments through fields and pastures under a late summer sun. By 3:00 p.m. the exhausted troops reached the southern outskirts of Sharpsburg, here mostly an expanse of rolling farm fields undulated by tree lines and woodlots. As the 12th South Carolina pulled up to the scene in the column, the men were met with a demoralizing sight: The Union IX Corps, having mostly crossed Antietam Creek via a stone bridge in the valley, was forming on the Sharpsburg side of the creek and methodically moving forward in long battle lines. If unchecked, Lee's army could be cut off from the Potomac River. While some Confederate forces remained to check the Federal advance, help was needed to add weight and support to any Confederate resistance.

Hill, mounted on what was described by one soldier as a "stately steed," had little time to ponder his options but reacted swiftly. He sent forward a combined force of Gregg's, Branch's, and Archer's greatly reduced brigades. As the column approached the open fields south of Sharpsburg, Gregg had Company B of the 12th South Carolina conduct a brief reconnaissance mission to determine the Federals' position.[21]

There would be little time to stem the massive Union wave heading their way. Burnside's bluecoats, flushed with the prospect of victory, were slowly but surely advancing on Sharpsburg along a broad, sweeping line. Gregg dispensed with formal orders to his regimental commanders. Wheeling his horse away from the column, he yelled to Barnes as the 12th steered off the road into action:

20 Ibid., 75; *SHSP* 24:271; "Reunion of Old Comrades," *Yorkville Enquirer*, Aug. 26, 1880: 1; Daly, *Alexander Cheves Haskell*, 79–80; Brown, *A Colonel at Gettysburg and Spotsylvania*, 70; William S. Dunlop, "The Confederate War: Company B, Twelfth S. C. V. in Bivouac and Battles," *Yorkville Enquirer*, Nov. 6, 1889, 1 [hereafter cited as *Bivouac and Battles (Part III)*].

21 *OR* 19(1):988. The area where the regiment formed and fought is today east of the home and outbuildings of Antietam Creek Vineyards, which has its address as 4835 Branch Ave, Sharpsburg, MD 21782. As such, much of the maneuvering and fighting of the 12th took place on ground that is not owned by the National Park Service.

"[C]ommence firing men and form the line as you fight." With so much ground to cover, Gregg began sending units to bolster the most threatened areas. The 14th South Carolina advanced to the right, holding the extreme right flank of Lee's entire army and missing the subsequent fighting. He aligned the 13th, 12th, and 1st from left to right, with Orr's Rifles in reserve. The 12th served as the regiment of direction, responsible for guiding the brigade forward. Because of significant straggling that day, however, the 12th engaged with only about 175 men.[22]

As the IX Corps advanced, intending to cut off Lee's escape route to the Potomac, the South Carolinians prepared for a clash. To the brigade's front was a 40-acre "luxuriant cornfield" in a valley with two slight hills and a ravine featuring a long stone wall. Behind the 12th's lead, the three regiments rushed up one hill to the cornfield's highest point, bellowing the Rebel yell. As one soldier in the 12th recalled, "tired and footsore the men forgot their woes in that supreme moment, and without a minute's rest sprang to their duty as if fresh from the bivouac."

Across the ravine, Barnes spotted Federals advancing down the ravine from the other hill "in force," planning to join fellow troops already straddling the stone fence. The three South Carolina regiments halted at the top of the hill and began firing at the 4th Rhode Island and 16th Connecticut, part of Col. Edward Harland's 2nd Brigade in the IX Corps' 3rd Division—the left flank of Burnside's column. The fire temporarily halted the enemy's progress.[23]

As the 12th focused its fire on the 16th Connecticut, the 1st struck the 4th Rhode Island with deadly precision. Recalled a soldier in the 1st:

> Running rapidly forward through the corn, we stopped at the top of the hill and poured a galling fire into the fleeing foe. Many of them stopped in a little hollow in the corn at the foot of the hill, afraid to attempt the passage of the open slope beyond. Into them grouped here in a crouching disorderly line, we poured volley after volley, doubtless with terrible execution. I say volleys, and here was the only time in battle that I now remember firing to be done by command. Maj. Alston many times gave the command, 'Right wing—ready—aim—fire—Load! Left wing—ready—aim—fire!—Load!' with splendid effect, for the line obeyed as a drill.[24]

22 *OR* 19(1):996–997, 988–989; Daly, *Alexander Cheves* Haskell, 80, 84.

23 *OR* 19(1):996–997, 988–989; Daly, *Alexander Cheves Haskell*, 80, 84; Dunlop, *Bivouac and Battles, (Part III)*, 1.

24 Susan Williams Benson, ed., *Berry Benson's Civil War Book* (Athens, GA, 2007), 28.

With the enemy checked in the ravine, and with bullets buzzing through the stalks of corn, the South Carolinians had to decide whether to go forward or stay on the defensive. "There was some difference of opinion at this time as to Gen. Gregg's orders," J. F. J. Caldwell recalled, "Col. Edwards regarding them as defensive, Col. Barnes as offensive. I am not able to say which was right." Edwards guided his 13th away from the 12th to a stone wall along the crest of the hill and ordered his men to hunker down and continue firing. The 1st was content to continue firing volleys at the enemy; Barnes, on the other hand, had other intentions. With the Yankees stymied across the hill and positioned precariously along the stone wall in the ravine below, Barnes sensed an opportunity to destroy the 16th Connecticut and 4th Rhode Island with one aggressive stroke. By nature, he favored an attack.

"In that awful moment," a soldier standing near the colonel recalled after the war, "the clarion voice of the lamented Barnes rang out for the last time above the din of battle: 'Forward; charge!'" Unsheathing his sword and pointing it at the mass of Federals in the ravine, Barnes led an inspiring assault against the enemy troops along a stone wall in the ravine. The two sides were about 30–40 yards apart when they opened fire on each other. The firefight in the ravine lasted several minutes, which included limited hand-to-hand combat, before the stunned Federals withdrew up the other hill, as Barnes and his men continued firing at them from the ravine.

Despite the success in flushing the 16th Connecticut and 4th Rhode Island from the stone wall, the 12th could not stay in that position for long without support as it was not well-suited for either defense or offense. As the Federals regrouped on the hill, the South Carolinians were subjected to a fierce cross fire from the front but also on both flanks once other enemy units entered the fray. Whether by order or by necessity, the regiment gradually started to flee up the hill it had just charged down. As the men of Company H fell back on the left, a Yankee bullet slammed into Pvt. John Harris, passing completely through one of his legs. Cringing in pain, the Catawba Indian from Rock Hill watched helplessly his company's retreat. With enemy troops approaching and fearing capture and imprisonment in a Federal prison, Harris begged his comrades to kill him on the spot rather than allow him to be captured. John Harris might not have been aware of it, but his brother James, shot in the foot as well, was being carried off the field by comrades at that very moment.

The mass of men was halfway up the hill when the Federals counterattacked and retook their original position along the stone wall in the ravine. Barnes halted and about-faced the regiment, swiftly ordering a counterattack, and though they drove the enemy back a short distance, they were unable to secure the position. The Connecticut and Rhode Island troops pushed back and re-formed at the wall.

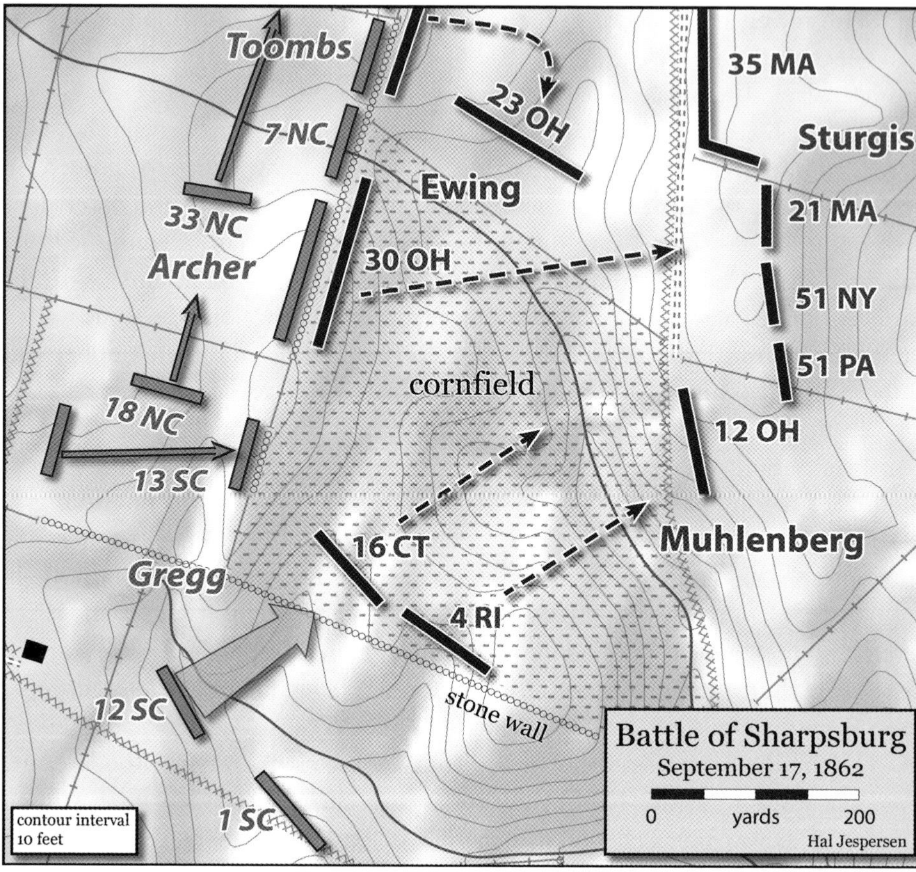

The Federals were close to enveloping the 12th's right flank and also had Colonel Hamilton and the 1st South Carolina, farther up the hill and to the 12th's right, in danger. Receiving withering fire from his front and facing a flank attack, Barnes again withdrew the regiment up the hill. Rather than leave the 12th without support, the 1st South Carolina attacked the flanking Federals, and with help from Orr's Rifles drove them away in confusion. This momentarily relieved the pressure on Barnes's right flank. "It was a severe struggle," recalled Lt. William Miller of Company H. "All day we were in a tight place."

As the 12th regrouped on the hill, Barnes again eyed the stone wall in the ravine. His obsession with dislodging the Yankees from that position had reached a heightened fury. If they could be cleared from this area, it would make Burnside vulnerable to a flank attack. The 16th Connecticut and 4th Rhode Island had actually crossed over the wall and were reforming their ranks for what looked like another attack against the 12th. It did not matter to Barnes, however, that he faced nearly 1,000 men. For the third and final time that afternoon, he ordered a charge. In a whirlwind of smoke, musketry, and Rebel yells, what was left of the regiment raced down the hill. A severe, hand-to-hand struggle ensued near the stone wall, and, as Dunlop recalled, "men fell . . . like leaves before an autumn gale."

During the melee, a Federal grabbed the staff of the 12th's battle flag. Barnes rushed forward and seized the standard with his left hand while using his right to cut down the man with his sword. The flag secured, Barnes cheered on his men, buoyant that the tide had turned, as the Federals began to give way. And then a bullet slammed into one of Barnes's knees, passing completely through it and lodging in the other. The tenacious and revered colonel lay prostrate near the stone wall that had been his center of focus for at least an hour.

The furor and aggressiveness of this third assault sent the 16th Connecticut and 4th Rhode Island scurrying to the rear. With Barnes down, Major McCorkle assumed command, later writing that the fight that day "was the only time I drew my pistols and shot at any person." The 12th, he wrote, "drove them behind the fence . . . putting them completely to rout as they ran through the plowed ground and up the opposite hill." As the Federals retreated up the hill, the men of the 12th capitalized, leveling their rifles and taking aim "with great slaughter."[25]

Gregg's aide, Alexander Cheves Haskell, who witnessed all three assaults, wrote glowingly that "the 12th swept forward and gained the stone fence. This was the wedge that split Burnside's line." Indeed, the 12th's attack was a turning point on the southern end of Lee's line, and in a sense, the battle of Antietam itself. As the Yankees fled, support from other Light Division brigades arrived and pressed the attack farther into Burnside's exposed left flank, which soon gave way. This action halted any attempt to cut Lee's army off from the Potomac. The 12th, however, could go no farther. With their colonel down, few men were left for further action, and the wounded from the three assaults required attention. That would occur as fresh Confederates overtook the position and pressed forward.

Major McCorkle and the few survivors of the regiment held the position at the stone wall until sundown, when he ordered the regiment to fall back and support the 13th South Carolina, still in its original position at the top of the hill. About this time, there would be more tragedy in the command ranks. General Branch

25 Ibid., 28; *Lancaster Ledger*, Oct. 15, 1862, 1; Caldwell, *The History of a Brigade of South Carolinians*, 76–77; Daly, *Alexander Cheves Haskell*, 81; *OR* 19(1):996–997; *OR* 12:2, 694; Carol Reardon & Tom Vossler, *A Field Guide to Antietam* (Chapel Hill, NC, 2016), 254; Dunlop, *Bivouac and* Battles *(Part III)*, 1; Blummer, "Record of the Catawba Indians Confederate Service," 225–226.

rode up, and while conversing with McCorkle and Colonel Edwards of the 13th was shot in the head and killed as he viewed the field.[26]

* * *

The battle of Sharpsburg cost the 12th South Carolina dearly. The regiment suffered 63 percent of all casualties in Gregg's Brigade that day. In addition to Barnes, Capt. F. A. Erwin of Company H, Lt. J. B. Blackmon of Company E, and Lt. William J. Stover of Company I were mortally wounded. Captains John Miller of Company B and H. C. Davis of Company C were wounded, as was Lt. R. M. Kerr of Company H. The casualty count for the enlisted men was astounding, with 20 killed outright and 82 wounded in only an hour. To put that in perspective, the four other regiments in the brigade suffered a *combined* 61 killed *and* wounded.

Heading into the battle with a mere 175 troops, by the end of the fight, only about 70 members of the 12th remained ready for duty—less than a regulation-sized company. After one of their most grueling days in the war, those survivors slept on the field within a few hundred yards from the stone wall.

Scores of the wounded would be carried or helped from the ravine to a bed of wheat straw. They were cared for there by J. Ford Prioleau, the regimental surgeon who had recently rejoined the regiment after staying behind at Manassas after that battle. He was assisted by several privates who were detailed as nurses, among them Joseph Templeton.[27]

Barnes's men carried their wounded commander up the hill, and from there to a hospital at the rear—accompanied by Cadwallader Jones Jr. of Company H, the son of Lt. Col. Cadwallader Jones. Surgeons believed Barnes stood a reasonable chance of survival with amputation of both legs, but the proud colonel would have none of it. "He said he would rather die than to live without legs," recalled the younger Jones, who pled with Barnes to reconsider. The man's mind was made up, however, and with amputation off the table, nothing could be done to save him.

As the sun went down, a rickety ambulance passed Maj. Andrew B. Wardlaw, one of Gregg's brigade officers. Inside was the wounded Barnes, in agonizing pain. "It was very distressing & a sad commentary on the horrors of war to hear such a man shrieking out with pain as the vehicle passed over rough places in the road"

26 *OR* 19(1):996–997. No reference is made to Lt. Col. Cadwallader Jones assuming command until after the fighting concluded. It is presumed that Jones, who was elderly and not in the best of health, fell out somewhere on the march and caught up later that day. Joseph Pierro, ed., *The Maryland Campaign of September* 1862*–Ezra Carman's Definitive Study of the Union and Confederate Armies at Antietam* (New York, 2008), 355.

27 Caldwell, *The History of a Brigade of South Carolinians*, 78; Daly, *Alexander Cheves Haskell*, 82, 84.

Colonel Dixon Barnes, as he looked in the antebellum years. *South Carolina Relic Room and Military Museum, Columbia, SC*

Wardlaw confided to his diary that night. During the army's subsequent retreat across the Potomac into Virginia, Barnes was transferred to Charleston, in what would become West Virginia in 1863. Just 46, he died there on September 27, 10 days after the battle. His loss was felt not only in the 12th, but throughout the entire brigade. Indeed, he had molded the regiment into one of the most aggressive and well-drilled regiments in Lee's army. The tributes to his memory spoke volumes about the respect and admiration he had earned. Recalled Caldwell:

> Of all our losses in the summer campaign, [Barnes's] was certainly the greatest. In camp he drilled his regiment with remarkable care and exactness, and governed it with admirable discipline, while on the field of battle he led it with a gallantry and coolness unsurpassed in this army. I think that all who have witnessed his conduct will bear me out in saying that no officer in the brigade executed so many brilliant charges and successful charges as he. He was the head and heart of his splendid regiment, commanding the attention and admiration of all by his handsome form and martial bearing, and animating and fortifying them with his clear, ringing voice. No appearances staggered him, no obstacles stayed him. When he was ordered against a line of the enemy, he invariably broke it, and with slaughter. Indeed, so fierce and impetuous were his charges, that it was sometimes necessary to recall him. Nor was he less cool and obstinate in defence than gallant in attack.
>
> In unofficial life he was equally noteworthy. A clear, quick apprehension marked all his writings and conversations, his manners were full of courtesy and refinement, and through the whole ran a most pleasant vein of cheerfulness and humor.

> A skillful officer, a brave soldier, an honest man, his name deserves to be recorded in the first list of those who gave their lives for the Southern Confederacy.[28]

Colonel McGowan of the 14th South Carolina, who would eventually assume command of Gregg's Brigade, recounted in his after-action report: "Where all did so well it may not be unpardonable to declare that in this battle the palm was borne off by the intrepid Colonel Barnes, who nobly fell while leading the invincible Twelfth in their victorious charge. Colonel Barnes was as amiable and generous in peace as he was gallant and irresistible in war. Having large wealth and high position at home, he left all to fall at the head of his beloved regiment, gallantly struggling for the independence of his country." A soldier in the 1st South Carolina was more succinct: "The state never lost a more nobler or generally esteemed officer."[29]

The battle would be a tactical draw, but McClellan and the Federals could claim, as they did, a strategic victory because Lee's army retreated to Virginia. The timely arrival of the Light Division on the field that afternoon and the placement of Gregg's Brigade in the 40-acre cornfield had blunted and thrown back Burnside's advance just as it seemed poised for victory. As it had at Second Manassas, the 12th South Carolina had figured significantly in saving Lee's army—and the small regiment also justified A. P. Hill's decision to override Jackson's arrest edict of Colonel Barnes at Harpers Ferry, as Barnes's aggressive tactics had been so instrumental in turning the tide that bloody afternoon of September 17.

It can never be known whether a contrary decision by A. P. Hill not to interfere and leave Barnes under arrest would have resulted in more tactical successes for the regiment later in the war assuming Barnes survived the campaign. However, it is reasonable to infer that without Barnes's determination and inspiration, the three attacks by the regiment at the stone wall would never have been made, the battle of Sharpsburg would have evolved differently, and the Army of Northern Virginia could have suffered a war-ending defeat rather than a tactical draw. It seems unlikely that Major McCorkle would have responded in a similar vein as Barnes did. He very well may have, but given Barnes's default and sometimes rash penchant for aggressive maneuvers, McCorkle, leading the regiment for the first time in combat, may have yielded the momentum to the New Englanders in the ravine as the other regiments in Gregg's brigade were content to do that afternoon.

28 Caldwell, *The History of a Brigade of South Carolinians*, 79–80. Wardlaw, Andrew B., Diary entry, Sept. 17, 1862. Copy in the collection of Robert K. Krick, Fredericksburg, VA.

29 *OR* 19(1):989; Daly, *Alexander Cheves Haskell*, 85. For a good description by a soldier in Company I of Colonel Barnes's leadership style in battle and his death, see LOCAL, "The 12th South Carolina Regiment," *Lancaster Ledger*, Jan. 28, 1863.

With Barnes gone and the ranks depleted to a mere handful of men, the 12th South Carolina and the rest of Gregg's Brigade remained at their positions astride the hill on September 18. Before dawn on September 19, the brigade joined the entire Light Division and marched toward the Potomac. Hill's command comprised Lee's rear guard, with Gregg's Brigade at the rear of the Light Division. Except for some skirmishing by pickets in the 14th South Carolina, the entire division reached Boteler's Ford on the Virginia side of the Potomac relatively unscathed about 9:00 a.m. Unfortunately, because of the hasty withdrawal and lack of ambulances, many wounded comrades were left in Maryland, along with regimental surgeon Prioleau, who would not make it back to the regiment for several weeks.[30]

After crossing, the brigade marched several miles and bivouacked in a stand of woods. Early the next morning, the men were roused and ordered to fall in. The entire Light Division countermarched to Boteler's Ford, where McClellan had begun crossing his forces, attempting to gain a foothold on the Virginia shore. About a half-mile from the ford, Hill deployed the division in two lines. Gregg's Brigade formed the center of the front line, flanked by Pender's and Thomas's brigades.

Advancing as choruses of the Rebel yell rang out, the division swept forward in a well-dressed line and, under heavy artillery fire, drove the Federals into the river. "Our whole first line of three brigades moved as one man, as steadily, coolly, deliberately as if on the drill ground," Caldwell recounted. "Indeed, our brigade performed better than I ever saw it on a regular brigade drill. What a spectacle it must have been to the enemy!"[31]

Despite the martial pageantry, most of Gregg's command—save Orr's Rifles, deployed as skirmishers—did not a fire a shot. The 12th, in fact, spent most of the engagement behind a hill, shielded from any real danger. Largely confined to the brigades of Pender, Thomas, and Archer, the assault drove the Yankees back across the river in confusion and stopped McClellan cold. A number of Federals would be shot in the water during the retreat; their floating bodies would be an eerie revelation for many Confederates. "It was one of the horrible sights of the war," one would comment.

McCorkle reported one man in the regiment slightly wounded, probably from artillery fire. About midnight the Light Division began marching toward Martinsburg and the Shenandoah Valley. Robert E. Lee's ambitious foray north had come to an end.[32]

30 Caldwell, *The History of a Brigade of South Carolinians*, 80; *OR* 19(1):989; *OR* 12(2):694.

31 *SHSP* 27:215; *OR* 19(1):989; Caldwell, *The History of a Brigade of South Carolinians*, 82.

32 *OR* 19(1):997; Caldwell, *The History of a Brigade of South Carolinians*, 82, 85; *SHSP* 27:216.

Chapter Six

Reorganization, Rest, and Recrimination: The Battle of Fredericksburg

THE TREK TO Martinsburg the morning of September 20 was especially harsh for the weary soldiers of the 12th South Carolina, many in perhaps their worst physical condition of the war to date. During a stop on the outskirts of the railroad hub town, Lt. Col. Cadwallader Jones, now in command of the regiment, searched an abandoned Federal military depot in vain for shoes for his barefoot troops.[1] As he re-emerged from the depot, Jones ran into none other than Stonewall Jackson, who happened to be lurking nearby. Jackson queried the startled colonel on whether he had found anything of value inside, drawing a quick concession from Jones that he had come up short. Informed by the colonel that he required a "dozen or more" pairs of shoes for his desperate troops, Jackson reassured him, "I have just captured a box of shoes and will send you some tonight." Whether Jones smiled, sighed, or remained impassive at the news was apparently never recorded.

True to his word, at about 10:00 that evening, one of Jackson's staff officers brought Jones the needed footwear, which would be "speedily delivered" to the men as they sat around fires at their encampment near Opequon Creek, roughly two miles outside Martinsburg. Given the tense relationship between the domineering Jackson and the officers of the Light Division in the preceding weeks,

1 Cadwallader Jones's presence at the battle of Sharpsburg remains a mystery. After Dixon Barnes was mortally wounded, it is clear that Maj. William McCorkle assumed command of the regiment, indicating that Jones was likely not on the field. Jones, however, apparently assumed command of the regiment at some point after the battle and before the withdrawal across the Potomac. As suggested previously, it is possible that Jones, like many others, simply fell out of the column during the demanding march to Sharpsburg on Sept. 17 but rejoined the regiment later that day.

the delivery was a kind gesture surely appreciated by the men at this challenging time. With Lee's army facing uncertain prospects after the bloody Sharpsburg setback, the benefits of even the smallest action could be monumental. "The men hurrahed for Jackson," Jones recalled, though he admitted—perhaps sheepishly—that he too had reaped the reward: "I slipped my feet into a pair of them with extreme satisfaction."

Shoes, however, were not all that was needed. "It is difficult to describe the condition of the troops at this time, so great and various was their wretchedness," lamented brigade historian J. F. J. Caldwell. "They were sunburnt, gaunt, ragged, scarcely at all shod, spectres and caricatures of their former selves. Since the beginning of August, they had been almost constantly on the march, they had been scorched by the sultriest sun of the year, they had been drenched with rain and the heavy dews peculiar to this latitude, they had lost much night rest, they had worn out their clothing and shoes, and received nothing but what they could pick up on the battlefield, they had thrown away their knapsacks and blankets, in order to travel light, they had fed on half-cooked dough, often raw bacon as well as raw beef, had devoured green corn and green apples, they had contracted diarrhea and dysentery of the most malignant type, and, lastly, they were covered with vermin."

Orders for all men to bathe went out, and company commanders literally marched their men to the creek to comply. "We got orders to clean up," recalled William Miller of Company H. "The men had only the clothes they had on their persons and had had them on nearly two months, so you can imagine our condition. No washing in two months. We stripped off and got into the creek. We had no soap but we had plenty of cold water and did the best we could washing our clothes. We got through, got out of the creek and hung out our clothes to dry. We sat around on stumps and on the grass, waiting for them to dry so we could put them on again. No one but a Confederate soldier knows what they had to endure—the want of rations and need of clothes. Many were barefooted by this time and foot sore."[2]

After the long-overdue cleanse, the brigade took advantage of a chance to rest and reorganize in the wake of the arduous and costly campaigns of the summer and fall. In late September, the brigade moved its encampment south, about 10 miles north of Winchester, in a range of rolling hills known as Bunker Hill. Elections were held for company grade officers, with A. P. Hill himself determining promotions for higher ranking officers. The regiment soon learned of Colonel Barnes's death, and Jones would be promoted to colonel, Maj. William McCorkle

2 Miller, "My Experience," 221; "Colonel Cad. Jones"; Caldwell, *The History of a Brigade of South Carolinians*, 86–87.

Cadwallader Jones as he appeared in the postwar years. *Confederate Veteran*

to lieutenant colonel, and John Miller of Company B, the regiment's senior captain, to major.[3]

Bunker Hill delivered a constructive and well-timed reprieve for the entire brigade, the 12th in particular. As a fitting tribute to their slain commander, the men named their new bivouac "Camp Barnes," and other than the occasional drill, military review, or dress parade, the men were afforded ample time to reconstitute their health. Opequon Creek, a Potomac River tributary roughly 35 miles long, offered decent drinking water, and the weather mercifully cooled. Several factors also helped increase the ranks for both the regiment and the brigade: (1) Emphasis was placed on collecting stragglers from the countryside who had fallen out of line during the long marches of August and September and had not returned; (2) new recruits from South Carolina joined the army, adding to the regiments originally established near their homes, meaning relatives and friends could fight together; and (3) officers and enlisted men recovering at various hospitals from wounds or illnesses rejoined the ranks, as did many of the soldiers temporarily assigned duty as nurses after Second Manassas, some of them even traveling from Richmond to do so.

William R. Sims of Company A was one who joined the regiment at Bunker Hill. Having fallen out of the ranks on the brutal march from Harpers Ferry to Sharpsburg on September 17, Sims spent that battle in a Confederate hospital but had finally been given a clean bill of health. Sims, like the thousands of other returnees to their home regiments, slowly breathed new life into the Army of Northern Virginia.[4]

3 Caldwell, *The History of a Brigade of South Carolinians*, 86.

4 *SHSP* 43:20–21; Gallagher, ed., *Fighting* for *the Confederacy*, 155; Daly, *Alexander Cheves Haskell*, 85–86; McLean, *Recollections and Reminiscences*, 6:226; William Templeton to Catherine Templeton, Sept. 22, 1862.

All the same, health issues sidelined a few in the regiment, among them William Miller, thus negating some of the gains. The summer campaign had taken its toll on Miller, even though he had remained resolute and continued to tough it out. But by the time the regiment reached Martinsburg, gangrene in Miller's feet proved too great to keep him in action; sent to a temporary hospital in Winchester, he would lose a toe and half of two others. At Winchester he was subjected to substandard care by male orderlies and nurses, whom he complained were "ignorant and careless of their duties."

In December, along with others at the Winchester hospital, Miller traveled for further care to Staunton, Virginia, about 100 miles away. Miller recalled that during the evening, the ambulance drivers simply relaxed in camp and paid no attention to the needs of the wounded and sick, many of whom were unable even to walk. "We crawled around on our hands and knees," Miller remembered. For most, the situation improved significantly in Staunton, and Miller and many of his wounded comrades were soon transported by rail to Richmond and would receive treatment from a doctor who had once practiced in South Carolina. Despite the loss of his toes, which left him with a "crippled foot that has impeded me in walking ever since," Miller returned to duty with the regiment in the spring of 1863.[5]

Assorted vermin, however, again beleaguered those lucky enough to avoid wounds or illness but now continued to live in unsanitary conditions without proper hygiene. "Lice, until recently, considered too disgusting to be even mentioned in polite circles, become a common theme of discussion and employment. . . . The earth literally crawled with them," one South Carolinian recalled. "Besides the pressure of thumbnails, it seemed that only boiling water or hot, strong smoke effectually destroyed them." New uniforms, as well as blankets, remained in short supply, and as the fall weather settled in, many of the men continued to suffer without footwear. A smallpox outbreak added to the misery, and Lee ordered vaccinations for his entire army. Many of the men of the 12th received theirs in late October.[6]

The otherwise beneficial stay at Bunker Hill ignited more drama between Stonewall Jackson and the brigade, however, with Jackson this time setting his sights on Colonel Daniel Hamilton of the 1st South Carolina. Shortly after the brigade arrived at Martinsburg, Hamilton apparently failed to have his men "clear their weapons" as ordered. The mistake was a minor transgression, due probably more to

5 Miller, "My Experience," 221–222.

6 Caldwell, *The History of a Brigade of South Carolinians*, 87; *SHSP* 43: 21; Welch, *A Confederate Surgeon's Letters to His Wife*, 34; Daly, *Alexander Cheves Haskell*, 86.

the colonel's exhaustion than an intentional disobedience to orders. Nevertheless, in true Stonewall form, Jackson immediately had Hamilton arrested.[7]

Hamilton's arrest was the final straw for General Gregg. For nearly three months, Jackson's authoritarian leadership had directly impacted his South Carolinians, particularly his brother officers. On August 22, he was professionally embarrassed and fretted as Jackson had all five of his regimental commanders arrested for exhausted and nearly starved soldiers burning palings of an ornamental fence. On September 4, he received what he considered an inappropriate tongue-lashing from Jackson on the road to Leesburg and then later that morning watched as his division commander, A. P. Hill, was arrested for alleged insubordination. He remained quiet when one of Jackson's staff officers falsely accused and arrested his top subordinate, Colonel Barnes, over utterly false allegations that soldiers from the 12th had stolen apples from a roadside orchard. Adding insult to injury, Gregg was compelled to enforce that disputed arrest by having Barnes relinquish his sword—the one the colonel had wielded so gallantly in saving Jackson's left flank at Second Manassas and would again nearly three weeks later during the 12th's heroic clash at Sharpsburg.

It pained Gregg that the courtly commander had died knowing the false allegations against him for the apple orchard incident were never dismissed. And now another regimental commander, Hamilton, had been arrested for a minor infraction involving something as mundane as clearing rifles.

Enraged, the proud general fired off a communique to General Lee outlining his displeasure and offering a complete defense of Hamilton. It is possible the correspondence contained actual charges against Jackson, as well as a request for either a court of inquiry or court-martial. Regardless of the contents, protocol mandated that the communique be sent first to Jackson, who forwarded it without comment to Lee for review and action. A few weeks passed without a response, and Gregg directed his adjutant, Lt. William C. Haskell, to communicate directly with Lee for a resolution. Haskell rode from Bunker Hill to Lee's headquarters on a cold day in early November, but when he announced the reason for his visit, Lee's demeanor turned "grave" and he invited Haskell into his tent. Lee was adamant he did not want the matter pursued, that the Confederate cause could ill afford to have valued warriors such as Gregg and Jackson at odds with one another. When

7 Caldwell, *The History of a Brigade of South Carolinians*, 85, fn. 1. Note: A "clear the weapons" directive was a safety precaution commonly ordered after a battle or in the wake of an extended march such as Gregg's Brigade had endured.

Haskell relayed Lee's message to Gregg, the commander reluctantly dropped the matter. Gregg's animosity toward Jackson persisted, however.[8]

* * *

Other than picket duty and the occasional foray to tear up Yankee railroad track near Berryville, Virginia, Gregg's command spent the rest of October and most of November encamped at Bunker Hill. To break the monotony in camp, the men often amused themselves with incidents of lightheartedness and frolic. Veterans recalled in particular the great squirrel chases that fall, led by none other than A. P. Hill, in which the hapless rodents would be yelled at and harassed as they jumped from tree to tree. If one fell during a chase, Hill was usually there, pistol in hand, yelling, "Stand aside, boys, and let me get a crack at him."

Despite the opportunities for fun, duty and unrelenting war continued to take center stage. After Antietam, the Army of the Potomac rested and reorganized on the other side of the Potomac until late October. The Federal lines were spread between Hagerstown, Maryland, and Harpers Ferry. On October 26, McClellan finally began moving south. Instead of marching through the Shenandoah Valley, however, he crossed at Harpers Ferry and Berlin, Maryland, and then moved east of the Blue Ridge Mountains, holding the gaps and finally concentrating his forces near Warrenton, Virginia, by November 6. This posture ostensibly protected Washington while keeping his army supplied via the Orange and Manassas Railroad.

In response, Lee ordered Longstreet to transfer his command to Culpeper Court House, leaving Jackson and his troops well west in the Shenandoah Valley and positioning Longstreet between the Army of the Potomac and Richmond. Lee also officially reorganized the Army of Northern Virginia from two wings to two corps of infantry and promoted Longstreet and Jackson to lieutenant general. Longstreet's Right Wing became the First Corps, Jackson's Left Wing the Second.

8 Gallagher, ed., *Fighting for the Confederacy*, 157–158; Robertson, *A. P. Hill*, 152–154. Whether Gregg bounced the letter off A. P. Hill before sending it is unknown but likely. Hill and Gregg had borne the brunt of Jackson's wrath the past three months. During this period, Hill also urged Lee to review the matter of his Sept. 4th arrest, requesting a court of inquiry. Jackson softened his position on the charges following Hill's flawless performance at Sharpsburg, and Lee, as he would later with Gregg's charges, wanted nothing to do with the controversy. Despite Jackson's inference that he would drop the matter and Lee's intimation that he did not view the matter as particularly important, the proud Hill persisted in trying to clear his name, convincing Lee to formally intervene as a mediator and counselor. The parties met with Lee both individually and together in the fall of 1862, but each had dug in, refusing to drop their charges against the other. Having done all he could to effect a reconciliation, Lee simply ignored the issue, hoping that time would solve what their egos could not.

Whether they liked it or not, A. P. Hill and his Light Division, including Gregg and his South Carolinians, remained under Jackson's command.[9]

On November 7, Abraham Lincoln removed McClellan as commander of the Army of the Potomac, replacing him with Ambrose Burnside—perhaps Little Mac's most loyal subordinate. With the capture of Richmond still among Lincoln's primary strategies to end the war, Burnside began moving his forces toward Fredericksburg on November 15, intending to occupy the lightly defended town before striking at the Confederate capital by closely following the Richmond, Fredericksburg and Potomac Railroad. By November 20, most of Burnside's army was in the vicinity of Falmouth, north of the Rappahannock and Fredericksburg itself. Burnside, however, had to wait for the arrival of pontoon bridges before his troops could cross the Rappahannock. By then, Lee already had Longstreet's Corps en route from Culpeper. Arriving on November 22, Longstreet established a formidable line west of town along Marye's Heights as a frustrated Burnside continued to wait for his pontoon boats.

Lee hastened to consolidate Longstreet's and Jackson's corps at Fredericksburg, and Jackson began his march from the Valley on the 22nd, the day Longstreet established his position along Marye's Heights. Marching up the Valley Turnpike through Winchester, the Light Division crossed both forks of the Shenandoah River, then passed through the Blue Ridge Mountains at Thornton's Gap. According to one South Carolinian, the march was a spectacle of martial beauty: "The scene, ascending and descending the mountains, was grand, the long line being visible for miles, as it wound up and down and around, with glittering arms and accoutrements, like some huge serpent." All the same, the march was not without its difficulties. Snow and rain pelted the column for several days. With a large contingent of troops still barefoot or poorly shod, many struggled to keep pace, their already cracked and bleeding feet abused further by the icy mountain roads.[10]

From Thornton's Gap, the column marched through Madison Court House toward Orange Court House, where a pleasant, unexpected surprise awaited. Mail had finally arrived from South Carolina, and many of the men would receive treasure troves of packages containing sorely needed clothing, uniforms, and other essentials. In fact, some of the men accumulated such an abundance

9 Caldwell, *The History of a Brigade of South Carolinians*, 88; B. F. Brown, "A. P. Hill's Light Division," in *Confederate Veteran*, 40 vols. (Nashville, TN, 1893–1932), 30:246; Allan, *The Army of Northern Virginia*, 455–456; Caldwell, *The History of a Brigade of South Carolinians*, 88.

10 Allan, *The Army of Northern Virginia*, 459–464; *SHSP* 14:206–207.

of these that they resorted to writing loved ones at home with requests not to send anything more.

After leaving Orange Court House, the column wound its way to the outskirts of Fredericksburg by December 3, having traversed 175 miles in 12 days. The brigade, now with about 1,500 men, encamped in the Massaponax Hills, about four miles from the town—coincidentally the site of Gregg's 1st South Carolina camp in 1861, prior to his promotion to brigadier general.[11]

Burnside's pontoon boats finally began to arrive at Falmouth on November 25. The general prevaricated for various reasons, however, and the designated river crossings at key sites would not begin until the fog-shrouded predawn hours of December 11, with one regiment assigned to construct the portable bridges—the 50th New York Volunteer Engineers—meeting heavy resistance from Confederate marksmen hidden within buildings that lined the river. The resulting bloodshed forced a delay at an attempted crossing directly opposite the heart of Fredericksburg, compelling Burnside to shell the town with massed artillery on Stafford Heights. The artillery barrage would last four hours but proved ineffectual, as the enemy riflemen—part of Brig. Gen. William Barksdale's Mississippi Brigade—resumed their onslaught once the engineers returned to work.

Eventually, Michigan and Massachusetts soldiers crossed the Rappahannock by boat above Fredericksburg and established a bridgehead to help clear the Confederate threat near the river. The 15th New York Engineers had already succeeded in erecting two bridges about a mile south of town, and now the 50th New York Engineers could complete their work at their position with relative security. By December 12, Burnside had the bulk of his army across the river, prepared to assault Lee's consolidated forces the following day.

Deep woods, thick underbrush, and marshy terrain made the hilly ground the Confederates occupied a morass. Longstreet had his five divisions extended left to right from Taylor Hill to Marye's Heights, where his First Corps connected with Jackson's left flank. The Second Corps extended from there to Hamilton's Crossing, and J. E. B. Stuart's 8,000-man cavalry corps roamed on Jackson's right flank, closest to the Rappahannock. The Light Division formed Jackson's front, with the other three divisions (under Jubal Early, William Taliaferro, and D. H. Hill) aligned to its rear. Troops were arrayed along this front in two distinct lines, and the relative positions of the brigades would be an important factor in the coming battle.

11 Caldwell, *The History of a Brigade of South Carolinians*, 89, 95; Welch, *A Confederate Surgeon's Letters to His Wife*, 36–37; Joseph Templeton to Jane Templeton, Dec. 8, 1862.

From left to right, Hill placed the brigades of Dorsey Pender, James Lane, and James Archer (as well as two regiments from Field's Brigade, commanded here by Col. John Brockenbrough) closest to the Rappahannock. Behind the first line, several hundred yards to the rear but parallel, he placed Thomas's Georgians, Gregg's South Carolinians, and Brockenbrough's remaining two regiments left to right respectively. These second-line brigades straddled a crude, recently dug military road at the foot of a hill but were obstructed entirely from the first line by the thick woods and marshes.

Not only were there lengthy intervals between units on the first and second lines, but significant gaps also existed between the brigades at the front: The Archer–Lane gap straddling the railroad, for instance, was an estimated 600 yards wide, and the one between Lane and Pender was nearly as extended as that. To offset this, Thomas's Georgians were placed directly behind the breach between Lane and Pender, and Gregg's South Carolinians directly behind the Archer–Lane opening.[12]

Gregg's five regiments (each about 300 men) were arrayed from right to left both in the woods and along the military road as follows: Orr's Rifles; 1st South Carolina; 12th South Carolina; 13th South Carolina; and 14th South Carolina. Because of the wooded terrain and thick underbrush, the South Carolinians could not see Archer's men ahead to their right or Lane's to their left, both roughly 500 yards away. It was a disaster waiting to happen.[13]

Blame for the glaring deficiencies and gaps in the Light Division's position belongs primarily to Hill and Jackson, two men still barely on speaking terms because of their unresolved feud during the march to Sharpsburg. There is also some question how much each brigade commander knew about the area they defended and the troop dispositions in general. Gregg's comprehension as such will undoubtedly always remain a mystery. Although he was aware that Lane's and Archer's troops were ahead, he surely never realized just how significant the separation was between their brigades.

Lane claimed he conveyed information on the gap to Gregg and its relation to the South Carolinians in his after-action report. Gregg's actions, however, cast doubt on that. Indeed, no skirmishers from any of the South Carolina regiments were sent forward to the marshy thicket, and Gregg did not order his men to entrench or fortify the position—a telling sign that he believed only friendly troops were *directly* on his front. It is also possible that Gregg, Hill, and Jackson were convinced it was highly unlikely enemy troops would venture into an icy, unpredictable quagmire

12 *CMH*, 169; Caldwell, *The History of a Brigade of South Carolinians*, 90–91.

13 Caldwell, *The History of a Brigade of South Carolinians*, 92; *SHSP* 10:446.

with any force even if they breached the gap between Archer and Lane. Again, Hill and Jackson must be held to account for Gregg's mindset and inadequate preparations on December 12 and early on the morning of the 13th.[14]

* * *

As December 12 closed, Gregg's men occupied the military road in relative tranquility. Their muskets stacked, they acknowledged their role as a reserve should fighting break out. The men huddled around low-burning fires lining the road, doing what they could to sleep. The following morning started pleasantly enough, although a foreboding heavy fog cloaked the skies as they calmly boiled their coffee and cooked what rations they had. Exhibiting little apprehension himself, Gregg simply informed his commanders that the brigade held the second line and advised his men not to fire should any troops suddenly appear, as they no doubt would be fellow Confederates.

When the fog lifted about 10:00 a.m., however, the Federal threat before Hill's first line became unmistakable: three expansive double lines of infantry pushing in their direction across an open plain. As Confederate artillery opened in earnest, Federal batteries across the river on Stafford Heights answered, raining shot and shell into Hill's lines. Some of the shots that missed those in front fell among the South Carolinians on the military road, who quickly abandoned their cooking fires and took cover in the woods.[15]

The attacking troops belonged to Maj. Gen. George Gordon Meade's division of Pennsylvania Reserves, about 6,500 in all from Reynolds's I Corps. Confusion regarding orders had influenced Federal plans that morning. Burnside intended for Maj. Gen. William Franklin's Left Grand Division to make an early drive against Stonewall Jackson's position on the right, which, if successful, might draw reinforcements from Longstreet's command on Marye's Heights and make Lee's left vulnerable to a planned concentrated attack by Maj. Gen. Edwin Sumner's Right Grand Division from the city of Fredericksburg itself. Franklin had discussed the outlines of the attack with Burnside the previous evening and would later claim that the formal orders he received the morning of December 13 had changed. Originally believing he was to lead a full attack on Lee's right, Franklin now seemed convinced his assault would be merely a diversion.

14 Caldwell, *The History of a Brigade of South Carolinians*, 92; *OR* 21, 654.

15 Caldwell, *The History of a Brigade of South Carolinians*, 92–93; *SHSP* 10:445.

In addition to misconstrued orders, the heavy fog affected Franklin's decision-making. With the obscured visibility, an all-out attack was impractical this early, but Burnside had directed Franklin to send part of his command toward Hamilton's Crossing and neutralize a concentration of artillery on nearby Pleasant Hill that posed a significant threat. He assigned this to Meade, positioned on Franklin's extreme left near the Smithfield House, a local residence. That plan quickly went awry. Meade did not begin moving until about 9:00 a.m. Franklin also instructed the Pennsylvanians to follow the incorrect road, which diverted them away from their target and toward Jackson's infantry. Worse, two guns in Stuart's horse artillery under Maj. John Pelham moved forward and began menacing Meade's left flank.

The Keystone State boys found themselves funneled toward the heart of Hill's Light Division. Striking Lane's front, they would be flung back and forced toward the Confederate right, actually nearer the still-undetected gap on Archer's left flank. A subsequent attack was likewise repulsed, but the extent of the gap was finally apparent to the Federals. The 1st and 6th Pennsylvania Reserves managed to peel around Archer's left and find the opening with a frantic push, putting them directly in line with Gregg's position on the second line.

As the firing increased to the front, anxiety understandably increased for some in Gregg's Brigade, including members of the 12th, who scurried to secure their weapons from the stacks along the military road. That, according to one soldier, produced rebukes from the regimental commanders, agitated entreaties to "Let the guns alone! Lie down!"[16]

Gregg evidently still did not suspect that Lane and Archer had been flanked and that his men were in the eye of a Federal storm with Meade's men swarming through the breach. Because the Union advance had actually pushed Lane and Archer farther apart, the troops that began to appear on Gregg's front were not friendly Confederates falling back as he had expected. For a unit positioned in reserve, the sight of retreating troops normally was a call for action. But shock consumed the men in Orr's Rifles who had been lounging on Gregg's right, as the shadowy figures of the Pennsylvania Reserves materialized and unleashed a "withering" deadly volley at them.[17]

Additional Federal troops, the 2nd Pennsylvania Reserves and the 121st Pennsylvania Infantry, had followed the initial assault, and as the familiar popping sounds of scattered gunfire echoed among the trees, most of the men in Orr's Rifles broke for the rear, not bothering to grab their rifles from the stacks. A few, though,

16 Caldwell, *The History of a Brigade of South Carolinians*, 92; Benson, *Berry Benson's Civil War Book*, 32.

17 *CMH*, 170–171.

lunged for their guns and returned fire, which spurred a frantic ride by Gregg to stop what persisted in his mind as friendly fire.

By his actions, it is clear Gregg had no inkling the troops in the woods were Yankees, and because the general was partially deaf, it is also likely the intense gunfire and chaos contributed to his continuing perplexity. Remaining in the saddle amid sporadic fire, Gregg implored his troops to refrain from firing on their comrades, even knocking down a few aimed rifles with his sword. Soon enough, however, the Pennsylvanians' onslaught had enveloped the few earnest soldiers in Orr's Rifles who were still engaged, with hand-to-hand combat breaking out in some spots. Within minutes, according to one Confederate, Orr's Rifles had been "broken, slaughtered, and swept from the field." Gregg tried his best to rally his retreating men, but as he turned at one point to yell out either encouragement or reproach, a Yankee bullet struck his spine and he would fall from his horse and collapse helplessly to the ground.

Panic-stricken, the companies on the right headed directly for the rear while those on the left raced down the military road toward the brigade's center, passing the hesitant 12th South Carolina in the process. As the 1st, 2nd, and 6th Pennsylvania worked around the brigade's disintegrating right flank, Lt. J. D. Charles, commanding a company on the extreme left of the Orr's Rifles line, wheeled his men to make a stand—appealing for help from others in the regiment still standing. That contingent then rallied upon Colonel Hamilton's 1st South Carolina, next in line. Hamilton was now commanding the entire brigade in place of the mortally wounded Gregg. He quickly mounted his horse, and after directing the 1st to angle its right wing toward the Federal advance, galloped down the military road to inform the other regiments that he was in command and exhorted them to hold steady.[18]

First in line to Hamilton's left was the 12th South Carolina, under newly-minted Colonel Cadwallader Jones. Revered by his men, the 48-year-old Jones undoubtedly detested Yankees and had no fear in battle—he was well-known for being both bold and reckless. There were plenty in the ranks, though, convinced that his aggressiveness and daring meant that either capture or death was inevitable. His son, Cadwallader Jones Jr., was among those to marvel at his swagger, calling him a "gamecock." Fredericksburg would be the elder Jones's first and last battle as the regiment's commander. As Dixon Barnes had done at Sharpsburg nearly

18 Caldwell, *The History of a Brigade of South Carolinians*, 92–93; *OR* 21:646–647, 651; Dunlop, *Bivouac and Battles (Part III)*, 1.

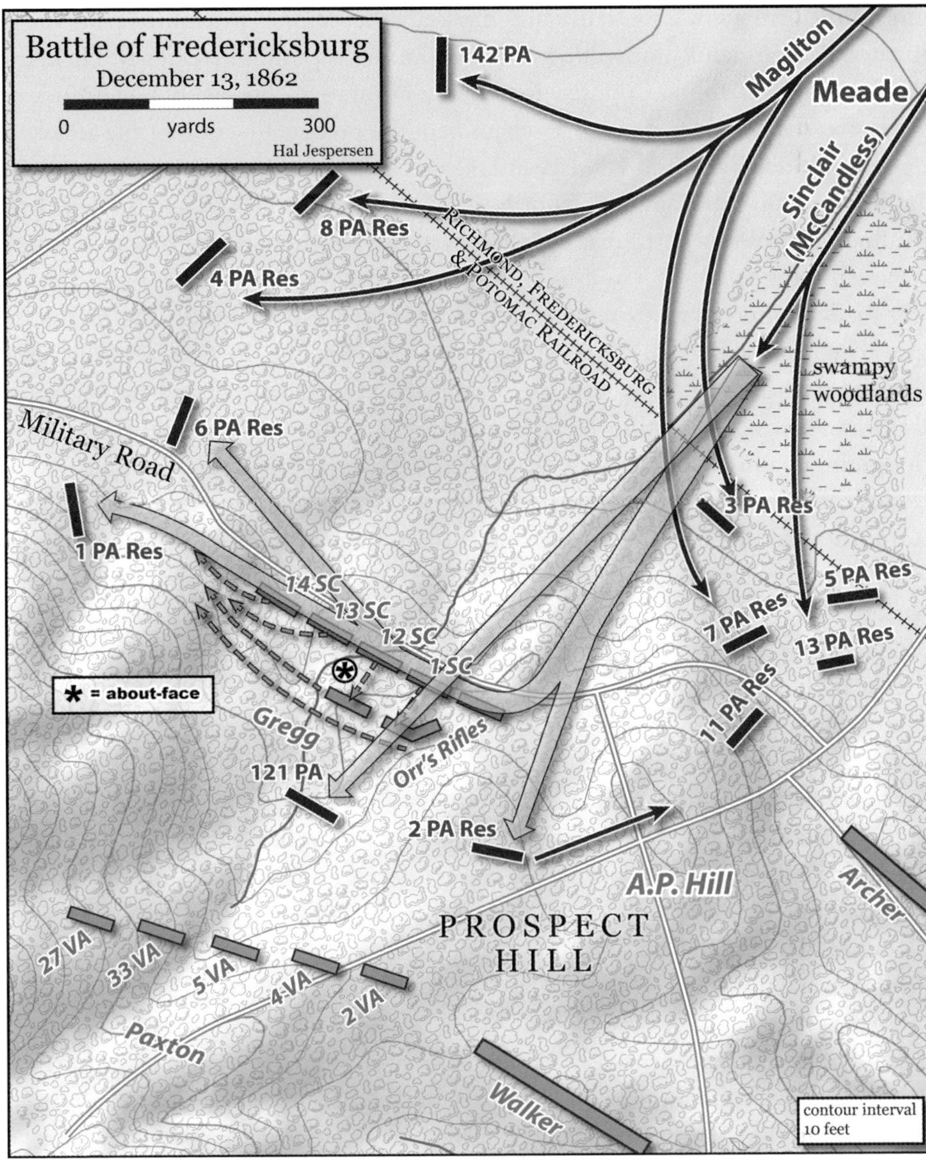

two months earlier, Jones performed laudably this day, managing to avert what promised to be outright disaster for his men.[19]

As Hamilton sped by on horseback, Jones looked down the line and immediately grasped the gravity of the situation, ordering the men to grab their

19 Cadwallader Jones Jr. to My Dear Sister, Jan. 11, 1862, UNC.

guns and form ranks. Remaining composed, the colonel prudently paused for further developments, not willing to compromise his position recklessly. He knew the 1st South Carolina opposed the enemy advance to his right, but echoes of gunfire in the woods and the sheer chaos kept the precise direction of the attack in question. Indeed, the 2nd Pennsylvania Reserves and the 121st Pennsylvania were approaching on the regiment's front (toward the marshy thicket) and its right (the 1st South Carolina's position), but there was also considerable commotion in the regiment's rear.

Jones conducted an extremely difficult set of maneuvers amidst the chaos. He quickly about-faced the 12th so that the rear rank became the front and the front rank became the rear. Although this maneuver admittedly inverted the regiment from its normal orientation in line of battle, it immediately brought the 12th's fire power against the 1st Pennsylvania Reserves, now gaining a foothold on the rear of the brigade. Because of the 12th's about-face, most of Hamilton's 1st South Carolina remained facing the other direction but a portion of the 1st's right flank was refused (or bent back) at an acute angle to face the Pennsylvanians. This bent back portion of the 1st was now to the left of the 12th's (new) about-faced front and somewhat blocked a portion of the 12th's men from being able to gain clear shots at the enemy. To avoid hitting the men refusing the 1st's flank and to gain a clear field of fire, Jones now had to extricate the 12th by uncovering the bent back portion of the 1st South Carolina. Amidst increasing gunfire, shouts, and pandemonium, Jones ordered the regiment forward and slightly obliqued or wheeled the regiment to the left after clearing the bent back right flank of the 1st. Halting and dressing the 12th on this bent back portion of the 1st, Jones ordered return fire against the 1st Pennsylvania Reserves and a short and intense firefight erupted along the line. Now, the two regiments could fire in opposite directions; most of the 1st firing toward the original front and the bent back or refused portion of the 1st and 12th firing toward the rear.

What Jones had executed was palpable to observers down the line in the 13th and 14th South Carolina. Following his lead, Colonel McGowan about-faced those two regiments and conducted similar maneuvers as Jones had, creating a unified front in the brigade's rear against the surging Federals. The Four regiments (minus the shattered Orr's Rifles) were soon slugging it out with the 1st and 6th Reserves. As J. F. J. Caldwell recalled, it was all accomplished as though on a drill field or parade. "Never did soldiers behave with more coolness and intrepidity," he proudly wrote after the war.[20]

20 Caldwell, *The History of a Brigade of South Carolinians*, 92–94; *OR* 21:646–647.

Nevertheless, with the 2nd Pennsylvania Reserves and 121st Pennsylvania swarming through the marshy thicket on one front, the enfilading Minié balls from multiple directions wreaked havoc. To dodge the whistling projectiles, several men close to Jones sought shelter on the ground. That did not impress the colonel, who exhorted the men to stand firm. When an artillery shell then shrieked past Jones's head, he too dropped to the ground and would be chided by his men, obviously amused at the irony. Collecting himself, Jones, ever the gamecock confidently walked down the line and qualified his former order, yelling: "You may dodge the big ones!"

"The combat was short, sharp, and decisive," conceded A. P. Hill. Despite its best efforts, the brigade had been all but enveloped on three sides. Slowly but surely, the men began falling back, with clusters breaking from the sheer weight of the attack. Although disorder marked the eventual retreat down the military road, fortune would somehow shine on the brigade in the nick of time, as John Brockenbrough's Virginians and Jubal Early's Division appeared seemingly out of nowhere. Wrote McGowan:

> The rattling musketry and charging yell of the Fifth Alabama Battalion, the Forty-seventh Virginia, and Twenty-second Virginia Battalion, the withering fire from Hamilton's regiment right in their faces, was more than the Federals could stand. In addition to this, that gallant old warrior, General Early, to whom I had sent, requesting that he would move down to my support, came crashing through the woods at the double-quick. The enemy, completely broken, fled in confusion. The two regiments of Brockenbrough's brigade, Archer, with the First Tennessee and Fifth Alabama Battalion, and Early's troops, chased them across the railroad and back to their reserves.

Hamilton, Jones, and the other regimental commanders moved what remnants they could in support of Early's advance but quickly fell back to the original position along the military road. Given what they hoped would be a reprieve of some length, the men attended to the wounded, constructed crude breastworks by felling trees, and even found time to sleep. There would be no relief to their left, however, as victory or defeat was being decided in front of Marye's Heights.[21]

Just past noon, Sumner's assault on Longstreet's defenses began. Major General William French's 3rd Division in Maj. Gen. Darius Couch's II Corps would be sent forward first, his three brigades under Nathan Kimball, John Andrews, and Oliver Palmer advancing mostly exposed across open fields against what would become

21 Caldwell, *The History of a Brigade of South Carolinians*, 92–94; "Colonel Cad. Jones."

known to history as the "Sunken Road." Fourteen Federal attacks on the position failed that day, costing the Federals a once-unthinkable 6,000–8,000 casualties, Despite the unabated carnage, Burnside refused to reconsider his battle plan and ordered the attacks to continue as late as 4:00 p.m.

On December 15, the mauled Army of the Potomac retreated across the river. A campaign that had begun with great promise for the Federals, especially after George McClellan's success at Antietam, had come to calamitous, humiliating finish. Although it had not been a perfect performance by Lee or his top subordinates, the Confederates had recorded yet another remarkable victory against stacked odds.

* * *

As Burnside considered renewing the attack, December 14–15 would be spent with both armies burying their dead and tending to the wounded. On Jackson's end of the field, the men in Gregg's Brigade observed Federal crews on the military road collecting their dead for burial during a brief truce. It was a spectacle, Private Carter of the 12th's Company I recalled, that the men "enjoyed . . . with pleasure." Some Union troops took the opportunity to trade coffee for tobacco, with some purportedly deciding to shake hands with men whom they had fought just two days before.[22]

Casualties in the brigade were commensurate with the relative positions the regiments occupied when the surprise attack began. Not surprisingly, the two regiments hit first—Orr's Rifles and the 1st South Carolina—suffered the highest casualty count: 170 killed and wounded in Orr's Rifles; 73 killed and wounded in the 1st. The 13th and 14th South Carolina had 55 and 28 killed and wounded, respectively, and for the first time in the war, the 12th suffered the fewest casualties in the brigade: one killed and seven wounded, and no officers lost. Colonel Jones's quick thinking had helped save the regiment and the brigade from complete disaster.[23]

In the fighting's aftermath, J. M. Anderson, the regimental chaplain of the 12th South Carolina, found the partially paralyzed Maxcy Gregg on the ground. Lying near Orr's Rifles' original position, Gregg could only watch helplessly while his men were struck down and routed. Dismounting from his horse, Anderson inquired of Gregg the location of his wound, with the general confirming his back. In the habit of carrying whiskey with him, Anderson offered some to Gregg, who

22 LOCAL, "For the Lancaster Ledger," *Lancaster Ledger*, Jan. 7, 1863, 1.

23 Caldwell, *The History of a Brigade of South Carolinians*, 95.

accepted. The chaplain also removed two blankets from beneath his saddle and spread them under Gregg's bloody body. Grimacing from the pain, Gregg asked Anderson to remove his boots, as they were tight and causing him aggravation. It proved a struggle, so Gregg suggested that Anderson use a knife to cut them off. With the help of some nearby soldiers, Anderson located an ambulance to transport the general to an "elegant" mansion about a mile away owned by Thomas Yerby, where Gregg was laid on a bed in one of the bedrooms.

Dr. Powell, the Light Division's chief surgeon, arrived to examine and dress the wound. Gregg informed Powell he initially believed the wound was mortal but now had a measure of hope, having gained some feeling in his body. Powell made no reply, prompting Gregg to ask the surgeon to give him an opiate if the wound was, in fact, mortal. Powell delivered his answer by duly administering the pain reliever.

In a touching gesture given the bad blood between them, Gregg had the presence of mind to send a message through intermediaries to Stonewall Jackson requesting a visit as soon as possible. Accompanied by a staff officer, Jackson immediately rode to Gregg's bedside, where the two men made amends. Gregg expressed remorse for the recent charges he endorsed against Jackson for the arrests of Barnes and Hamilton. No doubt playing naïve, Jackson told Gregg he had no idea to what the general was referring.

Taking Gregg's hand in his, Jackson added: "The doctors tell me that you have not long to live. Let me ask you to dismiss this matter from your mind and turn your thoughts to God and to the world to which you go." As tears streamed from his eyes, Gregg replied, "I thank you, I thank you very much." And with that, Jackson took his leave. Before the end of the day, Gregg would indeed die, one of two Confederate brigadiers slain during the fighting (Georgian Thomas R. R. Cobb the other).[24]

Gregg's death, as well as the deaths and injuries of numerous men in the brigade, was unfortunate and avoidable. The 600-yard gap between Archer and Lane and the failure by his superiors to communicate what had occurred before the battle allowed the Federals to catch the South Carolinians exposed and vulnerable along the military road with their rifles stacked. Clearly, Gregg believed that his men would not be engaged, or believed he would receive sufficient notice of a Confederate retreat on his front and therefore have time to get his men in line and prepare a defense. His attempt to stop the men in Orr's Rifles from

24 J. M. Anderson to Misses Gregg, Jan. 9, 1863, Maxcy Gregg Papers, University of South Carolina, Columbia, SC.

firing on supposedly friendly troops proved an egregious, avoidable error that ultimately cost his life.

The void in the brigade created with Gregg's death was immeasurable. He had been an exemplary commander and in a year of command had instilled in all five regiments a sense of pride and discipline that made his brigade among the Army of Northern Virginia's most formidable fighting units. Under his guidance, the brigade fought well at Gaines's Mill and its performance at Second Manassas was critical to victory. At Sharpsburg, his instincts and decision-making had helped thwart Burnside's brimming momentum when the Federals seemed on the verge of cutting off Lee's army and winning a decisive, war-changing victory.

Beyond the fighting, Gregg was a fair man and not afraid to put his reputation on the line when he felt his men had been handed a raw deal, even taking a stand against the celebrated Stonewall Jackson. Known as a tough, stern, and unrelenting man, Gregg's tender side showed on several occasions, as evidenced by his heartfelt discussion with Dixon Barnes at Harpers Ferry and his deathbed reconciliation with Jackson.

With numerous tributes to Gregg coming in from all corners of the Confederacy, a soldier in Company I offered perhaps the finest honor to his beloved and respected general: "We are much pained at the death of Gen. Gregg. He fell in front of his brigade encouraging his men, displaying such bravery as is not generally exhibited by our commanding generals. The country, in his death, has lost one of its best Generals. He had won the confidence and respect of his men. Although a strict disciplinarian, his *word being law*, he was liked by his command, and none never plead for redress but what they received justice at his hands."[25]

Kindred spirits in terms of their offensive philosophies in warfare, in 1862 Maxcy Gregg had counted heavily on Dixon Barnes and the 12th South Carolina to perform difficult maneuvers in the face of daunting odds. Now both men were gone, and as 1863 approached, their boots needed to be promptly filled.

25 LOCAL, "Near the Rappahannock River, Va.," *Lancaster Ledger*, Jan. 17, 1863 (emphasis in original).

Chapter Seven

Winter and Spring on the Rappahannock

The Confederate victory at Fredericksburg had again changed the trajectory of the war in the Eastern Theater, but as 1863 began, those in the 12th South Carolina and Gregg's Brigade were not necessarily looking at the big picture. As they settled into their winter quarters at Moss Neck Manor on the Rappahannock, several miles south of Fredericksburg, command assignments were at the forefront. The primary concern? Who would, or could take the fallen Maxcy Gregg's place?

The answer came on January 20. For more than a month after the battle, Col. Daniel Hamilton of the 1st South Carolina had ably filled Gregg's shoes, but A. P. Hill and the Confederate high command handed the reins instead to Col. Samuel McGowan, commander of the 14th South Carolina. For many observers, it was only a modest surprise, as McGowan's promotion to brigadier and elevation to brigade command bypassed both Hamilton and Col. Oliver Edwards of the 13th South Carolina, each senior in rank.

A South Carolina native, the 43-year-old McGowan had been a trial lawyer and politician in Abbeville before the Civil War. His military bona fides were solid. During the war with Mexico in 1846–48, he served with the Palmetto Regiment, becoming a captain and serving on the quartermaster general's staff. He would marry Susan Caroline Wardlaw, the daughter of a local judge, and soon became one of the top attorneys in the Abbeville region. He also represented his hometown in the South Carolina legislature for 12 years.

As war beckoned in 1861, South Carolina Governor Francis Pickens appointed McGowan to command a brigade of state troops, which he led during the bombardment of Fort Sumter in April. By that summer, however, his commission lapsed and his troops were transferred into Confederate service; he would join Brig. Gen. Milledge Bonham's staff as an aide-de-camp and served at First Manassas in July. In the fall of 1861, he would be elected lieutenant colonel of the 14th South Carolina.

McGowan assumed command of the 14th in the spring of 1862 following the resignation of Col. James Jones, which corresponded with Col. R. G. M. Dunovant's departure as commander of the 12th South Carolina. He was with the regiment during the Seven Days' fighting and at Cedar Mountain, but the serious wound he received at Second Manassas sidelined him for the Maryland campaign. He was back in action for the 12th's November march from Bunker Hill to Fredericksburg and the epic battle on December 13.

Described as intelligent, energetic, popular, and affable, McGowan also was recognized for his oratory skills—honed during his many years in the courtroom and on the floor of the state legislature. He was not as rigid, aloof, or exacting in military matters as his predecessor, Gregg, but he was an excellent drill instructor and maintained good order in the ranks and in camp, both well-liked and respected by his men. "He is a good officer, a good man, and we are all pleased," Private Carter of the Lancaster Hornets would write to his hometown newspaper, the *Lancaster Ledger*.[1]

If anyone decried his passing over Hamilton and Edwards, McGowan's leadership over the next two and a half years vindicated the decision to place him in charge of the brigade.

* * *

Forested terrain near Moss Neck Manor would be chosen as the brigade's winter quarters, where the South Carolinians would be amenable neighbors of the North Carolina brigades of Dorsey Pender and James Lane. It was christened "Camp Gregg" in honor of the slain brigadier, and the men spent the end of December and early January clearing nearly 100 acres of trees to build their huts and shanties.

1 Caldwell, *The History of a Brigade of South Carolinians*, 101–104, 107; LOCAL, "For the Lancaster Ledger," *Lancaster Ledger*, May 13, 1863, 1. Fears, whether justified or not, were prevalent in the 12th's camp just prior to McGowan's promotion that the brigade would be disbanded and the regiments assigned to other commands. Assistant surgeon Willis Keith wrote in a letter home: "There is some talk too of our Brigade being broken up, and the Regts. distributed among others. We think some will be put with [Micah] Jenkins's Brigade. I think, that that would be a shame, and hope that instead the President will appoint Col. McGowan Brigadier, and put him in command." See Willis Keith to Anna Bell Keith, Jan. 19, 1863, Wilkinson-Keith Family Papers, College of Charleston, Charleston, SC.

Returning to the 12th South Carolina after a lengthy furlough was Sgt. J. R. Boyles of Company C, who in June was wounded during the Seven Days' fighting outside Richmond. Boyles was sad to hear of Gregg's death and became disheartened observing the number of civilians and soldiers lounging about the Confederate capital as he traveled toward Fredericksburg. It gave him a premonition of ultimate Southern defeat. "I began to feel, for the first time, that we would eventually be overpowered," he would write. "There were too many gaily dressed gentlemen wearing citizen's clothes, besides hundreds, yes, I might almost say thousands, who sported the uniforms of the Confederate officers—these uniforms were new and clean, and showed plainly that they had never seen any service; they evidently held some soft, bombproof offices of some kind. A great many of them professed to be provost marshals. There were also hundreds of soldiers here in the same capacity, who had never been to the front, and had never seen the smoke of battle. . . . Altogether, there were too many soft places and too many idlers."[2]

At Camp Gregg, Boyles worked feverishly alongside his messmates to prepare their quarters before the onset of more bad weather. The designs, shapes and constructions of the various huts took as many forms as the individual messes. "Our tents, bunks, or whatever they could be called, were made with poles or split timber, about 12 feet long, leaned against a ridge pole in a slanting position," he recalled. "[They were] covered like old time potato sacks with leaves and dirt, having a chimney at one end, the funnel being empty barrels; they were quite warm and four or five men slept, cooked and eat in each."

Other men constructed more elaborate log huts, which one soldier remembered was a difficult endeavor, as the troops were "extremely unskillful in fitting together the logs that composed our houses and in constructing, for houses or tents, chimneys that would draw or throw out heat." These log huts were daubed with mud, very damp, and prone to flooding. "As the spring came in we ventilated by knocking out the daubing," he stated. Apparently, there were heated debates during construction on the engineering aspects of the dwellings. "The chimneys were curiosities," another soldier lamented. "I had many arguments on the subject, but am not sure I ever reasoned a man out of the belief that a deep, rectangular fireplace was the warmest and most economical."

Some of the men gave up any attempt at construction, choosing instead to burrow in the ground and use captured Yankee tent flies and shelter halves to cover the hole. "Yesterday was a very wet day," one conceded, "but we can keep fairly comfortable with the little Yankee tents we have captured during the summer campaign."

2 Boyles, *Reminiscences*, 30–31.

Each of the line officers was issued one 10-foot square canvas fly per company to use as he wished for his own quarters, a provision every 20 enlisted man received as well. These proved quite versatile and were put to good use. "We usually pitched these tents flat on the ground, built a chimney at one side of the door, and hung up an oil cloth or other thick cloth for a door," one soldier recalled. "Afterwards, we almost universally adopted the system of raising a basis of log, three or four feet high, and stretching the tent over this, thereby adding much to the room and comfort of our dwellings," added another.[3]

Cadwallader Jones Jr. of Company H was among those whose tent was furnished with a chimney. It "makes it very warm and comfortable—[and] is a vast improvement on the fires out of doors," he wrote to his sister in mid-January, also noting: "It would really amuse you to see how much ingenuity & skill had been displayed by the men in making themselves comfortable by putting up every kind of little, but warm huts and shelters, with rough chimneys."[4]

A reunion of brothers would occur about Christmas as well when Joseph and William Templeton were united in the field. In August, William had traveled with other recruits from Lightwood Knot Springs to Virginia to join the 12th but was too late to make the march to Manassas and was assigned instead to the 5th South Carolina, part of Longstreet's command. William served as a teamster in Longstreet's ordnance train and came close to being wounded at Antietam. Because the Templeton brothers had always desired to fight together, however, they convinced Pvt. Martin Rawls of the 12th to trade spots with William in the 5th. Such trades apparently were common as long as there were willing parties.

"I am going to the 12 reagment to day," William wrote to his sister on December 21 from the 5th South Carolina's camp near Fredericksburg. "Me and Martin Ralls [*sic*] maid a swoop. He came hear yesterday I will go to the 12 today." It would take a little longer than expected, but by the end of December the brothers were together again at Camp Gregg.[5]

* * *

"General Orders No. 12" of January 30, 1863, would be one of General McGowan's first official acts as the brigade's new commander. It authorized the South Carolinians to incorporate on their regimental battle flags the names of the

3 Ibid., 32; Caldwell, *The History of a Brigade of South Carolinians*, 104–105.

4 Cadwallader Jones Jr. to My Dear Sister, Jan. 12, 1863, UNC.

5 William Templeton to Sarah Templeton, Dec. 21, 1862; Joseph Templeton to Sarah Templeton, Dec. 29, 1862.

Brothers Joseph Templeton (left) and William Templeton (right) pose for the acclaimed Richmond photographer Charles Rees. Presumably taken sometime in the winter of 1863 after William transferred from the 5th South Carolina to Company B, both men are wearing the standard uniform of the Army of Northern Virginia during this time period: short waisted jackets and trousers manufactured in Richmond and the typical civilian slouch hat common amongst Confederate soldiers. *South Caroliniana Library, University of South Carolina, Columbia, SC*

engagements in which they had fought to that point. The orders, one of only a few distributed to the brigade to survive the war, also paid tribute to all five regiments in the brigade, instilling a deep sense of pride in each unit's accomplishments:

> The list of battles is a long one. The flag of the 1st South Carolina Regiment S.C. Volunteers was at Fort Sumter, where the first gun of the revolution was fired, and those of the 12th and 14th Regiments S.C. Volunteers were first unfurled in battle at Port Royal Ferry, S.C. on the 1st of January 1862, where they marked with bloody significance the advent of the eventful year which has just closed; whilst the 13th Regiment and Orr's Regiment of Rifles, S.C. Volunteers have stood shoulder to shoulder with their comrades in all of the great battles fought by the army of Virginia, from Mechanicsville to Fredericksburg.

After Maxcy Gregg's death at Fredericksburg, Colonel Samuel McGowan of the 14th South Carolina was promoted to brigadier general and commanded the South Carolina brigade for the rest of the war. *Library of Congress*

It was McGowan's objective to keep the achievements of each regiment unique. Directed to list 11 engagements on its flag, the 12th was tied with the 1st for the most engagements of any of the five regiments: Bay Point, Port Royal Ferry, Mechanicsville, Cold Harbor (Gaines's Mill), Frasier's (Frayser's) Farm, Second Manassas, Ox Hill, Harper's Ferry, Sharpsburg, Shepherdstown, and Fredericksburg. Other battle honors were to come, of course, and would be inscribed alongside those names by the end of the war.[6]

In the new year, 20-day furloughs were instituted (two per company at a time), the men received eight-months' back pay, and some were issued their first government-made attire from the Richmond Clothing Bureau. It is unknown how many were issued new uniforms and in what frequency they were issued, but at least some men received regulation uniforms featuring two-piece sleeve jackets with epaulettes and belt loops. These were lined with unbleached osnaburg and were made of various dyed jean cloths, and the men in highest need of clothing were given priority.

Reviews of the new jackets were decidedly negative. "[T]he quality was more to be complained of than the quantity," wrote one soldier. "Most of the men rubbed out a jacket in two or three months—a pair of pantaloons in one. It was coarse, stiff and flimsy . . . the cut was worst of all. Anybody could put on the clothing, but scarcely any object in nature, except a flour barrel, would find a fit. Shoes were scarce, blankets curiosities, overcoats a positive phenomenon."

6 "General McGowan's Brigade," *Edgefield Advertiser*, Feb. 11, 1863, 4. The regiment's flag from the latter stages of the war, now located at the South Carolina Confederate Relic Room in Columbia, was not the same flag the regiment used at this stage in the war. The flag referred to in this quote was virtually destroyed during the battle of Spotsylvania Court House on May 12, 1864, and replaced later that year through the fundraising efforts of patriotic citizens. More information concerning the replacement flag is found in Chapter 12.

In addition to the government-issued uniforms, provisions and clothing were constantly being shipped to the front from South Carolina, and at least some of the men continued to get all of their clothing from home. In one letter, a soldier requested two pairs of drawers, two pairs of socks, and one pair of pants—all to be brought to him care of the regimental chaplain, J. M. Anderson, who was making a trip to South Carolina to gather goods for the men.[7]

The men's attention to clothing needs seemed unremitting, but they were equally torn by a desire to assist the beleaguered citizens nearby in war-torn Fredericksburg. During the battle, the beautiful colonial-era city had been ravaged not only by the shelling of the Federal guns from Stafford Heights but also by enemy soldiers during the short Union occupation, many of whom resorted to vandalism. Each regiment in the Light Division's six brigades collected contributions for the affected citizens, passing around a hat. The 12th would raise $241.50, the 1st $479, the 13th $414, the 14th $154, and Orr's Rifles $232. The entire Light Division raised $11,870.60 for the "Fredericksburg sufferers"—an astounding feat given the daily suffering of the soldiers that winter and that their pay often came months late.[8]

The endeavor, which Anderson coordinated, coincided with another supply source for the men not only of the 12th but also all South Carolinians serving. The South Carolina Central Association, created early in the conflict, would provide supplemental provisions in the form of uniforms, undergarments, clothing, shoes, foodstuffs, and blankets—all donated from the state's citizenry. It served primarily as a collecting bureau for such items to be distributed to those most in need as well as a means to transport specific items to individual soldiers from families back home. With offices in both Columbia and Richmond, donations could be sent to either location and earmarked for a specific soldier or unit or to the troops at large.

The charity could also be earmarked for those soldiers suffering in Northern prison camps. With supplies from the Richmond government often inadequate to fully equip and clothe the troops, the association became a major contributor and supplier to the men on the front lines and became a de facto quartermaster partner to the Confederate government. "It is right to inform the public that the Government needs help in this matter," chairman M. Laborde averred in a plea to citizens for supplies, "and that private and State Associations must co-operate with it, or great suffering and destitution will be the necessary consequence."

7 Joseph Templeton to____, Dec. 25, 1862. It cannot be determined to whom this letter was addressed.

8 "Hdqrs AP Hill's Light Division," *Richmond Dispatch*, Jan. 27, 1863, 2.

Donations took the form of both raw materials to be converted into things such as shoes and uniforms as well as items already constructed. Spearheaded by a committee of 11 prominent Columbia citizens, the association's main tenets were patriotism to the Confederate cause; an admission that the Union armies operating in the field were larger, better equipped, and better fed than the Army of Northern Virginia; that the Army of Northern Virginia was the sole institution capable of keeping Federal armies at bay and out of South Carolina; and lastly that everyone—from the wealthiest of landowners and bankers to the downtrodden yeoman—had a vested interest in donating whatever they could so that the soldiers could continue to subsist and resist the enemy in the field.[9]

Although the Richmond government did what it could to provide uniforms, it simultaneously reduced the men's rations that winter. Brigade historian J. F. J. Caldwell recalled that each man was issued one pound of flour (down from one-one/eighth pound), half a pound of bacon (down from three-fourths of a pound), and one-quarter pound of beef (if any beef could be had, which was rare). Sugar was in abundant supply, though the men lacked access to coffee.

"We fell into more fashionable habits, breakfasting late and dining at four or five," one man recalled. "There was not often a third meal—we were only too happy to get two full ones." Complained another soldier in the regiment, "[E]verything is scarce here and cannot be had for the money." Nevertheless, the men of the 12th consistently received supplemental food from home in the form of sausages, ham, jelly, candy, cake—all greatly appreciated and devoured.[10]

Despite the decrease in rations, the weather in January was mild and the men's general health remained stable, a noticeable improvement after the draining campaigns of 1862. "It is seldom that we have a man die now," Caldwell wrote. A brief bout of scurvy would break out in early January but was quickly terminated through treatment and isolation of the affected men.

In February, the weather turned wintry again and snow fell regularly, with accumulations of a foot or more. The snowstorm on February 22 was particularly brutal. "It is the most severe storm we have had yet," wrote assistant surgeon Willis

9 *Charleston Daily Courier*, Oct. 30, 1862, 1; "Bureau of Central Association," *Camden Confederate*, Nov. 28, 1862, 1; "Central Association," *Charleston Mercury*, Aug. 8, 1863; "A Card," *Charleston Mercury*, Aug. 12, 1863, 2; "Central Association," *The Spartan*, Oct. 27, 1864, 3; M. Laborde, *Central Association for the Relief of the Soldiers of South Carolina: The Plan, and Address, Adopted by the Citizens of Columbia, October 20, 1862* (Charleston, 1862), 3–15.

10 Caldwell, *The History of a Brigade of South Carolinians*, 105–107; Welch, *A Confederate Surgeon's Letters to His Wife*, 42; Joseph Templeton to Sarah Templeton, Jan. 11, 1863; Cadwallader Jones Jr. to My Dear Sister, Jan. 12, 1863.

Keith in a letter home that day. "It is now about sixteen inches deep on level ground and many feet where it drifts."

The snowfall provided a great wartime memory for many of the men: a series of snowball fights pitting several regiments and even brigades against one another. "On one occasion," recalled J. R. Boyles, "our brigade and General Pender's became engaged, and the field officers were out on horseback and took part in the sport—it was pretty rough, although seldom any serious casualties." Private Gilmer Greer of Company A recalled that the Tar Heels got the best of the South Carolinians on that occasion as they started to "sling mud." The rains came later in the month, forming a proverbial swamp between the camps of the 12th and Orr's Rifles on one side of the camp and those of the 1st, 13th, and 14th on the other. Mud would cover the men as they went about their daily activities. Despite this, the men enjoyed "rousing" fires at night while listening to songs alternated by the bands of the 14th South Carolina and 13th North Carolina, as they relaxed, smoked their pipes, sang, or chatted.[11]

The men of the 10 companies also filled command vacancies during this period. That would include a showdown between Boyles and John Rosbrough for lieutenant in Company C, in which politics had a hand. In his bid for rank, Rosbrough resorted to doling out free commissary sugar in exchange for votes, and one soldier whom Boyles had arrested for an infraction during the regiment's trek to Virginia the previous spring delayed his furlough for an entire week simply to vote against him. Nevertheless, Boyles won the election, passed his officer's examination, and was commissioned a lieutenant. "I now received double rations," he recalled, "but instead of deserting my old mess I continued to remain with them and we all eat together."[12]

The habits and desires of the respective regimental commanders dictated the consistency (or inconsistency) of drill in the brigade. As such, some regiments drilled more than others. As a soldier in the 1st South Carolina stated bluntly, "There was little drilling done, and that carelessly." The 1st's colonel, Edward McCrady, concurred: "There was, it is true, very little drill in our army." Boyles, however, stated affirmatively that Col. Cadwallader Jones and the 12th South Carolina kept a consistent routine of training every day as weather permitted during this first winter in Virginia.

11 Caldwell, *The History of a Brigade of South Carolinians*, 106; Welch, *A Confederate Surgeon's Letters to His Wife*, 39–42; Boyles, *Reminiscences*, 33; *Recollections and Reminiscences*, 7:241; Willis Keith to Maddie Keith, February 22, 1863, College of Charleston..

12 Boyles, *Reminiscences*, 32–33.

The primary military endeavor during this period was picket duty along the Rappahannock. Since they were camped near each other, McGowan's, Pender's, and Lane's brigades occupied the same picket line along the river, about two miles from camp near a home owned by a man named Burress and the regiments each took a 24-hour shift. With three five-regiment brigades, guard duty for each regiment occurred approximately twice a month.

Colonel McCrady recalled after the war that the 1st was not adept at guard duty, noting that few regiments knew much about "the niceties of guard mounting." Whether that was the case for the 12th is unknown, but given Colonel Jones's penchant for continued drilling, it is presumed the regiment had at a better grasp of such protocols than the 1st.[13]

Whether guards were posted according to the manual or not, picket duty along the Rappahannock was anything but formal. William Templeton recalled that he routinely saw Yankee pickets across the river. Informal truces among opposing sentries happened frequently, allowing men on both sides to fish in the river without fear of being shot. In some instances, and contrary to orders, enemy soldiers even agreed to carry unloaded weapons on the picket line and traded items during informal truces. Boyles recalled that one of these truces would be broken by a few Alabama troops farther downriver. As Federal troops floated by in a boat, he noted, the Alabamians "could not resist" firing and killing them all, admitting that the event "started again the daily picket firing across the river."

On another occasion, Boyles and his guards were fired at as they headed to their picket line. "We found that the balls did not come from the post opposite us, but from one further out of sight," he wrote, adding:

> I proposed to some of our fellows that we slip down and try to get a shot at them—four of our men and myself started in search of this post; we had to crawl on our hands and knees a quarter of a mile before getting opposite them; we could hear them—they were playing cards, completely hid by a clump of undergrowth; while peering glimpses of them we heard horses feet coming up to where they were; we leveled and fired as they dashed in and heard them cursing, as if it hurt; we reloaded as soon as possible, waiting to see the result; in a few moments the party they had relieved started out at a gallop in single file; we discharged our five guns at them, and it was amusing to see how they lay flat and endeavored to get on the opposite sides of their horses; if we touched any of them, we never knew it; the river was pretty wide at this point and they were probably 500 yards from us.

13 Ibid.; Caldwell, *The History of a Brigade of South Carolinians*, 106; *SHSP* 14:207–208.

Once, during a blinding snowstorm, the regiment embarked on fatigue duty several miles from their camp for a few days to corduroy a road for supplies.[14] And there was also plenty of time for foraging. The men of the 12th were adept at it, just as they had been a year earlier while encamped near Pocataligo in South Carolina. Two of the most renowned and celebrated foragers in the regiment were Bob Easler and Tom Howell of Company C. One night, the two men raided a nearby farm for cabbage they had spotted growing. While procuring the produce, a guard posted in the yard fired at them. After skedaddling back to camp, they wasted no time cooking and consuming "a hearty meal" with their commanding officer to avoid others finding out.

On another outing, Howell scoped out a plump turkey in the yard of a local house, following the gobbler at a distance into a ravine intent on stealing it. Confronted by the owner on where his turkey had gone, Howell pointed in the other direction, grabbed the bird, and then "lit out" with it.

"Some of the best foraging done during the war, I believe, occurred while camped here," Boyles remembered fondly.[15]

* * *

A significant transition took place in late February with the dual resignations of Colonel Jones and Lt. Col. William McCorkle. Both men had directed the regiment ably since Barnes's mortal wounding at Sharpsburg but were leaving the army now because of failing health. The war had been especially tough for Jones, who had recently returned from a leave of absence. Cadwallader Jones Jr. asserted that the rigors of campaigning had shortened his father's life by 10 years (although the elder Jones would live until December 1899).

On February 27, at a special dress parade held on the camp's muddy grounds, Jones called the regiment to attention one last time. He addressed the troops with a touching and poignant farewell speech, paying tribute to the regiment's heroic deeds and exhorting them to continue the struggle in defense of their state and country:

> Officers and Men: I have tendered my resignation to the War Department, being no longer [able] to perform the duties of my office.
>
> For eighteen months, in heat, or in wintry woods unsheltered—on the toilsome march, on the embattled field, we have stood together. Now, when I come to

14 Boyles, *Reminiscences*, 31–32, 34.

15 Ibid., 33–34.

> look for the last time on the regiment, it fills me with painful emotions. At my distant home I shall often recur to the past, and though I may no longer be your commander, the good name of the 12th South Carolina Volunteers, will always be near my heart.
>
> In ten pitched battles, and through many skirmishes, you have already born the blue Palmetto with honor to yourselves and to your State. You have never met the enemy but to conquer. How you performed your part at Manassas, let the heroic Gregg bear witness. When he saw the regiment returning victorious from the gallant charge of the 29th of August, exhausted of ammunition and nearly one half killed or wounded: "Your Regiment, Col. Barnes, has covered itself with glory—let the men rest until further orders."
>
> Such was the language of the departed General of the Brigade, to our own gallant and beloved Colonel.
>
> Officers and Men: You have done enough for Glory; you have assisted in driving back McClellan, Pope and Burnsides, but until those worse than savage invaders shall be driven from all our borders, you have not done enough for your country. When that glorious day shall come, as come it must, then your native State will open her arms to receive you. Let me beseech you, stand by the flag of the Twelfth, advance its banner as you did through the dark and bloody woods of Manassas, and again in the terrific fight at Sharpsburg! Your country can ask no more!
>
> Officers and Men: I bid you an affectionate farewell and may the God of battles nerve your hearts to the deeds of valor, and shield you in the day of trial.[16]

Jones's passionate oration before the regiment made a significant impact on at least one soldier, who, after hearing it, wrote in a letter that he would "not come home until peace is made."

With the resignations, Maj. John L. Miller was named a colonel and assumed command of the regiment; Capt. Henry Davis of Company C was promoted to lieutenant colonel; and Capt. Edwin Bookter of Company D was promoted to major.[17]

Miller was a native of York County and born in 1829. After graduating from North Carolina's Davidson College in 1847, he practiced law in Yorkville, South

16 "Resignation of Col. C. Jones"; Cadwallader Jones Jr. to My Dear Sister, Jan. 12, 1863, UNC. A surgeon's certificate in Jones's compiled service record states that he was suffering from "inflammation of the bladder." Copy in author's possession.

17 Caldwell, *The History of a Brigade of South Carolinians*, 108; Joseph Templeton to Sarah Templeton, March 10, 1863.

Carolina. In 1851, the state legislature appointed Miller "commissioner in equity" for the York District, performing duties similar to today's circuit court judge. Unlike judges making rulings according to the letter of the law, however, commissioners in equity heard cases in which litigants demanded equitable or "fair" remedies given the facts of a particular case. That made equitable courts distinct from law courts, with commissioners given the flexibility to make judgments according to what they believed was fair and just, not necessarily what precedent and the letter of the law demanded.

Miller, who also worked as the proprietor and senior editor of the *Yorkville Enquirer* newspaper at this time, served two terms as a commissioner and was elected to the state legislature when his term expired. A devout Presbyterian, Miller was a first cousin of Mary Boykin Chesnut, the noted Civil War diarist and wife of Confederate Senator James Chesnut. As war approached in 1861, he was one of the first to answer the call, raising what would become Company B of the 12th South Carolina, its men drawn primarily from York County. Miller had fought with the regiment in every engagement thus far, wounded at Gaines's Mill and then again Sharpsburg. By the time of Colonel Barnes's death in September 1862, Miller had already established himself as an adept company commander and, as the senior captain in the regiment, he was a logical choice for promotion to major. Now, a few short months later, he would skip a rank and receive a third star on his collar.[18]

While in their winter quarters, the men were exposed to dramatic differences in the command styles and personalities of the Light Division's various officers involving discipline and punishment. As the 12th was encamped near Dorsey Pender's North Carolinians, the men often witnessed firsthand the stark difference between discipline in their camp and in that of the Tar Heels. On one occasion, they would witness two of Pender's men stripped to the waist and whipped 39 times for attempting to desert. A distant sound of volleys on any given day typically meant a deserter in Pender's command had been executed, and members of the 12th also watched a condemned Tar Heel shot by a 12-man firing squad as he sat on a coffin with his hands tied.

Other punishments in Pender's Brigade consisted of men marching either with their heads stuck through a barrel, riding a wooden horse, or carrying a heavy load of wood throughout the camp, and one offender had his hands and feet tied to a cannon for 16 hours. Boyles noted that almost daily a large number of conscripts

18 "Death of Col. Jno. L. Miller," *Edgefield Advertiser*, May 25, 1864, 3; Caldwell, *The History of a Brigade of South Carolinians*, 185.

arrived to replenish Pender's ranks; whether that was related to discipline problems or not was never confirmed, however.[19]

McGowan avoided administering such punitive measures in his brigade, clearly a testament to the officers who set the expectations and tone and the men who followed their lead. The brigade no doubt benefited from having strong leadership with positive examples set by Maxcy Gregg and Dixon Barnes permeating to the line officers. Though they were men with different personalities, successors such as Samuel McGowan and John Miller continued many of the same practices as administrators and leaders once they assumed command.

As the spring of 1863 neared, the Light Division featured six strong, veteran brigades: McGowan's South Carolinians, Thomas's Georgians, Pender's and Lane's North Carolinians, Archer's Alabamians and Tennesseans, and Field's and Brockenbrough's Virginians, now commanded by Brig. Gen. Henry Heth. As McGowan organized his own staff, one of his appointments was Pvt. Robert G. Center of the 12th South Carolina's Company D, as a mounted courier.

Writing from camp that spring, D. J. Carter remarked that the brigade and army had grown "immensely, both in numbers and discipline." Along with the new recruits, wounded men from earlier campaigns were returning in droves. Spirits and confidence in the camp were high. In a letter to his despondent sister in mid-April, Lieutenant Cadwallader Jones Jr. reassured her: "You need not entertain any doubt about our ability to keep back the rascals in this quarter; for it is quite certain that, if 'old Joe [Hooker]' has the boldness to cross this River any where near here, he will be laid upon the shelf, like his other predecessors."[20]

The weather was blustery, with occasional snow, in March and early April, and the men's activities primarily involved picket duty along the Rappahannock. Camp rumors abounded concerning a likely spring campaign, amplified by Lee's decision to send two divisions in Longstreet's First Corps (Pickett's and Hood's) for operations in Suffolk, Virginia, south of Richmond.

By late April, the weather turned relatively pleasant, a sign that campaigning likely would soon commence in earnest. On a rainy April 29, the South Carolinians in McGowan's Brigade were ordered to be ready to march at a moment's notice and to have their extra baggage and surplus equipment transported to Richmond. Ordered to cook three days' worth of rations, the men had barely finished packing

19 Boyles, *Reminiscences*, 33–34; Welch, *A Confederate Surgeon's Letters to His Wife*, 44–45.

20 Caldwell, *The History of a Brigade of South Carolinians*, 107; LOCAL, "For the Lancaster Ledger," *Lancaster Ledger*, May 13, 1863, 1; Cadwallader Jones Jr. to My Dear Sister, April 15, 1863, UNC. For an interesting account of larceny taking place in the 12th's camp during which Willis Keith's ax, frying pan, and tobacco were stolen from his servant's tent, see Willis Keith to Anna Bell Keith, March 7, 1863, College of Charleston.

their knapsacks and rolling their bedrolls when the long roll sounded and they were called into line. As that call had come sooner than they expected, much of their excess baggage from the winter remained at their camp.

With the 13th South Carolina left behind to picket the Rappahannock, the brigade marched quickly to A. P. Hill's headquarters and joined the Light Division's five other brigades in what surely was a spectacular sight. From there, the division headed toward Fredericksburg, pausing after several miles at the position they held during the December fighting, with McGowan's command again occupying the crude military road there.

Breaking ranks, the men built breastworks on their front and rested in this position the rest of the day and for most of April 30. McGowan then sent the 12th South Carolina as skirmishers into the woods from which the Yankees had surprised them during the battle. As the regiment crept forward in open order to gain a foothold on the Rappahannock, Federal artillery checked it by lobbing shells from Stafford Heights, followed by an advance of troops, now across the river on pontoon bridges. That Federal force engaged the 12th in a hot but brief contest, eventually compelling Colonel Miller to move the regiment back to the cover of Confederate artillery.

That night, the men slept on their arms in the open, enduring a relentless mix of rain and sleet; the rest of the brigade remained behind them in the woods, relatively covered. Whether they realized it, more fighting lay ahead and the brigade would soon be on the move again, as a sudden push north of Fredericksburg by the Army of the Potomac—now under Maj. Gen. Joseph Hooker's command—had exposed the Confederate army's left flank and rear.

Lee initially addressed that push by sending the First Corps' division of Maj. Gen. Richard Anderson up the Orange Turnpike. On April 29, McLaws's Division would follow Anderson, but Lee knew he needed to bolster Anderson's and McLaws's commands with the bulk of Jackson's Corps. What would become known as the Chancellorsville campaign had begun.[21]

* * *

Hooker, the 49-year-old commander of the Center Grand Division during the battle of Fredericksburg, had assumed command of Burnside's army on January 25 following the bungled Union "Mud March" of January 20–22. Known as "Fighting

21 Welch, *A Confederate Surgeon's Letters to His Wife*, 47; Caldwell, *The History of a Brigade of South Carolinians*, 108–109, Boyles, *Reminiscences*, 34–35; Daly, *Alexander Cheves Haskell*, 98; Cadwallader Jones Jr. to Dear Sister, April 15, 1863, UNC.

Joe"—a nickname for which he actually had no fondness—he immediately set out to restore the army's sagging morale and discipline. Hooker reorganized his new command into seven corps, which continued to make their home on ground north of the Rappahannock, occupying a line running from Stafford Heights at Falmouth to Aquia. The army would be supplied principally along the Union-controlled section of the Richmond, Fredericksburg and Potomac Railroad.

Lee's line that winter was significantly longer than Hooker's, by roughly 25 miles. Longstreet's First Corps occupied the hills behind Fredericksburg, extending from the Rappahannock to Hamilton's Crossing, along with positions at both the Banks' Ford and the U.S. Ford. Jackson's Second Corps occupied a line extending south from Hamilton's Crossing to Port Royal.[22] The Confederates, however, were undermanned because of the aforementioned departure of two of Longstreet's four divisions in February. George Pickett's and John Bell Hood's commands, accompanied by Longstreet himself and two artillery battalions, had gone south to guard Richmond against potential threats from the Virginia Peninsula or North Carolina.

In late April, Hooker launched the offensive that he was confident would finally break the stalemate on the Rappahannock line. On April 27, the V, XI, and XII Corps (under Maj. Gens. George Meade, O. O. Howard, and Henry Slocum, respectively) left Falmouth on a stealth march up the Rappahannock above Fredericksburg. They crossed the river at Kelly's Ford on the 29th and then crossed the Rapidan at the Germanna and Ely's Fords, congregating in the wilderness near the Chancellorsville homestead. The next day, the II Corps under Maj. Gen. Darius N. Couch crossed at the U.S. Ford, and Maj. Gen. Daniel Sickles's III Corps would follow suit on May 1, giving Hooker five of seven corps in close proximity, a total of approximately 80,000–90,000 troops.

Having crossed the river at Fredericksburg, Hooker's other two corps (Maj. Gen. John Reynolds's I Corps and Maj. Gen. John Sedgwick's VI) had become a distraction for Lee as well, forcing the Confederate commander to contend with a possible simultaneous Federal advance against his front and rear.[23]

Hooker had approximately 134,000 men at his disposal—what one Confederate observer later labeled "the greatest [army] this country had ever seen"—while Lee had fewer than 61,000. The Federals' moves thus far had been well-executed and had Lee potentially caught in a deadly vice. Lee, however, correctly surmised that the 40,000 or so Federal troops at Fredericksburg were

22 *SHSP* 40:48, 52.

23 Ibid.; *CMH*, 214–215.

there merely as a demonstration. To stall them, he left Jubal Early's Division in the hills west of the city, as well as William Barksdale's Brigade and a sizable portion of the army's artillery, and turned his focus up the Orange Turnpike toward Orange Court House. With Anderson and McLaws already ahead, now positioned along the turnpike near the Zoan Church, Lee wasted no time ordering Jackson to launch a hurried march.

The Light Division held its familiar position in Jackson's ranks, accompanied by D. H. Hill's former division, now commanded by Brig. Gen. Robert E. Rodes, and Isaac Trimble's Division, commanded by Brig. Gen. Raleigh E. Colston. Beginning well before dawn on May 1, the march would take place under a dramatically moonlit sky. That allowed the men an opportunity to get clear views of a few key sites from the December battle, most notably the Confederate entrenchments and the stone wall on Marye's Heights where Longstreet's veterans had famously devastated those repeated Union attacks.

As Hooker's troops consolidated in the vicinity of Chancellorsville on April 30–May 1, unabated confidence continued to frame the brash general's outlook, as well as many of his subordinates. That would begin to change as May 1 progressed when elements of the Army of the Potomac clashed with McLaws's Division along the Orange Turnpike and Anderson's Division on the roughly parallel Orange Plank Road. With timely support from Rodes, McLaws engaged and forced back Maj. Gen. George Sykes's Federals from Meade's V Corps, then marching east along the turnpike. As the Light Division plunged ahead, McGowan's men could hear the booming of artillery and firing toward the front and soon saw the debris of war—felled trees and sharpshooters on both sides of the road.[24]

Hill's Light Division marched at the rear of Jackson's column, eventually veering off the turnpike toward Anderson's position on the Orange Plank Road. Ahead lay Union Maj. Gen. Alpheus Williams's 1st Division in Slocum's XII Corps. "We now heard heavy firing in front," recalled J. R. Boyles, "and in the afternoon came up to where the fighting had commenced."

The vigorous outbreak of fighting and reports that additional Confederate troops were headed in his direction spurred Hooker to make what some subordinates and observers proclaimed at the time was an egregious miscalculation, a sentiment in which many modern historians concur. Rather than remaining aggressive to keep Lee off-balance, and with Slocum's Federals making progress near the Confederates' Zoan Church position, the Union commander at 2:00 p.m. halted operations for the day and instructed his five corps to pull back and entrench at

24 *CMH*, 215–216; *SHSP* 40:65; H. P. Griffith, *Variosa—A Collection of Essays, Sketches, and Verses* (1911), 57.

Chancellorsville. Hooker still had a significant advantage in numbers and seemed to bank on the supposition that Lee would never devise an attack against such stacked odds or might even order his forces to retreat toward Richmond either to fight on more reliable ground or at least keep the capital secure. As Hooker's predecessors tended to learn, ceding the upper hand to Lee as "Fighting Joe" just had rarely ended well.

* * *

Well after sundown on May 1, McGowan's Brigade assumed the advance of Jackson's column, eventually filing to the right of the road near a depression forming a battle line in a small clearing surrounded by woods. As the troops peeled off to the right, enemy bullets struck their position with minimal damage. The men also caught a close glimpse of an excited A. P. Hill, standing in the midst of several officers, "gesticulating vigorously with his right hand" while holding the reins of his horse with his left.

In their position perpendicular to the Orange Plank Road, the men formed a battle line and were instructed to sleep on their arms without fires. Other than having to deal with a few artillery shells thrown in their direction and occasional friendly fire from jittery troops to the rear, the brigade was not engaged that night. Each regiment, however, kept strong picket lines posted. "I slept but little, if any, brooding upon the morrow; all night I could hear thousands of axes in front of us," Boyles remembered of the entrenching Federals ahead. Recalled another soldier: "We were on the edge of an old field that skirted a belt of scrubby forest not more than two hundred yards wide between us and the enemy's main works. Our men lay down in line on the ground with guns loaded and capped, to await the coming of the morning and to get some needed rest after a toilsome march and a rather exciting day."[25]

It would be a breezy and unseasonably brisk night, and the stars shone brightly above the trees. Meaningful sleep would be wishful thinking for most, however. Continuous picket fire created an almost continuous drone, and artillery wagons rumbling to the rear of their line and the noise and tramping of additional brigades arriving augmented the men's unrelenting anxiety.[26]

Those who had slept even a little were awakened to the blare of enemy bugles, compounded by Federal artillery shells whistling through the woods— "crashing

25 *OR* 25(1):901; Boyles, *Reminiscences*, 35; Caldwell, *The History of a Brigade of South Carolinians*, 109–110; Griffith, *Variosa*, 59–61.

26 Griffith, *Variosa*, 61–62.

over our heads," one veteran recalled. It was an especially cold and damp morning, with most of the men, according to one solider, "chilled to the bones." Some in the 12th were apparently shivering so much that their teeth chattered and bodies shook violently.

As the sun rose, the Confederates could make out enemy breastworks to the front and U.S. flags hanging from standards in the distance. Amid the shelling, they quickly rolled their blanket rolls and packed their knapsacks while attempting to eat what few rations they had. An order to pile up the knapsacks and bedrolls was the signal they would soon be on the move. Calling his men to attention, McGowan led the brigade forward in a battle line for several hundred yards toward a wooded thicket, only to be greeted with unexpected volleys from a solid line of Yankee infantry, with a few of the South Carolinians wounded.

In response, the 12th hit the ground or joined their comrades in seeking protection behind trees, firing only when an enemy soldier emerged from one of their hiding spots. The brigade remained engaged in this position, trading shots, for at least an hour before being relieved about 10:00 a.m.[27]

As the men fell back by the left flank to the Orange Plank Road, they likely did not realize that they were about to embark on what would prove to be perhaps the most famous march of the entire Civil War. Overnight, Lee consulted with both Jackson and J. E. B. Stuart and had conceived a plan to hurl a portion of the Army of Northern Virginia against Hooker's position. Intelligence provided by Stuart's troopers showed that the Federal right flank, held by Howard's XI Corps, was in the open and surprisingly vulnerable. If that flank could be compromised, there was a good chance that, despite the numbers, the entire Federal line would collapse like dominoes.

To succeed, however, Lee would have to risk dividing his already outnumbered forces. While Anderson and McLaws, with about 13,000 men, remained opposite Hooker's well-entrenched front, Jackson would lead his 28,000 men in three divisions on a circuitous 12-mile march to the left, doing what he could to remain undetected, and strike the unsuspecting Howard from the rear. With Longstreet absent, Jackson was the only lieutenant general on the field and Lee predictably and wisely entrusted this difficult endeavor to him.

27 Boyles, *Reminiscences*, 35–36; Caldwell, *The History of a Brigade of South Carolinians*, 110; Griffith, *Variosa*, 61–62.

Jackson began the march sometime about 7:30 a.m., with Rodes's Division in the lead. Colston's Division followed, and Hill and the Light Division brought up the rear. For that reason, Hill's men did not begin moving until mid-morning.[28]

To reach their target, Jackson's ranks would have to follow a rustic amalgamation of roads, trails, and paths. Despite the ultimate outcome, for McGowan's men it was a long, tedious, and frustrating march, featuring several abrupt halts and starts. "We kept up our march all day—first South, then West, then North and Northwest, passing an old iron foundry on the way," recalled an apparently irritated Boyles, a belief echoed by Colonel Hamilton of the 1st South Carolina: "[W]e were subjected to the most trying ordeal to which any troops could be subjected. As soon as we reached the open ground, we were exposed in open and full view to the batteries of the enemy, and, under a deliberate and annoying fire, we passed these batteries in review."

"The roads were, fortunately, just wet enough to be easy to the feet and free from dust," recounted J. F. J. Caldwell. "The weather was fine, but we suffered for water. . . . We marched regularly and rapidly until about an hour before sunset." About 1:00 p.m. a halt was ordered. "Arms were stacked in the road," recalled a soldier in the 14th South Carolina, "knapsacks unslung, and the men lay down on the ground and at their scanty rations from their haversacks, while the skirmish line stood and kept watch in the woods." Ten minutes later, they were back on the road marching.[29]

Although Jackson's column proceeded essentially undetected, on a few occasions the Confederates came within range of nervous Federal pickets, who began firing away, drawing a response from individual units as the main body "poured on" down the road. At about 4:00 p.m. Rodes's Division, in the vanguard, neared Howard's line, reaching the same Orange Turnpike they had occupied that morning but now headed east. Jackson deployed his command in three lines. Rodes remained the first, Colston the second, and Hill the third. Hill was still deploying his division when the surprise flank attack began after 5:00 p.m., as three brigades—McGowan's among them—were still marching in column.[30]

As Lee and Jackson had hoped, the onslaught led by Rodes scattered the startled Federals like an "irresistible avalanche." But for only a few pockets of

28 Boyles, *Reminiscences*, 35–36; Caldwell, *The History of a Brigade of South Carolinians*, 110; *CMH*, 216–217; *SHSP* 40:71.

29 Boyles, *Reminiscences*, 36; *OR* 25(1):901; Caldwell, *The History of a Brigade of South Carolinians*, 112; Griffith, *Variosa*, 67–68.

30 Daly, *Alexander Cheves Haskell*, 102; *SHSP* 40:76; Caldwell, *The History of a Brigade of South Carolinians*, 112.

resistance, the position crumbled as Southern soldiers ran pell-mell through the enemy camps, capturing or killing scores of Yankees. Indeed, as one Confederate wrote, "There was nothing left but to lay down their arms and surrender, or flee." The wooded terrain created some problems, however, and command and control were lost as the attack rolled forward, forcing Rodes to halt and rectify his lines. About then, Colston's Division surged in to join the fight, and the two lines quickly swept everything in their path toward Chancellorsville; using the Orange Turnpike as a guide.[31]

The Light Division had struggled to keep pace, and only three of the six brigades were fully deployed behind Rodes and Colston when the attack began. There were reasons for it, but unfortunately McGowan's Brigade was among the three lagging behind. "We marched pretty quickly down the plank road, and before long came upon the evidence of battle," wrote one soldier.

At some point during the hectic attack, the 12th South Carolina was ordered to stay behind to guard Jackson's ordnance trains against a potential cavalry attack and to collect and guard the mounting number of Federal prisoners being captured. There is no record why the 12th was chosen for this task or which officer ordered it, whether McGowan, Hill, or Jackson.[32]

By sunset, as the battle still raged ahead, the men of the 12th continued to bring in and hold prisoners. According to William Dunlop of Company B, the regiment was stationed at the junction of the Orange Turnpike and the Culpeper Plank Road. It is likely that the men hunkered down that evening in or near the captured Federal camps, cordoning off an area for the prisoners and probably dividing the regiment between guard duty for those prisoners and for Jackson's ordnance trains.

Although the 12th remained detached from the rest of the brigade, their fellow South Carolinians played a role in completing Jackson's historic rout, eventually joining forces with Colston's surge toward Hooker's main line. Halting at one point, the brigade maneuvered into a thick pine wood, deployed into battle line to the right of a road, and exchanged volleys with an enemy force making a stand.

At the conclusion of that brief skirmish, the South Carolinians bivouacked along the road. During that respite, many of the men had the misfortune to witness a wounded Stonewall Jackson being carried to the rear. Jackson had been the victim of friendly fire as he reconnoitered with his staff between the lines, mistakenly shot in the left arm by a nervous picket in the 18th North Carolina.

31 *SHSP* 40:77–78.

32 Ibid.; William S. Dunlop, "The Confederate War: Company B, Twelfth S. C. V. in Bivouac and Battles," *Yorkville Enquirer*, Nov. 13, 1889, 1 [hereafter cited as *Bivouac and Battles (Part IV)*].

Jackson would have that arm amputated and then was transported 15 or so miles by ambulance to Guinea Station, where he died of pneumonia on May 10.[33]

On May 3, the fighting continued in earnest well in front of the 12th's position. In addition to its responsibilities guarding the ordnance trains and Federal prisoners, the regiment received orders to serve as the Second Corps' de facto provost guard, charged with gathering Confederate stragglers and sending them to the front and into the fight. "It would seem incredible," wrote Boyles, "but it was nevertheless true, we gathered up hundreds—yes, I may say thousands—of men who had run out of the fight, officers as well as privates; we formed them in squads and sent them to the front."

With the intense fighting enduring well into the evening, hospitals were set up in the vicinity for the wounded. "We had occasion to visit our hospital where the wounded were being brought," Boyles recalled, "and I tell the untarnished truth when I say there was a pile of arms and legs as large as a good sized house." The rest of McGowan's Brigade remained engaged throughout the day; McGowan went down with a wound below the knee and Colonel Edwards of the 13th, next in line, was shot in the shoulder. Command of the brigade devolved to Col. Abner Perrin of the 14th South Carolina.[34]

As May 4 dawned, the magnitude of the victory resounded among the Confederate ranks. Lee not only held the field, but Hooker's supposedly unconquerable army had begun retreating across the Rappahannock, making a distressing return to Falmouth. Still on provost duty in the rear, the 12th South Carolina's morning reports from its 10 companies listed approximately 350 men present for duty. And though words filtering in from the front confirmed the victory, not all the news was positive. In addition to Jackson's ultimately fatal injury, A. P. Hill had been wounded by a shell behind his knees. With Both Jackson and Hill sidelined, Lee's cavalry commander Stuart was the only major general in the vicinity and assumed temporary command of the Second Corps.

Early on May 4, with the 12th now guarding nearly 2,000 prisoners—mostly German troops from Howard's XI Corps, which bore the brunt of Jackson's flank attack—Colonel Miller received orders for his regiment to march the prisoners approximately 65 miles to Richmond. Miller realized it would probably be a while before he and his men had time to notify families and friends at home regarding the regiment's status after the battle and wanted them to know they had been spared

33 Caldwell, *The History of a Brigade of South Carolinians*, 113–114; Dunlop, *Bivouac and Battles (Part IV)*, 1. Dunlop likely meant that the regiment was deployed at the intersection of the Orange Turnpike and Orange Plank Road.

34 Boyles, *Reminiscences*, 36; Caldwell, *The History of a Brigade of South Carolinians*, 114–118.

the bloodshed. In a hastily drafted note that he sent for immediate publication in various newspapers, he wrote: "The 12th regiment South Carolina Volunteers have not been engaged in the fight. It was detached to guard prisoners. Corporal Ellis, Company E, of Lancaster district, was wounded in a skirmish severely."

As the regiment departed the wilderness of Chancellorsville with a prisoner force five times its own size, it was essential that each soldier remained vigilant. "We had no relief—it took every man to stand guard day and night—no rest, no sleep, nothing to eat," Boyles recalled. Captain Dunlop reported that the 12th marched for two days to reach Guinea Station on the Richmond, Fredericksburg and Potomac Railroad. After their arrival, the men endured an unrelenting rainstorm without food or adequate shelter. The regiment also received orders to march the 75–100 Federal officers to the train depot, board them on cars, and send them to Richmond.

On May 6, Mississippians in Brig. Gen. Joseph Davis's command were called to guard the remaining prisoners briefly while the 12th drew rations of "salt horse" and hard tack. The prisoner march then continued, with the regiment reaching Milford Station the evening of May 7, Hanover Junction on May 8, and the outer reaches of Richmond on May 9. Only four prisoners were lost, left behind along the way because of illness.[35]

Watching the 12th march the prisoners down the Brooke Turnpike from his home on the outskirts of Richmond was John Beauchamp Jones, the gossipy and observant assistant clerk in the Confederate War Department. In an entry in his diary dated May 10, Jones described the regiment's appearance and the spectacle of the 12th conveying nearly 2,000 prisoners into the capital:

> May 10th—Detachments of Federal troops are now marching into the city every few hours, guarded by (mostly) South Carolinians, dressed in home-spun, died yellow with the bark of the butternut-tree. Yesterday evening at 7 o'clock, a body of 2000 arrived, being marched in by way of the Brooke Pike, near to my residence. Only 200 Butternuts had them in charge, and a less number would have sufficed, for they were extremely weary. Some of them however attempted to be humorous.
>
> A young officer asked one of the spectators if the "Libby" [Richmond's famed prison] was the best house in the city to put up at. He was answered that it was the best *he* would find.

35 Joseph Crute, *Units of the Confederate Army* (Gaithersburg, MD, 1987), 258; Boyles, *Reminiscences*, 36–37; John L. Miller, "Guineas Station, May 5," *Abbeville Press and Banner*, May 15, 1863, 1.

A view of Libby Prison in Richmond circa 1865. *Library of Congress*

> Another passed some compliment on a mulatto wench, who replied: "Go long you nasty abolition Yankee."
>
> One of our soldiers taken at Arkansas Post, just exchanged, walked along with the column, and kept repeating those words: "Now you know how *we* felt when you marched us through your cities."
>
> But generally, a deep silence was maintained, and neither insult nor indignity offered the fallen foe. . . .

The trek to Richmond was an incredible feat that highlights the regiment's resolve, discipline, and reliability. With 350 men, the 12th marched more than five times that many prisoners to the Confederate capital. "These fellows could have overpowered us at any time on this march," Boyles recalled, "but most of them appeared to prefer imprisonment to fighting."

Richmond's residents welcomed the sight of the enemy prisoners, and the city turned out in droves to witness the spectacle of downtrodden Yankee soldiers led along its streets to prison. Recalled Boyles: "A goodly number were young men, dudes, home guards, who taunted our captives but were gotten the best of, being met with the reply that they had better be at the front, that if their capture had depended on them, they would never have been taken, etc.; very true, too."

At Libby Prison, located on the banks of the James River, the prisoners were turned over to Confederate authorities. Boyles would write, however, that the detainees profusely thanked the men of the 12th for the kind treatment they received during their capture and march "and assured us that if ever they captured a member of our regiment they would treat him with the utmost kindness; told us good-bye and blessed us as long as they could see us."

The regiment then drew rations from a nearby depot and promptly marched out of the city, camping along the RF&P rail line. The bivouac provided welcome relief from the stress of war, as the men enjoyed the company of throngs of women who came to visit the "heroes" from the front lines. "Young ladies paid us great attention," Boyles recalled, "and many roguish glances were exchanged."

At 7:00 a.m. on May 12, reality resurfaced, as the men were ordered to pack their knapsacks and board a train for Fredericksburg, which they reached about 6:00 p.m. Although Chancellorsville had been a costly victory after the deaths of Stonewall Jackson and thousands of Confederate troops, the combined brilliance and determination of Lee's army in routing and humiliating a Federal army more than twice its size had found a fitting place high on the shelf of Civil War renown.[36]

36 John B. Jones, *A Rebel War Clerk's Diary*, 2 vols. (Philadelphia, 1866), 1:318 (emphasis in original); Boyles, *Reminiscences*, 36–37; Dunlop, *Bivouac and Battles (Part IV)*, 1. For an interesting story in which a 46th Pennsylvania soldier describes Colonel Miller stealing a watch from a fellow prisoner on the march to Richmond, see *National Tribune*, February 13, 1919, 3.

Chapter Eight

Witnesses to Defeat: The Battle of Gettysburg

Shock rather than relief or joy greeted the "broke down" 12th South Carolina at the Moss Neck Manor encampment following its grueling journey to and from Richmond. "Shambles" probably best described what the men found on their return to Camp Gregg. Charred tents and huts used by both officers and men had been ravaged, a few still smoldering. Some personal baggage had been carried away to Guinea Station apparently, and much of the men's other personal items were either strewn about the camp or missing altogether. All that could be salvaged were certain valuables that some soldiers had stowed for safekeeping in nearby homes before the current campaign—that and whatever they wore or had with them while marching toward Chancellorsville, Richmond, and back.

The culprits responsible for the devastation and loss were never identified, but the other four regiments in McGowan's Brigade had returned to Moss Neck Manor immediately after the battle, and other units had passed through in the preceding two weeks. Left with little choice, an irritated Colonel Miller ordered the regiment's camp moved to a nearby grove of "beautiful" pines the following day. The new camp, according to Company B's William Dunlop, "was systematically laid off in streets and alleys, and the regiment placed in regular order."[1]

Changes were also in store for the Army of Northern Virginia's high command that would have lasting effects on McGowan's Brigade. On May 10, as the 12th marched the Federal prisoners to Richmond, Stonewall Jackson succumbed to

1 Caldwell, *The History of a Brigade of South Carolinians*, 125–126; Dunlop, *Bivouac and Battles (Part IV)*, 1; Joseph Templeton to Sarah Templeton, May 13, 1863.

pneumonia contracted after his accidental wounding eight days earlier. The loss of Jackson sent shockwaves through the army and the Confederacy at large; he was also deeply mourned by McGowan's South Carolinians, despite their tempestuous relationship with the general during their one year of service in the Army of Northern Virginia. "I had no idea that I could be so depressed by the death of any man, as I have been by the death of Gen. Jackson," one 12th South Carolina officer wrote to his wife on May 25. To compensate for the loss of the commander whom he had long considered "my right arm," Robert E. Lee reorganized the Army of Northern Virginia in late May. Longstreet continued as the First Corps' commander, assigned three divisions under Maj. Gens. John Bell Hood, Lafayette McLaws, and George Pickett. Newly promoted Lt. Gen. Richard Ewell, finally recovered from his grievous wounding during the Second Manassas campaign and, walking now with a wooden left leg, would be Lee's replacement for Jackson atop the Second Corps. Like Lee and Jackson, Ewell was a fellow Virginian to his three division commanders: Maj. Gens. Jubal Early, Robert Rodes, and Edward "Allegheny" Johnson.

Ewell's new command, however, would be smaller than Jackson's, as Lee created a new Third Corps and handed the reins to A. P. Hill, whom he also promoted to lieutenant general. Lee created three divisions for Hill by shuffling units from Longstreet's command, bringing in units from other areas, and reducing the number of brigades in the Light Division. Major General Richard H. Anderson's Division, formerly of Longstreet's Corps, was among those transferred to the Third Corps, and Maj. Gen. Henry Heth would command another division, formed by joining Heth's and Archer's brigades from the Light Division and combining them with the brigades commanded by James Johnston Pettigrew and Joseph Davis. Colonel Brockenbrough assumed command of Heth's old brigade.

Reduced from six brigades to four, the Light Division would be commanded by newly promoted Maj. Gen. Dorsey Pender, a North Carolinian. In addition to McGowan's South Carolinians, there were Lane's North Carolinians, Thomas's Georgians, and Pender's old North Carolina brigade, now under Brig. Gen. Alfred Scales—the former commander of the 13th North Carolina and a particular standout during the Chancellorsville fighting. The choice of Pender as Hill's replacement was met with trepidation by many of McGowan's soldiers, among them J. R. Boyles of Company C, who labeled him a leader "of whom we had a perfect horror, as being a strict disciplinarian." It was warranted disdain, as the South Carolinians witnessed firsthand Pender's draconian punishments while the brigades camped near each other the previous winter.[2]

2 *OR* 25(2):840; Boyles, *Reminiscences*, 38; "Extract of a Letter," *Yorkville Enquirer*, June 3, 1863, 2.

With the death of Stonewall Jackson, A. P. Hill was promoted to command of the newly created Confederate Third Corps and Brigadier General Dorsey Pender of North Carolina was promoted to Major General in command of the reduced Light Division. *Library of Congress*

With the wounded McGowan sidelined, Col. Daniel Hamilton of the 1st South Carolina again assumed temporary command of the brigade. Hamilton, however, had his own health problems and quickly relinquished command to Col. Abner Perrin of the 14th South Carolina, the brigade's senior colonel. The 12th South Carolina therefore entered the summer of 1863 with a new regimental commander (Miller), a temporary new brigade commander (Perrin), a new division commander (Pender), and a new corps commander (Hill). Despite the potential chaos created by such extensive turnover, the men's morale was high and the 12th remained an exemplary unit.

There was, however, a buttoning down in all facets of military protocol under Pender's regime in the now smaller Light Division. Pender's reputation for discipline extended to the drill field as he ordered all his brigades to drill with knapsacks and bedrolls—a "hardening" that one soldier insisted was unnecessary for veteran troops and risked leaving them disenchanted with service. The drill field would not be the lone venue for the restrictions either, as Pender increased discipline in the camps and provost areas, too. Previously, men under guard for infractions were dismissed in the evening, allowed to spend the night in their bivouacs, and then return to continue their sentences the following day. Now, each regiment was ordered to have a chain of guards always on duty, day and night, to enforce the use of passes and to prohibit men from leaving camp without authorization.

McGowan's South Carolinians returned to picket duty along the Rappahannock, occupying the positions held during the winter and early spring, though they were forbidden to converse with enemy pickets as before. "Here we rested and recuperated for nearly a month, with nothing to do in the way of military service except to keep up our picket and drill," recalled Captain Dunlop.

The warm weather did allow the men time to enjoy a new favorite pastime: fishing. The entire brigade would benefit, as details meandered along the

Rappahannock with rods or nets to bring back the "proceeds" in the form of shad and herring, which would be shared among the men in the ranks. It proved a downright "feast," according to one 12th South Carolina soldier.

The men also were pleased by delivery of a large lot of shoes, and with more uniforms arriving either from Richmond or home, the men found themselves "comfortably clothed" for a change.[3] Yet, despite the provender, pleasant weather, and new shoes, Joseph Templeton would describe the regiment's overall health as poor during this period. Dysentery prevailed among the men, leading to fatalities on some occasions. On May 16, Company B's T. W. Ramsay died of the ailment. He was laid to rest in the woods near the new regimental camp. Others, such as Joseph Templeton's brother William, were sent to hospitals in Richmond to be treated.[4]

With idle time on their hands and good weather, many of the soldiers were drawn to regular sermons by the 12th's "esteemed" chaplain, J. Monroe Anderson, in an area cleared by the troops in a shady grove of trees—complete with a pulpit and seats made of unhewn timber. During his service on May 24, Anderson administered communion to the men in attendance. As one soldier noted, it would be the last time many of the men received the sacrament.[5]

* * *

In late May, General Lee began planning a second major offensive north. Two years of war had produced a bloody stalemate along the Rappahannock line between Richmond and Washington. During the Maryland campaign, Lee weighed a march into Pennsylvania before he was drawn into battle at Sharpsburg. The victory at Chancellorsville had given the commander considerable hope he could triumph north of the Mason-Dixon Line and this time sway northern

3 Benjamin Flowerday, "Painting a Picture of a South Carolina Regiment Marching into Pennsylvania: An Analysis of Clothing Requisitions of the 12th South Carolina during the Second Quarter of 1863," unpublished paper in author's possession, Dec. 18, 2024. Researching each of the regiment's companies and their requisition requests using the Compiled Military Service Records, Mr. Flowerday's insightful paper sheds light on the interesting yet often overlooked aspect of uniform distribution in the Army of Northern Virginia.

4 Caldwell, *The History of a Brigade of South Carolinians*, 125–127; William S. Dunlop, "The Confederate War: Company B, Twelfth S. C. V. in Bivouac and Battles," *Yorkville Enquirer*, Nov. 20, 1889, 1 [hereafter cited as *Bivouac and Battles (Part V)*], 1; Joseph Templeton to Margaret Templeton, May 22, 1863.

5 Dunlop, *Bivouac and Battles (Part V)*, 1.

sentiment against the war enough to compel Lincoln to reconsider his stance on forcing the southern states back into the union.[6]

In the initial stage of Lee's plan, portions of his army would head north from the Fredericksburg/Rappahannock line toward the Shenandoah Valley to assess how Hooker would respond. On June 3, Ewell's and Longstreet's corps began moving toward Culpeper, Virginia, while the men in Hill's Corps remained in their camps, keeping an eye on the Federal forces across the Rappahannock and guarding against a possible Yankee advance from Fredericksburg against Richmond.

What one soldier remembered as a brief period of "quiet comfort and peace" was interrupted in the late afternoon of June 5 with the sound of distant artillery. Having crossed the Rappahannock with a portion of his army, Hooker attacked Hill's lines. One 12th South Carolina company, then on picket duty, took part in the action, with no reported injuries. At about 10:00 p.m., the regiment struck its tents and fell in, with the men ordered to leave their "forest sanctuary" and all unnecessary baggage behind. Soon, the 12th joined their fellow South Carolinians and followed Colonel Perrin toward Fredericksburg.[7]

At sunrise the following day, Perrin's command found itself on familiar ground—the position they had occupied during the fighting at Fredericksburg on December 13. The South Carolinians remained there for several days, patrolling the river to keep an eye on the Federals, now clearly more active around Falmouth.[8]

While encamped, Pender organized special sharpshooter battalions for each of his brigades. In McGowan's Brigade, the handpicked detail included at least one marksman from each company for a total of about 120 men in three newly created companies. Lieutenant Sharpe of the 12th South Carolina commanded one of these companies, which marched at the head of the brigade and were used for special assignments and skirmish duty.[9]

On June 15, pickets in Hill's Corps at Fredericksburg discovered that the Federals had withdrawn from their positions and disappeared. The men in the 12th wondered specifically what to make of the situation. "We are ignorant as to [Longstreet's and Ewell's] whereabouts or intentions," wrote one Company I soldier, adding that Hill's strong defensive position—combined with general Federal inactivity across the river—meant it was unlikely "we will have another fight

6 *SHSP* 23:210.

7 Boyles, *Reminiscences*, 38; Dunlop, *Bivouac and Battles (Part V)*, 1; LOCAL, "For the Lancaster Ledger," *Lancaster Ledger*, June 17, 1863, 2.

8 Dunlop, *Bivouac and Battles (Part V)*, 1; Caldwell, *The History of a Brigade of South Carolinians*, 129.

9 Caldwell, *The History of a Brigade of South Carolinians*, 129–130.

here." This soldier, and assuredly others, felt confident that with Lee, Longstreet, and Ewell out of sight and on the move, "another Maryland campaign" north was in the works.

On June 16, Hill's entire command began a march of approximately 17 miles, following the Plank Road and crossing the Rapidan at Ely's Ford before bivouacking in a range of hills north of the river. Traversing some of the wreckage from the Chancellorsville fighting, the regiment filed by the Chancellor House ruins that had been Hooker's headquarters during the battle and eventually destroyed by Confederate artillery. The scene, one solider recalled, was a "horrible spectacle, indescribable," and D. J. Carter described seeing half-burnt bodies of Yankees in and around the house as they marched by, still unburied more than a month after the battle.

The men received another blow as rumors began circulating that the regiment's surplus baggage, left in camp more than a week earlier, had been destroyed—the second such loss of personal items in as many months. "Word came to us that our baggage had all been piled up and burned," recalled J. R. Boyles, who lamented that the loss included his personal diary, "in which I kept a strict account of each day's events from the time of our arrival at Lightwood Knot Springs." Nevertheless, spirits remained high. "Our men were full of enthusiasm and nearly every member of Co. O was in ranks, expecting a little fun," he remembered.[10]

During the march, commenced in stifling heat, Pender's Division formed the rear of Hill's advance, which meant the men dealt both with stragglers from other units who infiltrated their ranks and considerable dust generated by the shuffling feet of the thousands of troops to their front. After a solid 15-mile march that day, the column halted near Stevensburg. That evening, the men of the 12th were issued their first round of beefsteak of the season, and each man in Company I managed a "refreshing" bath in a mill pond close to camp.

The next day, the column trudged another 12 miles on dusty roads through Culpeper "under a burning sun," which a soldier in another regiment remembered as "the most oppressive heat I ever felt." Dunlop noted great numbers of men falling by the wayside from sunstroke and lack of water. One who succumbed was Joseph Templeton. Sent to the rear, he was confined to a hospital for the duration of the campaign.[11]

10 Boyles, *Reminiscences*, 38–39, Dunlop, *Bivouac and Battles (Part V)–* 1.; LOCAL, "For the Lancaster Ledger," *Lancaster Ledger*, July 22, 1863, 2; D. J. Carter, "Campaign of 1863," *Lancaster News*, Dec. 18, 1889, 1; LOCAL, "For the Lancaster Ledger," *Lancaster Ledger*, June 17, 1863, 2.

11 Caldwell, *The History of a Brigade of South Carolinians*, 130–131; Dunlop, *Bivouac and Battles (Part V)–* 1; Joseph Templeton to Sarah Templeton, June 23, 1863.

Despite the rugged marching and the heat and dust, the men's spirits remained high, and purportedly Pender's "generous" treatment of the troops during the trek toward the Shenandoah Valley and beyond earned him their newfound respect. Wrote Boyles: "Gen. Pender, of whom we had entertained such fears, proved quite humane and treated kindly, halting and resting in the middle of the day."

On June 19, the troops marched another 18 miles through the Virginia countryside, crossing two rivers in the process, and encamped in an open field that evening, with an afternoon rain providing the hot, dusty men some needed relief. A 10-mile march ensued on the 20th, as the column snaked through Flint Hill and ascended the Blue Ridge Mountains—marching "through the clouds," as one Company I soldier remembered it—before bivouacking atop a mountain at Chester Gap. Although men continued to fall from the ranks during the marches, according to one report, all had succeeded in catching up with their comrades by the morning of June 21.[12]

Wrote one 12th South Carolina soldier: "We passed through many towns and villages in Virginia where first one and then another army had held sway, but everywhere could be witnessed genuine and true devotion to the Southern Cause. The ladies cheered us and expressed the hope that the enemy would never more be allowed to pollute their homes." The march resumed at 4:00 a.m. on June 21. The column descended into the valley, passing through Front Royal before toiling across both forks of the nearby Shenandoah River. Deep water and strong currents added to the struggle, but the resolute hordes buoyed themselves with cheers, serenaded in the process by the 14th South Carolina's band. The day's 12-mile advance was productive. At each stop along the way, men from the regiment visited homes to "forage"—"not to steal," one soldier explained, "but to beg, and they always brought in something nice."[13]

By the evening of June 22, following a 13-mile march, Perrin's command had reached Berryville, Virginia, the site of Lee's temporary headquarters. Now traveling with portions of the Army of Northern Virginia was Lt. Col. Arthur Lyon Fremantle of the British army, who had been granted permission by officials in Richmond to seek a meeting with General Lee as his army marched north. Fremantle left the Confederate capital on June 19 and reached Berryville on the 22nd. A day earlier, he had encountered Pender's Division as he traveled and later offered his observations on the condition of the men:

12 Dunlop, *Bivouac and Battles (Part V)*, 1; Boyles, *Reminiscences*, 39; Caldwell, *The History of a Brigade of South Carolinians*, 131; Carter, "Campaign of 1863."

13 Caldwell, *The History of a Brigade of South Carolinians*, 131; Dunlop, *Bivouac and Battles (Part V)*, 1; Boyles, *Reminiscences*, 39; Carter, "Campaign of 1863."

> The soldiers of this division are a remarkably fine body of men, and look quite seasoned and ready for any work. Their clothing is serviceable, so also are their boots; but there is the usual utter absence of uniformity as to color and shape of their garments and hats: gray of all shades, and brown clothing, with felt hats, predominate. The Confederate troops are entirely armed with excellent rifles, mostly Enfields. . . . The colors of the regiments differ from the blue battle-flags I saw with [Braxton] Bragg's army. They are generally red, with a blue St. Andrew's Cross showing the stars . . . most of the colors in this division bear the names of Manassas, Fredericksburg, Seven Pines, Harper's Ferry, Chancellorsville &c. . . . I saw no stragglers during the time I was with Pender's division.[14]

With marches of nine and fifteen miles on June 23–24, respectively, Hill's Corps reached the Potomac and encamped near Shepherdstown in what was now formally West Virginia, not far from the site of its post-Sharpsburg engagement in September 1862. Captain Dunlop's slog on June 23 would be particularly memorable. Suffering from an infected boil on the back of his neck, which he had bandaged, Dunlop recalled that he drew the attention of women in the towns through which they passed. To honor his service, convinced the wound had come in battle, they went out of their way to offer him pies and cakes. Dunlop in turn offered no resistance, and perhaps even shared the spoils with the men in his company.

June 25 would be memorable as well for the regiment. After marching through the heart of Shepherdstown, the soldiers descended the rocky hillside to the Potomac, stripped off their clothes, and crossed the river as the 14th South Carolina's band played "Dixie." Boyles was among those who viewed the river as the "great dividing line between the contending armies." Despite the rough waters, the men kept their ranks closed effectively and crossed into Maryland without incident, ready for the next stage of their excursion. There was no longer any doubt an invasion was imminent, and they advanced beaming with optimism. On his first northern invasion in September 1862, General Lee hoped the presence of Southern troops in Maryland would spur pro-Confederate boys to rally to the cause. Although Boyles and others in the regiment echoed that sentiment now, they would be quickly disappointed. The Marylanders, he recalled, "didn't rally worth much."[15]

Passing through the battlefield of Sharpsburg during their advance that day left many in Hill's Corps with mixed emotions. Some took advantage of a brief

14 Arthur Fremantle, *Three Months in the Southern States* (New York, 1864), 226.

15 Caldwell, *The History of a Brigade of South Carolinians*, 131, Boyles, *Reminiscences*, 39.

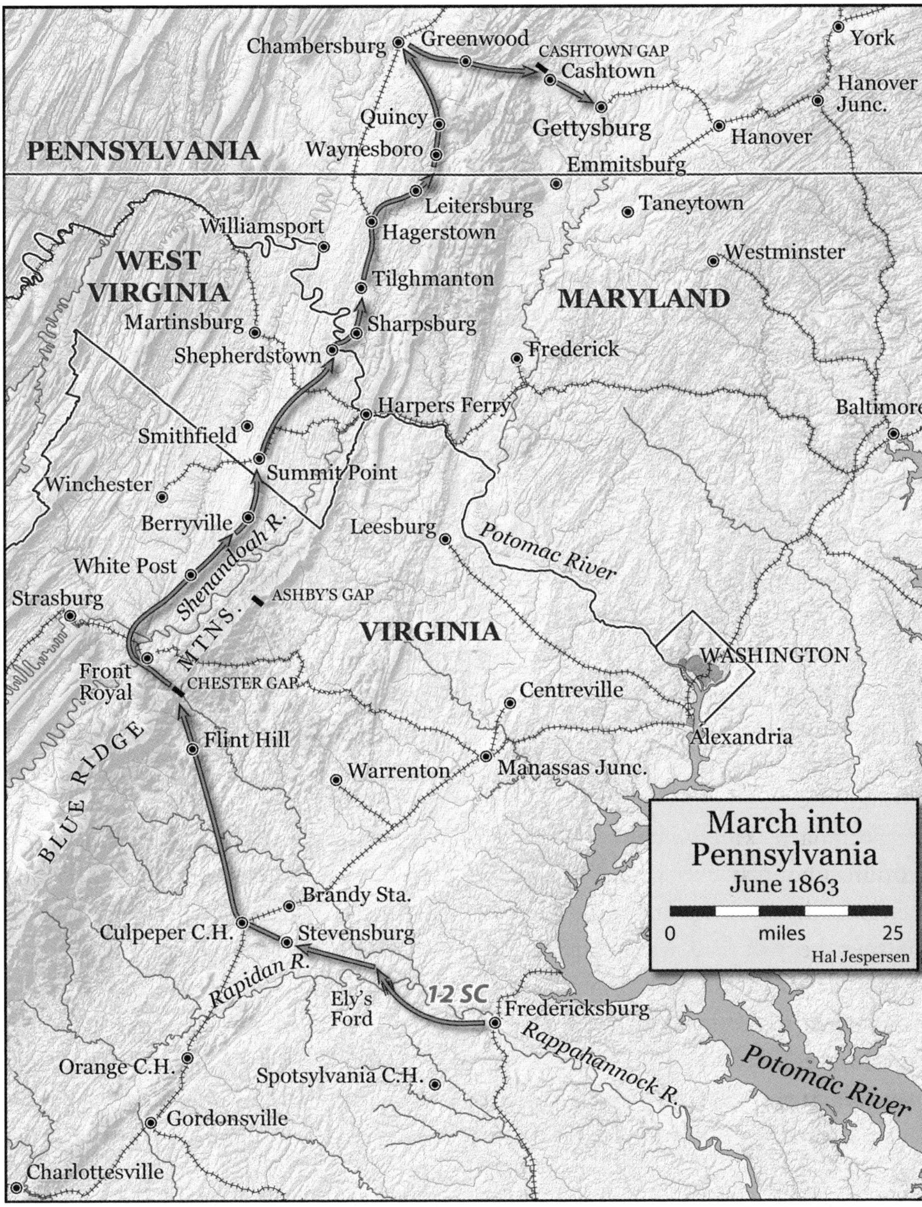

break to roam the ground upon which they had fought 10 months before and to visit the graves of fallen comrades buried on the field after the epic battle. "Some we found had been roughly dealt with, some undisturbed," wrote one soldier, and D. J. Carter and Ben Powell of Company I located the grave of one comrade and "fixed it up anew" before rejoining the column as it marched through town.

They bivouacked that night near Tilghmanton, Maryland, and approached the Pennsylvania state line on June 26 after a 15-mile trudge over mud-caked roads.

While marching through Hagerstown on the 26th, some of the men visited the offices of the *Herald of Freedom and Torch Light*, a pro-Union newspaper, disappointed to find that the Unionist editors had fled rather than confront oncoming Confederate troops.

The march through western Maryland would be markedly different for the men than it had been in Virginia. "Some towns through which we passed appeared to be intensely Southern," Boyles recalled, "while in others, if a Confederate flag was seen, some lady waved a tiny one away back from a window, evidently afraid of her neighbors to see it, lest she should be reported, arrested and thrown into prison." Despite the cool reception, provisions were abundant and the roads were in good condition. Still, the daily marches and the heat, dust, and frayed clothing again took a heavy toll.

At each stop, men immediately broke ranks to bathe or wash their clothes to rid them of vermin and lice. One evening, Boyles recalled, he and his messmates spread their oil clothes on the ground along with some blankets and, using their knapsacks as pillows, lay down under another oil cloth and additional blankets during a pelting rainstorm.[16]

* * *

With spirits high, Hill's Corps entered Pennsylvania on June 27. "I do not suppose any army ever marched into an enemy's country with greater confidence in its ability to conquer and with more reasonable grounds for that confidence than the army of Gen. Lee," Perrin recalled. Other than what Perrin labeled "a few cavalry skirmishes," the column met no enemy resistance as it advanced toward Chambersburg. Boyles made note of a collection of local ladies watching the Confederates as they passed, and also relished coming upon a line of cherry trees from which the men enjoyed their share of sweet fruit.

The South Carolinians found a serene and restful bivouac south of Chambersburg—for the next two days at least. For some soldiers, the lush Pennsylvania countryside and abundant throng of farms was too tempting to resist. Many slipped past guards patrolling their camp's perimeter in search of food from locals. While lounging in camp, many also wrote letters home. The men's

16 Dunlop, *Bivouac and Battles (Part V)*, 2; Boyles, *Reminiscences*, 40; Caldwell, *The History of a Brigade of South Carolinians*, 132; LOCAL, "For the Lancaster Ledger," *Lancaster Ledger*, July 22, 1863, 2; Carter, "Campaign of 1863."

confidence in General Lee was a prevailing sentiment in this correspondence. As one soldier proclaimed: "We have a large and effective force here—an army which has never been defeated—so you may know that success, in whatever Lee undertakes, is bound, by all the glorious achievements which have heretofore crowned our arms, to accompany us."

As was his custom, Lee issued strict orders for the troops not to molest private property in the region, and the men in the regiment (and brigade) for the most part obeyed. According to a 1st South Carolina soldier, there was no great need to forage as many locals voluntarily provided the Rebel soldiers supplies and food, and one 12th South Carolina soldier complimented the citizens on their kindness, noting they "always have a smile on their face." While encamped near Funkstown, Maryland, the troops encountered one particularly generous individual whose only request was that they not take his home.[17]

An alarming difference in the Confederates' approach to foraging during the Gettysburg campaign would not become apparent for at least another year. Lieutenant Boyles was among the 12th South Carolina soldiers to comment bitterly after the war that the respect he and his comrades had shown local citizens in June–July 1863 was not replicated by Maj. Gen. William Tecumseh Sherman during the Atlanta campaign, his March to the Sea, and the Carolinas campaign, when the Yankees ruthlessly devastated local homes and farms in their path as part of Sherman's "Total War" tactics.

The stark contrast, Boyles railed, was particularly distressing for the South Carolinians when Sherman drove through their home state in January–March 1865 during the waning days of the war. In Pennsylvania, the lieutenant bluntly recalled, "[p]rivate property was protected, but if we had known what was in store for our homes and families by Sherman and his vandals, we would have made a clean sweep and left them homeless."[18]

* * *

Expecting to march toward Chambersburg on the morning of June 30, the South Carolinians and the rest of Pender's Division headed instead toward Greenwood and then Cashtown along what was known as the Chambersburg Pike. Leaving camp in

17 Dunlop, *Bivouac and Battles (Part V)*, 2.; Caldwell, *The History of a Brigade of South Carolinians*, 133; Boyles, *Reminiscences*, 40; LOCAL, "For the Lancaster Ledger," *Lancaster Ledger*, July 22, 1863, 2; Abner Perrin to Governor Pickens, July 29, 1863, in Milledge L. Bonham, ed., "A Little More Light on Gettysburg," *Mississippi Valley Historical Review* 24 (1937–1938): 519–525.

18 Boyles, *Reminiscences*, 40; Caldwell, *The History of a Brigade of South Carolinians*, 133.

a light rain, the men funneled through extraordinary stretches of countryside that would continue to impress them long after the war. The tightly aligned farms they passed, inhabited mostly by the Pennsylvania Dutch (and some Shakers), were rich in cattle and boasted plentiful fields of hay and corn. Boyles recalled a conversation he had with one farmer lamenting an earlier loss of his horse to unidentified Confederate soldiers. The old man had apparently attempted to hide his horse from capture "mit a hay-sthack, but it was no use, de tam rebels find him anyhow."

During long halts along the turnpike, the troops feasted on apple butter from local farms. They also had an opportunity to view the charred remains of the famed Caledonia Furnace in the hamlet of Greenwood, owned by U.S. Rep. Thaddeus Stevens, a noted abolitionist. Jubal Early's passing column had torched the place only days earlier.

As Hill's men snaked along the gentle slopes of South Mountain, the terrain quickly turned from lush fields to thick woods. About 2:00 p.m., the corps halted and encamped just west of Cashtown. The South Carolinians' bivouac would be in a region known as Miller's Gap, referred to in one report simply as "rough" countryside and a "basin" in the mountain in another.

After gathering wood for their campfires, the men received a whiskey ration on General Hill's orders and were also directed to prepare one-day rations, a sign that fighting was likely in store. Once the wagons came up later that evening, company officers made requisitions and men in need were issued brand new jackets, shirts, pants, drawers, and shoes. As the men enjoyed the whiskey, cooked their rations, and tried on their new clothing, speculation spread through the camp that enemy troops were not too far away. Several companies of the 12th South Carolina were ordered to conduct an evening picket around Cashtown.[19]

The speculation was valid. A foraging/reconnaissance expedition that day by one of Heth's brigades revealed a Yankee force of unknown size and makeup near Gettysburg, about seven miles away. Little else could be determined. Lee himself was uncertain about the enemy's dispositions or intentions, as he had heard nothing directly from Stuart's cavalry, operating to the east, for at least a week. With his forces still uncomfortably spread apart, Lee responded by ordering his army to concentrate east of South Mountain without delay. The advance of Pender's command to Cashtown was the product of that order.

At 5:00 a.m. on July 1, Heth advanced with his 7,000-man division from around Cashtown toward Gettysburg to determine the enemy force on his front.

19 Dunlop, *Bivouac and Battles (Part V)*, 2; Boyles, *Reminiscences*, 40; Welch, *A Confederate Surgeon's Letters to His Wife*, 61–63; Carter, "Campaign of 1863"; Perrin, "A Little More Light on Gettysburg," 521; Flowerday, "Painting a Picture."

Pender's four Light Division brigades (6,500 or so men total) followed in support, led by Perrin's command. There was evident urgency in the camp, a telltale sign that something was afoot. About 5:00 a.m., the 366 men present for duty in the regiment quickly packed their knapsacks, rolled their bedrolls, and formed without eating breakfast, while those on picket duty double-quicked back to camp. Men fortunate enough to be left with their whiskey rations from the previous evening made sure those were duly consumed.

The air was heavy that humid July morning, and the column waited impatiently for Heth's massive division to vacate in an early mist. Perrin had approximately 2,000 men in five regiments and the recently formed sharpshooter battalion. The sharpshooters, under Capt. William Haskell, would lead the way, followed by the 13th South Carolina, Colonel Miller's 12th, and then the 1st and 14th. Orr's Rifles remained behind to guard the mountain gap as well as the division's immense wagon train. Reports vary about the time of the brigade's departure, but J. F. J. Caldwell recalled that Perrin's men marched off "at once" after falling in "just after daylight." Most likely it was 8:00 a.m., as Maj. Joseph A. Engelhard, Pender's assistant adjutant general, recorded in the Light Division's November 1863 after-action report.[20]

After Pender's command streamed down the mountain through Cashtown—passing the Cashtown Inn, which would serve as headquarters for several Confederate commanders during the campaign—the countryside beyond began to open, featuring a collection of stately homes and orchards. The long, snaking line of gray and butternut troops along the Chambersburg Pike presented a remarkable vista. Behind Heth, the South Carolinians held the front of Pender's advance in the middle of the 13,000–14,000-man column. They had progressed about a mile or two when distant artillery fire began to reverberate from the direction of Gettysburg. With the ominous sound, the usual chatter among the ranks decreased, as men sensed the gravity of the moment, and the column's pace slowed. As the booming to the front increased, couriers on horseback pounded past the column heading toward Cashtown.

The rate of march alternated from there, varying between a regular pace and the double-quick. Regardless, there was no straggling in the ranks. Before long, men saw playing cards scattered alongside the road, an indication that the troops to their front were discarding items that could be deemed scandalous if they were killed in battle and their personal items sent home. About 9:00 a.m., as the

20 Caldwell, *The History of a Brigade of South Carolinians*, 137–138; Dunlop, *Bivouac and Battles (Part V)*, 1; *OR* 27(2):656; Perrin, "A Little More Light on Gettysburg," 521; Crute, *Units of the Confederate Army*, 258.

artillery and small-arms fire intensified ahead, Pender halted the division near what is today the Seven Stars Road, letting the men rest for about an hour. As Heth's men deployed into line of battle, Pender's men quickly filled their canteens.[21]

Under rising temperatures, Pender moved his division again about 10:00 a.m. Heth had James Archer's and Joseph Davis's brigades heavily engaged at this point, with the Federal presence in Gettysburg stronger than believed; it soon became apparent to all that these enemy soldiers were not merely local militia. Boyles noted seeing Federal prisoners headed in their direction under guard as well as numerous civilians, including a woman leading a cow followed by her crying children. He also recalled rapid bursts of artillery and the rattle of musket fire as the regiment splashed across Marsh Creek about three miles from Gettysburg, what he described as sounding like fire in a cane-brake.

Once across Marsh Creek, the column filed to the right and followed a farm path (today's Knoxlyn Road) along the ridgeline. Perrin aligned his brigade along the ridge, fronted his regiments generally facing east and was joined shortly by General Scales's North Carolina brigade; Scales arrayed his men to Perrin's left, resting his left flank at or near the turnpike. Left of the turnpike, Pender deployed General Thomas's Georgia Brigade and General Lane's North Carolinians on Thomas's left. The entire line extended approximately a mile, with the four brigades divided in half by the turnpike.[22]

From their slightly elevated position, Perrin's South Carolinians assessed the surrounding countryside. The undulating ground was mostly open but also featured a few fences, hedges, and narrow bands of timber. Visible in the distance was Herr's Ridge, where Heth had a line of battle advancing. "It was really a magnificent site," a South Carolina surgeon accompanying the column wrote to his wife after the battle.[23]

After Perrin deployed Haskell's sharpshooters as skirmishers on his right, the brigade descended the hill through a band of trees and dressed on Scales's right. The fences, gardens, and hedges were only minor obstacles for the men as they moved ahead slowly, their spacing roughly a half-mile to Heth's rear. About a mile into their advance in this formation, Pender ordered a brief halt, the men soaked in

21 Welch, *A Confederate Surgeon's Letters to His Wife*, 63–64; Thomas Littlejohn, "Recollections of a Confederate Soldier," Manassas National Battlefield Park Collection, copy, Vertical File V7-SC1, Gettysburg National Military Park Library, 5; Caldwell, *The History of a Brigade of South Carolinians*, 137; Carter, "Campaign of 1863"; Perrin, "A Little More Light on Gettysburg," 521.

22 Boyles, *Reminiscences*, 40; Littlejohn, "Recollections," 5; *OR* 27(2):656; John A. Leach to John B. Bachelder, Sept. 12, 1882, in David L. and Audrey J. Ladd, ed., *The Bachelder Papers*, 3 vols. (Dayton, OH, 1994), 2:904 (hereafter cited as *BP*); John A. Leach to John B. Bachelder, *BP* 2:1046.

23 Welch, *A Confederate Surgeon's Letters to His Wife*, 64; *OR* 27(2), 661; *BP* 2:904.

A postwar photograph of the Chambersburg Turnpike just west of Gettysburg. Perrin's Brigade advanced to the right of the turnpike on July 1 toward McPherson's Ridge in the background and beyond that to Seminary Ridge. *Author*

perspiration. As one soldier recalled: "These advances in line of battle are the most fatiguing exercise I had in the army."

Now within range of the enemy's artillery, they endured a continual shower of shell fire. As they waited, the furious thunder of the fighting ahead, particularly the repeated pitch of the famed Rebel yell, was breathtaking. To relieve the tension, some of the men began to eat the rations they had cooked the previous evening. Before long, Lane's North Carolinians arrived from across the turnpike and would be placed on the extreme right of the division, extending the flank previously held by the 13th South Carolina.[24]

* * *

After another half-mile advance to Herr's Ridge, the men halted again, waiting for further orders. The fighting that day had been unexpectedly intense for Heth's division. While conducting a reconnaissance-in-force with Archer's and Davis's brigades, Heth had stumbled into battle still unsure of the forces he faced. The waiting Yankees, in fact, comprised two brigades commanded by Cols. Thomas Devin and William Gamble in Brig. Gen. John Buford's 1st Cavalry Division. As Buford conducted a fighting retreat toward Seminary Ridge by dismounting his men

24 Boyles, *Reminiscences*, 41; *OR* 27(2):661; Caldwell, *The History of a Brigade of South Carolinians*, 138.

and having them fight on foot, Archer and Davis established battle lines on both sides of the Chambersburg Pike—Davis to the left (north) and Archer the right (south).

Confederate expectations, however, that only Federal cavalry was ahead would soon be negated by the arrival of portions of Maj. Gen. John Reynolds's I Corps, in particular, Brig. Gen. Solomon Meredith's famed "Iron Brigade" in Brig. Gen. James Wadsworth's 1st Division. Although Davis enjoyed initial success against New York and Pennsylvania units in Brig. Gen. Lysander Cutler's 2nd Brigade before his brigade was stopped in an unfinished railroad cut, Meredith outdueled Archer's forces on McPherson's Ridge, inflicting approximately 375 casualties. Not only was Archer wounded in the showdown, but he was also among 240 of his men captured. Reynolds, however, was among the critical losses for the Federals, shot in the head and killed as he was shouting orders to his men.

A lull would settle over the battlefield for several hours, but the fighting resumed in the afternoon, with the Confederates gaining the upper hand. The arrival of Ewell's Corps, which had marched that day from Carlisle and York, figured significantly in that development. Lee, who had reached the battlefield by this point, had hoped to avoid an engagement until his entire army had consolidated near Gettysburg. With Ewell's men engaged on Oak Ridge now, Lee authorized Heth to attack with his other two brigades, Brockenbrough's Virginians and Pettigrew's North Carolinians (commanded by Col. James K. Marshall after Heth was wounded and Pettigrew assumed division command).

* * *

At about 4:00 p.m., Pender rode up to Colonel Perrin near the 12th South Carolina's position on the brow of Herr's Ridge to let him know it was time to reinforce Heth's stalled brigades. Perrin's orders were clear: Combined with an advance by Scales's Brigade, the South Carolinians were to sweep forward and contest the Yankees at close range, allowing Heth's battered command to disengage. In doing so, Perrin stressed, the men were to move forward without firing or stopping under any circumstances. There was no doubt Perrin intended to avoid what Dixon Barnes referred to as useless "long taw firing." One fearsome, devastating charge, he hoped, would prove too much for the stubborn enemy force.[25]

Perrin and Scales occupied a pie-shaped area between the Chambersburg Pike and the Fairfield Road, two of the roads that intersected Gettysburg like spokes in a wagon wheel. Hugging the turnpike, Scales advanced through Herbst

25 *OR* 27(2):661; Boyles, *Reminiscences*, 41; Perrin, "A Little More Light on Gettysburg," 521–522; Brown, *A Colonel at Gettysburg and Spotsylvania*, 77.

Woods (commonly called McPherson's Woods) and up McPherson's Ridge while Perrin occupied the undulating terrain to Scales's right adjacent to the Fairfield Road, with the 14th, 1st, 12th, and 13th South Carolina deployed from left to right. Lanes's Brigade was to Perrin's right, on the other side of the Fairfield Road. Ideally, the Tar Heels were in position to support the 12th and 13th if they became engaged. Because they remained out of sight during the advance, however, Perrin was uncertain whether the support was there. As the advance commenced, Lane's Brigade was not connected to the brigade's right flank regiment, the 13th South Carolina.

His sword drawn, Colonel Miller led the 12th off Herr's Ridge a little after 4:00 p.m. The regiment "advanced through an open field across the small stream [Willoughby Run]," Captain Dunlop recalled, "and mounted the smooth hill beyond." Wounded men from Pettigrew's Brigade headed in their direction, joined by elements of Archer's command from the morning fighting, who were in the same vicinity.

In the ravine leading to Willoughby Run, Perrin halted the brigade to redress his lines and to reiterate that the men were not to fire as they advanced. Engaged ahead were Heth's exhausted troops, and beyond that stood the Lutheran Theological Seminary building astride what was known as Seminary Ridge. Making a stand in an open field about halfway between the advancing Confederates and the Seminary building were stubborn fragments of the Iron Brigade and Colonels Chapman Biddle's and Roy Stone's brigades from Maj. Gen. Abner Doubleday's 3rd Division. Behind the ragged Federal line and west of the Seminary were hastily constructed breastworks as well as a stone wall that extended south from those works along the crest of the ridge.

Resuming the advance, the men of the 12th and 13th passed Emmanuel Harman's burning farmhouse (sometimes spelled Harmon) before crossing the stream. On the slight rise just beyond, they soon found themselves amid soldiers in Pettigrew's Brigade, participants in the afternoon clash with the Iron Brigade. "The field was thick with wounded hurrying to the rear, and the ground was grey with dead and disabled," J. F. J. Caldwell recalled. Private Thomas A. Littlejohn of the 13th South Carolina later wrote that some Tar Heels vowed "we would all be killed if we went forward." With extensive casualties, the sense of disillusion on those soldiers' part was perhaps forgivable, as the Federals had pulled back and established a relatively strong position on Seminary Ridge, aided by the arrival of fresh artillery. But the battle's tide had begun to turn with the arrival of Pender's Division and units from Ewell's Second Corps. At about the same time, Early's forces were overwhelming Howard's XI Corps north of Gettysburg, forcing a retreat toward Culp's Hill and Cemetery Hill, and Rodes's victory on Oak Ridge to

Pender's left soon gave the Confederates' control of the battlefield north and east of the town. The Federal holdouts were clinging to their tenuous Seminary Ridge line directly ahead of the South Carolinians.

Despite the warnings, the 12th and 13th continued their advance, even opening their ranks to allow some of Pettigrew's survivors through. Given the contours of the ground, the 14th and 1st South Carolina drifted left toward Scales and the turnpike while the 12th and 13th gravitated somewhat toward the Fairfield Road as the line advanced.[26]

As the 12th ascended the rise beyond the creek, it came within sight of a ragged line of Federal infantry from the Chambersburg Pike extending to the right nearly to the Fairfield Road. It also came within range of the Federal artillery posted along Seminary Ridge north of the turnpike as well as artillery posted near the Seminary to their front. Dunlop noted that the enemy guns unleashed "with fearful accuracy" an assortment of shot, shell, canister, and grapeshot at the 12th, both direct and enfilade. Recalled another soldier: "We advanced through a wood and up a hill at the top of the hill we came into an open field where we were saluted by a volley of grape and canister from a battery on our left."

Men began to fall as the regiment crested the rise. Capt. John A. Hinnant, commanding Company C, went down with grapeshot in his left leg, and Robert Hagins of Company H and Lt. R. L. Simmons of Company B, along with dozens of others, met a similar fate. Despite the artillery fire, the 12th did not falter as it steadily advanced about 200 yards, abiding by the order not to fire. Boyles, now in command of Company C because of Hinnant's wounding, went down with his own severe wound during the onslaught. "I received a grape shot in my right leg below the knee, which shattered the bone into splinters, the shoe on that foot flying off some distance," he recalled. Two comrades, John Robertson and Jim Williamson, would be wounded in short succession, too.

"Here, we met the most destructive fire of musketry, grape & canister I have ever been exposed to during the war," remembered Perrin, who had advanced mounted at the rear of the regiment. The artillery and small-arms fire not only checked the South Carolinians, it also put them in danger of relinquishing the position. Ahead of the 12th, arrayed from left to right, were the 142nd Pennsylvania, 80th New York, and 121st Pennsylvania in Biddle's brigade, and shortly, Lt. Col. George McFarland's 151st Pennsylvania arrived, deploying to the 142nd's right. For the 12th at least, it was clear that remaining stagnant in the field without firing was no longer an option. Colonel Miller finally ordered his men to shoot, and the

26 Dunlop, *Bivouac and Battles (Part V)*, 1; Littlejohn, "Recollections," 4; *OR* 27(2):661; *BP* 2:904, 1046. Brown, *A Colonel at Gettysburg and Spotsylvania*, 78–79.

sudden volley felled several enemy soldiers. McFarland's arrival had bolstered the Union position, and the additional fire had the 12th and 13th South Carolina in danger. Miller and Colonel Brockman of the 13th ordered an immediate response. The 12th's response was particularly notable, as the regiment's left companies fired obliquely toward the 151st Pennsylvania and 142nd New York, with the right companies doing likewise against the 80th New York and 121st Pennsylvania to the right. The 151st's casualty count was heavy, McFarland conceding that the 12th's return fire was "at least two to one, was very severe and destructive, and my gallant officers and men fell thick and fast."

Embroiled in a desperate standoff, Perrin knew he needed help from Scales to his left. As they emerged from Herbst Woods, however, Scales's North Carolinians faltered, hesitated, and then halted under the withering Federal artillery fire that ripped through their ranks from near the Chambersburg Pike. Without Scales's support, the 12th and the other regiments in Perrin's command began to waver in the face of additional artillery coming from near a farm lane with rail fencing on their left front. Rather than ordering a retreat or staying in place, Perrin resolved that a hasty charge was his best option. Drawing his sword, he yelled "Forward!" and spurred his horse through the gap between the 1st and 12th. With a round of cheers, the South Carolinians dashed forward behind their battle flags.

Perrin's fortitude would be the turning point on this portion of the field. "This action gave new life to the brigade," wrote Boyles, who watched the drama unfold as he lay on the ground writhing in pain and shock. The sight of the charging Confederates compelled a wide retreat for Seminary Ridge, where Federals took position behind the breastworks and stone wall. The disorganized ranks of the three Pennsylvania regiments and the 80th New York became a shooting gallery for the pursuing South Carolinians—"crushing," conceded Maj. Alexander Biddle of the 121st Pennsylvania, who lamented that his "ranks were broken and became massed together" as they fled.

At this time, however, dismounted Union troopers of Col. William Gamble's brigade (the 8th New York, 12th New York, and 3rd Indiana) congregated behind a stone wall in a skirt of trees to the far right of the Seminary on the other side of the Fairfield Road. As the Union infantry established defensive positions on the western fringes of the Seminary grounds, the artillery continued its deadly work on Perrin's men. Within minutes, the re-formed Federal infantry to the front and Gamble's dismounted cavalry on the Confederate right poured small-arms fire into the 13th and 12th South Carolina from behind the stone wall.

Colonel Miller took a moment to re-dress the 12th's line. Soon, the brigade moved forward once more. While the 14th and 1st South Carolina on the left received the brunt of the artillery fire from across the turnpike during the advance,

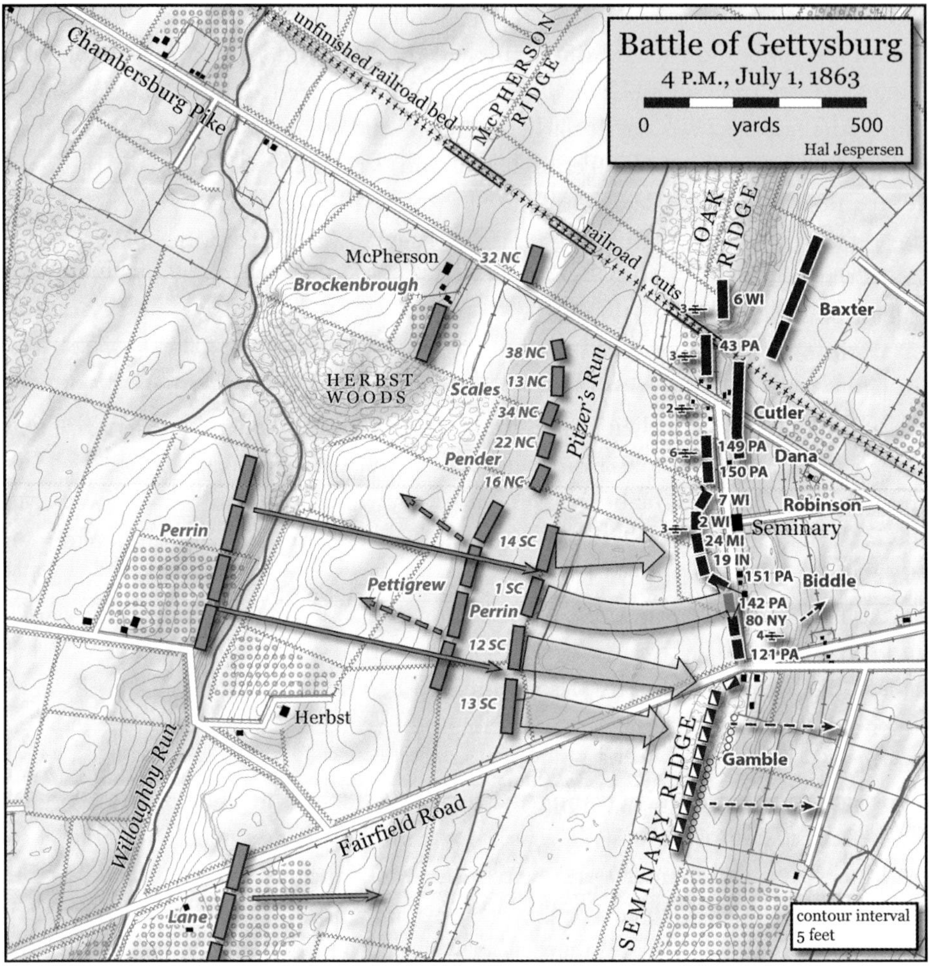

the 12th and 13th staggered under the blistering fire of Gamble's troopers and Biddle's infantry, taking heavy casualties. "We opened a sharp and rapid carbine fire, which killed and wounded so many of the first line of the enemy, that it fell back," Gamble wrote in his after-action report.

Pressing on through the enemy fire, many of the men threw off their knapsacks and bedrolls to help maintain their strength and momentum in the stifling heat. Then, within 200 yards of the Seminary, the 12th and 13th were slammed by a hail of bullets and artillery. "They began throwing grapeshot at us by the bushel it seems," one soldier recalled.

The deluge for the 14th on the far left, mostly small-arms fire, was even worse. Assessing the casualty count after the battle, Perrin grieved: "[I]t looked to us as though this regiment was entirely destroyed." Though stationed well behind the lines, a surgeon in the 13th South Carolina could distinctly hear the fighting's fury, noting in a letter to his wife that "such a rattle of musketry I never heard surpassed."

The Light Division continued its determined push on the Federal position, but as men fell and the fog of war grew thicker, the gaps between the regiments became more pronounced, affecting the alignment both in Perrin's command and the division as a whole. Two of the three Light Division Brigades intended to take part in the advance were of little to no assistance to the four regiments of Perrin's Brigade. James Lane's Brigade, supposedly covering Perrin's right flank on the other side of the Fairfield Road by engaging with and defeating Gamble's dismounted cavalry at a low stone wall on Seminary Ridge, lagged far behind at this critical moment due to an unconfirmed threat of lurking enemy troopers on his right. Alfred Scales's Brigade, on Perrin's left flank, had done an admirable job keeping pace with the South Carolinians initially, but were beginning to receive devasting short range fire by Federal artillery along the Chambersburg Pike which compelled it to halt. The lack of support from Lane combined with the trouble that Scales's Brigade faced as it emerged from the Herbst Woods would impact the assault's effectiveness.

Only Perrin's four regiments remained an operational fighting force and they would have to go it alone if Seminary Ridge was going to be taken. "Lane's Brigade never came up at all," Perrin wrote bitterly after the battle, meaning the 8th New York, 12th New York, and 3rd Indiana Cavalry, armed with breach-loading carbines, could keep their attention exclusively on the 13th and 12th. The enfilade fire on 13th's right flank, in fact, limited the regiments' effectiveness, and it was forced to halt for a moment. Wrote Buford in his after-action report: "My troops at this place had partial shelter behind a low stone fence, and were in short carbine range. Their fire was perfectly terrific."

As it waited for the lagging 13th to catch up, the 12th endured another onslaught of fire on its right. "There was no giving back or wavering exhibited by any of the 12th, but rushed forward leaving its supports behind," recalled a soldier in Company I's Lancaster Hornets. His commanding officer, Lt. William J. Stover, exhorted the men to press on, which drew praise from one soldier: "There is no officer more worthy of notice."

Company B held the regiment's right flank, with Company K to its immediate left. To counter their isolated position due to the 13th's temporary halt and the salvos from Gamble's men, Dunlop quickly wheeled those two companies to the right and began firing volleys in return, hoping it would buy time for the 13th to come up. James Ware, James Brigman, John Quinton, and J. H. Smith were among members of Company B to fall once Dunlop made his right turn. In the center of the regiment, volleys from Biddle's three regiments felled two color-bearers. As the 12th's flag fell to the ground, Sgt. S. H. Huey, a file closer in Company I, rushed forward and seized the standard, holding it high and waving it defiantly at the Yankees. In the heat of combat, the ranks inevitably opened, with the regiment soon resembling more of a strong skirmish line than a shoulder-to-shoulder, two-rank line of battle.

The 13th South Carolina finally caught up to their comrades in the 12th, and the regiments began trading fire with the Yankees on their front and to the right. To their left, however, a plank fence forced the 1st to oblique right before executing a "change front forward on the left"—undeniably a difficult maneuver on a drill field, let alone under fire on a battlefield. Now angled to the left of the Federal infantry and artillery positioned near the Seminary, the 1st fired away, getting timely support from remnants of the 14th South Carolina. With this onslaught from close range, the rout was on; Federal infantry and artillery soon began a desperate scramble toward Gettysburg. A rally by some Yankees troops at the stone wall on Seminary Ridge was quickly squelched as well, and the 1st and 14th joined in an energetic pursuit down the Chambersburg Pike.

Hundreds of prisoners were captured during the chase, which would halt near the town square. Meanwhile on the brigade's right, the 12th and 13th continued to slug it out with Gamble's troopers and elements of the 80th New York and the 121st, 142nd, and 151st Pennsylvania. Another critical moment had arrived. The stand conducted by the 12th and 13th resulted in a deadly impasse, accomplishing little other than mutual destruction. With the 1st and 14th South Carolina now on the heels of Yankees fleeing into Gettysburg and other Federal units beginning to fall back, Perrin conferred with Colonels Miller and Brockman, convinced that another charge was necessary to finish this clash. Perrin directed Miller and Brockman to march their respective regiments at an oblique angle to the right to engage Gamble's troopers at close range. That, he believed, would give his men a foothold on their flank and drive a wedge between Gamble and Biddle. "[T]hese two regiments had necessarily to change direction to the right somewhat, as to meet the enemy full in front," Perrin would note.

Miller and Brockman responded to the order without hesitation. Whether intended or not, as the left regiment of the two, the 12th obliqued and charged right at a harder angle, reaching the stone wall near the Fairfield Road first. With that, it was able to effectively pour galling fire into Gamble's unprotected right flank. As the Federal troopers focused on stopping Miller's onslaught, the 13th hit the position more directly in front, spurring another mad retreat across the fields south and west of Gettysburg. The South Carolinians would pay a price, however. Sergeant Huey, still bearing the 12th's colors, was struck down with a severe wound to his neck. Anthony Raines of Company C grabbed the standard

A view of the Chambersburg Turnpike looking east toward Gettysburg. As the Federal line on Seminary Ridge disintegrated, the 1st and 14th South Carolina chased the retreating Union troops toward Gettysburg down this road while the 12th and 13th South Carolina drove off the troopers of William Gamble's cavalry brigade several hundred yards to the right of this photograph. *Library of Congress*

from the ground but was promptly killed. The 12th would lose six color-bearers during an engagement that lasted 15–20 minutes: four killed, two wounded.

As Perrin hoped, the attack was so quick and intense, and the movement so unexpected, that Biddle preemptively ordered a retreat through the Seminary grounds rather than risk a subsequent assault on his regiments. "Our entire line now swept down the hill in pursuit of the fleeing enemy and across the field into the city," Dunlop recalled. "The enemy took refuge upon Cemetery Hill, a strong position south of town." The combined strength of the 12th and 13th during that last push has not been determined, but it is unlikely it exceeded 300–400 men. Gamble nevertheless asserted that his command was forced back from the stone wall by "overwhelming numbers."[27]

The defeat was total. "Now the Yankees limbered up about thirty pieces of artillery and moved off with it within plain view of us & the Yankee infantry literally swarmed through the streets of Gettysburg," Perrin would glowingly recall. While the 12th and 13th warmly chased the defeated Federal cavalry, the 1st and 14th South Carolina poured into town via the Chambersburg Pike, with

27 Boyles, *Reminiscences*, 41; Dunlop, *Bivouac and Battles (Part V)*, 1; *OR*, 27(1):323, 330; *OR* 27(2):661–662, 665; Michael C. Hardy, *General Lee's Immortals—The Battles and Campaigns of the Branch-Lane Brigade in the Army of Northern Virginia, 1861–1865* (El Dorado Hills, CA, 2018), 221–222; Hoyt, Recollections and *Reminiscences*, 6:284; Welch, *A Confederate Surgeon's Letters to His Wife*, 65; Littlejohn, "Recollections," 6; LOCAL, "For the Lancaster Ledger," *Lancaster Ledger*, July 22, 1863, 2; *OR* 27(1):927, 934, 315, 327; Boyles, *Reminiscences*, 62; Perrin, "A Little More Light on Gettysburg," 522–523; Brown, *A Colonel at Gettysburg and Spotsylvania*, 82, 85.

small firefights erupting in the streets that resulted in either capture or death for clusters of troops from Stone's and Biddle's brigades. Adding to the Federal army's misfortune was the concurrent rout to the northeast of town by Early's Division in Ewell's Corps. Perrin could take immense pride in the performance of his four regiments, with the 12th South Carolina clearly carrying its share of the load. Not since Sharpsburg, when the intrepid Col. Dixon Barnes was in command, had the regiment shown such offensive efficacy during a pitched battle and routed an enemy so thoroughly.

Not all who watched the South Carolinians in action, however, felt assured of victory. As the brigade disappeared from Seminary Ridge and out of view from his vantage point to the rear, an anxious Dorsey Pender wondered aloud whether it had met destruction or capture. The general spurred his horse across the stream searching for any information he could obtain. Encountering Lieutenant Simmons of Company B, wounded and headed toward the rear, Pender asked whether the brigade had indeed suffered misfortune. "No," Simmons replied, "it is over the hill yonder." Kicking his mount in the side, "Dorsey" galloped fiercely ahead to find his victorious men and share in their triumph.

* * *

As the next two days revealed, Perrin's charge up the slope toward Seminary Ridge that afternoon was one of the few bright spots in the Confederate effort at Gettysburg. The assaulting troops of the 1st, 12th, 13th, and 14th South Carolina regiments were disciplined and aggressive, carried out difficult orders at the regimental and company level, and dislodged the enemy from strong defensive positions. In truth, Perrin's brigade fought as two separate commands that afternoon, with the 12th and 13th on the right and the 1st and 14th on the left. Each regiment had to react to changing tactical conditions and carry out difficult maneuvers in the face of tremendous fire.

The charge of the South Carolinians elicited high praise from at least one Federal commander, Col. Charles Wainwright, who wrote with admiration in his journal: "Never have I seen such a charge. Not a man seemed to falter. Lee may well be proud of his infantry; I wish ours was equal to it."

The 12th had performed well and done its share under its new colonel, John Miller. In his after-action report, Perrin praised both Maj. Edwin Bookter and Capt. T. F. Clyburn, commanding Company E. Of Bookter, Perrin wrote: "I remarked particularly the cool and gallant conduct bearing of Major Bookter, and the force and judgment with which he managed the men under his control." Clyburn was cited for acting with "uncommonly good conduct in the action."

In addition to hundreds of prisoners, the brigade captured thousands of small arms, two field pieces, several caissons, and four flags, including a I Corps standard and a "beautiful" flag of the 104th New York. According to Perrin, the success could have been greater had support or reinforcements been available to continue the pursuit to Cemetery Hill, where the Federals had begun to establish a stronger line with the Seminary Ridge position overtaken. In private correspondence just a few weeks after the battle, Perrin wrote that Pender immediately realized that it was urgent for the Confederates to augment the hard-earned victory with an organized pursuit. "The very batteries which we had run off & which we saw them take off through Gettysburg were the first to form a line of battle at their new position," Perrin admitted. "The first shell fired by them from that position was aimed at my brigade."

With time critical, Pender sent word to the rear requesting that Maj. Gen. Richard Anderson's Division, resting on Herr's Ridge, come forward and engage. "I suppose," Perrin wrote shortly after the battle to the governor of South Carolina, "you will be curious to know where Anderson was & why he was out of the way at so important of a juncture. His failure to be up was the cause of the failure of the campaign. . . . [I]t may have been Gen Hill's fault & it may have been the fault of Anderson himself."

Perrin also did not withhold his feelings about Longstreet, writing that Lee's old warhorse "as usual was out of the way and was not seen on the field until the next day."

Without support and with the sun setting, Perrin recalled the two halves of the brigade to the Seminary grounds. With the four regiments reunited, Perrin ordered detachments from each to scour the area for prisoners. As the brigade assembled and took stock of its losses (approximately 500 men total), Pender rode among the troops. In a somber tribute, he raised his hat and complimented Perrin on his men's performance. As he passed the 12th near the Fairfield Road, Pender specifically sought out Miller, then holding a meeting with Lt. Col. Henry Davis and a few other officers. "Colonel," he remarked, "this brigade has done the fighting for my division, in vain I have endeavored to bring up the remainder of my command." Although Pender did not formally castigate the efforts of Lane's and Scales's Tar Heels, his disappointment at that moment was unmistakable. The weary men of the 12th responded with "three hearty cheers" for the commander, a man whom many had looked upon with manifest apprehension when he assumed command of the Light Division in May.

Shortly after Pender's sortie among the ranks, troops of Maj. Gen. Robert E. Rodes's Division in Ewell's Corps marched toward Seminary Ridge from the north. In their wake was none other than Robert E. Lee, who would praise the decimated regiments before him as "the South Carolina brigade that captured

Gettysburg." Indeed, the commanding general had only a few moments earlier congratulated Pender on the victory and in doing so had erroneously credited the Tar Heel troops for taking the ridge by stating, "All honor to the noble North Carolinians." Pender, no doubt embarrassed at having to correct Lee and reverse an honor bestowed on his native state in the same breath, nevertheless set the record straight: "Permit me, General, to correct an error—the brave *South* Carolinians saved my division to-day."

* * *

The brigade was allowed only a brief rest east of the Seminary and adjacent to the Fairfield Road. It would not be long, however, before the men were ordered to form and move a short distance across the Fairfield Road, placed in a line of battle facing east behind the skirt of trees and stone fence that Gamble's troopers had occupied earlier that day. The 12th was posted directly south of the road, with the 13th, 14th, and 1st extended in that order to the right (south), with the right-most regiments positioned near the McMillan House and what the men described as a "fine orchard." Aligned a few hundred yards to the 12th's left, just across the Fairfield Road, was Junius Daniels's North Carolina Brigade of Ewell's Corps.

As the men settled down for the evening, Perrin ordered his battalion of sharpshooters forward about 300 yards, directing them to take position behind a rail fence in an open field. Sleep would be a challenge amid the constant rumble of supply wagons and artillery caissons, not to mention mounted couriers pounding up and down the line delivering orders to and from Lee at his nearby headquarters on the turnpike. Supply wagons would traverse almost to the front lines, delivering ammunition and rations.[28]

The day had not been kind to Lieutenant Boyles. His experience that day was a microcosm of what many wounded would endure and the care received in field hospitals behind the lines. The severe artillery wound Boyles received had shattered his leg, and he lay helpless in the July heat for some time on the ground between Willoughby Run and Seminary Ridge as bullets and shells fell around him. Desperate for water, he could only wait for the infirmary corps to come to his aid. Two orderlies finally arrived; however, they were without a stretcher. Losing blood and anxious to get to the rear, Boyles directed the duo to grab two sturdy sticks from

28 *OR* 27(2):662–663; Caldwell, *The History of a Brigade of South Carolinians*, 140; John Bachelder, Gettysburg Battlefield Map (New York: Endicott & Co. Lith.); Littlejohn, "Recollections," 7; LOCAL, "For the Lancaster Ledger," *Lancaster Ledger*, Sept. 16, 1863, 2; D. "Camp Notes," *Abbeville Press*, Aug. 7, 1863, 1; *OR* 27(1): 3, 30, 318, 934; Perrin, "A Little More Light on Gettysburg," 522–533; Brown, *A Colonel at Gettysburg and Spotsylvania*, 72, 82–83, 86.

the nearby brush, cut his sword belt into straps, and tie his blanket to the poles as an ad-hoc stretcher. As they approached Willoughby Run, Boyles begged them to lay him in the water to cool off. "[F]or a time, my life's blood caused the water to run red," he would write after the war. "I knew that if I lived I was ruined forever."

Placing him back on the makeshift stretcher, the orderlies carried Boyle about a half-mile farther to Herr's Ridge, coming upon an entire division of fresh Confederate troops with stacked arms—"cooking and eating, as if nothing was going on, while our poor boys were catching death at every step," he bitterly recalled. Those troops belonged to Anderson's Division, the same troops Pender had requested to come forward and continue the fight. After locating a surgeon, Boyles was informed that the hospital for Pender's Division was another three miles to the rear, roughly halfway to Cashtown. With all ambulances in use on other areas of the field, the kind surgeon procured a small wagon and sent Boyles along the Chambersburg Pike for care.[29]

At the hospital, set up near Andrew Heintzelman's tavern on the Chambersburg Pike, not far from Marsh Creek, Boyles would be laid on a pile of straw. As he waited in almost unbearable agony for attention, he had serious apprehensions about the quality of treatment he would likely receive from the 12th's surgeon, Dr. Bailey. Knowing amputation of his mangled leg was a certainty, Boyles made it clear he wanted the brigade surgeon, Dr. Thomas Evins, to perform the operation and not Bailey, who had a poor reputation and a fondness for the bottle. As tears streamed down his cheeks, the young lieutenant implored Evins to perform the operation, and Evins promised he would. "I was given something and laid out until next afternoon," Boyles would write. "Was too near dead to know how the night passed."

Amid the moans and cries of the wounded, the hospital's brigade and regimental surgeons worked methodically all evening and throughout the next day, the amputation of limbs their prime objective. Boyles vividly recalled the loss of his leg: "The next day I was lifted upon a table, which roused me a little, chloroform was placed to my nostrils and I felt as if I rose up and flew away. When I next remembered anything, I was on a pile of straw on my back in a tent, my right leg gone; some parties were whispering that I was gone, no chance for me; I felt that my time had come and was resigned to my fate."

* * *

As Boyles and the other wounded received treatment at the field hospital, their comrades in the 12th South Carolina rested as best they could in their bivouac astride

29 Boyles, *Reminiscences*, 41–42.

the Fairfield Road. That night, the Army of the Potomac strengthened its defensive positions on Cemetery Hill and Culp's Hill and along Cemetery Ridge, roughly a mile from where Perrin's command was camped. Despite putting Union forces to flight on July 1, the Army of Northern Virginia's failure to occupy the elevated ground south of Gettysburg, allowing the Yankees to fortify several strong positions, proved decisive. After Meade conferred with his generals, he decided to prolong the fight at Gettysburg. With fresh troops arriving continually, the high ground in and around Cemetery Hill became a metaphorical Gibraltar for the Union army.

As the weary men of the regiment awoke on July 2, Miller formed the regiment—now at half strength—into a line of battle and moved it directly behind the stone wall on Seminary Ridge. From this position, across a mile of sloping pasture, the men could see clearly the enemy positions on Cemetery Hill and Cemetery Ridge, bisected by the Emmitsburg Road. It was evident the Yankees were reinforcing and aimed to fight. At about sunrise, Federal batteries across the field began firing. Limited fighting broke out as well. Union skirmishers in a farm lane several hundred yards from the Confederate lines on Seminary Ridge engaged Captain Haskell's sharpshooter battalion which Perrin had operating in front of the brigade. The sharpshooters, Dunlop recalled, responded "defiantly" and, with aid from Confederate artillery on Seminary Ridge, joined in the fight. The Federal guns on Cemetery Hill managed only "small" damage to the brigade during the barrage, but the loss for the sharpshooters proved more severe.[30]

As the morning progressed, troops in Longstreet's Corps arrived in the South Carolinians' rear and eventually shifted to Hill's right (south) to prepare for an attack Lee had ordered on the Federals' purportedly vulnerable left flank. Hill's Corps now occupied Lee's center, flanked on the right by Longstreet and by Ewell north of town opposite Culp's Hill and Cemetery Hill.

The skirmishing between the Federals in the farm lane and the sharpshooters would continue all morning. Eventually the Federals in the lane began targeting Confederate artillerists with long-range rifles, prompting additional response by Perrin. About 1:00 p.m., the colonel summoned Dunlop, who recalled that Perrin instructed him to "take Companies B & K of the 12th regiment, reinforce the sharpshooters, and drive those fellows out of the lane." The order, Dunlop wrote, came not from Miller but directly from Perrin, complete with unadorned reassurance: "I know you will do it."[31]

30 Littlejohn, "Recollections," 8; Kent Masterson Brown, *Retreat From Gettysburg* (Chapel Hill, NC, 2005), 57; D. Augustus Dickert, *History of Kershaw's Brigade* (Dayton, OH, 1973), 231–232; Welch, *A Confederate Surgeon's Letters to His Wife*, 67–68; Dunlop, *Bivouac and Battles (Part V)*, 1.

31 Dunlop, *Bivouac and Battles (Part V)*, 1; *OR* 27(1):457.

Captain Dunlop was a seasoned officer who had fought in each of the 12th's engagements thus far. As he called Companies B and K to attention, he scanned the area to his front. Haskell's sharpshooters were several hundred yards forward, posted behind a snake-rail fence. Dunlop ordered the two companies over the stone wall and quickly deployed them into a skirmish line. "Moving slowly we advanced down the hill through a shower of whistling bullets and bursting shells until we got nearly to the fence where the sharpshooters lay," he recalled.

Reaching the snake-rail fence, the men crouched alongside the sharpshooters. They had no time even to catch their breath before a "double quick" sounded, and the entire contingent swarmed over the fence and down the hill, plowing headlong into the lane. The strike caught the Federals by surprise, leading to a frantic retreat to the Federal lines on western Cemetery Hill. These men, troops of the 4th Ohio, redeployed along the Emmitsburg Road, using fence railings, barns, and other outbuildings for protection. "An incessant fusillade was kept up between the opposing skirmish lines from this time forth," Dunlop recalled, "and repeatedly during the day their line was heavily reinforced and advanced to drive us from the position, but we held it the live-long day."

The skirmishing with the Ohioans gradually thinned the ranks of Dunlop's two-company command, already at reduced strength due to the previous day's fight. Eventually, the 8th Ohio advanced from Cemetery Hill and fed two of its companies into the skirmish as well. By day's end, Dunlop's command had suffered significantly. Among the killed was Cpl. I. T. Brown of Company B and Haskell, the sharpshooter battalion's commander.

About 6:00 p.m., as Longstreet's attack to the south was in full swing, Perrin ordered Major McCreary to take the 1st South Carolina (reduced to only about 100 men) forward to reinforce the Confederate force in the farm lane.[32]

By nightfall, Confederate momentum across the battlefield had been blunted, the prospect of victory for both armies still very much in the balance. Through a combination of factors, Longstreet's attack on the Confederate right had veered off course and had met stiff resistance in the Peach Orchard, Wheatfield, and on Little Round Top, and had also finally been stalled well short of its intended target on Cemetery Ridge. Longstreet's inability to drive in the Federal flank started a domino effect along Lee's entire line along Seminary Ridge. General Richard Anderson's supporting division of Hill's Corps started its attack but it broke down in plain view of the South Carolinians' position on Seminary Ridge. This breakdown, in turn, stalled the Confederate effort in the center of Lee's line. In an attack on the Confederate left, troops in General Johnson's Division of Ewell's

32 Dunlop, *Bivouac and Battles (Part V)*, 1; *OR* 27(2):663; *OR* 27(1):456–457.

Corps had breached the Union line on lower Cemetery Hill and taken a portion of the Federal works, though they could not reach the summit. Jubal Early's assault on East Cemetery Hill had initial success but was defeated in large part by the failure of Rodes to get his division deployed in a timely manner to support him. Deficient coordination, strong Federal leadership, tenacious Union troops, and a lack of support had deprived Lee of victory across the field.

At the height of those final assaults, the Light Division would suffer another incalculable loss. As General Pender prepared to send his men forward to support the Confederate offensive, he was hit in the leg by a shell fragment and knocked out of action. The wound proved mortal; he would die on July 18 in Staunton, Virginia, shortly after surgeons amputated his wounded leg.

Command of the Light Division fell to General Lane, who, without delay after Pender's wounding, attempted to support Ewell's attack against Cemetery Hill by ordering Thomas's Georgians and the rest of Perrin's command forward and into the farm lane on their front. About 10:00 p.m., Perrin moved his men to the right of Brig. Gen. Stephen D. Ramseur's Brigade in Rodes's Division. It was too late, however, for any real fighting. One 13th South Carolina soldier noted that the farm lane they occupied was closer to Seminary Ridge than the Federal line on Cemetery Ridge, though it actually was about equidistant between the two. From left to right, Perrin posted his regiments: the 12th, 13th, 14th, and 1st.[33]

After posting the brigade, Perrin had Dunlop and Companies B and K withdraw to an unoccupied redoubt 600 yards to the rear, where they could rest and finally

33 *OR* 27(2):659, 663; Littlejohn, "Recollections," 8; Brown, *A Colonel at Gettysburg and Spotsylvania*, 85–86. The author's interpretation of the order of regiments for Perrin's brigade in the farm lane (now known as "Long Lane") is based on two main factors. It appears that the 12th South Carolina spent the evening of July 1 on the very left of the brigade near the corner of present-day Confederate Avenue and Fairfield Road. This is the exact location where the regiment ended its fight with Gamble's dismounted troopers. It seems logical that the 13th South Carolina camped to the immediate south of the 12th extending toward the McMillan Woods based on its relative position to the 12th during the battle and where that regiment ended its respective fight with Gamble. Those regiments were closer to this area after the first day's battle. With the 1st and 14th being the last to rejoin the brigade after their forays into Gettysburg, it appears that they were formed up near the Seminary after their extrication from the town, with the 1st assuming its relative position to the right of the 14th when they formed facing east. When those two regiments faced right and marched down past the 12th and 13th across the Fairfield Road, they halted nearer the McMillan house and orchard and fronted toward Cemetery Hill (the 1st on the right of the brigade and the 14th to its left). Essentially, the wings of the brigade swapped positions for the rest of the battle; the 1st and 14th holding the brigade's right flank and the 12th and 13th holding its left. This order was preserved all day on July 2 as there are no accounts of the regiments shifting positions. When they were moved forward into Long Lane on the evening of July 2, the regiments kept these relative positions, which is consistent with the Bachelder Isometric Map with one exception: Bachelder identifies the 11th South Carolina as being in line. That was not possible, as the 11th was not part of the brigade. Taking the 11th out of the line, the regimental order is consistent with the analysis above.

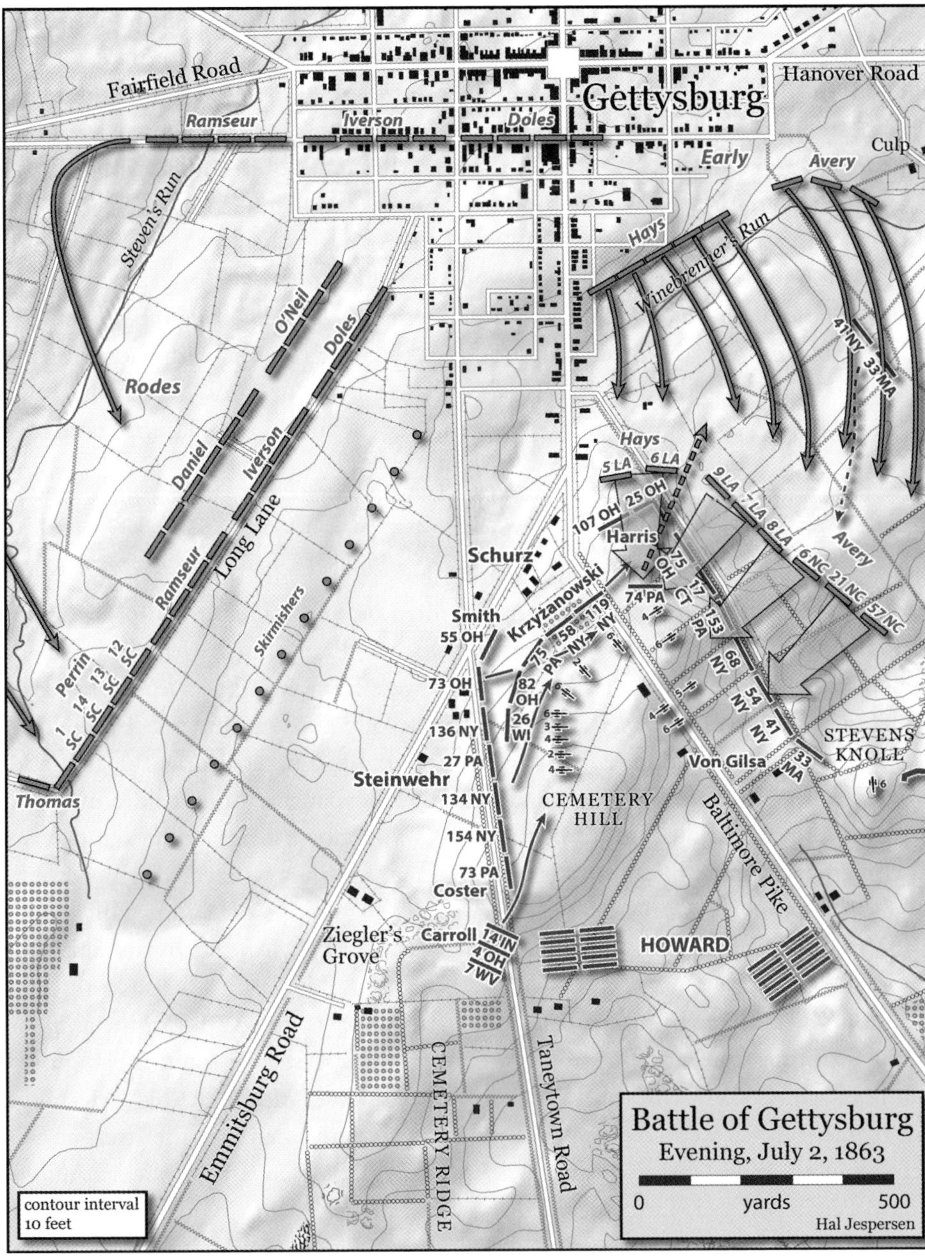

clean their weapons which were in rough shape from the sustained fighting that day. Several men carried unserviceable rifles with rounds still tamped at the bottom of the bore. One such soldier was Pvt. R. A. Mullineaux of Company B, who attempted to resolve the problem by inserting a ball screw down the barrel and into the ball itself, hoping that would dislodge it, to be pulled out with his ramrod. The ball, however, remained lodged. Seeking help, Mullineaux asked a comrade to hold the butt of the rifle while he pulled on the ramrod, only to have the rifle discharge unexpectedly as he did so. Mullineaux screamed in pain, Dunlop reported, as both the ramrod and ball passed "squarely through the center of his body." Even worse, the end of the ramrod broke off and struck another soldier, George Sherrer, in the head, causing a severe wound. As surprised comrades rushed to Mullineaux's aid, Dunlop found that the ramrod had passed partially through the private's body. He would die that evening, and Sherrer's head wound never fully healed. By this point of the war, however, the men found it easier to come to grips with these horrific moments. Life would go on as usual. "We cleaned our guns, replenished our cartridge boxes and returned to the front early in the morning," Dunlop recalled.[34]

* * *

At dawn on July 3, the South Carolinians rose in the dusty farm lane that had been their home overnight, later described by one soldier as simply a "worn out" roadway. To their front was the Emmitsburg Road, lined with a number of Federal skirmishers. On their immediate left were Ramseur's Brigade and Iverson's and Doles's brigades in Ewell's Corps, and beyond those units was the town of Gettysburg. Meanwhile, to Perrin's immediate right, hunkered down in the lane, were General Thomas's Georgians, adjacent to an expansive, open field. Given the proximity to the Yankee position, the men pulled down fence railings and posts to construct breastworks along the embankment. As they worked, the men could hear the fighting between the Federals and Ewell's troops on Culp's Hill, and a 13th South Carolina soldier recalled artillery fire over their heads in the direction of Seminary Ridge.[35]

Long-distance fighting broke out that morning to the 12th's front, and the South Carolinians began firing from the lane with "increased vigor and effect," noted Dunlop, whose command had rejoined the regiment. Although this long-range engagement never evolved into a pitched battle, it continued into the afternoon—according to Perrin, "the "heaviest skirmishing I have ever witnessed." At one point, Perrin ordered skirmishers from each of his regiments to advance from the lane to feel the enemy. Miller assigned that duty to Lieutenant Stover's Company I.

34 Dunlop, *Bivouac and Battles (Part V)*, 1.

35 Ibid.; Littlejohn, "Recollections," 8; John Bachelder Map.

In response, the Federals massed for an assault and drove the skirmishers back. In the process, several Lancaster Hornets from Company I were shot. Lieutenant Pogue of Company H, one of the sharpshooter company commanders and the regiment's former adjutant, would be killed as well. Perrin then advanced the 14th South Carolina to check the oncoming Federals, which he later wrote they did "in the most gallant style." These spirited clashes notwithstanding, the majority of the brigade, including the 12th, remained in position in the farm lane and traded rifle fire with the Federals throughout the day, with neither side gaining an advantage.

"The daylight of the 3rd was a signal for renewed hostilities," wrote Brig. Gen. Alexander Hays, commanding the Federal troops on Perrin's immediate front, "and during the forenoon was a repetition of the practice of the previous day, excepting that their skirmishers appeared more pertinacious in their assault." Throughout the long morning and into the afternoon, the area between the Emmitsburg Road and the farm lane became a no man's land that changed hands several times.[36]

Huddled in the farm lane about 400 yards from Cemetery Hill, the men of the 12th were exposed to the extreme July sun without shade and did what they could to keep low and protect themselves from small-arms and artillery fire. "You know," Lt. Cadwallader Jones Jr. of Company H wrote after the war, "it was in July, and the burning rays of the sun that day was so penetrating we could scarcely stand it so being almost overcome with heat." Jones and his men did what they could to shield themselves by throwing down a rubber blanket on the roadbed. When Jones sat up, hoping to catch some of the breeze, a Union shell whizzed by and struck the ground where he had been reclining. "It missed me not one half inch," he wrote. "[I]f I had been lying down, it would have taken me just about the middle. It plowed up a furrow along the ground under the company and wounded several men [but] fortunately did not explode."[37]

As Jones coordinated removing the wounded men of his company to the rear, he took stock of what men he had left in Company H. Looking around, he could count only eight, including himself. In a few moments, Colonel Miller yelled over to Jones and ordered him to take Company H forward to the picket line. "I hollowed [*sic*] back to him, I had no company," Jones recalled, "that I had only eight men—he said take them and go forward—of course I had to do so—it certainly seemed pitiful to go out in an open field in front of that stronghold of Yankees with a little squad of eight men."

36 Dunlop, *Bivouac and Battles (Part V)*, 1; *OR* 27(2):663; Carter, "Campaign of 1863," 1; *OR* 27(1):454.

37 Cadwallader Jones Jr. to My Dear Brother, July 19, 1922, UNC.

Nevertheless, Jones ordered Company H forward over the fence rails. After moving forward about 100 yards, Jones halted his small command at another pile of rails, which provided some protection, and returned fire. During the advance, he unfortunately would lose another man, W. H. Hand, who was shot and killed.[38]

Lee decided overnight that a better-coordinated resumption of his attack early on the morning of July 3 would provide the victory that had seemed so agonizingly close on July 2. If Ewell on the left and Longstreet and A. P. Hill on the right could now move in conjunction, he felt Confederate numbers and the sheer power of a tandem onslaught would prove too great for the Federals to withstand. It became evident fairly early this was not possible. Even with Maj. Gen. George Pickett's Division now on the field, Longstreet did not have his corps ready for an early-morning attack. Yankee artillery and troops on Culp's Hill also began to engage Ewell preemptively after 4:00 a.m., foiling three separate attempts by General Johnson's Division and maintaining possession of the critical elevation.

With that setback, Lee turned his attention to a concentrated assault on Meade's center on Cemetery Ridge. Anderson's attack late on July 2 had come close to breaking the position. To complete the task and chase the Army of the Potomac from the field, Lee now turned to Pickett's three fresh brigades and portions of both Pender's and Heth's divisions (commanded by Trimble and Pettigrew, respectively)—approximately 12,000 men total. He also directed J. E. B. Stuart, who had arrived on the field the previous day, to lead his four brigades of cavalry east of Gettysburg and guard the army's left flank.

The massed attack by Pickett, Pettigrew, and Trimble would begin about 3:00 p.m. It would be preceded by an artillery barrage featuring approximately 170 guns intended to weaken, or ideally tear apart, the assembled Federal units on Cemetery Ridge. The daunting barrage opened at 1:00 p.m., described by one South Carolina soldier as a "deafening echo." From their position in the farm lane, the men of the 12th would have a front row seat to the assault, which would include contributions from General Lane's and Col. W. J. Lowrance's North Carolinians (Scales's Brigade) in the Light Division, led here by Trimble. Curiously, none of the five brigades posted in the farm lane would be included in the attack, however.

Shortly after the artillery barrage concluded, the Confederate lines based on Seminary Ridge began their breathtaking march into history, an incredibly

38 Ibid. Jones writes that this advance occurred when "Pickett made his famous charge." Because of the length of time that had elapsed at the time this letter was written in 1922 and the lack of a corroborating source that any of the South Carolinians advanced during the actual charge—combined with the presence of the 8th Ohio, which advanced and flanked some of Pettigrew's men—it is believed that this advance by Company H occurred during the various back-and-forth skirmishes that morning.

steady advance of more than a mile into the heart of a Federal stronghold. Dunlop remembered the spectacle:

> In a few moments a column of 15,000 men under Pickett and Heth [Pettigrew] and Wilcox [Trimble], in three lines of battle, separated by intervals of about one hundred yards, debouched from the skirt of timber on Seminary Ridge and moved to the attack. The Federal batteries opened at once; but their practice upon the advancing lines was comparatively harmless so long as one line stood above another on the face of the ridge as they descended. With streaming banners and glittering arms the triple column moved down into the valley and across the Emmitsburg road—to the right, and in full view of McGowan's (now Perrin's) brigade, and with quickened pace began the ascent of Cemetery Ridge.
>
> Suddenly a lurid line of fire and smoke shoots forth from the enemy's works that belt the brow of this modern Gibraltar, and a perfect storm of iron and lead bursts upon the Confederate column. To this fearful assault the Confederates respond with a shout of defiance, and with a sheet of lead from their deadly rifles, comb the Federal parapets. Closing its gaps, the front line swept forward through the tempest of death that beat against it until it reached a point some two hundred yards in front of the enemy's works, when it recoiled upon the second line. Onward the two supporting lines urged their way, far beyond, when the first line broke.
>
> As the issue narrowed, the fury of the conflict increased, and the face of the sloping hill, at first dotted here and there, now became strewn with the Confederate killed and wounded. Staggering beneath the blows that rent their ranks at every step, the second line gave way. And now the third and last line rushed forward with a yell over the prostrate forms of their fellow comrades and closed with the enemy. To and fro the contending lines surge and sway in the death-grapple. The Federal artillerists for a moment yield to the contest and limber their guns for flight.
>
> Victory hovers over the rival standards, and in an agony of suspense every eye is turned toward the desperate struggle. Oh! for the life of the Southern cause, why does not Perrin charge? But he has no orders. The little band of 5,000 Confederates under Pickett, now the sole arbiters of the great issue, for a little while held their ground against Meade's heavy columns as they closed upon them from every side. But Garnett is dead; Armistead is dying, and Kemper, the last of the three brigade commanders, is stricken down with a fearful wound, and men are falling by scores on every hand. At length, reeling and staggering beneath the terrific blows that fell upon them, the little remnant of immortals gave way and

> retired from the unequal contest, leaving more than one-half their number killed and wounded on the field.[39]

Following the repulse of what has become known to history as "Pickett's Charge," the 12th South Carolina and Perrin's remaining regiments held their position in the farm lane for the remainder of July 3. Casualties were severe for both the regiment and the brigade. The 12th alone lost 129 men (20 killed, 105 wounded, and four captured/missing), with Company H particularly devastated (44 officers and men on July 1; only eight remaining on July 4). The 13th, fighting on the 12th's right flank on July 1, sustained a similar casualty count: 35 killed, 105 wounded, and four captured/missing for an aggregate of 144. The regiment suffering the largest toll in the brigade was the 14th: 26 killed, six missing/captured, and an astounding 220 wounded for a total of 252. The brigade's total casualties were 647, just short of half of all men engaged.

"Not a gun to be heard today," D. J. Carter of Company I wrote in his diary on July 4. Both armies remained in place that day, and Lee then prepared to evacuate his army to Virginia the following day. The brigade's wagon train was ordered to the rear, and the ambulances were filled with wounded who could be safely transported. Meanwhile, both sides did their best to bury the dead on the battlefield.

By day's end, the trains were headed toward Williamsport, Maryland, in a driving rainstorm, and after midnight on July 5, the 12th withdrew from the farm lane back to Seminary Ridge to await the wagons near the Fairfield Road. Once the wagon train cleared the road, the infantry followed, with rain drenching the men as they marched. The unmacadamized Fairfield Road had become a quagmire, almost impassable after the horses and wagons cut through. The torrential rain continued well into the day. The soaked, mud-stained men would halt at Fairfield and rest until evening before resuming their march and crossing the Blue Ridge Mountains at Monterey Pass.

The retreat continued on the 6th, with the brigade halting at Waynesboro. As many as 60 men had fallen from the ranks because of exhaustion. On July 7, Perrin's command reached Hagerstown, wet, filthy, and drained of strength. Because of the unrelenting rain, the Potomac River was too high to ford by foot. As he waited for his engineers to erect a pontoon bridge, Lee had to dig in and prepare a defense,

39 Dunlop, *Bivouac and Battles (Part V)*, 1.

aware that the pursuing Federals were on his heels. Meade would establish his own strong position once he closed within a mile of Lee's earthworks.[40]

For six long days, Hill's men remained miserably entrenched with their backs to the flooded Potomac near Hagerstown, improving their fortifications and waiting for Meade to launch a direct assault on their lines. Federal skirmishers probed Perrin's lines, but a full attack never materialized. At times, the skirmishing became quite spirited, and on one occasion pickets from the 12th, acting in conjunction with pickets from other regiments, were driven back into the main lines.

Soon, a severe shortage of flour meant the men had to do without bread for three days. Beef became scarce, too, and the quartermasters impressed a flock of sheep in order to feed the troops in the muddy trenches. The often-violent rain would not let up, and the waters of the Potomac remained at high levels. As the men held on, Lee's engineers worked feverishly to complete the bridge, using any scrap of lumber they could find. From the earthworks on July 8, a soldier in the 12th wrote home to the *Lancaster Ledger* that the regiment had "just passed through the 3 days of hardest fighting of the war," giving an accounting of the battle and the casualties of Companies I and E from the Lancaster area:

> Company "I," Lieut. Stover commanding. Killed–Sergt. P. B. Lindsay, Corporal W. M. Barton, Privates James B. Fleming, J. P. Caskey, and J. A. Nesbit. Wounded–Lieut. Stover, slightly, Sergt. S. H. Huey, severely in neck, Corp. W. G. A. Porter and D. L. Adams, flesh wound in the arm, Wesley Blackmon, W. Crenshaw, J. B. Langley, J. T. Vincent, B. M. Powell, E. M. L. Williams, severe flesh wounds, J. J. Montgomery, right leg amputated above the knee–is doing well. Slightly wounded–Sergt. J. H. Harper, J. B. Adams, R. J. Hughes, J. M. Hagins, T. C. Langley, E. K. Plyler, W. Mathis, Phillip Shehane, and W. W. Terry.
>
> Company "E," Capt. T Frank Clyburn commanding. Killed–none. Wounded–Lieut. J. B. Blackmon, in hand, Corpl. S. A. Johnson, right arm amputated, Privates T. L. Gardner, left arm amputated, S. B. Ingram, severely in face, R. A. Ingram, severely in left hip, F. M. Gardner, seriously in ankle, J. W. Gardner, flesh wound in leg, J. [last name illegible], flesh wound in leg, W. A. Williams, in left shoulder, W. J. Williams, in left arm, J. F. Hill, seriously in shoulder, J. L. Dunlap, slightly in leg, J. J. Roberts, slightly in hip, W. L. D. Lucy, slightly in

40 Welch, *A Confederate Surgeon's Letters to His Wife*, 70; Caldwell, *The History of a Brigade of South Carolinians*, 144, 147; Cadwallader Jones Jr. to My Dear Brother, July 19, 1922, UNC; *OR* 27(2):664; Carter, "Campaign of 1863," 1.

leg, H. P. A. Haile, supposed mortally, Thos Talbert, through thigh, G. W. Liles, slightly in right arm.[41]

By July 13, the river had fallen to a level that the wagons could ford, and with the pontoon bridges finished, the infantry could cross as well. That evening, the brigade left its position near Hagerstown and marched quickly and quietly toward the Potomac, the rain pelting the men as they marched miserably through deep mud, with some straggling. Some of Perrin's men would be captured by Federal pickets when they wandered into the woods hoping to find shortcuts. On the morning of the 14th, Heth's and Pender's divisions arrived near Falling Waters, Maryland, to make the crossing—the last troops in Lee's army to do so. Awaiting the order to cross, the weary men of the 12th stacked arms and dropped out of line to rest about two miles from the river, most of them falling asleep with no trouble.

It would prove to be a critical, deadly misstep that no one at the corps, division, brigade, or even regimental level had posted guards in their rear. None of the men's rifles were loaded and the powder in their cartridge boxes was wet from the incessant rain. As some of the men slept, a few others detected the approach of cavalry on their flank. Believing they were Confederate troopers, particularly by the almost nonchalant manner in which they moved, the tired infantrymen were not alarmed. Before they realized what was happening, a Federal contingent from Company B and Company F of the 6th Michigan Cavalry, in George Custer's 2nd Brigade, formed a line and rushed the resting southerners, striking Pettigrew's North Carolinians first.

Perrin's men were about 50 yards to Pettigrew's rear, although the weapons were again unloaded and useless and their powder wet. Perrin ordered a rally to the right, extending his line to a canal under enemy pressure. "The wildest excitement ensued," wrote J. F. J. Caldwell. "There was no time for arrangement, but every man must depend on his own reason, or rather his own instincts. The enemy dashed in, firing pistols and sabering everything in his way. Some men recovered their arms in time to fire upon them, some ran away, some fought with empty pieces, some even had recourse to stones. . . . The din was horrible, the confusion inextricable. . . . It was a most unfortunate affair. We should have utterly destroyed them."

One South Carolinian was more blunt: "The attack was a complete surprise and is disgraceful either to General Hill or General Heth. One is certainly to blame."[42]

41 Caldwell, *The History of a Brigade of South Carolinians*, 149; Perrin, "A Little More Light on Gettysburg," 525. LOCAL, "For the Lancaster Ledger," *Lancaster Ledger*, July 22, 1863, 2.

42 Caldwell, *The History of a Brigade of South Carolinians*, 149–150; Welch, *A Confederate Surgeon's Letters to His Wife*, 71; *OR* 27(2):664; *OR* 27(1):1000.

General Pettigrew was among the casualties, shot in the abdomen and mortally wounded. His men rushed him across the Potomac, and he was transported from there to Bunker Hill, West Virginia, but would die on July 17. During the melee, Hill ordered a retreat toward the river, which the men did in "in good order," according to a surgeon in the 14th South Carolina. After Perrin extricated the brigade to the pontoon bridge, the South Carolinians formed along the road and held off the Federals as the rest of Hill's Corps crossed. The affair was costly, with more than 500 estimated casualties in Heth's command. In the five South Carolina regiments, 98 men were listed as missing, presumed captured—the highest such total for the brigade until the Appomattox campaign—as well as four killed and 19 wounded.

The 12th's casualty count was 18 (one killed, four wounded, and 13 missing/captured). Because the wounded men were treated in Williamsport, we know three of their names: Pvt. W. T. Blackman, Pvt. W. Blake, and Sgt. G. W. Gardner. They were eventually sent north as Federal prisoners.[43]

"Our army again crossed the Potomac River, back to old Virginia," recalled William Miller of Company H, overlooking that they actually were now in West Virginia. His commander, Lt. Cadwallader Jones Jr., remembered being issued rations once across the Potomac, the first in several days. Cooking their rations in dirty utensils, Jones recalled their bread was black as gunpowder, but the men didn't mind. "We ate heartily," Jones recalled, "the men were in good spirits and ready to cross back over the river." After getting into Virginia, the brigade headed south to Martinsburg and then on to Bunker Hill where it went into bivouac for two days, camping in the same position it occupied following the battle of Sharpsburg in 1862.

On July 18, Pender died from the wound sustained on July 2. "We feel the loss of General Pender in our division," recalled one soldier. "He was a very superior little man, though a very strict disciplinarian."[44]

With the army back on southern soil, the invasion of Pennsylvania came to an end. Never again would the men of the 12th South Carolina enter enemy territory or push as far north as they had over the past month. Although the invasion had not resulted in a victory, there were positives, however. The brigade itself had fought well and claimed victory on its part of the field. Morale in the brigade remained high despite the strategic setback. "I do not think our army ever fought better. . . . I know so far as our own brigade is concerned it never fought

43 Caldwell, *The History of a Brigade of South Carolinians*, 149–150; *SHSP* 27:241–250.

44 Miller, "My Experience," 222; Cadwallader Jones Jr. to My Dear Brother, July 19, 1922, UNC; Welch, *A Confederate Surgeon's Letters to His Wife*, 72.

as well," wrote Perrin, who added that the South Carolinians "showed more dash and fought more desperately and more effectually than ever before. It now stands second to no Brigade in the army."

His assessment of the battle and the campaign was valid. The South Carolinians' July 1 fighting on McPherson's Ridge and Seminary Ridge produced one of the Army of Northern Virginia's top tactical victories in the war, giving Robert E. Lee justifiable hope that he would leave Gettysburg with another signature triumph. The men of the 12th concurred with their commander and downplayed the turn of events at Gettysburg. William Miller labeled the battle simply as "unfortunate," and a Company I soldier wrote home after the retreat, "We are looking for another battle soon."

This simplistic, yet realistic attitude served the men in the regiment well after the Army of Northern Virginia's first real defeat since Robert E. Lee had taken command thirteen months earlier. Despite the setback in Pennsylvania, they were not giving up and were acutely aware that the war would continue in bloody earnest. The Federals had managed to win one battle; not the war, and if it took additional sacrifices and renewed hardship to win the day, they were ready to do what was needed to assure victory. Little did they know that the worst of the war and their suffering was yet to come.[45]

45 Miller, "My Experience," 222; Perrin, "A Little More Light on Gettysburg," 524. 222; LOCAL, "For the Lancaster Ledger," *Lancaster Ledger*, July 22, 1863, 2.

Chapter Nine

Revival at Orange Court House

Despite the torrential rain, the mud-caked marches, and the close call at Falling Waters, the 12th South Carolina managed to cross the Potomac River into West Virginia by July 15, for the time being beyond the clutches of Meade's army. Although Lee and his subordinates welcomed a chance to recover and rebuild the Army of Northern Virginia's strength, there could be no argument that, with the concurrent Union victories at Gettysburg and Vicksburg, the course of the war had taken a turn against the Confederacy. How abrupt that turn was, however, remained to be seen. Even after these setbacks, the men in Lee's army remained determined, lamenting that victory had seemed agonizingly close at several points during the three-day clash at Gettysburg. Their commander knew, however, there was little room for error in the Eastern Theater. It would be critical to recapture the momentum and success his army had enjoyed in early May at Chancellorsville and before that at Fredericksburg.

The South Carolinians in McGowan's Brigade were among those hoping to use the reprieve to reenergize their battered ranks. Those in the 12th also worried about the welfare of their wounded comrades left behind in the field hospital near Marsh Creek and likely captured—their future considerably more uncertain. In that lot was Lt. J. R. Boyles of Company C.

After his grueling venture behind the lines on an improvised stretcher late in the July 1 fighting, Boyles pled in vain to have the brigade's surgeon, Thomas Evins, amputate his severely damaged right leg and not the 12th's own Dr. Bailey, a poorly regarded surgeon with a fondness for the bottle. Despite his pleas, Boyles recalled that Bailey indeed performed the procedure "so drunk that he had to lean against the table to keep from falling." Several witnesses confirmed the lieutenant's recollection, with Boyles grieving: "I suppose he deemed me a good subject to experiment on. Amputated my limb twice and left me with such an imperfect stump that I could never wear an artificial limb, but will go on crutches the balance of my life, having already been on them 25 years."

Lying nearly naked on a bed of straw, close to death, Boyles received a visit from a 1st South Carolina soldier bearing food on the morning of July 4. He would learn that Lee's army was in full retreat and undoubtedly watched helplessly as its immense wagon train filed past the hospital astride the Chambersburg Pike. Left to the mercy of a few "awkward" Federal cavalrymen, the lieutenant and his fellow wounded comrades were captured the next day. Adding to Boyles's duress was the filthy blanket they wrapped about him, infested with lice so thick that he remembered almost seeing the blanket move. With no way to bathe or clean, the wounded Confederates suffered in the oppressively hot July weather.

Alongside Boyles in a field tent were his captain, J. A. Hinnant, and Company C comrades D. L. Carter, Wylie Wyrick, and R. K. Moses, as well as Jim Harvey and Sam Proctor of Company F and Billy Crosby of Company D. Wyrick and Moses would not last long from the exposure, dying within a few days, as would Crosby.[1]

Boyles and his fellow wounded comrades remained at the field hospital under Federal surveillance until the morning of July 17, when they were transported by ambulance to the Gettysburg train station destined for internment at assorted Union prison camps. Some would be sent to Fort Lafayette in New York Harbor, some to Elmira in south-central New York, some to Fort Delaware near Philadelphia and Wilmington, and some to Camp Chase in Columbus, Ohio. Women at the station provided some temporary relief, handing out refreshments as the men waited to be loaded onto a train headed for Jersey City, New Jersey.

At Jersey City, the men were loaded on steamboats and transported to David's Island in Long Island Sound, about 25 miles from New York City. Here, Boyles recalled, the men were "tenderly carried ashore and placed in a pavilion, each man having a separate bed, on which were new and soft mattresses, clean sheets and pillowcases. After undergoing a thorough bath, shaving, and being furnished with clean clothing, our wounds were dressed, cards placed at the head of each bed, giving name, rank, and State of each occupant. They tried to make us just as comfortable as possible."

1 Dolph Dunlap of Company C and Tom Harris of Company F had also remained behind and acted as assistant nurses during the ordeal. Whether more men from the 12th were left at the hospital is unknown, but evidence suggests that Gilmer Greer of Company A and Thomas Faris of Company H were there as well.

Unexpectedly, the Federals treated their prisoners well during what became a four-month stay. They even furnished daily whiskey provisions and allowed a physician from South Carolina who had relocated to the north to oversee their care. Boyles reported that his daily allotment of whiskey was eight ounces, noting, "I scarcely ever drank half of it[;] consequently, my nurse got a good drink every morning and appreciated it by showing me marked kindness." A mail system was also established, and female visitors from South Carolina were permitted to stop by, providing the men with Yankee greenbacks and other items to make their temporary stay more comfortable.[2]

* * *

As Boyles and his fellow prisoners recuperated in New York, the 12th South Carolina and the rest of the Army of Northern Virginia encamped for a few days near Martinsburg before embarking on a demanding march south along the Valley Turnpike, enduring intense, particularly debilitating heat during the slog. Following stops in Winchester and Kernstown, the troops diverted east at the Shenandoah River and camped just west of Front Royal. Notable was the lukewarm fanfare the men experienced the next day while marching through Front Royal, a far cry from their energetic reception during the trek north a month earlier.

On August 4, McGowan's Brigade crossed the Rapidan River at Barnett's Ford and completed a nearly three-week excursion by encamping about a mile from Orange Court House. "Here," J. F. J. Caldwell recalled, "we rested from the labors of active campaigning."[3]

The brigade's encampment, Caldwell noted, was in a stand of oaks, with the five regiments aligned in column, each separated by intervals of roughly 30 yards: the 12th in front followed by the 1st, 14th, 13th, and then Orr's Rifles. "The lines were loosely dressed, so as to give room behind the front of each company street, for two rows of flies and a street of twelve or fourteen feet," he recalled, noting with pride that many of the men had "small 'Yankee' flies" (probably a shelter half)—a telling sign that the Confederates "had held many a battlefield" in the war thus far. Officers were issued the larger Confederate-made flies to replace those lost during the retreat from Gettysburg.

Joseph Templeton of Company B, who rejoined the regiment after falling out from exhaustion during the march north, had only good things to say of the

2 Boyles, *Reminiscences*, 43–46; Hoyt, *Recollections and Reminiscences*, 7:241; 8:285.

3 Caldwell, *The History of a Brigade of South Carolinians*, 153–155; Welch, *A Confederate Surgeon's Letters to His Wife*, 75.

encampment: "Wee are camped in a helthy place and have good water," he wrote his sister. "[W]e see the best times we have ever seen since wee came to virginia we get plenty of beef and corn bread to eat."

The men quickly settled into routine camp life. Rations of beef, bacon, flour, sugar, and potatoes were abundant, and new uniforms and footwear would be issued. Each regiment would conduct 24-hour picket duty every 20 or so days, though the requirements were fairly light. Organization and discipline markedly tightened, however, and drilling commenced in earnest: company-wide during the morning and battalion-wide in the afternoon.

To assure competency, officers in line for promotion faced rigorous review by examining boards filled by fellow officers. Camps were required to be kept neat and clean at all times, and a chain of sentinels guarded the outer perimeter so that only officers or men with passes, or those going for water or wood, could leave. The health and morale of the brigade improved considerably during this time, and troops who had been ill or wounded in previous engagements would return to replenish the ranks on a daily basis. "The army is in excellent trim and we believe ready and willing to go wherever General Lee directs—even into the enemy's country," wrote a Company I soldier. The prospect of fighting, however, was less likely according to others: "[I] do not think wee will have any fight here soon," Joseph Templeton wrote on August 18. "Each successive day was the exact reflection of its antecedent," recalled one officer.[4]

In the wake of the Gettysburg campaign, the men sorely needed not only the routine of normal army life but also rest, and some took the respite to reflect on the recent foray across the Potomac. Writing from camp on August 28, the usually upbeat and optimistic Cadwallader Jones Jr., Company H's new commander, sounded a somewhat melancholy tone: "We are having a nice time in camp now or at least a time of good rest, which so many of us needed after the severe campaign across the Potomac. Never have I seen a set of men, nor could I ever imagine so many men more broken down & completely worn out with the fatigue of so much hard marching and hunger that could almost be call[ed] starvation."

Jones lamented the loss of life and the hardships the regiment had suffered during the invasion, stating that they had "accomplished nothing or little by it" and that it disturbed him so many of the 12th's men had been left behind in the hands of the Yankees who might desecrate their graves. He took issue, however,

4 Caldwell, *The History of a Brigade of South Carolinians*, 156–157; LOCAL, "For the Lancaster Ledger," *Lancaster Ledger*, Sept. 16, 1863, 2; William Templeton to Sarah Templeton, Nov. 20, 1863; Welch, *A Confederate Surgeon's Letters to His Wife*, 73; William Dunlop, "Bivouac and Battles," *Yorkville Enquirer*, Nov. 27, 1889, 1 [hereafter cited to *Bivouac and Battles (Part VI)*].

Cadwallader Jones Jr. *Don Ernsberger*

with those outside the army who characterized the recent campaign as an outright loss. "[I]t is perfect folly," he would write, "to say that the army was whipped and as some will have it completely demoralized at the battle of Gettysburg, for it was not so; and those that thought so were not in the army." Ending on a more defiant note, Jones posited that the army was anxious to get back to Virginia to defend Richmond, which, he wrote, "never can be taken while the Army of Northern Virginia is kept together."[5]

On September 1, A. P. Hill took an opportunity to review the Light Division's four brigades, accompanied by Maj. Gen. Cadmus Wilcox, who had replaced the fallen Dorsey Pender as its commander. One soldier described the "gala day" in detail: "The several brigades made a splendid appearance, and all seemed delighted and well pleased with the looks of their new General. Among the observers, we noticed General Ewell and lady, and hundreds of others of the fair sex, among the number Mrs. Hill and Wilcox. All the observers seemed to enjoy the occasion finely, but not so much the rank and file. It reminded us very forcibly of our old field reviews in Lancaster, though executed in a more military style and dispatch."

Another review, this one for all three divisions in Hill's Third Corps, took place on September 10, attended by Lee himself. That review was the first, and probably last, time the entire corps would be reviewed during the war; it proved quite the affair. Cavalrymen and their officers, encamped near the Rappahannock River, made the trek over to Orange and infantrymen and their officers from other corps stationed in the area sought leave to witness the spectacle. In addition, a number

5 Cadwallader Jones Jr. to Dear Sister, Aug. 28, 1863, UNC.

Cadmus Wilcox was promoted to Major General following the Gettysburg campaign and was transferred to command the Light Division following Dorsey Pender's death. *Library of Congress*

of citizens from the surrounding countryside attended, some riding out in carriages. Hill arranged the nearly 20,000 veterans in three battle line columns of divisions, one behind the other. Thirteen brigades, representing nine states, stood patiently at attention waiting for a glimpse of the gray-haired commander. Captain Robert E. Lee Jr., in attendance with several cousins from Richmond, described his father's reactions during the emotional day:

> The general was mounted on Traveller, looking very proud of his master, who had on sash and sword, which he very rarely wore, a pair of new cavalry gauntlets, and, I think a new hat. At any rate, he looked unusually fine, and sat his horse like a picture of grace and power. The infantry was drawn up in column by divisions, with their bright muskets all glittering in the sun, their battle flags standing straight out before the breeze, and their bands playing, awaiting the inspection of the General, before they broke into column by companies and marched past him in review. When all was ready, General Hill and staff rode up to General Lee, and the two generals, with their respective staffs, galloped around front and rear of each of the three divisions standing motionless on the plain.
>
> As the cavalcade reached the head of each division, its commanding officer joined in and followed as far as the next division, so that there was a continual infusion of fresh groups into the original one all along the lines. Traveller started with a long lope, and never changed his stride. His rider sat erect and calm, not noticing anything but the gray lines of men who knew him so well. The pace was very fast, as there were nine good miles to go, and the escort began to become less and less, dropping out one by one from different causes as Traveller raced along without a check. When the General drew up, after this nine mile gallop, under the standard

of the reviewing-stand, flushed with the exercise as well as with pride in his brave men, he raised his hat and saluted.

Seeing Lee raise his hat, Hill's veterans responded with emotional applause and shouts of adulation for their general, waiving their flags and holding their own hats high—the sounds of 20,000 soldiers echoing across the countryside. The review itself was a "most imposing site," according to Lee's son; it also seemed to indicate that Hill's battle-hardened divisions had recovered from the horrific fighting at Gettysburg, let alone the taxing retreat to Virginia, and that the men were ready to re-engage with Meade's army. Also, with two divisions in Longstreet's First Corps headed south to bolster Braxton Bragg's Western army in Tennessee and Georgia, the rejuvenated Third Corps was essential to holding the Federals in check. Lee was undoubtedly reassured by what he witnessed during the day's review.[6]

Not all would be pomp and circumstance, however. Although systemic desertion was never a heavy concern for the 12th during the war, in August–September 1863, two men were captured attempting to desert. The culprits, described by Caldwell as "men who had never performed great service," were found guilty by court-martial and sentenced for execution before the entire Light Division in late September. Spencer Welch, the 14th South Carolina's surgeon, was among those who granted that the punishment was justified, writing, "There is no other way to stop it."

But as the day of execution approached, with the duo's coffins already constructed, General Perrin intervened to spare their lives. Still holding temporary command of McGowan's Brigade, Perrin encouraged each regiment in the brigade to circulate petitions endorsing pardons for the men. Perrin would take these petitions personally to Lee, who acquiesced and commuted the sentences in favor of imprisonment in Richmond.

Perrin's efforts were extraordinary in that executions were commonplace during this time—indeed, nine men from other brigades in the Light Division

6 LOCAL, "For the Lancaster Ledger," *Lancaster Ledger*, Sept. 16, 1863, 2; Carter, "Campaign of 1863," 4; Robert E. Lee Jr., *My Father, General Lee* (New York, 1960), 106–107. Two discrepancies must be addressed. First, despite the assertion that "Mrs. Wilcox" attended the divisional review, Cadmus Wilcox was a bachelor. Second, deserters—presumably from Edward Thomas's Georgia Brigade who were mistakenly identified belonging to the 47th Georgia Infantry—told their Federal captors on Sept. 15 that the corps' review took place on Friday, Sept. 11. That date, however, differs from Pvt. D. J. Carter's diary entry cited herein in which he affirmatively states that the review was on the 10th. Because of the contemporaneous nature of Carter's diary and the certainly unreliable memory of prisoners having just deserted, Carter's September 10 date is generally accepted as the correct date of the review. Cf. Alfred Pleasonton to George Meade, Sept. 15, 1863, in *OR* 51(I):1088. More likely than not, these prisoners belonged to the 45th Georgia.

were executed for the same offense on September 27. It is unknown what prompted Perrin's intervention and what circumstances might have prompted Lee to rescind the punishment.[7]

As summer faded to fall, religious fervor again came alive in the South Carolinians' camp, much as it had prior to the Gettysburg campaign. Preachers descended on the camps in large numbers, and many who had previously expressed little to no interest in religion found themselves drawn to the sweeping evangelism. The zeal and enthusiasm, in fact, was striking. "The most ordinary preachers drew large congregations," wrote one South Carolinian. "[S]carcely a day passed without a sermon; there was not a night but the sound of prayer was not heard." Several sermons were scheduled most days, and if none happened to be available, men would travel in small groups to hear ministers in other brigades. The 12th South Carolina even had its own Christian Association, led by its venerated chaplain, J. Monroe Anderson.[8]

By the fall of 1863, however, Anderson reluctantly resigned from service, as the rigors of campaigning had irreparably wrecked his health. His departure would prove severe, as he had taken care of the men both spiritually and physically. When they needed provisions such as socks and blankets, Anderson had often returned to South Carolina and implored families and citizens to donate items to the troops, at times personally traversing the countryside to gather supplies. He had also worked closely with the Central Association for the Relief of Soldiers, based in Columbia.

"He certainly has the confidence of every member of the regiment, both saint and sinner," wrote one soldier. "He accomplished more good by his kind sociable manners than all the other preachers we have ever had before put together. He was . . . respected by all . . . a gentlemen of high personal merit. Our prayers are with him, and trust that he may soon be restored to us again." Added another soldier: "[He was] a good strait forward man, and unlike a great many of the preachers in the army, he came here to effect good, and not to 'show off' in fine uniform."

At a meeting of the regiment's "Christian Association" after news broke of Anderson's resignation, the following resolution was submitted by Colonel Miller and unanimously adopted:

> We the members of the Christian Association, 12th Regiment, S. C. V., deeply lament that our valued chaplain, the Reverend J. Monroe Anderson, has found

7 Caldwell, *The History of a Brigade of South Carolinians*, 157, 169; *OR* 29(1):739; Welch, *A Confederate Surgeon's Letters to His Wife*, 78–89.

8 Caldwell, *The History of a Brigade of South Carolinians*, 157–158; LOCAL, "For the Lancaster Ledger," *Lancaster Ledger*, Nov. 25, 1863, 2.

it necessary to retire from his arduous duties and many hardships among us. We will long cherish with admiration and gratitude, the memory of his untiring zeal to promote the spiritual interest of the Regiment, the loveliness of his modest life, and the warmth of his Christian sympathy. Our prayers, too, will be earnest that his strength and health may soon be improved so that the army in which the Master has so eminently qualified him to labor with success, may not long be deprived of the blessing of his ministry.

Anderson, who lived until 1879, continued his service as a minister after the war and became a highly respected professor of philosophy and literature at Davidson College in North Carolina. His son, Dr. Neal Anderson, followed in his father's footsteps in the Presbyterian ministry.[9]

* * *

Fighting for the Army of Northern Virginia finally resumed in late September. When Federal cavalry feinted toward Liberty Mills on the Rapidan River, about five miles from Orange Court House on September 22, Wilcox's Division (minus Lane's Brigade) was ordered to support the Confederate cavalry posted there. For some reason, Caldwell reported that the division was not engaged. Private D. J. Carter recalled, however, that Company I and three others in the 12th South Carolina, led by Captain T. F. Clyburn, were thrown out as skirmishers and drove back a contingent of enemy troopers, capturing several. According to Carter, the 12th had no losses during the brief skirmish and the four companies then camped near Liberty Mills for two days before joining their comrades at the regiment's new camp along the Rapidan at Richardson's farm, about three miles from Orange Court House. At this new camp, some of the officers and soldiers wounded at Gettysburg returned to the ranks from their furloughs, including Captain Stover of Company I.[10]

9 LOCAL, "For the Lancaster Ledger," *Lancaster Ledger*, Nov. 25, 1863, 2; LOCAL, "For the Lancaster Ledger," *Lancaster Ledger*, May 13, 1863, 1; "Congregation will give a Reception to their Pastor," *Twin City Daily Sentinel*, Nov. 29, 1915, 2; "Spirits Turpentine," *Wilmington Morning Star*, March 25, 1879, 1.

10 Caldwell, *The History of a Brigade of South Carolinians*, 158–159. Caldwell indicated the cavalry engagement occurred on the 25th; however, given the contemporaneous nature of Carter's diary, his version is accepted as more accurate. Cf. D. J Carter, "Campaign of 1863," *Lancaster News*, Dec. 18, 1889, 4; LOCAL, "For the Lancaster Ledger," *Lancaster Ledger*, Nov. 25, 1863, 2. "LOCAL" writes that Miller, as the brigade's senior colonel, commanded the brigade during the skirmish with cavalry; however, brigade historian J. F. J. Caldwell is silent on this issue. See Caldwell, *The History of a Brigade of South Carolinians*, 158–159.

Eager to make the Richardson's farm encampment their winter quarters, the men quickly went to work prepping the site. "This camp was selected with the view of establishing winter quarters, and some preparations were being made, a few houses built," Carter would write. Added another soldier: "[C]ontrary to orders, the majority of our troops had put up comfortable quarters for the winter, and made every little necessary arrangement for the spending of the season in that locality."

Their hopes would be in vain, however. In late September, with the Army of the Potomac positioned in and around Culpeper, Meade received orders to send the XI and XII corps to the aid of Maj. Gen. William Rosecrans's besieged army in Chattanooga. Sensing an opportunity to catch Meade off-guard, Lee reached back into his exceptional playbook and drew up an offensive mirroring the one he had used successfully against John Pope's Army of Virginia in the summer of 1862. The terrain involved in the plan was essentially the same, as were some of the soldiers and principals in both armies. "The Confederate commander hoped to get behind Meade's army and cut off its escape route across the Rappahannock River," according to historian Jim Campi. "If Lee succeeded, the Army of the Potomac would be at his mercy."[11]

On October 9, Hill's and Ewell's commands left their respective camps and began moving in tandem around Meade's right flank, doing what they could to keep their advances clandestine. That day, the 12th and their fellow South Carolinians in Hill's Corps would cross the Rapidan and camp near Madison Court House. After crossing the Robinson and Hazel Rivers on October 11, the column bivouacked near Sperryville, then recrossed the Hazel River the following day and followed the Winchester & Culpeper Turnpike to within six miles of Culpeper.

By then, it was evident that the Federals were gone. On October 7, according to Campi, Union signalmen on Pony Mountain had intercepted messages from the Confederate signal station on Clark Mountain "that clearly indicated that some sort of movement was underway. Two days later, Meade and his chief of staff [Maj. Gen. Andrew A. Humphreys] saw for themselves the gray columns moving beyond the Union right flank."

Meade wasted little time abandoning his position, beginning a frantic retreat toward the Union stronghold at Centreville, approximately 50 miles away. Although Lee was naturally displeased by the abrupt escape, there was one unexpected benefit for his army: the bevy of Federal supplies left behind.

11 Jim Campi, "A Roar From the Portals of Hell," American Battlefield Trust, https://www.battlefields.org/learn/articles/roar-portals-hell, accessed Jan. 29, 2025.

The Army of the Potomac would follow the Orange and Alexandria Railroad as it hurried toward Centreville, but Hill and Ewell maintained a steady pace in their pursuit. Then, early on October 14, Maj. Gen. Gouverneur Warren's II Corps clashed with J. E. B. Stuart's cavalry and elements of Ewell's Second Corps at Auburn before escaping in the direction of Bristoe Station in Fauquier County, about 17 miles from Centreville.

As the skirmish unfolded at Auburn, Hill continued his own advance, reaching Bristoe Station later that morning. A Federal force was already there, he realized—Maj. Gen. George Sykes's V Corps, serving as Meade's rear guard. Hill, however, interpreted detritus before him as a sign the Federals were retreating in haste. "Campfires were still burning," Campi writes, "and the road was littered with blankets and haversacks." Hill was known not to back down from a fight. In his mind, the retreating Federals would be easy prey if he pounced immediately.

The supposedly fleeing Federals could be seen on both banks of a nearby stream called Broad Run. Although Henry Heth did not have his entire division available, Hill would not hesitate. He ordered Heth to attack with what he had available on the field: Brig. Gens. William Kirkland's and John Cooke's North Carolina brigades.

What neither Hill nor Heth realized was that the Union II Corps had by then arrived from Auburn and had assumed a position on the right, concealed behind a railroad embankment. As Heth's men rushed toward Broad Run, Warren's Federals began firing away at will. Startled, Heth turned to confront the sudden onslaught, with no luck. The Confederates would suffer 1,380 total casualties during the bloody repulse, with Kirkland and Cooke both sidelined by severe wounds and Brig. Gen. Carnot Posey in Anderson's Division mortally wounded. Many of the Confederate dead would be buried out of convenience in mass graves.[12]

With 540 casualties, the Army of the Potomac suffered comparatively less. Meade also had the time to complete his march to Centreville uncontested.

Wilcox's Division had been nearby during the fighting at Bristoe Station but would not be engaged. For the next two days, the 12th South Carolina occupied its time tearing up the railroad as far back as the Rappahannock River. Private Carter took pleasure in describing the regiment's destruction of railroad ties on those two days, creating what later became famous as "Sherman's Neckties" during William Sherman's notorious 1864 March to the Sea. "We piled up the cross ties then lay the railing across and set fire to the heap, bending the railing double," he proudly recalled.[13]

12 Caldwell, *The History of a Brigade of South Carolinians*, 159–160; Carter, "Campaign of 1863," 4.

13 Carter, "Campaign of 1863," 4.

* * *

On October 18, a Sunday, the men rested after their toil and attended church services in camp. Some also took the opportunity to wander through the Federals' deserted camps. The next day, the brigade crossed south of the Rappahannock and encamped a few miles from the river. Picket duty resumed along both the Rappahannock and Hazel rivers until November 6, when the troops relocated closer to Culpeper Court House. Here, the men commenced constructing winter quarters, an endeavor cut short on the 8th when they were called out and formed for battle three miles north of the courthouse. The regiment was soon on the move again, this time to the camp it had occupied near Orange Court House before its departure on October 9.

As the men began constructing winter quarters again, the first snow fell, giving them hope that now they would have leisure to settle down and wait out the winter. But then another big change hit the ranks, as Lt. Col. Henry Davis, seriously wounded at Sharpsburg, resigned his commission. Taking his place was Major Bookter, with Captain Clyburn of Company E promoted to major.[14]

On November 26—celebrated as Thanksgiving Day in the North—orders went out for the brigade to cook rations and prepare for a march toward Fredericksburg to begin the following morning. What would become known as the Mine Run campaign had begun. "The weather is extremely cold," recalled one soldier, who also noted that the brisk pace at which the men marched at least helped them maintain their body warmth.

As they marched the afternoon of November 27, the men could hear artillery fire to the front, with Maj. Gen. Edward Johnson's Division in Ewell's Corps already fighting. The South Carolinians bivouacked near Mine Run that evening and constructed breastworks amid continual firing. The next few days were spent falling back and moving forward, constructing earthworks, and skirmishing on and off with the Federals. Earthworks were constructed by felling trees, and the men camped in them. Sporadic fire would erupt from time to time between the lines, but little more than that.

Huddled in the works, the men of the 12th South Carolina struggled to keep warm as harsh winds blew across the field, piercing the men's bones and compromising the small fires they built to stay warm. "The weather became colder than ever," recalled one soldier. "[T]he men were almost frozen." A company from each regiment would be sent to the front every 24 hours to post pickets; however, with the men awaiting a possible Federal assault, no fires were allowed.

14 Ibid.

It was about this time that the men learned of the Army of Tennessee's disaster at the battle of Missionary Ridge near Chattanooga. Although Longstreet's Corps had joined Bragg's army at Chattanooga in September, it was away during the Missionary Ridge fighting, engaged with Ambrose Burnside's Army of the Ohio 100 or so miles north at Knoxville.[15]

On November 29, the Rev. John Watson, J. Monroe Anderson's successor as the 12th's chaplain, held a short service for the regiment in the cold earthworks. The service drew the attention of General Lee as he, Hill, and their respective staffs rode along the works inspecting the lines. Lee, on Traveller, reined up. "He halted, uncovered his venerable head, closed his eyes and in deep reverence sat upon his horse until the service closed," recalled Dunlop, who opined that it was "a scene for a picture worthy of the skill of Raphael, or the masterhand of Michael Angelo."[16]

The Federal movements over those few days in late November had the makings of a major battle, but Meade never launched an outright assault, apparently content to assess the Confederate position through a series of probing actions. On December 1, the Army of the Potomac began to fall back across the Rapidan. Hill's entire corps, with Maj. Gen. Wade Hampton's cavalry in tow, gave chase on the Plank Road on the 2nd but would halt after a few miles and eventually turn in the direction of Orange Court House. As the column trudged along the road, a soldier caught a glimpse of Lee as he passed, writing, "I remember that General Lee looked very much annoyed." On December 3, the South Carolinians were back at their winter quarters about three miles from Orange Court House. The short, anti-climactic Mine Run campaign was in the books.[17]

* * *

The 12th continued preparations for the onset of winter. In addition to picket duty and daily drill, the men spent the bulk of their time constructing a five-mile plank road from Orange Court House to Liberty Mills. Emphasizing what seemed sudden contentment in the ranks, one officer recalled that "our clothing was comfortable, rations were sufficient, and wood and water convenient and abundant. We were cheerful, contended and happy in our little city of tents and shanties."

Religious fervor also remained conspicuous, and before long the men of the 12th constructed a chapel out of slab wood for their services. In addition to the

15 Caldwell, *The History of a Brigade of South* Carolinians, 165–166; Carter, "Campaign of 1863," 4.

16 Dunlop, *Bivouac and Battles (Part VI)*, 1.

17 Caldwell, *The History of a Brigade of South Carolinians*, 167; Carter, "Campaign of 1863," 4.

new chapel, nine of the regiment's 10 companies erected altars in their streets for impromptu moments of worship. So important to the men that the wayward company establish its own altar or at least have a venue for religion, a collective mission was established to spread the gospel in that company's camp, and soldiers were routinely sent over to that company street to lead its members in services Wrote Dunlop: "It was an impressive sight, and a fact worthy of historical notice, to see ten companies of brawny veterans standing in line at the opening or close of the day with heads bowed and eyes closed, reverently rendering unto their gracious Benefactor the homage and worship due unto his name."[18]

It was testament to Colonel Miller's sense of duty and discipline that drilling remained a consistent enterprise for the 12th, which was not necessarily the case throughout the brigade. Good news arrived before Christmas when 21-day furloughs were instituted within the regiment, allowing many of the men to travel home to South Carolina. Nevertheless, there were complaints that the furloughs were not always issued to the troops who had been at the front the longest. In a letter to his sister, Joseph Templeton groused that as much as he wanted to come home, "there is no chance" since "the lofers and Hell hounds will get home" before he would.

Templeton also noted the influx of convalescents returning from the hospitals in Richmond, protesting that many of them had gotten furloughs before him: "The hospital rats is coming in to their companies and geting furlows and the men that has done the duty canot get any," he lamented. Some men went as far as having their wives write letters to them stressing a need to attend to important business at home, hoping it would grant them priority in the furlough line. Whether that ploy was successful was apparently never documented.

An equitable solution was soon established. Those yet to receive a furlough during their service were given preference over those who had. Officers were allowed furloughs as well, but only one furlough per company was granted and only if the officer had more than two other officers present in camp. "This falls very heavy upon some companies whose officers are absent from sickness, wounds and on detached duty," recalled one soldier. As a result, few company commanders or their subordinates were able to get home that winter.

The regiment's numerical strength at this point remains a mystery. Given the Gettysburg casualties, combined with the number of new recruits and soldiers who returned from rehabilitation in hospitals, the total was likely 450–500 officers and men (approximately 40–50 men and 1–3 officers per company). Company A, for

18 Dunlop, *Bivouac and Battles (Part VI)*, 1.

example, had 60 men on its roll (44 present) on January 1, 1864, and a Company H soldier sent home the following ledger during the winter:

Joined by Recruit	21
On roll 1st March	70
On furlough of indulgence	12
Absent, sick and wounded	5
Present, sick	3
In hands of enemy	1
Exchanged prisoners not returned	3
Present for duty	46
Total, present and absent	70[19]

Christmas was underwhelming for the men and highlighted the plight of the Confederacy in failing to obtain its independence. In a rare account written on December 25, 1863, one soldier expressed indifference to the holiday, though he did wish that his fellow soldiers remained positive despite the absence of peace:

Orange C.H., Va., Dec. 25, 1863

Camp 12th S. Regiment.

A Christmas greeting to you all. This once universal holiday is again at hand.—Yes, Christmas has come! But we do not enjoy it as in days of old; how happy should we have been, had it conveyed the welcome tidings of peace upon its wings; yet we should not despair that it has not. The coming of 'Santa-Clause,' the Christmas gift; the firing of crackers; the merry shouts of the boys on the streets, which once conduced so much to keep up the spirit of the occasion, must now, in a great measure, be suspended. There are other guns to fire, not in sport, but to send the deadly missiles into the ranks of our enemies. There are other gifts to make more sacred and lasting than the 'Christmas gift.' Though we do not underrate the Christmas gift, we regard it as a generous institution; 'tis good to give, especially to the happy little ones, whose minds have not been

19 Ibid.; Joseph Templeton to Sarah Templeton, Feb. 12, 1864, and Jan. 12, 1864. Caldwell, *The History of a Brigade of South Carolinians*, 167; "Company A, 12th Regiment," *Yorkville Enquirer*, Feb. 10, 1864, 2; Ensign, 12th Reg. S. C. V., "For the Yorkville Enquirer," *Yorkville Enquirer,* March 16, 1864, 2; LOCAL, "For the Lancaster Ledger," *Lancaster Ledger*, Jan. 13, 1864, 2.

> depressed by the sad state of the country—we should have a smile for them on such occasions—And though the peace which we so fondly wished for and expected to bless our efforts by this time, has not come, let us endeavor to be hopeful, cheerful and happy.
>
> The men in the camps manifest a disposition to make lively the day as far as in their power and means. Owing to the scarcity of the necessary materials, but few enjoyed the usual luxury of a nog, but other amusements, perhaps more respectable, enabled us to pass the time agreeable and pleasant.[20]

The fair weather in December gave way to bitterly cold conditions in January, accompanied by strong winds. "[T]he wether is very coald," Joseph Templeton wrote in a January 17 letter. "The snow is on the ground yet and looks lik it would stay all winter." Rations were also reduced about this time, and the men began requesting care packages from home to get by. As Templeton pled in another letter home: "I want you to send me a small box by J. S. Chambers [a comrade]. I want you to send me some Cow peas. I never was so starved in all my life and I want a poan of bread and some potatoes if you have them to spare."[21]

In late January or early February, McGowan's Brigade received orders to relocate its camp about a half-mile up the Rapidan. The scarcity of wood to fuel the men's fires in their huts was a contributing factor in that decision. The new camp was established on historic ground in an expansive forest—Montpelier, former President James Madison's estate. There, the South Carolinians cleared a portion of woods and began constructing new huts. "The regiments were now separated, so that wood was cut by each one all around its camp," Caldwell would write "This supply of wood lasted us for the rest of the winter."

By all accounts, the men favored the new location. Hygiene was also heavily stressed, and with the camps kept reasonably clean, the health of the troops improved. Rations also increased after the unpleasant downturn in January. Although no beef was issued, bacon and plenty of cornmeal were available.

Despite the cold weather, the supply of government-issued blankets, uniforms, and shoes became all but non-existent. General Wilcox, commander of the division, recalled, "[T]he troops were not regularly and well supplied with good and sufficient rations, nor was their clothing of the best. Their morale was, nevertheless, excellent."

20 LOCAL, "For the Lancaster Ledger," *Lancaster Ledger*, Jan. 13, 1864, 2.

21 Joseph Templeton to Sarah Templeton, Jan. 17, 1864, and Jan. 20, 1864; Welch, *A Surgeon's Letter to His Wife*, 87; Caldwell, *The History of a Brigade of South Carolinians*, 171.

The men again turned to their loved ones at home for help, and the Central Association and various aid societies in South Carolina collected considerable amounts of clothing and sent them north.[22]

Relief from the hemorrhaging of troops that had ravaged the brigade's ranks after Gettysburg increased as spring approached. Besides the continued return of wounded warriors, nearly 200 conscripts arrived from South Carolina. More than half of those were assigned to the 1st, as its ranks were the most depleted in the brigade, but the 12th got roughly 50 of the newcomers.

The increase in numbers did not necessarily add to the 12th's fighting prowess, however. According to one veteran, the quality of the new troops left much to be desired due to their "aversion to duty." One laudable recruit to arrive was Nelson George, the Catawba Indian from Rock Hill. He was joined by fellow Catawba William Cantey, a veteran of five battles whose service in Company K of the 17th South Carolina ended in 1863. Both joined fellow Catawbas James Harris and Alexander Tims in Company H ("Indian Land Guards") on March 11.

Also returning was General McGowan, sidelined for nearly 10 months after his wounding at Chancellorsville. McGowan's resumption of command meant Abner Perrin, a newly minted brigadier general, was handed command of Wilcox's old Alabama brigade. "We were very sorry to lose him as highly as we esteemed General McGowan," wrote one veteran. "He was an officer of remarkable gallantry and remarkable discipline, and perhaps, more distinguished than for these qualities by his devotion to, and concentration upon, the military life. He was always and entirely a soldier, and appeared to by far the greatest advantage amidst the greatest danger and tumult."[23]

During periods of downtime, the proximity of the brigade's five regiments usually led to generally friendly interaction among soldiers in different units, and banter often boiled down to the qualities of respective units and how they ranked among others. On one occasion, James McKeekin of Company F happened upon a soldier from the neighboring 14th South Carolina. The soldier from the 14th was unaware to which regiment McKeekin belonged. When McKeekin asked him his opinion of the 12th as they discussed the merits of the various regiments in the

22 Caldwell, *The History of a Brigade of South Carolinians*, 168; Cadmus Wilcox, "Lee and Grant in the Wilderness," in *Annals of War*, originally published in the *Philadelphia Weekly Times*, republished (Dayton, OH, 1988), 486; J. T. Parker, "Acknowledgment," *Yorkville Enquirer*, April 13, 1864, 2. McGowan's Brigade's winter camp was recently discovered on the grounds of Montpelier and featured in a Feb. 8, 2014 C-SPAN program titled "Confederate Winter Quarters." This program is accessible at https://www.c-span.org/video/?317592-1/ahtv-confederate-winter-quarters.

23 Caldwell, *The History of a Brigade of South Carolinians*, 169, 171; Blummer, "Record of Catawba Indians' Confederate Service," 224–225, 227; Joseph Templeton to Sarah Templeton, April 13, 1864.

brigade, the soldier replied with admiration: "Well, I don't know very much about them, but I'll be durned if they ain't pups to fight!"[24]

On February 9, an extraordinary meeting took place at the 12th's camp. It concerned the issue of reenlistment for the duration of the war—a matter then sweeping the Confederate armies. Men in several Army of Northern Virginia regiments, in fact, had already reaffirmed their desire to continue serving. As his men emerged from their huts, Colonel Miller read a prepared proclamation:

> BROTHER OFFICERS AND SOLDIERS: It is with heartfelt pleasure that I announce to you the re-enlistment of a great many brigades in the Army of Northern Virginia. A spirit of generous rivalry seems to exist among the war-worn veterans in devoting themselves to the service of their country. The spectacle presented is one that will challenge and receive the admiration of every friend of liberty. With implicit confidence in their leaders, both civil and military, they gather around the standard of their country, and beneath the folds of their battle flags, all tattered and torn, proclaim their determination never to yield to the vandal foe, who are seeking to deprive us of all that renders life desirable. Discarding all minor considerations, they only look to the momentous issues at stake—liberty and independence on the one hand; on the other subjugation and vassalage to the base hirlings of power, inconceivably worse than death. This note of preparation will not only cheer desponding patriotism, and re-assure the hopes of the country, but it will strike terror into the ranks of the enemy; and may we not hope that it will shame into silence the miserable croakers at home? And may stalk like a hideous spectre before the gaze of soulless extortioners and speculators, who are now fattening on the blood of fallen heroes, and gnawing at the very vitals of the country.
>
> We have met today, not to re-enlist, but as a war regiment, to show to our brave comrades that we are with them heart and hand in this noble work. It is simply intended to re-iterate our determination to remain in service until our independence is established. Animated by your past brilliant achievements on many well-fought fields, I can very readily anticipate your response. I will not insult you by my appeal to your patriotism or argument to convince you of your obligations to your country. I know you will still pursue the path of honor, and in the future, as you have ever done in the past, obey the high behests of duty.

24 "The Twelfth Regiment," *The News and Herald* [Winnsboro, SC], Aug. 23, 1879, 2.

At the conclusion of Miller's remarks, Sgt. J. C. Chambers motioned for appointment of a five-soldier committee to consider the reenlistment issue. Chambers would be selected, as were Pvt. D. J. Carter, Sgt. G. W. Smith, Sgt. T. B. Burnes, and Corp. S. C. Burkett. The committee met and returned shortly with the following resolution:

> Whereas we have learned with gratification the patriotic resolve of our brave comrades in arms, in re-enlisting for the war, notwithstanding we enlisted for the war in August 1861, to serve during the war, we are desirous of extending to them our hearty cooperation in this noble work; and whereas subjugation, confiscation and utter ruin are mild expedients by which our affection for the "glorious Union" is to be restored; be it therefore, RESOLVED, that the cruel persecution, the dangers, hardships, and privations to which we have been subjected, our deserted homes and desolated fields, have only inspired us with fresh zeal and an unconquerable determination never to yield to the mercenary hirelings of Yankeedom, nor lay down our arms until liberty is secured and the sovereignty and independence of the Confederate States be firmly established.

Holding the document in his hand, Miller called for a vote by the entire regiment, receiving unanimous affirmation. For their action in re-enlisting, the regiments of McGowan's Brigade were officially recognized by a joint resolution of the Confederate Congress which stated:

> Resolved by the Congress of the Confederate States of America, That the thanks of Congress are due, and are hereby tendered, to Orr's Rifles, the First, Twelfth, Thirteenth, and Fourteenth Regiments South Carolina Volunteers, composing McGowan's brigade, for their patriotic devotion to the cause of Southern independence, as manifested by their recent action, unanimously reiterating their determination to serve during the war. In thus renewing their pledges, after nearly three years of arduous and gallant service, they have met the expectation of their country, and are entitled to its approbation.
>
> Approved February 17, 1864[25]

The die was cast and there was no turning back. The men of the 12th would see their dream of a Confederate nation prevail or be defeated in the attempt.

25 "The 12th Regiment"; *OR* 33:1184.

Chapter Ten

A Spring of Misery and Mud

On March 1, 1864, General McGowan notified William Dunlop, Company B's energetic and enterprising commander, that he would organize another three-company battalion of sharpshooters to specialize as skirmishers, scouts, and for other special duty. The brigade's previous sharpshooter battalion served during the Gettysburg campaign but was disbanded after the invasion of Pennsylvania to compensate for excessive losses in the ranks. Captain Dunlop, just back from a furlough in South Carolina, would be promoted to major and handed command of this new battalion.

The rebirth of such a unit was a harbinger of things to come. As winter slowly turned to spring in Virginia, it would be only a matter of time before the fighting reignited in earnest. A vital component of that fighting, McGowan estimated, was a mobile force comprised of men known for their shooting prowess to carry out distinct functions during battle and on the march. He determined that each of the three companies would field a 60-man roster, led by one commissioned and three non-commissioned officers, and because McGowan held the 12th in high regard—perhaps his brigade's most dependable and hardest-fighting unit—he felt Dunlop was a fitting choice as the battalion's leader. The newly minted major had served notably for more than a year as Company B's commander, displaying heroism and competence repeatedly from Gaines's Mill to Gettysburg.[1]

1 William Dunlop, *Lee's Sharpshooters; or the Forefront of Battle* (Little Rock, AR, 1899), 17; Dunlop, *Bivouac and Battles (Part VI)*, 1.

Dunlop went to work filling the ranks, pulling between two and four marksmen from each of the 50 companies in the 1st, 12th, 13th, 14th, and Orr's Rifles. Training would last until the end of April. "Estimating distance, target practice, movements and dispositions against cavalry, bayonet exercise, etc. were prominent features of the system," Dunlop recalled.

Drilling in open-order skirmish formations and being able to form for battle quickly and efficiently were important requisites, and those unable to withstand the rigors of training were replaced with others more adept in such skills. "With this training," Dunlop wrote, "the battalion of sharpshooters awaited the opening of the campaign of 1864 in the hope that under the blessings of God it might strike some blow that would tell for the freedom of the south."[2]

As a return to campaign fighting drew near, the men of the 12th South Carolina waited out the harsh end of winter and slow onset of spring in the rustic camps near Orange Court House. Snow continued to fall at regular intervals well into March, the snow on the ground still knee-deep as late as March 23, and the weather was hardly better in early April, as a combination of rain, sleet, and snow deluged the camp.

A visit by North Carolina Gov. Zebulon Vance, meeting with soldiers from the brigade's nearby Tar Heel contingent, would provide a memorable distraction for the men of 12th South Carolina. Many walked the short distance from their own camp to listen as the popular Vance delivered speeches before his fellow Tar Heels. In one such speech to Alfred Scales's Brigade, William Templeton recalled that Vance "made the beast speach i ever heard. He toald them to fight to the last an never giv up nor desert. . . . [W]hen he spoke of the brave boys who had falin in defence of their country the tears run down his cheak."[3]

* * *

The 12th, as well as the entire brigade, would depend on an influx of food and clothing from various sources that miserable winter. Writing to the *Yorkville Enquirer* on March 28, Capt. J. T. Parker, commanding Company A, thanked William McCorkle for "six pairs of wool socks" that the company's former commander had sent to the front. "We appreciate the gift, not only on account of its intrinsic value to the destitute soldiers," Parker wrote, "but with it is conveyed to us the pleasing assurance that we are still kindly remembered by our 'old captain.'"

2 Dunlop, *Lee's Sharpshooters*, 18–23.

3 William Templeton to Sarah Templeton, April 4, 1864.

Captain William S. Dunlop of Company B was promoted to Major and commanded McGowan's Brigade Sharpshooter Battalion during the last year of the war. *Lee's Sharpshooters*

"To know that while here exposed to all the toils, hardships and privations of a soldier's life, we are remembered and cared for by our friends at home. . . . Articles of clothing, especially socks, are much needed by many of our soldiers, who cannot be supplied by either home or from the Quarter-Master's Department. Let other friends imitate the example of Colonel McCorkle."[4]

In addition to donations sent directly to the front, the South Carolina Central Association continued its critical work as the middleman between those eager to donate items and the men in the ranks. With trains departing frequently to Richmond, individuals hoping to send items to a specific soldier or make a general donation to one of the regiments needed only get the package to the headquarters in Columbia with assurances that the quartermaster of the brigade would compensate the benefactor for any articles furnished. Particularly important that winter was the association's purchase of 15,000 pounds of hides and 11,000 yards of fabric that would be converted into shoes and uniforms for the troops. And even in his retirement from active field service, the Rev. J. Monroe Anderson continued to entreat the citizenry in the various counties for supplies and material, reiterating passionately that the government was simply incapable of adequately supplying the men with socks, blankets, and clothing. He also promised that he would personally take the donated articles to the association as assurance they would reach the troops as intended.[5]

In addition to the work of the Central Association and direct mailings, private citizens also took matters into their own hands. Jonathan N. McElwee Jr., a resident

4 Parker, "Acknowledgment," 1.

5 "Items," *Yorkville Enquirer*, Feb. 17, 1864, 2; J. Monroe Anderson, *To the Ladies of York Dist.*, Nov. 25, 1863, 2.

of the Taylor's Creek region in York County, advertised in the *Yorkville Enquirer* that he would "take charge of any boxes of provisions, uncooked, and clothing that you may please send" to the troops "free of any charge for my time and services." McElwee offered two dates within a two-week window for families to meet him in Yorkville. "I hope that the friends will respond to this call," he appealed, "as much praise and gratulation is rendered for all such favors."[6]

Despite the supply challenges and blustery weather, good news arrived for the 12th in mid-March. Several soldiers of the regiment, including some wounded and captured at Gettysburg, had been exchanged and allowed to go home from various northern hospitals and prison camps. Among the fortunate were Lieutenant Boyles, H. Dogins of Company G, and E. S. Danvin of Company B. The news, however, was not entirely positive: P. P. Hall of Company K, W. P. Wyrick of Company C, and J. H. Smith and G. W. Cobb of Company B had perished while in captivity at either David's Island, New York, or Point Lookout, Maryland.[7]

Picket and fatigue duty intensified in April. Company B was frequently stationed near the home of a Mr. Houser, where the wives of both Colonel Miller and General Thomas were staying. One of the soldiers stationed as a guard at the home was William Templeton, who confided in letters to his sister that his duties were considerably light. "I onley stay in day light to keep horses out of his wheatfield an to keep the soldiears from throwing down the fence. He boards me. . . . I don't have to stay [out] wen it is raining."

As the weather continued to warm, rumors of a pending campaign filtered through the camp and that the army would begin moving any day. On April 18, the 12th received orders to send all its surplus baggage to the rear. The opponent this spring would be the same Army of the Potomac, but with a twist. Although George Meade remained the formal head of the largest Federal army, he would now command in the field under the watchful eye of Lt. Gen. Ulysses S. Grant, whom Lincoln had named commanding general of all United States armies in March.[8]

On May 4, Colonel Miller notified his company commanders that the regiment would move out that day. As the men scurried to gather and pack their belongings and cook their rations, "a universal stir ensued," wrote one veteran. Some officers' tents were torn down, cut apart, and distributed among the soldiers for use as shelter in the coming campaign. Fielding approximately 480 men, the 12th marched out of the camp about noon, joining the brigade's other units in

6 Jona. N. McElwee Jr., "To the Friends," *Yorkville Enquirer*, Feb. 10, 1864, 2.

7 "Our Soldiers," *Yorkville Enquirer*, March 16, 1864, 2.

8 William Templeton to Sarah Templeton, April 16, 1864, and April 28, 1864; Joseph Templeton to Sarah Templeton, April 30, 1864; Welch, *A Confederate Surgeon's Letters to His Wife*, 90.

a centralized area between the camps. Before long, McGowan had the South Carolinians on the move. After marching through Orange Court House, they struck the Orange Plank Road and headed purposefully toward familiar ground and Fredericksburg. "The gait was not slackened until sunset," recalled one veteran.

The brigade marched behind Henry Heth's Division and would bivouac near Verdiersville. That evening, Hill received the consent of General Lee and Jefferson Davis to commute the sentences of 12 soldiers in McGowan's Brigade either under arrest or facing court-martials—part of an army-wide push to help bolster the ranks for the pending fighting. Four soldiers from the 12th were in that group, each sentenced to execution for desertion: Privates David Ramey, I. W. Ramey, and S. H. Bothel of Company K and J. W. H. Ramey of Company G. Lee told Davis he consented on Hill's behalf "in consideration of their former character as soldiers for gallantry and the faithful discharge of their duties—And in Private David Ramey's case, further in consideration of his refusing to listen to the persuasions of his Uncle and quitting the party of deserters and returning to his duty, his extreme youth and unanimous recommendation from the court."[9]

The men were on the road again by dawn, with the 12th in front. Speculation swirled that the Army of the Potomac had crossed the Rapidan and was advancing toward Spotsylvania Court House. As the morning march progressed, the South Carolinians began to hear artillery fire to the front as well as evidence of battle in the form of wounded Confederate cavalrymen, Union prisoners being sent to the rear, and dead Federal soldiers lying along the road. As the men entered the tangly thickets of the area that would become known as "The Wilderness," brush fires could be seen at a distance. About 2:00 p.m., McGowan halted the column, allowing the men to rest. To the left was an open field surrounded by woods where the artillery battalion of William T. Poague was positioned.[10]

As skirmishing increased to the front, McGowan ordered Miller to file the 12th to the left and lead the brigade through that field containing Poague's guns. While tramping through the tall grass behind the cannons, the men caught a brief glimpse of both Lee and J. E. B. Stuart. It was about 4:00 p.m., and many doubted any serious fighting would take place given the late hour.

McGowan advanced another half-mile and placed his brigade to the right of Ewell's Second Corps in another tangle of woods, forming a battle line on a "clear,

9 Caldwell, *The History of a Brigade of South Carolinians*, 173; *Supplement to OR* 6(1):774–778; LOCAL, "Army Correspondence for the Ledger," *Lancaster Ledger*, Nov. 8, 1864, 1; Douglas S. Freeman, ed., *Lee's Dispatches: Unpublished Letters of General Robert E. Lee, C.S.A., to Jefferson Davis and the War Department of the Confederate States of America, 1862-1865* (Baton Rouge, LA, 1994), 149–150.

10 Caldwell, *The History of a Brigade of South Carolinians*, 173; *Supplement to OR* 6(1):774–778.

commanding ridge" between Ewell and Poague's artillery. The men, however, had no sooner caught their breath when orders arrived by courier from Hill for McGowan to return his brigade to the Plank Road. There, Lee ordered McGowan to advance up the road toward the position occupied by Heth's Division, already heavily engaged.[11]

During their scramble toward the fighting, Heth rode back to meet with McGowan, instructing him to deploy the South Carolinians on both sides of the road—three regiments on the left, the other two on the right. Firing could be heard to the front right, so McGowan amended Heth's orders slightly on the fly, directing Miller to deploy on the extreme right of the road, to be joined by Orr's Rifles to the 12th's left and the 1st South Carolina adjacent to the road, while the 13th and 14th occupied the ground left of the road. It was about 5:30 p.m. "[A]s the formation was made under fire, I soon perceived that the enemy pressed heaviest on the right of the road," McGowan recalled.

Miller ordered the 12th to march to the right and led the regiment into the woods perpendicular to the Plank Road. As McGowan's Brigade deployed, the North Carolinians in Scales's Brigade jetted off behind the 12th and moved farther to the right—a move designed to extend the South Carolinians' flank, though Scales men, perhaps mistakenly, roamed out of sight and adequate supporting distance. Once the 12th, Orr's Rifles, and the 1st cleared the Plank Road, Miller ordered the 12th to front and advance toward the increasing sound of fury in the woods ahead.[12]

His dispositions set, McGowan ordered a general advance toward Heth's fragmented lines. Spurring his horse forward and waving his sword over his head, McGowan led the cheering South Carolinians through the dense foliage. "We entered the conflict alone," recalled one veteran. "As soon as the line was formed and dressed, the order to advance was given."

With full-throated cheers that echoed through the woods, according to J. F. J. Caldwell, the 12th traversed the thick underbrush with its "accustomed gallantry"—the advance encumbered substantially by "thickly set saplings that covered probably several hundred acres of ground" and "logs, brush and other impediments." After passing through Heth's stalled lines, the men continued another 400–500 yards—"like a gale through the woods," in the words of an impressed Wilcox—to finish what turned into a rout of Brig. Gen. George W. Getty's 2nd Division in Maj. Gen. John Sedgwick's VI Corps. Chaos reigned

11 Caldwell, *The History of a Brigade of South Carolinians*, 174; *Supplement to OR* 6(1):774–778.

12 *Supplement to OR* 6(1):774–778.

absolute due to the rough terrain, the difficulty keeping the men in formation, enemy fire, smoke, and the worn out soldiers of Heth's division, who "mostly lying on the ground, kept up a scattering fire through our ranks and over our heads it was difficult to say which, after we passed in their front." For many veterans, the unremitting surge summoned memories of similar onslaughts at Second Manassas, Sharpsburg, and Gettysburg. Watching the impressive charge, Caldwell recalled that the 12th, "was soon lost to us in the great maelstrom of the enemy's lines."

Bullets whizzed by and caught not only men but the trees as the 12th and other regiments halted to commence firing. "[T]he range of the enemy's balls was very high," Caldwell remembered well after the war. "[I]ndeed I remember reaching up with my sword to the scars upon the trees to show the men around me how wild our adversary's aim was, and using that to impress upon them the importance of low, accurate firing on our part so as to destroy the line opposed to us before they ascertained our range." Once the Federals found their aim, however, the return fire was devasting, causing "fearful damage" to the ranks. As the advance grounded to a halt, the men instinctively found cover and knelt among the dead and wounded.[13]

Critically, Miller would be wounded, struck in the bowels as he raced ahead with his sword in the air, and so was Lt. Col. Edwin Bookter. Command of the regiment passed to Major Clyburn, now faced with the decision whether to continue the assault, hold fast, or fall back. The Federal defense had stiffened, and with the sun setting and the 12th's top two commanders out of action, Clyburn realized he was in a precarious position, on the verge of being surrounded—no support on his right and Orr's Rifles lagging to the rear. In the chaos, under darkening skies, his men in the jumbled lines had resorted to fighting and shooting in all directions. More bluecoats quickly massed in the woods on both the regiment's front and flanks.

Clyburn gathered his Federal prisoners and placed them behind his lines. He then ordered the 12th to about-face and return to the brigade's main line. That almost backfired. With the prisoners now at the regiment's front, Confederates in other units feared a Union attack was underway and considered opening fire. "The line behind us came near firing on us, thinking it was a Yankee line," one officer remembered, "and we had to holler and show them in every way we could, that we're not a Yankee line, [which] kept them from firing into us."

Meanwhile, on the other side of the Orange Plank Road, the 13th and 14th regiments had driven forward and captured a gun in Capt. R. Bruce Ricketts's 1st Pennsylvania Light, Battery F in the II Corps, commanded again by Maj. Gen. Winfield S. Hancock. One of the Palmetto State regiments even planted its flag

13 Caldwell, "McGowan's Brigade at the Battle of the Wilderness, *Newberry Herald*, Aug. 17, 1882, 1.

at the gun's position before it was compelled to relinquish the prize as enemy forces closed in.

With his five regiments sputtering against the reinforced Federal VI and II Corps, McGowan ordered a general withdrawal. Gravitating toward the Plank Road, the somewhat disorganized regiments created a narrow, finger-like line that traversed the critical thoroughfare. It became a three-sided clash, the South Carolinians fighting back-to-back as they fell rearward in danger of being enveloped.

"On our return the enemy was so near the road on both sides that their balls crossed each other," McGowan wrote in his after-action report. Another soldier would be more critical, claiming, "[O]ur line was miserably short. For a time, we had a front of but a single brigade. I do not judge anyone; but I think it was the shortest most huddled, most ineffective line of battle I ever saw. But for the gallantry of our troops, which even surpassed itself, all must have been lost."[14]

It did not help that other brigades to the left in both Wilcox's and Heth's divisions were also spread thin and faltering. As the sun set, the fire finally died down. McGowan shifted his command to the left of the Plank Road and attempted to reorganize the regiments. The line continued to resemble a semi-circle, though, and Major Dunlop recalled that there was "little order or distinctive organization."

Amid the creeping darkness, the South Carolinians hunkered down, and some members of the 12th even stole down to a small stream between the lines to secure water for their empty canteens. "Anxious and uneasy and under a felt sense of insecurity, these gallant men spent the live long night in this exposed and disorganized condition," Dunlop would write.[15]

The fight in the woods had left Wilcox's and Heth's lines in shambles, now a hodgepodge of regiments and brigades waiting the night out essentially in the spots where they stopped firing. Although the Wilderness was an ideal place to fix a line and defend against an overwhelming assault, it proved impossible for troops on the offensive to attack and keep order. McGowan did what he could to rectify his lines, but darkness, fatigue, and confusion would inevitably trump the effort this evening.

The 12th was positioned roughly parallel to the Plank Road at a southerly angle, its right flank closer to the road than its left. The regiment occupied the brigade's extreme right, with the 14th, 1st, and 13th extended to the left in that

14 Caldwell, *The History of a Brigade of South Carolinians*, 177–178; *OR* 36(1):677; *Supplement to OR* 6(1):774–778; Dunlop, *Lee's Sharpshooters*, 398; Cadwallader Jones Jr. to My Dear Brother, Oct. 3, 1922, UNC. J. Fitz James Caldwell, "McGowan's Brigade at the Battle of the Wilderness," *Newberry Herald*, August 17, 1882, 1.

15 Dunlop, *Lee's Sharpshooters*, 32.

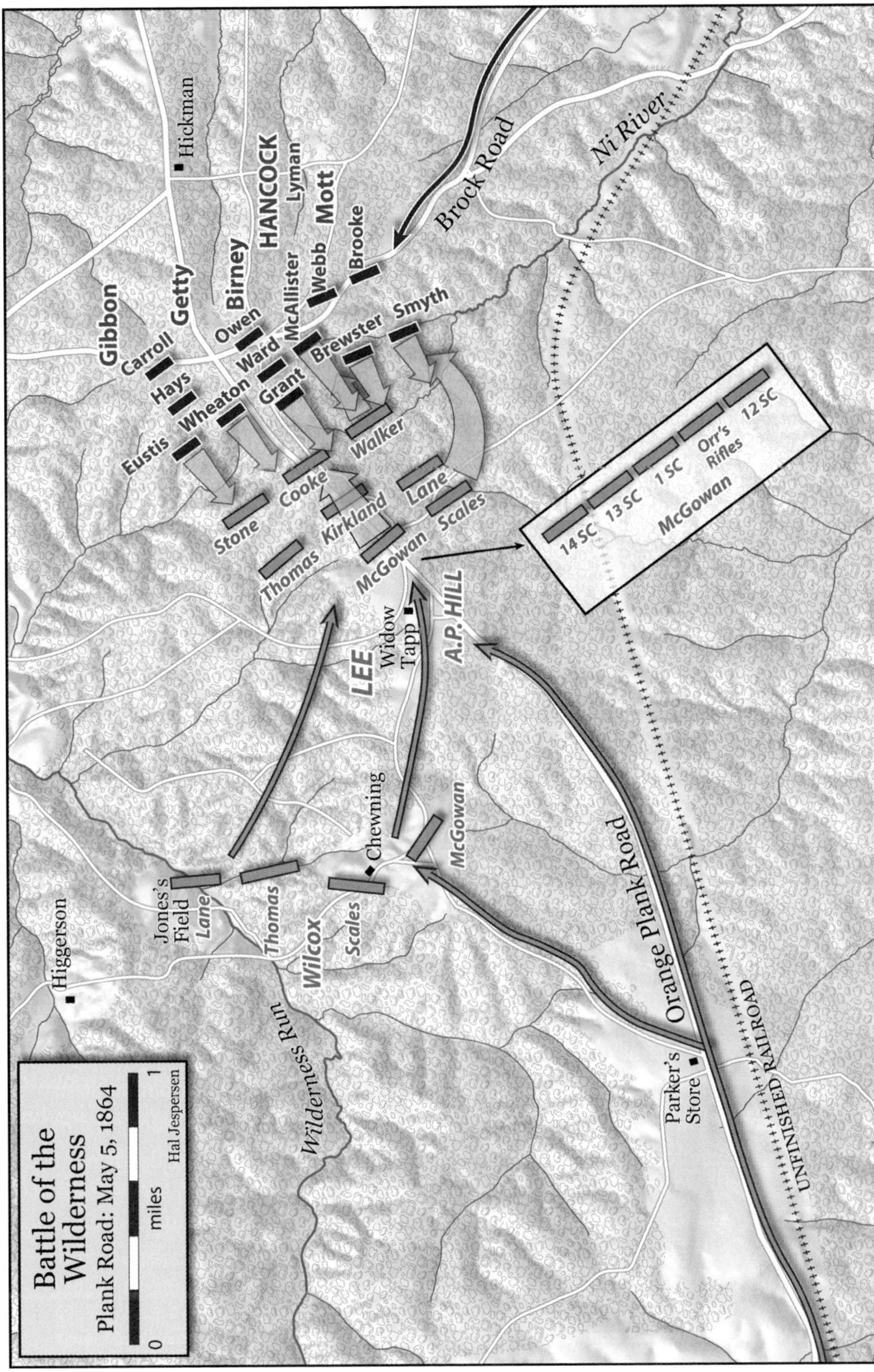

Battle of the Wilderness
Plank Road: May 5, 1864
0
miles
1
Hal Jespersen
Gibbon
Getty
Birney
HANCOCK
Mott
Lyman
Hickman
Carroll
Hays
Eustis
Wheaton
Owen
Ward
Grant
McAllister
Webb
Brooke
Brewster
Smyth
Walker
Cooke
Stone
Kirkland
Lane
Scales
Thomas
McGowan
A.P. HILL
LEE
Widow Tapp
14 SC
13 SC
1 SC
Orr's Rifles
12 SC
McGowan
Brock Road
Ni River
Orange Plank Road
UNFINISHED RAILROAD
Parker's Store
Chewning
Jones's Field
Lane
Thomas
Wilcox
Scales
McGowan
Higgerson
Wilderness Run

A view of hastily built breastworks constructed by the Confederates near the Plank Road during the battle of the Wilderness. *Library of Congress*

order, facing east. McGowan detached Orr's Rifles and Dunlop's sharpshooter battalion as skirmishers. Across the road from the 12th South Carolina, also at a standstill, was General Thomas's shattered Georgia brigade.[16]

General Wilcox, commanding the division for the first time in a major battle, was understandably worried about his position. About 9:00 p.m., he rode to the front for a personal examination, recalling after the war that his lines were "very irregular and much broken and required to be re-arranged." Wilcox rode from there to Lee's headquarters to recommend that his brigades be promptly withdrawn to reorganize. Before Wilcox could make his suggestion, Lee assured him that Longstreet's First Corps would be up early in the morning to relieve his battered troops.

Heth, meanwhile, had met with A. P. Hill to voice his concerns about the situation. Hill was adamant, however, that he did not want the exhausted troops bothered at such a late hour. Confirming that Longstreet was scheduled to arrive early, he shooed away the persistent division commander with a firm, "Damn it, Heth. I don't want to hear any more about it; the men shall not be disturbed."[17]

16 Caldwell, *The History of a Brigade of South Carolinians*, 178–180.

17 Wilcox, *Annals of War*, 495; James L. Morrison Jr., ed., *The Memoirs of Henry Heth* (Westport, CT, 1974), 184.

"The night of May 5 was an anxious one," McGowan recalled. "The troops stood to their arms all night in the same broken order in which they were at the close of the fight; the line, if any, was something like an irregular horseshoe—no two brigades touching each other. They had made a good march in the forenoon of that day and then had fought until after dark. Hungry, thirsty and fatigued, they had to pass a sleepless night, during the long hours of which the enemy could be distinctly heard in the thick cover of the Wilderness making arrangements to envelop them."[18]

Shortly after the firing ceased, Captain Cadwallader Jones Jr. of Company H dispatched a canteen detail to fetch water for his men. Incredibly, the detail crossed behind the Federal position and managed to return unscathed. As he rested in the dark forest, Jones opened a can of condensed milk he found on the ground earlier in the day. "I opened the can-and oh, my how good it then was," he recalled.

As the men did what they could to sleep, or at least rest, surgeons attached to McGown's Brigade worked feverishly to care for the wounded. One of the injured was an unidentified soldier from Company C who, along with several comrades, had been late getting into the fight. Those hardy souls had been ordered to the rear that morning to guide ambulances to the front lines and did not join the 12th until the latter stages of the clash. Trying to find the regiment in the dense foliage, one of the young men would be surprised by a Federal soldier, just a few paces away, and was shot through both thighs. As he lay on the ground losing blood, the poor soldier listened helplessly to the groans of his fellow wounded.

Ambulance stewards soon arrived and placed the soldier on a stretcher, carrying him to the regiment's field hospital, where he lay for some time desperate for water. One of the assistant stewards detailed at the hospital was D. J. Carter of Company I. Moved by the young man's distress, Carter provided him the much-needed water and even offered a drink from a bottle of brandy he pulled from his haversack, captured from the Federals earlier in the day. The water and liquor did the trick. "The sight of Mr. Carter, the drink of water and the sip of brandy had a wonderful effect on me," the man recalled years later. "I began to think I would not die." Carter and a surgeon bound the young man's wounds and reassured him that he would be among the first sent to the rear for better care.

Just before dawn, McGowan began to rectify the irregular alignments of his regiments on the left side of the Plank Road while General Thomas did the same on the right side. About this time, Wilcox rode up and concurred with McGowan that the brigade's right-most regiment (the 12th) should rest at a nearly a right

18 *Supplement to OR* 6(1):774–778.

angle on and to the road, informing him that Longstreet and his 25,000-man First Corps were expected to be "on the spot in a few minutes."

Before any major shifting or dressing of the line could take place, however, McGowan and Wilcox, as well as the weary men of the 12th just awaking, would see a distant sea of shadowy blue troops moving in their direction. They watched in horror as Thomas's Brigade, just across the Plank Road to the right, was consumed by what could best be described as a blue tidal wave. Dunlop and his sharpshooters began to engage the enemy but were slowly thrown back to the main battle line. Thomas implored help from McGowan, but before the South Carolinians could respond, the Georgia troops gave way, many of them streaming back through the woods and using the Plank Road as an escape route. In an instant, McGowan had lost support on his right and the Yankee onslaught in his brigade's direction showed no sign of abatement.[19]

These Union troops were from Hancock's II Corps, and they meant business. Clyburn and the remnants of his regiment opened fire and did their best to hold on as the swarming enemy troops struck their position. The void created by the Georgians' frantic retreat, however, allowed the Federals to envelop the 12th's right and rear.

Clyburn ordered his command to fire in all directions, with clusters of men fighting in no semblance of order behind trees and crudely constructed breastworks. Federal enfilade fire on the 12th's right threatened to cut McGowan's Brigade off from the rear. Federal soldiers began calling on the 12th to surrender. Nothing to date, not even the close call at Fredericksburg, had equaled this desperate moment in the regiment's history.

Incredulous at the suggestion of surrender, Clyburn and his men would have none of it. Doubling his calls for the return fire to continue, the major ran up and down the line to rally those able to fight. With hundreds, perhaps thousands, of Confederates streaming toward the rear on both sides of McGowan's Brigade, the only thing standing between the Federal army and Lee's supply lines were the 12th and their fellow South Carolinians. Clyburn quickly ordered the regiment to re-fuse its line to the west, but that bought only a few minutes of relief. With a retreat the only remaining option to avoid capture, Clyburn finally swallowed his

19 Caldwell, *The History of a Brigade of South Carolinians*, 180; *Supplement to OR* 6(1):774–778; "An Incident of the War," *Lancaster Ledger*, Jan. 29, 1898, 3; Cadwallader Jones Jr. to My Dear Brother, Oct. 3, 1922, UNC; Caldwell, "McGowan's Brigade at the Battle of the Wilderness," *Newberry Herald*, Aug. 17, 1882, 1.

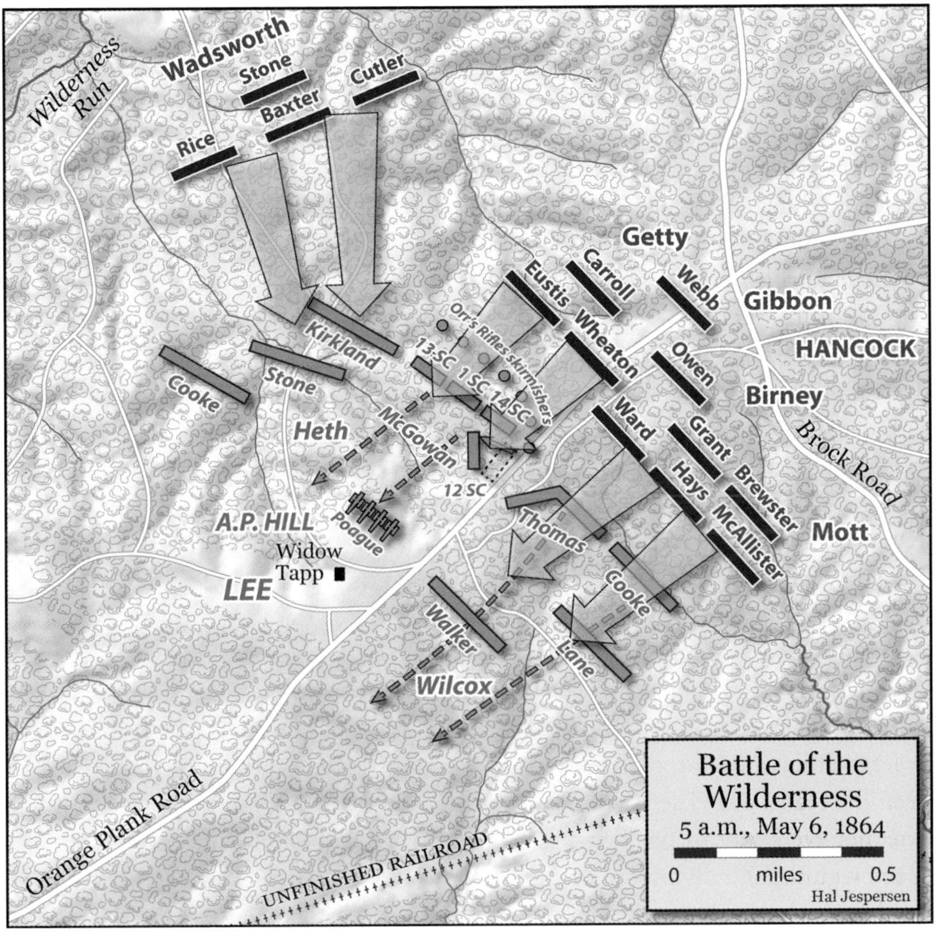

pride and had his men fall back. The 12th's retreat, in turn, sparked the other four regiments to follow suit.[20]

McGowan described the experience as "mortifying" but admitted that "under the circumstances it could not be helped." Conceded Captain Jones: "We did really almost get into a panic. I had never before seen such condition."

The South Carolinians' retreat would halt near the Widow Tapp farm, where Lee and Hill attempted to rally the Third Corps' shattered remnants. The sight of Heth's and Wilcox's men falling back in disorder horrified Lee, who, according to one South Carolinian, was "excited and chagrined" and "expressed himself rather roughly" to the officers and file closers who entered the field in chaos.

20 Caldwell, *The History of a Brigade of South Carolinians*, 180.

Descriptions of the retrograde movement from the woods vary: Some versions put the troops in full rout while others, such as Caldwell, described it as an orderly withdrawal. In reality it was probably a combination of both, with certain clusters of men running for their lives and other units maintaining more cohesion. When Wilcox emerged from the smoky woods and reported what was transpiring, an exasperated Lee implored, "Longstreet must be here; go bring him up." The major general, apparently believing he had been assigned duty as a mere staff officer, rode off in blind obedience, leaving his retreating division in the dust.

Lee then directed Lt. Col. Walter H. Taylor, his assistant adjutant general, to ride to the rear and prepare the army's supply train for a retreat, and in turn ordered Maj. Charles Venable, an aide de camp, also to find the absent Longstreet. Disaster for the Army of Northern Virginia seemed imminent.[21]

As he rode between groups of Hill's soldiers that chaotic morning, Lee saved perhaps his most intense frustration for McGowan. Finding the general on foot in one of the groups falling back, Lee could not contain his irritation. "My God! General McGowan is this splendid brigade of yours running like a flock of geese?" he scolded, stopping the veteran brigadier in his tracks. Recalled one of McGowan's aides: "I stood less than forty feet from him, when he spoke, and the words burned themselves into my memory. . . . I am not sure but his anger implied a sort of compliment to our past performances."

McGowan, having perhaps the worst day of his military career, shot back to Lee: "No, General! The men are not whipped. They just want a place to form and they are ready to fight as well as ever." As Lee rode off through the smoke, McGowan began rallying the men.[22]

Lee's annoyance was understandable but not completely justified. The troops, according to Venable, were not panicked—just disordered, having been outflanked by superior numbers. "The assertion, made by several writers, that Hill's troops were driven back a mile and a half is a most serious mistake," Venable wrote years later. "The right of his line was thrown back several hundred yards, but a portion of the troops still maintained their position."

21 *Supplement to OR* 6(1):774–778; Caldwell, *The History of a Brigade of South Carolinians*, 181; Wilcox, *Annals of War*, 496; *SHSP* 14:525; Cadwallader Jones Jr. to My Dear Brother, Oct. 3, 1922, UNC. For an assertive prosecution of Longstreet and the failure of his First Corps to be on the field (titled "Did Longstreet Loiter?") and an equally affirmative and full-throated defense and description of the brigade's rearward movement as an organized redeployment, see Caldwell, "McGowan's Brigade at the Battle of the Wilderness," *Newberry Herald*, Aug. 17, 1882, 1–2.

22 Caldwell, *The History of a Brigade of South Carolinians*, 181; Alexander, *Fighting for the Confederacy*, 357.

Captain Jones wrote that the brigade had been driven back only about a quarter-mile, and E. P. Alexander was among those to claim Hill's troops had not been devastated, shocked, or routed: "Indeed, the bearing of the men fully confirmed McGowan's statement, that they were not whipped out of their position, but flanked out."

Sergeant Berry Benson, a sharpshooter in Dunlop's battalion, recalled being within earshot of Lee and McGowan during their terse exchange, asserting that the troops almost immediately halted and formed. "The brigade was not demoralized or panic-stricken but acted from necessity," McGowan decreed in his after-action report, "[and] reformed at once in rear of Poague's Artillery, which opened upon and checked the advancing enemy."

With Wilcox to the rear on Lee's mission to find Longstreet, Hill began organizing the remnants of the Light Division and sent them down the Orange Plank Road. It was about then that the men saw Lee's "Old Warhorse" riding toward them, followed by a column of fresh troops. Hill directed his troops to the left of the road to wait for Longstreet to pass.

At that point, McGowan advanced to the same position his men held the evening before, on that open ridge about a mile from the Plank Road and closer to Ewell's position. Ahead of the line, Dunlop and the brigade's skirmish line soon made contact with Federal pickets, and sporadic gunfire broke out. Ordered to move back about 200 yards as a precaution, the South Carolinians began building breastworks out of logs and rails.[23]

Although Longstreet would be gravely wounded that day—like Stonewall Jackson at Chancellorsville, a victim of friendly fire—the arrival of his corps checked the Federal onslaught against Wilcox and Heth. As they furiously threw up breastworks, the men of the 12th could hear the gunfire and cheering erupting from Longstreet's clash along the Plank Road, as well as Ewell's engagement to their left. Although disaster had been averted, the men could not shake their disappointment, convinced they had been hung out to dry that morning and therefore flanked from their position. "It would have been a great relief to chastise somebody in reparation of our morning's misfortune," one soldier remarked drily.

As May 6 closed, the Army of Northern Virginia had restored its lines, turning the enemy back at several critical points—even managing a sweeping flank attack that rattled the Army of the Potomac's high command. Lying in their hastily built

23 Gallagher, ed., *Fighting for the Confederacy*, 357; Benson, *Berry Benson's Civil War Book*, 64; *Supplement to OR* 6(1):774–778; Caldwell, *The History of a Brigade of South Carolinians*, 181, 183; Cadwallader Jones Jr. to My Dear Brother, Oct. 3, 1922, UNC.

earthworks, the South Carolinians could at least sleep a little easier than they had the night before.[24]

With roll call the morning of May 7, the casualty totals were somewhat shocking. Of 1,700 rifles carried into the fight, the brigade had lost 481 men killed, wounded, or missing. The 12th had the second highest casualty count in the brigade at 102 (16 killed, 64 wounded, and 22 missing). Three officers were killed: Miller, who succumbed to his wounds the evening of May 5, and Lts. James R. McKnight and L. Armp Garvin. Three others were wounded: Lt. Col. Edwin Bookter and Lts. J. A. Watson and J. A. Beard.

The loss of Colonel Miller hit the regiment the hardest. He had been in command for more than a year and had led it to great success at Gettysburg, through the long retreat back to Virginia, and the subsequent harsh winter of 1863-64. His tactics in the field mirrored those of his mentor, Dixon Barnes, and he earned the deep admiration of all who knew him. Affable and courteous, he was well-respected not only in the regiment but also the entire brigade—the 12th's longest-serving commander. Just 33, Miller left behind a widow and several small children in South Carolina.[25]

* * *

The regiment had little time to mourn the loss. That afternoon, with a foul smell in the air and smoke above and through the trees obscuring sightlines, the brigade moved into the woods from its position between the wings of Lee's army. In that forest, the men were put to work constructing breastworks of rails and logs, though before long they would be ordered to continue moving a few hundred yards to the right, where they bivouacked for the evening. As they filed into this new position, the men participated in a cavalcade of shouting and cheering that began to sweep through the Confederate lines, many believing it signified good fortune. "It seemed to fill every heart with new life, to inspire every nerve with might never known before," Caldwell wrote. The Army of Northern Virginia had survived its first collision with Ulysses S. Grant.[26]

On the afternoon of May 8, McGowan's Brigade left its crude home in the earthworks and began marching south. Grant, foiled in his initial push through

24 Caldwell, *The History of a Brigade of South Carolinians*, 183.

25 Ibid., 185–186. Colonel Miller's body, along with wounded Brig. Gen. John Pegram, arrived in Richmond on the evening of May 7 via the Virginia Central Railroad. See "Arrival of Wounded," *Richmond Enquirer*, May 10, 1864, 1.

26 Ibid., 184.

the Wilderness, did not turn back, as most of his predecessors had done. Rather, he was moving to the left, headed for the crossroads town of Spotsylvania Court House, about 17 miles away. Lee had responded quickly; with the advantage of interior lines to that vital site on the road to Richmond, he wasted little time getting his men on the road.

Clyburn led his bloodied 12th on a path that cut through portions of the Wilderness battlefield. The sight, one veteran recalled, was "distressing." Shallow graves—holding the remains of many a comrade—and dead horses dotted the landscape. Amid a haunting tapestry of charred and burning trees, dropped or discarded rifles and various accoutrements littered the ground, and the stench of burning flesh and uniforms containing vegetable dye filled the air.

The men bivouacked that night near Shady Grove Church, about eight miles away, without much in the way of rations or water, resuming the march early the next morning and reaching the village of Spotsylvania without incident. As they approached the crossroads town, the brigade formed in a "column of regiments." About a half-mile from the courthouse itself, Wilcox placed the brigade on the army's extreme right. The men were directed to erect breastworks as Dunlop's sharpshooters moved forward to feel out the Federal positions.

"The system of fighting behind fortifications was now established," wrote a veteran. Their position was along a ridge of hills that commanded open fields from all views—"entirely secure" he remembered. Both armies spent the next few days waiting on edge, or perhaps skirmishing. Sporadic shelling from the Federal guns became a nuisance.[27]

As Dunlop's sharpshooter battalion probed the Federal lines on May 9, one of his top marksmen—Benjamin Powell of the 12th's Company I—would purportedly make history. Regarded as one of the finest shots in McGowan's Brigade, if not the entire Army of Northern Virginia, Powell was awarded a rare Whitworth rifle with a telescope sight just before the battle of Gettysburg—one of only two men in the brigade eligible for that honor. When the brigade's sharpshooter battalion was organized in the spring of 1864, Powell was a natural fit and even secured a commission as an independent, roving sharpshooter and scout allowed to operate generally as he pleased, often reporting directly to high-ranking officers such as McGowan and Wilcox. Regardless, he continued to identify proudly as a soldier in the 12th.

Sergeant Benson of the 1st South Carolina was one of Powell's friends and recalled that on May 9 Powell crowed he had killed a "big Yankee officer" that

27 *Supplement to OR* 6(1):774–778; *OR* 36(1):1093; Caldwell, *The History of a Brigade of South Carolinians*, 187.

morning. Benson was initially suspicious of the claim, convinced that Powell mistook the officer for a cavalryman. Powell, however, insisted his victim had been a prominent Federal, considering how the men around reacted once he went down. That evening, Federal pickets called across the picket line with news that a Confederate sharpshooter had indeed killed Maj. Gen. John Sedgwick, the VI Corps' commander. And in a postwar letter to his wife, Powell took credit for the feat, declaring that the Whitworth rifle he had been awarded "killed General Sedgwick at Spotsylvania Court House."[28]

* * *

On May 12, a long, meandering battle line had materialized for the Army of Northern Virginia at Spotsylvania. With Longstreet's wounding at the Wilderness, Third Corps division commander Richard Anderson was handed command of the First Corps, which occupied Lee's left flank. Ewell's Second Corps occupied the center, behind a salient a little more than a mile wide and roughly three-quarters of a mile deep that protruded from the main Confederate line and would become known as the "Mule Shoe" for its shape. And the Third Corps, now commanded by Jubal Early with Hill sidelined by illness, occupied the Confederate right flank.

Grant spent his first few days at Spotsylvania trying to ascertain Lee's defenses, particularly on the left, and on May 10 even attempted a direct attack on the salient by Col. Emory Upton, commanding 5,000 men in 12 regiments. Miscommunication among commanders and stiff Confederate resistance ultimately foiled Upton's attack, but it had shown promise. Determining that a similar attack on the position by a larger force would be successful, Grant planned for a second attempt to take place May 12. The larger force would actually be Hancock's entire 20,000-man II Corps. The hope was Hancock would grab control of the Confederate center with a massive attack on the Mule Shoe salient and that the sustained pressure from that would force the collapse of the rest of Lee's defenses.

To keep Lee from shifting reinforcements to the threatened center, Grant planned for simultaneous attacks from the east by Ambrose Burnside's IX Corps and from the west by Gouverneur Warren's V Corps. The VI Corps, now commanded by Brig. Gen. Horatio Wright with Sedgwick's death, was held back just behind Hancock's lines, ready to move in to exploit any gains made at the salient.

Before dawn on a miserable, rainy May 12, Hancock's assault began as directed. The Federals crashed through Ewell's lines and captured most of Edward

28 Berry Benson, "Who Killed General Sedgwick," *Augusta Chronicle*, Nov. 25, 1917; Benjamin Powell to Wife, Nov. 21, 1907.

Johnson's Division within an hour. Although Burnside moved from the east simultaneously, his attack was relatively half-hearted—"feeble," in the opinion of several historians—and would be blunted primarily by James Lane's North Carolina Brigade. Worse for Hancock, the planned attack by Warren on Lee's extreme left did not take place for reasons that were never adequately justified. That allowed Lee time to shift critical reinforcements to Ewell's threatened center, precisely what Grant had feared.

Just before 9:00 a.m., with Grant's attack well underway, McGowan's five regiments were ordered to march from their position near a brick kiln on the Confederate right toward the "sound of the guns" in the Confederate center and report directly to General Ewell. In the heavy rain and knee-deep muck, the South Carolinians would struggle to maintain a double-quick pace, but nevertheless reached Ewell within the hour.

Ewell informed McGowan that General Rodes, one of his division commanders, would lead the fight to reclaim the Mule Shoe. As the mud-caked South Carolinians continued moving ahead, Rodes inquired about the troops' identity. "McGowan's South Carolina brigade" came the reply from the ranks, drawing an ecstatic response from Rodes, who exclaimed to a group of officers: "There are no better soldiers in the world than these!"

As McGowan surveyed the field from his position near the ramshackle McCoull house and orchard, he focused on two lines of breastworks—a shorter, interior line about 200 yards away, the outer line roughly 100 yards beyond that. In creating these works in the Mule Shoe, the Confederates dug a series of traverses (perpendicular dirt walls) they intended to use for cover both while shooting and while receiving enemy fire. Those traverses figured substantially in the desperate fighting that day.

Continuing to scan the ground ahead, McGowan could also make out disorganized masses of troops in the interior works and what turned out to be Brig. Gen. Nathaniel H. Harris's Brigade of Mississippians in the Third Corps, engaged with the enemy in the outer works. Like a puppet master, Rodes was feeding units into the maelstrom to plug gaps the Federal attack had opened in the Mule Shoe. Although the Confederates had reclaimed portions of the salient to McGowan's right, considerable Federal pressure continued against the works on the left—one of those the ground on which Harris's Mississippians and nearby units were fighting.

Smoke billowed above the woods on their front, and the clips of musketry rattled ominously through the incessant rain. It was a little past 9:00 a.m. From right to left, McGowan deployed the 12th, 1st, 13th, Orr's Rifles, and 14th. For the South Carolinians, the moment offered a golden opportunity for redemption after the rebuke by Lee at the Wilderness, and there was no delay as McGowan sent his men forward at the double-quick. "Forward my brave boys," the general yelled out, mounted on his gray horse.

"There was a good deal of doubt as to how far we should go, or in what direction," McGowan conceded after the war. "At first, it was understood that we should throw ourselves into the woods, where the musketry was, but, somehow, this idea was changed to the impression that we were to move straight forward—which would bring only about the extreme right regiment [the 12th South Carolina] to the chief point of attack."[29]

Confusion would indeed reign as the brigade advanced, and the 12th felt the greatest heat, receiving deadly enfilade fire from the right. As they slogged forward, the men fervently screamed the Rebel yell—a haunting war cry that most veteran Yankees had experienced for some time now. Amid the frenzy of shot and shell, as well as unforgiving rain, the five regiments could not help but disconnect from one another.[30]

Inevitably, the units on the left gravitated toward Harris's rear, his Mississippians battling along the outer works. They halted, however, after reaching the inner works, which were manned at this point by Brig. Gen. William T. Wofford's Georgians and Col. John C. C. Sanders's Alabamians.[31] On the right, though, the "ever reliable" 12th maintained a steady advance toward the outer works, with the Federal fire so thick that the regiment's flagstaff was shot apart twice as the regiment advanced. Their target was a stretch of the salient near a stand of woods. Those woods provided some protection, whereas the remaining regiments remained in the open.

After planting their broken flagstaff defiantly in the outer works, the men began firing in earnest at massive columns of Federals to the right and front at nearly point-blank range. McGowan had been wounded by a Minié ball during the advance; his right arm shattered, he yielded command to Col. Benjamin T. Brockman of the 13th South Carolina. When Brockman was mortally wounded shortly thereafter, Col. Joseph N. Brown of the 14th assumed the reins. Following

29 Caldwell, *The History of a Brigade of South Carolinians*, 183–184; OR 36(1):1093–194; Brown, *A Colonel at Gettysburg and Spotsylvania*, 93–94.

30 Caldwell, *The History of a Brigade of South Carolinians*, 189–190; Brown, *A Colonel at Gettysburg and Spotsylvania*, 21; LOCAL, "For the Lancaster Ledger," *Lancaster Ledger*, June 7, 1864, 2.

31 With the death of a familiar face to McGowan's South Carolinians, Brig. Gen. Abner Perrin, Colonel Sanders assumed command of Perrin's Alabama Brigade. As Chris Mackowski and Kris White note in their book *A Season of Slaughter*, Perrin remarked that morning that he would come out of the fight a "live major general or a dead brigadier." During the early stages of the Mule Shoe fighting, Perrin would be shot seven times as he drove his men forward, fulfilling the unfortunate half of his vow that he would leave the fight a "dead brigadier." Chris Mackowski & Kristopher D. White, *A Season of Slaughter: The Battle of Spotsylvania Court House, May 8–21, 1864* (El Dorado, CA, 2013), 84.

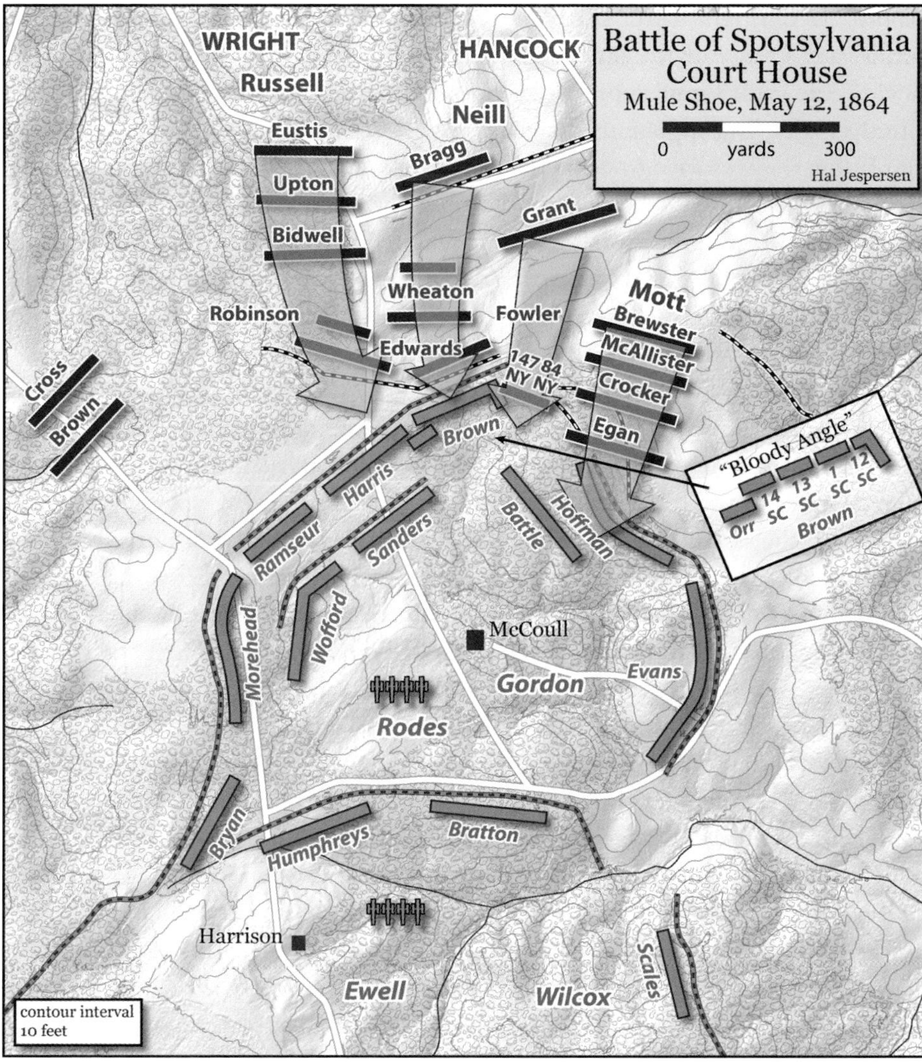

the 12th's lead, Brown quickly dressed the other four regiments still in the inner works and led them forward. As they plunged forward in the knee-deep mud, the 14th on the brigade's left significantly overlapped the right flank of Harris's Mississippians. Upon reaching the 12th's position Brown, or perhaps Lt. Col. Isaac Hunt of the 13th (who was organizing the regiments on that side), ordered Clyburn to shift the 12th right to uncover the brigade's left flank then lagging behind the Mississippians.

As Clyburn's men ducked and moved, using the breastworks' traverses for protection, the other regiments followed, quickly freeing the entangled 14th behind Harris's right flank. The point at which the full brigade finally aligned was a 200-yard stretch of the outer works that soon became known as the "Bloody Angle." The cataclysmic conflict there would endure for several more hours, well into the night. The opponents slugged it out at such close range that in addition to the gunfire they resorted to using bayonets, swords, and even hatchets.

"It was one of the fiercest and most bloody struggles of the war," Brown recalled. Added an officer on McGowan's staff: "The trenches, dug on the inner side, were almost filled with water. Dead men lay on the surface of the ground and in pools of water. The wounded bled and groaned, stretched or huddled in every attitude of pain. The water was crimsoned with blood."

Cadwallader Jones's Company H occupied the 12th's right flank that day. "We took the works in front of us extending far up as the big tree that was shot down by Minnie balls—beyond that up to the angle," he recalled. "My company was extended just to the tree, where the two lines overlapped—We holding one side of the works, and the Yankees holding the other side—for only a short distance, I suppose about ten yards, there was nothing between us except the works."[32]

As Jones worked his men into position, he shuffled them among the traverses, now caked with mud and standing water, to keep out of the line of fire. The Federals did literally occupy the ground just beyond the outer works, and some troops had even penetrated them to the 12th's right, using the traverses, too, to dump fire on Company H from only 15–20 feet. The torrential rain continued to be a factor as the two sides exchanged point-flank fire, with some ammunition water-logged and rendered unusable. Men fired in all directions and at times resorted to reaching their rifles over the traverses to fire away at an unseen enemy. "[I]t was plainly a question of bravery and endurance now," one survivor aptly noted.

In what seemed a repeat of the May 6 struggle in the Wilderness, the men of the 12th were being hammered on the front and right with devasting effect as the battle progressed. Out of necessity, Clyburn bent his right wing at an angle to meet the threat from the right, again using the traverses for cover. With mounting casualties and regimental and company organization broken down, the 12th's position became tenuous. Sensing the urgency on his right, Colonel Brown instructed Hunt to send the 12th reinforcements. For the next few hours, Hunt shuttled as many men and as much ammunition as he could to Clyburn.

As the day wore on, command and control further deteriorated on both sides of the Bloody Angle. The initial push by McGowan's Brigade had driven the Excelsior Brigade in the II Corps out of the salient. The 2nd Rhode Island and 37th Massachusetts of Brig. Gen. Henry L. Eustis's 4th Brigade in the VI Corps gained

32 Cadwallader Jones Jr. to My Dear Brother, July 15, 1922, UNC.

a foothold on the left, however, and poured devasting enfilade fire into the 12th South Carolina as Col. Francis Miller's 147th New York and Col. Edward Fowler's 84th New York (14th Brooklyn) in the V Corps lodged within the traverses on the right and hammered away at Cadwallader Jones's Company H.[33]

Fighting for their collective lives, McGowan's South Carolinians and Harris's Mississippians eventually found themselves intermingled, engaged nearly back-to-back. At one point, soldiers from the 12th stacked up partially filled ammunition boxes as cover as men behind them loaded rifles and passed them up to be fired. The Minié balls were flying so thick, one soldier recalled, some of the men's clothes were ravaged.[34]

"It was almost certain death to try to shoot so we got down to where we merely held the works and did not try to shoot," Jones noted. "Our dead was so thick on the ground at this point, that in some places, the men had to sit on dead bodies—they could not stand up because it would be certain death to do so—occasionally a man would pop up, shoot quick & drop back, and when a man was shot, he was generally killed, for he was hit in the head or neck—so he would fall in his tracks & lie there."

Recalled William Miller of Company H: "It looked as if we were all to be killed. [T]he fighting was fearful and continuous."

* * *

A key factor for the Confederates in the seemingly endless seesaw fight at the Bloody Angle was that it provided Lee a crucial opportunity to finish building a new line of earthworks across the base of the Mule Shoe, which his engineers and survivors of Ewell's Corps completed as darkness fell over the battlefield. At about 3:00 a.m., Lee ordered his men at the front of the salient, including McGowan's Brigade, to begin withdrawing to this new line. It would be a gradual exodus, Lee doing what he could to keep his intentions under wraps. Learning of the withdrawal at daylight, the Federals sprang into action and captured a fair share of Confederates yet to reach the new works.

In addition to the bloodshed, the fight that day sprung a number of stories of both incredible heroism and disbelief. One is perhaps unmatched in Civil War lore. During the afternoon struggle, firing by both sides on the 12th's right abruptly ceased and an argument broke out. A Federal officer from the 26th Michigan

33 Gordon Rhea, *The Battles for Spotsylvania Court House and the Road to Yellow Tavern, May 7–12, 1864* (Baton Rouge, LA, 1997), 275.

34 Caldwell, *The History of a Brigade of South Carolinians*, 96–97, 120; *CMH*, 319–320; Brown, *A Colonel at Gettysburg and Spotsylvania*, 291–292.

in Col. Nelson Miles's II Corps brigade jumped atop the works, sword in hand, and shouted that the 12th had surrendered by order of an unnamed Mississippi colonel. Captain Jones witnessed the spectacle as the Union officer walked up and down the works for about a minute exhorting the 12th to surrender. "You can't imagine what a hubbub it was," Jones recalled, with enemy soldiers hurling insults and demanding the other side give up the fight.

Clyburn ran up to Jones and ordered his men to resume firing, that no surrender was under consideration at any part of the line. Jones, on the other hand, was convinced the Federals were surrendering and countermanded his commander by telling the men not to shoot. "We thought they had surrendered—They thought we had surrendered," Jones recalled. "They had the butts of their guns turned toward us."

That spurred Brown to intervene. He called on the Federals to lay down their arms and come across to their side of the works. The Federal officer who raised the commotion, however, shouted back that he was waiting on the South Carolinians' surrender, as he believed a white flag had been raised by the Confederates. Brown retorted that he "commanded here, and if any flag was raised it was without authority and unless he came in, firing would be resumed."

The Federal officer requested a conference with Brown. Meanwhile, the arguments by both sides continued—the men, Brown recalled, "gesticulating, arguing, and what not." A subordinate officer, probably Clyburn or Jones, informed Brown that a white flag had indeed been raised on the Federal side of the works far to the right. Brown summarily notified the Federal officer of that and again demanded a surrender or the firing would resume. With no accord, the enemy commander headed back to his side and actually would be killed when gunfire erupted a minute or so later. Like that, the men in the 12th crouched again within the works, the slaughter resuming with "unabated fury."[35]

One touching story involved A. J. Samson of the 1st South Carolina and the 12th's battle flag. Its staff already struck twice during the advance, that flag continued to draw the attention of Yankee fire as the day progressed. At one point,

35 Cadwallader Jones Jr. to My Dear Brother, July 15, 1922, UNC; Brown, *A Colonel at Gettysburg and Spotsylvania*, 100–101; Cf. *OR* 36(1), 373–374. Colonel Brown's report, allegedly written the day after the battle, is not found in the *Official Records*. For an interesting view of the interplay between the confusion during the "Bloody Angle" fighting regarding the intermix of troops from other commands, surrenders, captures, desertion in the face of the enemy, mid-19th century codes of honor, and gossipy rumor mills in Lancaster County, see C, "For the Lancaster Ledger," *Lancaster Ledger*, June 28, 1864, 2. In this lengthy defense of Sgt. William B. Twitty of Company I, a soldier from his company counters "ugly rumors" about Twitty's speculated desertion during the fight, offering first-hand witness testimony that Twitty performed his duty and was likely captured with troops from other commands. Writes his anonymous advocate, known only as C": "[T]he rumor is too absurd and ridiculous to occupy the mind of a sensible man for one moment."

"riddled with bullets" and the regiment's color-bearer killed, it fell into the mud. Seeing the tattered banner draped over the fallen color-bearer, without hesitation Samson grabbed it off the ground. He kept it with him until after the fighting and then returned it to its rightful home with the 12th's color company.[36]

* * *

The stalemate at Spotsylvania Court House continued for another nine days, with serious fighting breaking out on only two days, before Grant decided to continue his advance on Richmond with another flank march. A Federal attack on May 18 was quickly cut short by Confederate artillery, and an engagement at the Harris farm between Ewell's Corps and a portion of Hancock's II Corps the next day also ended deadlocked.

The Bloody Angle would be the 12th's most searing, destructive clash in the entire war. Fighting on the brigade's flank for the second time in less than a week cost the regiment dearly. Of McGowan's five regiments, the 12th had the highest number of casualties by far: 118 (28 killed, 38 wounded, and a staggering 52 missing). It also had two line officers killed and three wounded. The next highest total was in Orr's Rifles, with 95 killed, wounded, or missing.

An early casualty in the 12th was Corp. W. A. Williams of Company E, shot in the head as he shouted orders to his comrades in the front rank. He was the fourth brother and son of the Williams family of Lancaster County to perish during the war, in addition to three cousins.[37]

What the men in the regiment—and McGowan's entire brigade—could say with pride was that they had redeemed themselves for the inglorious retreat down the Orange Plank Road at the Wilderness. Indeed, the men had fought valiantly and stubbornly and held the Bloody Angle for 18 hours, gaining Lee and his engineers the time necessary to create that new line of works at the rear of the salient. Without that hard-won time, the battle's outcome could clearly have gone the Federals' way.

The intense gunfire slackened as midnight approached. Sometime during the night, a few men were unexpectedly injured when an oak tree 22 inches in diameter near the 12th's position fell to the ground, the result of being shot

36 Cadwallader Jones Jr. to My Dear Brother, July 15, 1922, UNC; "Survivor's Reunion," *Yorkville Enquirer*, Aug. 7, 1879, 2; "Items," *Yorkville Enquirer*, June 8, 1864, 2.

37 Caldwell, *The History of a Brigade of South Carolinians*, 191; Brown, *A Colonel at Gettysburg and Spotsylvania*, 94–95; "For the Lancaster Ledger," *Lancaster Ledger*, June 7, 1864, 2; "Obituary," *Lancaster Ledger*, Sept. 27, 1864, 2.

through by both Federal and Confederate bullets. Scores of men simply sank into the mire of the bloody, flooded trenches and fell asleep. Others, undoubtedly riding waves of adrenaline, keenly watched for any movement of the enemy behind the works or peered through holes in the crudely made breastworks they had built extending the traverses.

Those in the regiment who survived the horrific fighting were consistent in boasting of their accomplishments. In a letter home on May 21, D. J. Carter beamed: "Our brigade has suffered more than any other in the army; it was detained from the Division by Gen. Lee and sent up to retake some breastworks that a portion of Ewell's corps had shamefully given up—the Stonewall Brigade."[38]

"I think we will be successful here," a Company I soldier wrote on May 14, "but it has been the most terrible battle of the war, and has taxed the courage and fortitude of our soldiers to the fullest extent."

William Templeton of Company B acknowledged in a letter to his sister Sarah: "We have been fighting ever since the 4th. We have had some of the hardest fighting I have ever seen. I hope it is over but am afraid it is not."[39]

Templeton's fear was justified. The fighting that erupted that May was not even close to being over. The 12th's ordeal would continue for another 11 months.

38 Caldwell, *The History of a Brigade of South Carolinians*, 196; LOCAL, "For the Lancaster Ledger," *Lancaster Ledger*, June 7, 1864, 2.

39 William Templeton to Sarah Templeton, May 21, 1864.

Chapter Eleven

From Spotsylvania to Deep Bottom

One would be hard-pressed to find a regiment in the Army of Northern Virginia that had been placed in more precarious situations, done more hard fighting, and suffered more casualties than the 12th South Carolina from May 4 to May 13. In clashes at the Wilderness on May 5–6 and at Spotsylvania Court House on May 12, the regiment had operated as the right flank of McGowan's Brigade, had fought without reliable support each time, and had driven back or held the enemy in check against high odds—all at a cost of 220 casualties, including its two highest-ranking field commanders and a handful of officers. The battle of Spotsylvania Court House would end on May 21 with the two armies locked in a stalemate, but plenty of fighting, bloodshed, and horror lay ahead for the 12th during Ulysses S. Grant's dogged crusade to defeat Lee's army, capture the Confederate capital of Richmond, and finally end the war.

As contemporary historian Gordon Rhea aptly wrote, the Wilderness and Mule Shoe fighting had left the 12th "wrecked." Indeed, the price the regiment—and, for that matter, entire brigade—paid for its grit and perseverance in combat was in many ways immeasurable. With the loss of so many veterans over those nine days, the 12th South Carolina would never be the same for the remainder of the war.

The toll started at the top, with Col. John Miller's death and Maj. Edwin Bookter's severe wounding at the Wilderness as well as the loss of both McGowan (wounded for the fourth time in the war) and his second-in-command, Col. Benjamin Brockman, at the Mule Shoe Salient. The highly competent Maj. T. F. Clyburn continued to lead the regiment as it emerged from the May 12–13 fighting, but many of the 10 companies were now commanded by lieutenants and were well below half-strength. Company B, for example, left the winter camp near Orange Court House on May 4 with 51 men. By the conclusion of the Spotsylvania Court House fighting, that total would be 31.

William Templeton of Company H was among those to express his dismay, acknowledging bluntly in a letter to his sister: "[W]e have lost a heap of men." Although some slightly wounded or previously missing men returned to boost the numbers as the campaign progressed, it was not enough to compensate for the loss of so many veterans. On May 14, only an estimated 260 men answered the regiment's roll call.

The extent of the carnage did not show only in the ranks. The staff of the regiment's battle flag, for instance, had been so riddled with bullet holes during the Mule Shoe fighting that it was completely unusable as a banner. After A. J. Samson of the 1st South Carolina returned it to color-company, it was sent to Richmond and burned respectfully at one of the capital city's soldiers' homes. The flag would not be replaced for several months, and then only through the benevolence of the citizens back home.[1]

* * *

While the men of the 12th absorbed this latest round of devastation and the heartbreak of lost friends and comrades, many continued to hold a positive outlook. That included D. J. Carter of Company I in the missives he sent to the *Lancaster Ledger*. Carter did not ignore the regiment's heavy losses and respectfully relayed the names of the Lancaster-area soldiers who were killed, wounded, or missing, but he also painted a vivid picture of the Mule Shoe fighting for his readers and made sure to commend the leadership of "the invincible Clyburn."[2]

The remaining eight days at Spotsylvania Court House were relatively uneventful when compared to the previous two weeks for McGowan's Brigade. On May 13, the South Carolinians rested and recuperated behind the new line of works that had been erected at the rear of the salient. The next day, they redeployed to the right, moving closer to the village of Spotsylvania and bivouacking near a church. Each regiment spent the morning of Sunday, May 15, at worship services in their

1 William Templeton to Sarah Templeton, June 7, 1864, and June 18, 1864; LOCAL, "For the Lancaster Ledger," *Lancaster Ledger*, June 7, 1864, 2; "Survivor's Reunion," *Yorkville Enquirer*, Aug. 7, 1879, 2; Rhea, *The Battles for Spotsylvania Court House and the Road to Yellow Tavern, May 7–12, 1864*, 274.

2 "For the Lancaster Ledger," *Lancaster Ledger*, June 7, 1864, 2.

camps, but that afternoon the brigade moved west of Spotsylvania Court House, reassuming the position on Lee's right that it occupied on the morning of May 12.

Despite the aggravating rain, the men enjoyed the calm. "Everything now remains quiet along the lines except an occasional fire from the outposts," recalled Company I's D. J. Carter writing from the breastworks. "Never was respite more welcome than the comparative rest that followed the terrible battle of the 12th, and which continued up to the 18th for we had been marching and fighting without intermission since the 4th of May," recalled one officer, a sentiment echoed by William Templeton in a letter to his sister: "I wish the fight was over for I am nearly wourn out."

There would be an unexpected and welcome benefit besides the rest: the assorted delicacies extracted from the haversacks of dead Federal soldiers, principally coffee and sugar. In addition, quality rations were reissued, such as cornbread and bacon, and meat, onions, rice, and potatoes would be added to the soldiers' diets.[3]

The miserable conditions remained a factor, however, as there would be no relief from the rain. Even when the sun finally broke through on May 17, the saturated ground remained a concern. Nevertheless, Grant planned to renew the fighting on May 18. Convinced that Lee's army was probably more vulnerable on the right, the commander considered an all-out attack down the Fredericksburg Road by the II and VI Corps. He would reassess after Brig. Gen. Joseph Kershaw's Division in Richard Anderson's First Corps collided with and nearly defeated troops in Maj. Gen. David Birney's 3rd Division, positioned at the tail end of Hancock's moving column on May 15.

Through Kershaw's clash and a subsequent skirmish between Thomas Rosser's cavalry and the 23rd U. S. C. T.—a brief engagement that the African-American soldiers, fighting for the first time, had won—Lee now had a better grasp of Grant's dispositions. Grant, now conceding that he likely could not surprise Lee, ordered Hancock and Wright to reverse course, march back to the positions they essentially held the morning of May 12, and launch an attack on Lee's left flank, yet to be truly tested in the battle thus far.

Grant still did not have the benefit of cavalry, as Phil Sheridan's troopers were in the midst of an epic raid on Richmond that had led to the mortal wounding of J. E. B. Stuart at Yellow Tavern on May 11. He was unaware that Ewell's Second Corps, now occupying Lee's left, had spent the past five days adding to and reinforcing the line of works on the hill that surrounded the home of local farmer Edgar Harrison. As Chris Mackowski and Kris White write in *A Season of*

3 "For the Lancaster Ledger," *Lancaster Ledger*, June 7, 1864, 2; Caldwell, *The History of a Brigade of South Carolinians*, 201–202.

Slaughter, "Grant had no way to know he was about to assault the strongest field fortifications in the east to date."[4]

The attack by the II and VI corps went forward as ordered about 4:30 a.m. on May 18, but it would be turned back with relative ease by Brig. Gen. Armistead Long's massed artillery and the agglomeration of works that Ewell's men had constructed. Grant finally abandoned the attack after several hours, with Union casualties approximately 1,500 and those of the Confederates about 250.

Although Lee had contended with his share of setbacks in two weeks of fighting, he had gotten the better of Grant thus far. Admitting that any prospect of success at Spotsylvania was now highly unlikely, the Union general-in-chief began planning his next move on the afternoon of May 18. Rather than continuing to "knock our heads against a brick wall," as Meade wrote to his wife, Grant prepared the army for another shift to the southeast, still optimistic he could get the jump on Lee in the race toward Richmond.

The II and VI corps moved first, marching back toward the Fredericksburg Road—the army's main supply line—and Lee's center. Lee ordered Ewell to follow with a reconnaissance-in-force, instructing the general to attack that supply line if an opportunity arose. Ewell believed he had an opening on the afternoon of May 19, but what he was confident would be a brief engagement with Federals near the Harris Farm evolved into a protracted clash between the Second Corps' veterans and combat newcomers from Brig. Gen. Robert O. Tyler's 4th Division—five units of artillerymen now serving as infantry, the so-called "Heavies" from Maine, Massachusetts, and New York.

Ewell soon found himself on the wrong end of that clash, saved from an outright loss only by darkness, which allowed a retreat under cover. Although Ewell had suffered roughly 1,000 casualties to the Federals' 1,500, he had delayed Grant's planned move away from the battlefield. After both armies remained in place on May 20, Grant set the Army of the Potomac in motion overnight on May 20–21. Despite a shade of apprehension, Lee suspected Grant's intentions and soon had his army on the move, too.

The opposing armies' next major clash would be roughly 25 miles to the south along the North Anna River on May 23–26.

* * *

4 Chris Mackowski and Kristopher D. White, *A Season of Slaughter: The Battle of Spotsylvania Court House, May 8–21, 1864* (El Dorado Hills, CA, 2013), 114.

The respite for McGowan's men, as it were, finally came to an end on May 19 when Grant began moving Hancock's and Wright's corps toward the Fredericksburg Road as the precursor for the army's proposed flank march. That afternoon, when Lee learned Ewell had run into trouble at the Harris Farm, he requested help from portions of the Third Corps, with A. P. Hill back in command. Blocked by Hancock's II Corps, however, Hill was unable to comply.

With Ewell's reconnaissance-in-force that day, Thomas's and Scales's brigades were dispatched from the works, meaning McGowan's Brigade needed to conduct an extended shift to the left to cover the opening this created. The South Carolinians' new position straddled an interior line directly behind the position the 12th held during the Mule Shoe fighting. As members of the Second Corps returned that night from the Harris farm clash, McGowan's men could hear excessive grumbling and rightly determined that the assault had failed. Before long, the brigade returned to its position on the right flank where it had spent the previous week.

Ewell's time as the Second Corps' commander was nearing its end. Lee had expressed displeasure at the general's performance since the first day of fighting at the Wilderness, in particular his prominent meltdown during the Federals' initial attack at the Mule Shoe. As Chris Mackowski writes in *A Tempest of Iron and Lead*: "At one point, Gordon found 'Old Baldy' sputtering and pulling on his beard in a state of near apoplexy. Shortly thereafter, as the remnant of [Edward] Johnson's shattered division streamed to the rear, Ewell mocked and berated them. 'Yes, goddam you, run,' he bellowed. He was, according to one witness, in a 'towering passion' emitting a 'terrible volley of oaths.'"[5]

When Ewell became ill a few days later during the fighting at North Anna, Lee saw an opportunity and decided the time had come to replace him with Jubal Early. Lee sent Ewell to Richmond for "recuperation" on May 24 and handed Early temporary command of the Second Corps—a move that he made permanent a few days later.

In abandoning Spotsylvania and moving to circumvent the Federal slide to the left, Lee would, as usual, count on contributions from McGowan's South Carolinians. Like Lee, the men in the 12th had convictions about Grant's objectives. As William Miller of Company H wrote, "it seemed a contest between the two armies as to which would get to Richmond first."

Grant, unsure how Lee would react once he realized the Army of the Potomac had departed, ordered Hancock's II Corps to march down the Massaponax Road and through Guinea Station in the direction of Bowling Green. He hoped reports

5 Chris Mackowski, *A Tempest of Iron and Lead: Spotsylvania Court House, May 8–21, 1864* (El Dorado Hills, CA, 2024), 178.

of an isolated Union corps and a renewed threat to Richmond might lure Lee to open ground for a fight.

Lee would not be enticed, though. Instead, he sent his army directly south, keeping his corps on interior lines against the evolving Federal advance. As it marched south, Hill's Corps remained west of Anderson's and Ewell's commands, passing through Chilesburg and crossing the North Anna to bivouac at Noel's Station on the Virginia Central Railroad on May 22. Colonel Brown, still commanding the brigade in McGowan's absence, had the 14th South Carolina picket the river while the other four regiments rested.

On the afternoon of May 23, Union troops crossed the North Anna at various undefended or lightly defended points. The crossing of Gouverneur Warren's V Corps at Jericho Mills required a response by Wilcox's Light Division that would prove disastrous, in part because A. P. Hill did not try to engage support in time from Henry Heth's or William Mahone's nearby divisions.

Forming Wilcox's battle line from left to right were the brigades of Scales (temporarily commanded by Col. William J. Lowrance), Thomas, McGowan, and Lane. For the South Carolinians, Colonel Brown initially sent Orr's Rifles toward Jericho Mills to scout the enemy while deploying from left to right, the 12th, 1st, 14th, and 13th behind a railroad embankment. Orr's Rifles returned shortly and assumed a position to the 13th's right.[6]

Wilcox ordered the division forward about 6:00 p.m., supported by Lt. Col. William Pegram's artillery battalion. His plan was simple enough: Thomas, Brown, and Lane would lead their men directly at the gathering V Corps while Lowrance drove left and attempted to flank Warren. Following in the wake of skirmishers who soon became warmly engaged, Brown advanced his brigade across the railroad tracks through a wheatfield to the edge of a grove of trees. Occupying the brigade's left, the 12th and 1st veered in that direction as they entered the woods while the other three regiments bore right. The 13th, 14th, and Orr's Rifles were soon engaged with the enemy.

Pushing ahead, the 12th and 1st came upon another smattering of V Corps troops—the 22nd Massachusetts and 95th New York of Brig. Gen. Charles Griffin's 1st Division, posted in a clearing. Determining that there was an opportunity to surprise and overwhelm the Federals, Clyburn ordered an immediate charge, joined by the 1st. The Yankees quickly bolted at the sudden rush, fleeing in disarray with the two Palmetto State regiments in determined pursuit.

6 LOCAL, "For the Lancaster Ledger," *Lancaster Ledger*, June 7, 1864, 2; Caldwell, *The History of a Brigade of South Carolinians*, 203–204; Rosalind Todd Tedards, *Orr's Rifles* (Wilmington, NC, 1917), 58.

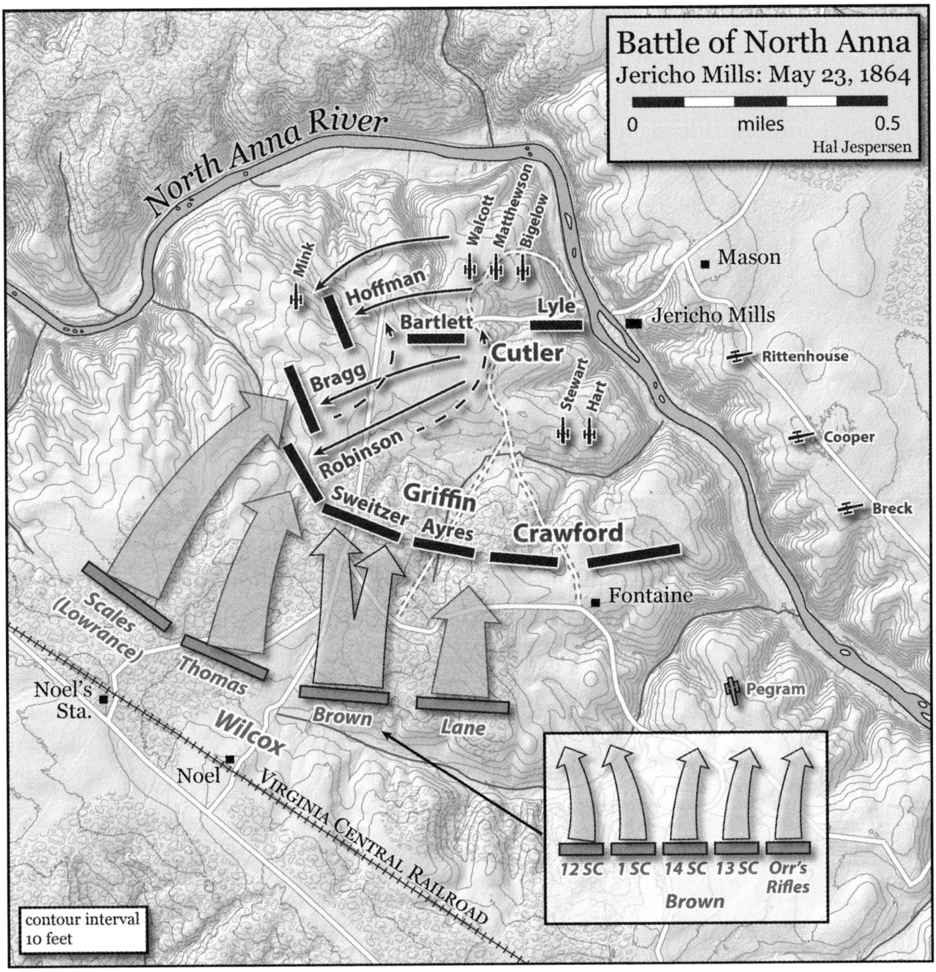

After scrambling down one hill and up another, the Confederates were momentarily inspired by what they saw as they ascended the summit: a mass of Yankee troops in retreat toward the North Anna. Wilcox's battle plan, it seemed, was working like a charm. While admiring the sight of fleeing Federals, the 12th and 1st South Carolina could not overlook something else on a ridge roughly 150 yards ahead: a well-laid line of artillery (12 guns) under Col. Charles S. Wainwright. They also began to realize that they were separated from their support. Clyburn and newly minted Lt. Col. Thomas P. Alston, commanding the 1st South Carolina, halted to dress their lines. As the regiments prepared to continue their advance, however, a strong line of infantry from Brig. Gen. Joseph Bartlett's 3rd Brigade in Griffin's division appeared and poured enfilade fire into the 1st's right flank.

Jericho Mill on the North Anna River. *Library of Congress*

With their regiments in danger of envelopment, the commanders ordered a retreat. As they fell back, however, Wainwright's waiting artillery unleashed several volleys of canister and grapeshot, ripping holes in the ranks. Clyburn attempted to redirect his men against the Union guns but was struck and severely wounded by grapeshot. Alston would be wounded shortly, too, and Colonel Brown was captured as he made his way from the left toward the 14th South Carolina's position on the right.

Falling back to the grove, the two regiments "suffered" due to punishing enfilade fire and as they retreated farther, grapeshot. There, the survivors met elements of Scales's Brigade, moving in support. In trouble of their own on the right, the 13th, 14th, and Orr's Rifles were retreating, and Thomas's Georgians to the left, exposed by the retreats, had halted their advance and were reassessing their options. Within an hour, the heavy artillery and quick response by the Federals quelled Wilcox's once-promising attack. As night fell, it was clear the battle's first day had gone Grant's way.

Wilcox never received formal blame for the uncoordinated attack that turned into a debacle. A. P. Hill was not as fortunate, however. Early the next morning, a frustrated Lee rode to the army's left, and, in a rare scolding, questioned the Third Corps' commander's response: "Why did you not do as Jackson would have done—thrown your whole force upon those people and driven them back?"

In Hill's defense, Lee had underestimated the threat posed by the V Corps. With intelligence provided by his own son, Maj. Gen. W. H. F. "Rooney" Lee, the Army of Northern Virginia commander determined that Grant had ordered Warren's crossing as a feint and even directed Hill by courier "to leave his men in camp." As the battle began to turn that evening, Hill called on Heth for support, although by the time Heth moved it was too late.[7]

* * *

By the evening of May 23, the 12th and 1st South Carolina were back at their bivouac at Noel's Station, joined by Thomas's Brigade and eventually the other three regiments. "We fell short of our usual success, and infinitely below the anticipations with which we entered the battle," Caldwell would write. Scouting problems at both the division and corps levels were behind Wilcox's miscalculation and obliviousness to the Federals' strong artillery presence. Despite the fragmented nature of the attack, there had been initial success, and men of the 12th interpreted the fight not as a loss, but rather a glowing success. "Yesterday, the enemy attacked our rear guard at this place, and were handsomely repulsed by Wilcox's division," Private Carter wrote. The attack, he added, had saved the division's wagon train and driven "back . . . the enemy about one mile, capturing and killing a large number. Our loss was small. . . . The troops are in good spirits and confident of success."

The brigade suffered 211 total casualties that day, and with Colonel Brown's capture, Lt. Col. Isaac Hunt of the 13th South Carolina assumed command. Losses for the 12th were 34 (2 killed, 21 wounded, and 11 missing); exact numbers are not available, but the regiment fielded only a little more than 200 men the morning of May 24. With Clyburn and Lt. W. H. Rives sidelined by wounds, Capt. Robert M. Kerr of Company H, the 12th's senior company commander, took the reins. Kerr's bona fides were solid, having commanded Company H since the September 1862 Maryland campaign.

Overnight on May 23–24, Hunt led the South Carolinians down the Virginia Central Railroad toward Hanover Junction. While this movement was part of a larger shift by Lee toward Richmond, D. J. Carter put a good face on the retrograde movement by writing to the folks back home from Hanover Junction: "It became necessary for the safety of our communication, for Lee to fall back to this place,

7 Gordon Rhea, *The Battle of Cold Harbor* (Eastern National, 2001), 10, 11; author conversation with Chris Mackowski, Jan. 25, 2025. L. C. Haskell, "Defence of McGowan's Brigade," *Daily Journal*, Nov. 5, 1867, 1. Haskell's account also contains vignettes from the battles of the Wilderness and Spotsylvania Court House.

so as to front both Grant and Butler and the better to protect Richmond." By daylight, the slow and tedious trek had covered only about 3–4 miles. When the exhausted troops halted about a mile west of the junction, they threw themselves down in a dusty field to rest. For the rest of the battle, they and McGowan's entire brigade remained in reserve. After digging a strong line of embankments in front of their camp, the South Carolinians held fast, encountering only routine shelling by Federal artillery.[8]

As at the Wilderness and Spotsylvania Court House, the battle of North Anna would end in stalemate on May 26, as Grant decided to make another swing to the left to try to get between Lee and Richmond. On May 24, Lee's army had recovered enough from the first day's setback to adopt a five-mile defensive line south of the river in the shape of an inverted "V." Hill's Third Corps would be on the left of that line.

Lee hoped Grant would believe he was retreating and launch an attack of some sort, unwittingly risking the separation of his forces that the Confederates could exploit. Grant made several moves that day but ultimately realized that Lee's defenses were simply too strong. Further probes by both Warren's V Corps and Wright's VI corps on May 25 would also be stopped short, and the armies spent the rest of the day staring the other down.

* * *

The Federals' subsequent flank march brought the two sides face to face again at the battle of Cold Harbor, where the engagement beginning May 31 would last nearly two weeks. Unlike the previous Overland campaign engagements, it produced a stunning, lopsided Confederate victory and a Union casualty count approaching 13,000 men that brought remorse even to the seemingly unflappable Grant. Grant's first campaign against Lee would officially end on June 12, but as before, the frustrated Union commander would not back down. The bloodshed would continue.

* * *

In his postwar history of the South Carolina brigade, J. F. J. Caldwell recounted the unit's movement as Lee followed Grant from the North Anna showdown:

8 Caldwell, *The History of a Brigade of South Carolinians*, 204–207; Brown, *A Colonel at Gettysburg and Spotsylvania*, 140; Gordon Rhea, *To the North Anna River* (Baton Rouge, LA, 2000), 304–319; *CMH* 3(1):460; LOCAL, "For the Lancaster Ledger," *Lancaster Ledger*, June 7, 1864, 2.

> On the 27th, Grant continuing the left flank movement towards Richmond, we were marched southward, across Little River and the South Anna, until some time after dark. Then we went into bivouac, not far from Kilby's mills, which are some twelve miles from Richmond, and on Stony Creek, I think. The next morning, the 28th, we marched to the neighborhood of Atlee's Station, on the [Virginia] Central Railroad. There was cannonading in our front and a pretty constant skirmish fire, but we were not carried up to the front line. On Sunday, we had divine service, and lay undisturbed until late in the afternoon. Then we marched and counter-marched until night; when we were put into a thicket and allowed to rest.
>
> On Monday the 30th, we took position on the Central Railroad, about the extreme left of the Confederate line, and fortified. Other portions of the division were sent out once or twice on reconnaissance; but we were undisturbed until the next day, when we were moved farther to the right, and relieved Kershaw's division. There was a good deal of confusion here, marching and countermarching, until we were separated from the other brigades of the division, and crammed into a swamp. Skirmishers were firing on the line in front, and occasionally a shell passed over us.
>
> One man in the Twelfth regiment was killed during these movements. Finally, however, we were restored to upper air, and ranged on the right of [John] Breckinridge's division. We erected earthworks, and lay still. On Wednesday, June 1, Breckenridge's skirmishers attacked those of the enemy, and we saw an interesting small fight in the open fields, which resulted in the capture of a few Federal prisoners and a right angry cannonade for a short while."[9]

The Army of the Potomac would be closer to Richmond on May 31 than it had been since June 1862, but thanks to the marching, countermarching, and maneuvering that Lee had choreographed that month, the Army of Northern Virginia was in a formidable defensive position in front of the Confederate capital, with both flanks resting on the Chickahominy River. Firmly entrenched along a seven-mile front, Lee had left Grant with limited options for a breakthrough. Even a colossal attack directly across the entire Confederate line—should Grant dare to call Lee's bluff—would be a daunting challenge, risking extensive bloodshed possibly worse than the collisions at the Wilderness and Spotsylvania Court House.

Union forces spent May 31 and June 1 probing and skirmishing as the armies solidified their positions and strength, helped by the arrival of troops on both

9 Caldwell, *The History of a Brigade of South Carolinians*, 208–209.

sides that had been fighting in the Bermuda Hundred campaign just to the south. One of those newly arrived units was Maj. Gen. William "Baldy" Smith's XVIII Corps of the Army of the James, which would join Wright's VI Corps in an attack against Anderson's position on the Confederate right at New Cold Harbor late on June 1. Colonel William Truex's 1st Brigade, part of James Ricketts's 3rd Division in the VI Corps, managed a limited breakthrough, crossing a small, unguarded "brush-lined" ravine between Anderson's two divisions, but would be turned back by Confederate reinforcements.

Grant planned for a larger assault the following morning on a wider front that was to include the II Corps but was postponed twice to give Hancock's men needed rest. Then, at daylight on June 3, the all-out Federal attack finally went forward. It would be short-lived and catastrophic—"a wanton waste of life," in the words of an anguished General Smith. From their strong line of earthworks, backed by a lethal array of artillery, the waiting Confederates simply mowed down Grant's troops as they advanced across open ground. Many of those wounded but not killed outright were forced to lie unattended between the lines, some for days.

Despite the bloodshed and havoc, Grant urged his subordinates to keep the pressure on throughout the morning, but he finally called off the attacks about 12:30 p.m. The extent of Federal casualties varies according to the source, but it was likely in the range of 6,000 killed, wounded, or missing on June 3 alone. The only success that day would occur in a separate action to the north, where an assault by the IX Corps—which Grant had officially attached to Meade's Army of the Potomac—breached a skirmish line in front of Early's Second Corps. After the initial success, however, Burnside mistakenly ordered a halt, intending to resume the advance that afternoon.

The 1,000 or so troops in McGowan's Brigade had assumed the extreme right of Lee's lines on June 2, straddling a high bank that overlooked the Chickahominy. It was familiar ground for the South Carolinians, the site of their clash at Gaines's Mill two years earlier during the Seven Days'—their first major engagement of the war. Surprisingly, they would not be engaged on June 3, meaning they would not see action in a major battle for the first time in the entire campaign. Nevertheless, the men could see portions of the fight unfold and clearly heard the din of battle. The only action for the brigade that day was a routine reconnaissance to the river by the 1st South Carolina.

On June 1, after receiving input and recommendations from Generals Wade Hampton, A. P. Hill, Jubal Early, and Richard Ewell, Lee promoted Army of Northern Virginia veteran James Conner from colonel to brigadier general and named him the brigade's temporary commander. Although the 35-year-old Conner was a South Carolina native, he had not served previously with Gregg's or McGowan's command. He had served, however, with Confederate militia at Fort Sumter in April 1861, with Hampton's Legion at First Manassas, and he commanded the 22nd North Carolina during the Seven Days' (wounded at Gaines's Mill) and at Gettysburg. A prominent United States district attorney before the war, Conner was serving as a judge of the military court of the Second Corps when he received orders to take the helm of McGowan's Brigade.[10]

The handsome Conner was thrilled with his new promotion and especially proud of Lee's endorsement. "The General was quite kind," he wrote in a letter shortly after his promotion. "I did not suppose that he had ever heard of me, or was aware even of my existence, but he spoke most handsomely of your humble servant, of the reputation he had always heard of me . . ." After almost a year serving on court martials behind the lines, Conner was equally eager to get back into the field and make his mark as a combat officer. "The being ordered to the rear with the wagons whenever the troops marched to the front did not suit my style," he wrote. "I could stay at home and be a District Attorney, and live cosily [sic] and comfortably unharmed by bullets, but would that suit me?" he asked rhetorically.[11] Other than news of Conner's placement, the record of the 12th South Carolina's activities in the days immediately following the June 3 fighting is sparse, little more than mention of picket duty and plentiful rations that included bread, meat, sugar, coffee, onions, rice, and potatoes. The proximity to Richmond no doubt contributed to the extent and diversity of the provender.

Writing from the entrenchments on June 7, William Templeton reported hearing cannon fire in a letter to his sister and that skirmishing had taken place along the lines, lamenting that he was "wourn out" from the fighting. Templeton, though, said he was optimistic about Confederate chances, predicting that Grant would not get closer to Richmond without bringing up substantial naval help on the James River. "We have got possession of all the hights hear," he wrote. "He has charged our brest works until I think he has lost one third of his army. We have lost a heap of men but not half as meny as the enemy." Many of the men in the regiment used their free time to attend to personal hygiene, both bathing and in washing their clothes. Indeed, many had not changed shirts in more than five weeks of constant marching and campaigning. Although he didn't mention it in his letter, that same day, Templeton and his comrades in the 12th caught a glimpse

10 Ibid., 209–210; *OR* 36(3):601; *CMH* 8, 386.

11 J. C. [James Conner] to My dear Mother, June 5, 1864, in Mary Conner Moffett, ed., *Letters of General James Conner, C.S.A.* (Charleston, SC, 1950), 132-33. The author is deeply indebted to Dean Chester for his cooperation in providing copies of pages from this rare book of letters and to Mark Wade for facilitating the introduction to the author.

James Conner temporarily commanded McGowan's brigade during the summer of 1864. *Confederate Military History*

of the new brigade commander for the first time. Riding down the line of entrenchments, Conner's bravado inspired the men worn down from weeks of fighting and marching and broke the monotony: "It was amazing to see the men crowd out of the trenches to get a sight of their new General," Conner proudly wrote. It was like the debut of a belle; I hope they were satisfied with their observation."[12]

Significant fighting would end after Grant's grievous attack on June 3. For the next nine days, he would reposition his forces around Cold Harbor in stages, preparing for a clandestine transfer of his army across the James, hoping capture of that critical railroad hub 20 or so miles south of Richmond would make Lee's position outside Richmond untenable. Simultaneous moves by Federal forces in the Shenandoah Valley and near Charlottesville forced Lee to respond by dispatching portions of his army in that direction, impacting his already limited numbers.

Through scouting reports, Lee was aware that Grant was repositioning the army, and he was not dismissing the possibility Grant would attempt to cross the James. Lee could also not rule out that the Union commander would retreat and, if so, he wanted to make that possibility particularly unpleasant for Grant while retaining solid defensive lines around the Confederate capital.

On June 12, Grant completed the transfer of his army across the James. Lee would learn about that on June 13, but to his good fortune he had already begun moving Hill's Third Corps south of the Chickahominy. Planning to disrupt a possible Federal retreat in that direction, Lee moved Hill toward White Oak Swamp, an area of inhospitable terrain that would be challenging for Grant's men to cross if contested.

12 William Templeton to Sarah Templeton, June 7, 1864; Dunlop, *Lee's Sharpshooters*, 99; J. C. to My dear Mother, June 15, 1864, in Moffett, *Letters of James Conner*, 134-135.

McGowan's Brigade joined the Light Division's forced march toward White Oak Swamp, about 12 miles away, on the morning of June 13. With unbearable heat pounding down on the men, officers did what they could to keep the ranks closed, but straggling was inevitable and the column would become drawn out during the rigorous excursion along dusty roads.

Approaching Frayser's farm, the brigade formed a battle line near Riddle's Shop on the Charles City Road. Under A. P. Hill's watchful eye, Conner sent forward his sharpshooters, with the rest of the brigade about 200 yards behind. A Federal skirmish line fronted the approaching South Carolinians in a heavy stand of timber. Engaged by the sharpshooters, the Yankees were slowly driven back. The rest of the brigade followed at a methodical pace, but, according to one soldier, Conner, a new brigadier, would unnecessarily pull up and halt the brigade every few minutes to dress the lines and rectify any "irregularities." Finally, Conner called a halt. The sharpshooters quickly dug rifle pits in the advance line while the rest of the brigade erected stronger breastworks in the woods. While many in the ranks cursed the constant stop and go that day, their new general had nothing but praise for his men's work ethic: "The way our men build fortifications beats the world. In three hours we had a capital line of works," he wrote in a letter to his mother after the engagement. That evening, Wilcox's entire division advanced and forced the enemy about a mile and a half away and returned to the works around 11:00 p.m.

Casualties were light that day. The 12th lost two men wounded in Companies C and D, likely sharpshooters but perhaps victims of artillery fire. McGowan's Brigade also inflicted 100 or so casualties on the Federal side, in addition to the capture of 30. That particular day was grueling as the men had been up at 5:00 a.m. to eat breakfast and did not get fed again until 1:00 a.m. the next day when the commissary delivered "dinner" to the front lines.[13]

The movement of Hill's Corps had shifted the axis of Lee's army, now extended in a southeasterly direction from the south bank of the Chickahominy to Malvern Hill. Fighting would break out in the vicinity of Petersburg on June 15–18 with limited Union success, but a smaller Confederate force commanded by Gen. P. G. T. Beauregard (only about 2,200 men) held firm against several poorly orchestrated attacks. The result would be the start of the horrific siege of Petersburg, which would last for another nine-and-a-half months.

Two days after the South Carolinians' engagement near Frayser's farm, Conner moved his brigade forward several hundred yards and constructed a set of "strong"

13 Caldwell, *The History of a Brigade of South Carolinians*, 211–212; Dunlop, *Lee's Sharpshooters*, 99–100; LOCAL, "Near Riddle's Shop, In Line of Battle," *Lancaster Ledger*, July 19, 1864, 2; J. C. to My dear Mother, June 15, 1864, in Moffett, *Letters of James Conner*, 135–136.

fieldworks in the woods, where they would enjoy some much-needed rest on June 15–16. "All has been comparatively quiet along our front for the last three days," wrote a soldier in Company I on June 17.

The heat and rigors of incessant campaigning were taking their toll on the 12th, however. While stationed in the lowland areas around Richmond, scores of men in the regiment went down with malaria. Some never returned to the ranks. On June 18, William Templeton informed his sister that in addition to the loss of six men killed or wounded and 12–15 missing from his Company B alone, many comrades were dealing with "bowel" issues. In his postwar history, Caldwell described the brigade's general health during this period:

> Our health was very bad. The constant exposure to sun and rain, the rancid bacon and half-raw cornbread that were issued us, the filth necessarily accompanying the scarcity of clothing, and the lack of opportunity for bathing or washing our clothes, the vile water of this section of the country, the atmosphere scarcely less unwholesome, the want of rest at night, (for we had still to keep one-third always awake at night and to rouse all at 3:00 o'clock in the morning,) and, perhaps as any of these causes, the constant, excited anxiety, had produced and aggravated diarrhea, dysentery, dyspepsia, and slow fevers, which were wasting men surely away."[14]

Although many of the men in the regiment were encouraged learning about the success Jubal Early and the Second Corps was having in threatening Washington, D.C. during a bold and ruthless raid through the Shenandoah Valley, the broader military picture looked bleak. Lee had allowed Grant to surprise him and the potential loss of the "Cockade City," as Grant intended, would be devastating. On June 17, Wilcox's Division began marching from its line of breastworks near Richmond toward the James, crossing the river on pontoons the next morning at Drewry's Bluff. Once across, the rush to Petersburg would resume immediately.

Clouds of dust literally choked the men under the unforgiving sun. "The day was burning hot," recalled one veteran, "and the water was so scarce that men fairly fought each other at every well we reached." As had happened during the march four days earlier, straggling was commonplace; soon, each of the five regiments—already greatly reduced because of casualties and sickness—had been reduced to the size of companies. Some companies in the 12th, in fact, had only a single soldier in the ranks by the end of the march.

14 William Templeton to Sarah Templeton, June 18, 1864; Caldwell, *The History of a Brigade of South Carolinians*, 213; LOCAL, "Near Riddle's Shop, In Line of Battle."

For seven or eight miles, the fanned-out brigade marched as incessant artillery fire resounded from the direction of Petersburg. Reaching a railroad, troops in the brigade's vanguard were quickly loaded into the cars and shuttled to the crossroads town. The remaining troops continued marching along the tracks, some arriving that evening and others the next day. By the night on June 18, Wilcox's entire division was in Petersburg; Conner's men were posted on the army's right near the Weldon Railroad. According to Caldwell, the brigade's march had covered 26 miles total.[15]

The exhausted troops were undisturbed on June 19–20, with many of the men catching up on rest and sleep and building arbors from sticks and branches to shield themselves from the hot Virginia sun. Many stragglers no doubt caught up with the regiment as well. On June 21, the brigade received hurried orders to march down the Weldon Railroad in support of Confederate cavalry and for a time pursued Federal troopers through a wooded area. No casualties were reported.[16]

During these frantic days of June 1864, it is difficult to ascertain the strength of the regiment at any one time or where it was located in the brigade's line of march. Records, both official and from soldier accounts, are scarce. The regiment's numbers had certainly reached a low point in the immediate wake of the fighting at Spotsylvania Court House, although a fair share of men returned to the ranks in the latter part of May and early June. Returns for the Army of Northern Virginia on June 30, 1864, indicate that Wilcox's Division had only 5,445 men present for duty from a 12,196-man roster. While official returns for McGowan's Brigade were not reported, Confederate deserters from Thomas's Brigade informed Union Maj. Gen. Benjamin F. Butler on July 11 that McGowan's command numbered no more than 1,000 men.

With five regiments and one sharpshooter battalion in the brigade, it is likely the regiments each numbered about 175–200 men. When one considers that the 12th had borne the brunt of the fighting in May and suffered the most casualties of the five regiments in the engagements at the Wilderness and Spotsylvania, its aggregate fighting force was probably below average—perhaps 150–180 men, with companies numbering 15–20 men each. The strength problem likely explains why only a captain (R. M. Kerr) continued to lead the regiment at this point.[17]

At the end of June, James Lane's North Carolina Brigade under the command of Col. J. D. Barry and McGowan's Brigade were ordered to march north of

15 Caldwell, *The History of a Brigade of South Carolinians*, 213–214; LOCAL, "Near Riddle's Shop, in Line of Battle."

16 Caldwell, *The History of a Brigade of South Carolinians*, 217–218.

17 *OR* 40(1):707; *OR* 41:168.

the James to relieve Henry Heth's Division stationed near Richmond. This two-brigade force would be under Conner's lead, and Lt. Col. Isaac Hunt the South Carolinians' provisional brigade commander. Sneaking out of the entrenchments in Petersburg just after dark on either June 29 or June 30, the two brigades passed through Petersburg, crossed the Appomattox River, and continued a stealthy march north toward Richmond.

The advance proceeded at a feverish pace, and despite cooler evening temperatures, the dust and lack of water made the ordeal as miserable for the men as the initial march to Petersburg two weeks earlier. During breaks, the men literally dropped to the ground, and some were purportedly so exhausted they managed to "sleep" as they marched.

After reaching Chaffin's Bluff in the late morning, the brigades crossed east of the James on a pontoon bridge and occupied works on the other side. They had marched nearly 30 miles in 15 hours. One veteran remembered that the brigade fielded only about 300 men when the column reached its destination. One company in the 1st South Carolina, for instance, had only two men remaining when the brigade arrived.[18]

McGowan's Brigade was on the right, anchored at Fort Harrison, and Lane's Tar Heels were on the left. Fort Harrison was an important part of the Confederate defenses around Richmond and the largest in a succession of fortifications extending from New Market Road to the James that included Forts Brady, Hoke, Johnson, Gregg, and Gilmer. These large earthworks were designed to protect strategically important Chaffin's Bluff and needed to be defended by both heavy artillery and infantry. It is unknown in what order the regiments were aligned in McGowan's command, but it is likely the understrength 12th was assigned a position near the center.

Heth's vacating division simultaneously moved back toward Petersburg. The line of earthworks ran in a northerly direction, commencing in the front of Fort Harrison. Confederate cavalry patrolled the left and heavy guns were placed in Forts Harrison and Gilmer and at Chaffin's Bluff to the east. McGowan's and Lane's brigades, however, were the only infantry in the area, besides the Richmond City Battalion. Each regiment conducted regular picket duty, and the men steadily improved the works in the area using abatis and other debris. Because enemy soldiers were well beyond the picket line, the chance the Confederates would be engaged on short notice was unlikely. That allowed them to decompress and rest. In fact, accounts from soldiers in the regiment indicated that they never saw or encountered Federal soldiers during this period.

18 Caldwell, *The History of a Brigade of South Carolinians*, 219–220.

The men, though, withstood horrible conditions. Rations consisted of rancid bacon and vermin-infested cornmeal and peas. There was a shortage of coffee as well, and many of the men had to go barefoot and wear inadequate uniforms—some of those had literally rotted since the outbreak of fighting in early May. To shield themselves from the sun, the men erected arbors of branches and kept busy picking blackberries when not on fatigue duty. They were aware that the heavy artillerymen in the forts, blessed with vegetable gardens and pigpens, seemed to have easier lives, but the men in the 12th welcomed having time away from the constant maneuvering and fighting they had experienced during the spring and early summer. There were even unfounded rumors that the brigade would be transferred to South Carolina that summer to recruit soldiers.[19]

Despite the hard conditions and unforgiving Virginia sun, the regiment recuperated quite nicely in July, and previously wounded men returned to the ranks, albeit gradually. A soldier from Company B recalled: "[F]or the first time in two months, we unbuckled our armor, relaxed our high nervous tension and laid ourselves down to rest. The days were hot but the nights were delightful . . . we had not a care."

William Templeton wrote that heavy summer rains had inundated the men as July progressed. Also, Kershaw's (Old) South Carolina Brigade, commanded now by Col. John Doby Kennedy, arrived from Petersburg to augment McGowan's and Lane's position. Men from the 12th had relatives and friends in Kennedy's command and capitalized on the spare time and close proximity to check on their comrades in arms. "It was interesting to see the two South Carolina brigades, Kershaw's and McGowan's, fraternizing with each other," one soldier fondly recalled. "I think both commands were rather desirous of a battle in company. They did not have long to wait."[20]

While the two longest-serving South Carolina brigades in Lee's army became reacquainted in the trenches near Fort Harrison, events near Petersburg soon disrupted the reunion. With the opposing armies dug in for a protracted siege, Grant and his subordinates explored options to break the impasse and take the city by force. For several weeks, Burnside and enterprising Pennsylvania coal miners in his IX Corps had dug a 500-foot mine under a section of the Confederate entrenchments that would be lined with explosives and blown up. By design, the explosion would kill scores of unsuspecting soldiers behind those defenses and

19 Ibid., 220–221; William Templeton to Sarah Templeton, _____, 1864; William Templeton to Sarah Templeton, July 16, 1864.

20 Caldwell, *The History of a Brigade of South Carolinians*, 221–222.

Partial views of Fort Harrison and the accompanying countryside. *Library of Congress*

open a massive gap through which the Federals could surge and capture Petersburg with Lee's lines broken.

The explosion was to be triggered early in the morning of July 30. To help keep the Confederates unsettled before then, Grant ordered troops from Hancock's II Corps and Phil Sheridan's Cavalry on an expedition to threaten Richmond and its accompanying railroads. Ideally, Lee would try to counter the attack by Hancock and Sheridan by sending troops away from Petersburg.

Hancock and Sheridan crossed the Appomattox on pontoons on July 26 and arrived at an area known as "Deep Bottom" to prepare for their diversionary advance on the city. Approximately 11 miles southeast of Richmond in Henrico County, Deep Bottom occupied land adjacent to a horseshoe-shaped bend in the James River known as Jones Neck. Throughout the war, it served as a convenient crossing point from the Bermuda Hundred region south of the river.

Another division from the Federal X Corps, commanded by Brig. Gen. Robert S. Foster, had crossed Deep Bottom earlier. Grant hoped to hold the Confederate infantry in place with his infantry while Sheridan's cavalry struck directly for Richmond. If all went as planned, the Federals would soon break through the lines at both Petersburg and the Confederate capital.

On July 27, Hancock and Sheridan crossed the James and advanced toward Fussell's Mill, sweeping through enemy resistance on the New Market Road and capturing four cannons. The Federals then established a battle line along the Long Bridge Road, with Hancock on the left and Sheridan on the right. Confederate reinforcements under Henry Heth and "Rooney" Lee arrived to stall the Federal advance, succeeding to do so only briefly.

The next day, Lee ordered McGowan's, Lane's, and Kershaw's brigades as reinforcements for the fight along Long Bridge Road. Conner remained in overall command of McGowan's and Lane's brigades, Hunt in command of McGowan's South Carolinians, and Captain Kerr in command of the 12th, which would assume the brigade's extreme left. Leading the advance was Lane's Brigade, then McGowan's, and finally Kershaw's. As the snaking column traversed the narrow Darbytown Road toward Fussell's Mill, shells from Federal artillery along the Long Bridge Road exploded in the men's midst. The 12th suffered no casualties, according to a Company B soldier; however, a shell landed within the color-guard of the 1st South Carolina, which was leading the brigade. Fortunately, despite the chaos created, there would be no significant casualties.[21]

The sounds of skirmishing escalated as the 12th continued to wind its way down the Darbytown Road. After his brigades cleared Fussell's Mill, Conner ordered them to file to the left and form battle lines "on the right by files into line"—facing south. With approximately 1,600 men in the two brigades, the maneuver created a logjam that took some time to untangle. For a brief period, as the 12th awaited Kennedy's arrival, the regiment assumed the column's left flank.

With the arrival of Kershaw's Brigade, the three units moved forward into a dense stretch of woods in the general direction of the enemy. There was a major problem, however. No one had indicated which unit in the attacking column was supposed to serve as the guide. In theory, this meant that the three-brigade force had no rudder to steer the expanded line toward an objective, a scenario that typically resulted in confusion, frustration, and disaster for the men in the ranks. In Civil War tactics, it was hard enough to maintain a battle line featuring a couple of thousand men in an open field; doing it without a dependable guiding element in the marshy forests of Virginia was all but impossible, and the absence of that guide now disrupted the formation's flow from the beginning.

"The line of battle now advanced through the swamp and tangled underbrush," a Company B soldier recalled after the war. "The numerous difficulties and exceeding roughness of the ground over which the lines moved soon resulted in the separation of the brigades one from the other, and even the differing regiments lost connection with their neighbors, right and left. All moved forward however, and each went at whatever appeared in their front."

With the formation's breakdown, each regiment had to fend for itself in the woods. On the brigade's right flank, the 1st and 14th South Carolina plunged into

21 Dunlop, *Lee's Sharpshooters*, 137–138; Caldwell, *The History of a Brigade of South Carolinians*, 222.

a roadbed running sharply to the left. In doing that, they lost touch with Lane's Brigade, which was also struggling to keep up, therefore opening a huge gap in that part of the line. On the brigade's left, the 12th and 13th also became separated and lost contact with Kennedy's men to their left. Units simultaneously crowded each other out or were spread too thin to bring sufficient force against a better organized Union force. Confusion reigned as the men slammed headlong into Brig. Gen. Henry E. Davies Jr.'s dismounted brigade of cavalry in Brig. Gen. David McMurtie Gregg's 2nd Division. In addition to fighting dismounted, Davies's troopers held a staggering advantage, carrying superior breach-loading carbines.

The Yankee troopers fought tenaciously and slowed the 12th and 13th's advance through the woods to a crawl, aided substantially by the rifled guns of Battery A, 2nd United States Artillery, which had unlimbered in a field outside the woods. Kerr and the 12th momentarily recoiled at this sudden Federal opposition and fell back alongside the 13th. Kerr, however, quickly decided that an attack on the enemy horsemen was the only reasonable option he had. In the tradition of his predecessors, Dixon Barnes and John Miller, the captain ordered a charge, joined by Maj. William Lester and the men of the 13th.[22]

As the two regiments—a screaming, gray-clad mass of soldiers—lunged forward, the line of Yankee troopers broke. "The suddenness of the attack, and the impracticability of forming my Second Brigade so as to bring it into action at once, gave the enemy an advantage which he used in forcing back the First Brigade to the road," Gregg would write.

The Confederate charge, however, began to unravel due to the thick underbrush, swampy ground and continued Federal artillery fire, as shells and splintered branches rained down steadily on the men. With every step, the 12th and 13th's position became more tenuous, though Kerr and Lester did not let up. Arriving at the edge of the woods, the two commanders realized they needed to organize the handful of troops they had (about 160 men) for a last push to maintain the momentum. Orr's Rifles would join the two regiments in this push, rolling forward in a "good line and advanc[ing] handsomely" toward the Federal artillery's two unsupported guns.[23]

Lieutenant W. N. Dennison, Battery A's commander, kept firing from his position along a crest in the field, hoping to hold the South Carolinians at bay, but soon he too decided the game was up. He ordered one of his cannons limbered and hauled away, while the second covered the retreat. "The enemy was steadily

22 Dunlop, *Lee's Sharpshooters*, 138; Caldwell, *The History of a Brigade of South Carolinians*, 223; *OR* 40(1):612–613, 619.

23 Ibid.

and rapidly advancing and it was impossible to withdraw more than one gun at a time," recalled a Federal officer. As Dennison's men limbered the second piece and prepared to fall back, a few enterprising South Carolinians emptied their weapons to kill off the gun's horses.[24]

Mortified at this turn of events, Dennison rode back and ordered the crew to unlimber the piece and remove it from the field by hand. But as the 12th continued to close in, Dennison's horse was struck by a bullet from one of the South Carolinians' rifles, flinging the lieutenant to the ground. At Dennison's urgent call for support, troopers from the nearby 10th New York Cavalry rode over and joined the gun crew in its attempt to get the piece away before it could be captured. The 12th and 13th were now about 50 yards away, however—advancing, in General Davies's opinion, "with great determination." Thwarted, the Federals abandoned the gun and fled for the rear.[25]

The lone cannon in the middle of the field and the Federals in full retreat was like waving a red flag in front of a bull. The South Carolinians stormed the crest and secured the piece—a remarkable battlefield trophy.

With Federal reinforcements forming beyond them, the men of the 12th began to wheel the artillery piece back to the woods, accomplishing the task with impressive speed. Later that afternoon, Davies attempted to reclaim the gun, dispatching an entire regiment, which followed the South Carolinians for nearly two miles. "[I]t could not be overtaken," the general conceded in his after-action report.[26]

* * *

The quick thinking and fearlessness of Kerr and Lester on the left contrasted completely to the disaster unfolding on the right. The 1st and 14th South Carolina were so intermingled after emerging from the woods that they were barely distinguishable from the other. Command and control at the company level ceased, and no one stepped in to bring any order. Caldwell expressed his frustration in his postwar history, opining that the jumbled mass of men could have simply aligned on a rail fence to their front to untangle the chaos.

By this time, Lane's Brigade had moved to McGowan's right, although it was still positioned an uncomfortable distance away. Lanes's men had struggled

24 *OR* 40(1):615–616, 619.

25 Ibid.

26 William Templeton to Sarah Templeton, Aug. 2, 1864; *OR* 40(1):615.

more than the South Carolinians in clearing the swamp. Despite their tardiness, the North Carolinians confronted Federal troopers that were bearing down on the disorganized 1st and 14th. Relieved temporarily from galling flank fire, the two regiments advanced toward the Yankee position, with the trailing Tar Heels not too far behind. The Federals, however, met the attack with withering fire, staggering both regiments. They then poured into the gap between Lane's and McGowan's men, delivering flank fire against both brigades to widen the interval. As the Federals moved to the rear to cut off the Confederates, Col. Thomas Devin's troopers in Sheridan's Cavalry Corps counterattacked to the front and began driving the North and South Carolinians from the field.

The attack was decisive. The 1st South Carolina broke, its men literally running through a Yankee skirmish line that had been forming at their rear. To the left, the 14th South Carolina fell back begrudgingly, rallying at different points to try to stop the onslaught but with no real success. Now on foot, having had two horses shot from beneath him during the attack, Conner drew his pistol to threaten the men. But even he finally accepted that the day was lost and "was obliged to retire," according to a staff officer witnessing the rout.[27]

On the left, the 12th and 13th lingered in the field for a period, basking in their stunning success. With Federal reinforcements moving in and no reliable support in place, however, the two understrength regiments fell back to the woods. Eventually, the entire brigade rallied and headed back to Fussell's Mill, near where the attack had commenced that morning. There, the brigade formed a line; the 12th occupied the extreme left, closest to the mill.

The brigade's casualty count was astounding: 239 out of 800–1,000 engaged. The 12th had the fewest at 18 (one killed, 12 wounded, and five missing), and the 13th had 42 (six killed, 33 wounded, and three missing). Orr's Rifles, in the center, also suffered 42 casualties (three killed, 34 wounded, and five missing). The highest losses, as expected considering the battle's trajectory, were in the two regiments on the right: the 14th with 77 (eight killed, 41 wounded, and 38 missing) and the 1st with 59 (three killed, 33 wounded, and 23 missing).[28]

Despite the gallantry displayed by Kerr, Lester, and their men, the battle of Deep Bottom was a bitter failure for Conner and the brigade in general. "The day was lost," Caldwell lamented. "The general carelessness of officers, and the excitement and stubbornness of the men, had lost us what should have been a brilliant success. We had surprised the enemy, terrified him, doubled him up in

27 Dunlop, *Lee's Sharpshooters*, 139; Caldwell, *The History of a Brigade of South Carolinians*, 224–225.

28 Caldwell, *The History of a Brigade of South Carolinians*, 226; William Templeton to Sarah Templeton, Sept. 19, 1864.

confusion, and yet we failed, because we were so foolish as not to keep a line. . . . This was the first time I had ever seen cause to be ashamed of the brigade, and I am glad to say, it was the last." In an acknowledgment of the poor showing, Conner simply stated in a letter home, "I have learned something from the fight, and will make some changes the next time I put them in."

One soldier in the 12th's Company B took a more optimistic view, declaring it a draw. "[B]oth sides were defeated," he would recall.

Writing about the battle after the war, William Dunlop claimed that Conner was "mortified" at the outcome and attributed the defeat not only to the terrain difficulties but also the failure of the respective commanders to conform his regiment's movement with that of the guiding regiment. It was unknown which regiment was intended as the "battalion of direction" in the advance, Dunlop would point out. It was likely either Orr's Rifles in the center or the 1st or 12th on the right and left, respectively.

Dunlop's stark admission revealed a recurring problem plaguing Lee's army at this point of the war. With the extensive loss of veteran officers at both the regimental and company level, few commanders remained not only to identify potentially troublesome issues *before* an assault but also to implement the proper commands *during* an assault.[29]

A glance at the command structure of McGowan's Brigade at Deep Bottom sheds light on this. Conner had been in command for only a month and had never been at the helm during a standup, close-quartered fight. Being charged as well with command of Lane's Brigade further complicated the situation. With Conner's attention diverted, Hunt assumed a central role for McGowan's Brigade, and Lester took up the 13th South Carolina's reins. None of the South Carolina regiments were commanded by colonels that day, and Kerr led the 12th as a captain.

As the bloody Petersburg campaign continued, the institutional knowledge of field and line officers would be sapped more and more as veteran officers were killed, wounded, or assigned to the sick list. Mounting casualties had also collapsed the rank structure of the various regiments. Not only were there new commanders leading regiments and brigades, but these commanders had few support staffers to assist them in their duties: "There now was really no commissioned officer on the regimental staff except the adjutant," Caldwell explained. This meant that the 12th, for example, had no available second or third officer, no one to take charge of the regiment's right or left wing and no one to assume command in the event the commander needed to head to the rear to seek or clarify orders.

29 Caldwell, *The History of a Brigade of South Carolinians*, 225; Dunlop, *Lee's Sharpshooters*, 140–141; J. C. to My dear Mother, July 30, 1864, in Moffett, ed., *Letters of General James Conner*, 144.

It is true, of course, that a regiment of 150–200 men was easier to handle than one of 800, but the lack of subordinate field officers created problems in assuring that orders were relayed as efficiently as possible during a difficult fight on rough terrain. That, probably more than anything else, explains why what promised to be a fairly straightforward advance at Deep Bottom became a bogged-down and disjointed affair.[30]

Given the circumstances, the 12th's performance at Deep Bottom was competent and workmanlike, if not flashy. Kerr proved he was a capable officer and that the regiment remained in good hands, capable of continuing its proud tradition of offensive-minded and aggressive tactics. Despite the failures on the right, the men of the 12th had performed impressively. They had routed the enemy and captured a cannon. While driving the Yankees from the field was nothing new for the veterans, hauling off a cannon was a novelty and bragging right enjoyed by few units, especially at this point in the conflict.

For the next two evenings, the regiment bivouacked near Fussell's Mill. Rumors circulated on July 30 that the brigade would return to Petersburg, but those proved false. By August 1, Lane's and McGowan's brigades were back at Fort Harrison. As they attended to picket duty and much-needed drill sessions—including morning and evening dress parades—the long and unrelenting summer of 1864 wore on.[31]

30 Caldwell, *The History of a Brigade of South Carolinians*, 227.

31 Ibid., 227–228.

Chapter Twelve

Showdowns on the Richmond-Petersburg Line

Despite the disjointed and lackluster performance by McGowan's Brigade during the fighting at Deep Bottom, the men in the 12th were in fine spirits on the return to their decrepit earthworks near Fort Harrison. "We had a fight last week," William Templeton beamed in a letter to his sister. "The Yanks came over on this side of the river [and] we drove them back again." Templeton would punctuate his elation with news of the stirring capture of the Federal artillery piece during the clash: "[Our] reagement and the 13 reg Captured one peace of artillery[.] we brot it off safe." Despite the unusual braggadocio, he signed off the letter in underwhelming fashion, offering only a restrained: "[I]t's all quiet hear for the last few days." Of course, as had happened more often than not in the war thus far, any harbinger of quiet would not last long.

In early August 1864, success in the war was being measured differently from theater to theater. In the Western Theater, Sherman's sweep through Georgia with Atlanta in his crosshairs—which had begun at the same time as Grant's toward Richmond—was almost a fait accompli. Atlanta finally surrendered in the face of relentless Federal pressure on September 2, and "Uncle Billy" would then plant an exclamation point on the destruction of the Peach State with his March to the Sea in November–December.

Uncertainty continued to rear its ugly head for Grant in the East, however. The battle of the Crater on July 30 had been humiliating, an unequivocal debacle that added to the growing distrust of the Union commander by Eastern Theater veterans, many still convinced that Grant was in over his head against Lee. Grant, though, was inured to the prospect of another bout with siege warfare, as he had endured at both Vicksburg and Chattanooga the previous year. He was not about to flinch in his determination to outwit Lee and capture Petersburg, no matter the cost.

* * *

The morale level of the men in the 12th was remarkably high at this point of the war, which was not necessarily the case for the brigade's other four regiments. The 12th's esprit de corps was justified in many ways. The regiment, led by Capt. Robert Kerr, had performed exceptionally throughout the recent fight. Under fire, Kerr responded with both gallantry and coolness. Holding the regiment together in the thick woods and swamps amid shelling and the fire of dismounted cavalry armed with repeating carbines had not been an easy task. Kerr's quick thinking in reorganizing his command after it had been thrown back and then spurring a frantic pursuit to capture a horde of fleeing Federals and one of their rifled cannons reaffirmed its fighting reputation after the setbacks at the Wilderness and Jericho Mills. Whether it was Dixon Barnes, John Miller, or now Robert Kerr in charge, the 12th South Carolina was still a force with which to be reckoned.

The men settled into their routines in the trenches near Fort Harrison, mostly picket duty, drill, and dress parade. The officers of the brigade received some good news while waiting for word on their next obligation or mission: the pending distribution of a long-awaited allotment of "fine gray cloth" that would be used to sew new uniforms. The only caveat? "There will not be enough for all," one officer wrote to his wife, "so we will draw lots for it."

On August 4, some of the men in the 12th also took part in an unexpected diversion when Maj. William Dunlop, Company B's former captain and now commander of the brigade's sharpshooter battalion, convened an important meeting of Companies A, B, and H. The soldiers continued to hold great interest in events back home, and this meeting was to officially endorse the regiment's former colonel, Cadwallader Jones, for the South Carolina senate as well as a member of the 12th still in uniform, Sgt. J. C. Chambers, for the state's house of representatives in that fall's election. Jones, whom the soldiers remembered fondly a year-and-a-half after he had resigned his command because of deteriorating health, received a unanimous endorsement from the three companies—each formed with men from the district in which Jones and Chambers were running. The resolution passed at the meeting read:

> Whereas, we, the Officers and Soldiers of Cos. A, B. and H, of the 12th Regiment of S. C. V., have learned, from a late issue of the YORKVILLE ENQUIRER, of the nomination of Col. Cad. Jones for the Senate, and J. C. Chambers, Esq., for

the House of Representatives, and being desirous of giving public expression of our appreciation of the patriotic course and past services of Col. Cad. Jones, as an officer and former commander; and as a lasting, though imperfect testimonial of our high regard for his ability, integrity and spotless character as a gentleman; and, also, as a tribute to the soldierly conduct, patriotism and talents of J. C. Chambers, Esq., our present companion in arms;

Be it therefore,

RESOLVED, That without any disparagement of the claims of others, or in the least pretending to dictate to the voters of York District, in reference to the offices alluded to above, we do hereby cordially and heartily concur in, and endorse the nomination of Col. Jones for the Senate, and J. C. Chambers, Esq. for the House of Representatives.

It is also moved and seconded that the proceedings of this meeting be sent to the YORKVILLE ENQUIRER for publication.[1]

The men finally had a chance to read mail early that month and readily devoured the news from home, although reports of Sherman's surge through Georgia and the possible loss of Atlanta were understandably difficult to digest. Sarah Templeton mentioned in a letter to her brother Joseph that rumors were circulating that the 12th had been transferred to Georgia to join the Army of Tennessee's defense of Atlanta. "Thair is no such good news," Templeton responded in his letter back on August 10, "for wee never will get oubt of Virginia while the war lasts."[2]

In the first week of August, the Confederate troops manning the Fort Harrison line at Chaffin's Bluff were shifted a few miles forward to establish new positions in the direction of Fussell's Mill, near the site of the South Carolinians' clash in late July. The shift was in response to a new threat to Richmond by Hancock's II Corps, the X Corps (now under General Birney's command), and Gregg's cavalry, all now across the James.[3]

For the next several days, the 12th remained posted in new entrenchments on the brigade's left. On August 13, Federal artillery shelled the position, and sporadic skirmishing continued along the lines as the Yankees inched closer to the Confederate works. They eventually drove in pickets from a brigade in Maj. Gen. Charles Field's 1st Division, part of Anderson's First Corps, in what many on the Confederate side suspected was a precursor to a larger attack. The next day, the

1 "Camp, 12th Regiment, S. C. V.," *Yorkville Enquirer*, Aug. 17, 1864, 2; William Templeton to Sarah Templeton, Aug. 2, 1864, and Aug. 10, 1864; Welch, *A Confederate Surgeon's Letters to His Wife*, 104.

2 Joseph Templeton to Sarah Templeton, Aug. 10, 1864.

3 *OR* 42(1):216.

entire line turned and marched to the left to extend the position. It rained that evening as the men waited anxiously for an attack that never came. The next day, the men shifted right again without any disturbance—"a day of perfect quiet," William Dunlop recalled.[4]

The rotation for the picket lines defending each of the brigade's five regiments at this time typically followed a consistent schedule (although William Templeton claimed in a letter that he once spent 50 consecutive hours on picket duty). As it turned out, Templeton's Company B was part of this rotation overnight on August 15–16 and would learn by courier at sunrise that the Federals were advancing in strength against the left of the line, threatening Field's Division. The 12th, short Company B, would lead the August 16 response by McGowan's Brigade—trailed in order by the 13th, Orr's Rifles, the 14th, and the 1st. Lane's Brigade followed McGowan's advance, with Conner still in command of both units.

After swinging around Field's rear, the two brigades fronted to the right. Lane's and McGowan's men deployed, respectively, to Field's immediate left, which put the understrength 12th on the line's extreme left flank. To maintain cover on his front, Conner ordered his command to align in a single rank—the first and only time in the war that McGowan's entire brigade would be deployed as such. One soldier labeled the alignment "loosely dressed," and another noted that the unusual deployment was intended to "keep up the appearance along our whole line." The lengthy yet skeletal line eventually stretched nearly 12 miles from White Oak Swamp on the Chickahominy to Chaffin's Bluff on the James.

While the troops on the main line hurriedly erected breastworks, Dunlop and his sharpshooters advanced in a skirmish line and were soon engaged when extensive fighting erupted to Field's right. At one point, Conner's men heard three lengthy volleys of fire followed by an ominous silence. Although the action ahead progressed out of their sight, word quickly spread that the Federals had driven Fields's entire division from its works. The extent to which this development impacted Dunlop's skirmishers remained uncertain, however.

Conner responded by moving McGowan's Brigade about a quarter-mile to the rear of the main works and then deploying the South Carolinians to the right, keeping them well back and concealed—ready to launch a counterattack, if needed. As they moved, the men were ordered to "close up" in two ranks, and a skirmish line was thrown to the left. After marching roughly a half-mile, the

4 Dunlop, *Lee's Sharpshooters*, 146.

column halted and dressed its line opposite Field's captured works. The 1st South Carolina remained on the right, closest to the enemy.[5]

Missing the companies still on picket duty, the brigade fielded about 600–800 men. Hunt ordered an advance into the woods lining the works, and to avoid a repeat of the communication mishap that had hampered their fight a couple of weeks earlier, he emphasized that the 1st was the "battalion of direction" and that the other four regiments should conform their movements to the 1st's. Hunt's prudence worked; the advance was conducted, in the opinion of one soldier, "not in the disorderly manner of the 28th of July." Despite the rough ground the South Carolinians traversed in the woods, the line moved effectively.

For McGowan's men, however, the frontal assault that was needed to reclaim the captured works would be a daunting challenge. Field's former stronghold ran at an angle to the line of battle, putting the South Carolinians' left flank at the front of advance. In this alignment, the 12th was posted on the left, and as the regiment entered a pine thicket, Col. Francis B. Pond's 1st Brigade in the X Corps' 1st Division opened fire. Fierce fighting broke out that before long would involve all five regiments.

Surging through the pines behind Kerr's lead, the 12th soon forced the first regiment it faced—the 85th Pennsylvania—to break and flee, in the process gaining a foothold in the works. The brigade's other four regiments could not mirror this success, however, which allowed the 62nd Ohio in Pond's brigade to divert its attention toward the 12th. The Buckeyes began to unleash deadly fire into the South Carolina regiment's right flank.

Realizing he had no support, Kerr ordered the 12th to retreat into the pine thicket. They swiftly rallied and renewed the attack, only to be turned back again by devastating enfilade fire. Kerr rallied the men once more, dressing on the 13th South Carolina's right, and reengaged. At some point, Brig. Gen. William Birney's 1st Brigade in the X Corps' 3rd Division entered the contested works to bolster the Federal position. Birney was the older brother of David Birney, the X Corps' commander. His brigade contained three USCT regiments—the 7th, 8th, and 9th—as well as the 29th Connecticut (Colored). The employment of black troops seemed to produce an effect on the South Carolinians once they realized who they were up against in this fight.

Hunt continued to inch the brigade forward and had closed to within about 20 paces of the works when the Federals delivered a "murderous" volley into their

5 Dunlop, *Lee's Sharpshooters*, 147–148; Caldwell, *The History of a Brigade of South Carolinians*, 230; William Templeton to Sarah Templeton, Aug. 18, 1864; LOCAL, "Army Correspondence of the Ledger," *Lancaster Ledger*, Aug. 30, 1864, 2.

midst. Stunned at the ferociousness of the volley, the Confederates wavered but at least managed to fire back as they retreated. With dense smoke hanging low in the pine woods, the shrieks of the wounded caught between the two lines kindled the South Carolinians' emotions. Cries for their comrades to return to the fight and drive the enemy were nearly impossible to ignore. "Rallying again a short distance back," recalled one soldier from the 12th, "and hearing their wounded comrades calling to them to charge, a wild impulse of desperate determination seized the entire brigade, when it rushed against the fortifications, stormed out the dense lines crowded there, and slew them by scores and hundreds as they fled in irretrievable panic." That latest attack against the Federal position, D. J. Carter would recall, had all "the violence of a tornado."

Almost simultaneously, Brig. Gen. John Bratton's Brigade in Field's Division swung in on the 1st South Carolina's right and slammed into the works. Hand-to-hand fighting broke out, but the Federals were soon desperately on the run, losing scores killed or wounded, and even more as prisoners. William Birney's USCT troops paid the higher price. Recalled Carter: "The slaughter of the enemy at this point was considerable, mostly negroes, who came up to restore the white Yankees."

The South Carolina brigades' tandem onslaught created the necessary pressure to crack the Federal line. A subsequent rally and attempted counterattack by the Yankees would be to no avail.[6]

Field's works were back in Confederate hands, and the men in the 12th were amazed to discover inside more plunder and supplies than many had ever seen. They were also startled to encounter Black troops face-to-face for the first time, both wounded and prisoners. The sight incensed the South Carolinians, their excitement already heightened after the severe clash. In an unconscionable scenario that mirrored the unabated slaughter of USCT troops by Confederate soldiers at the battle of the Crater on July 30, several men from the 12th refused to give quarter to Birney's men. "Our boys refused to take them as prisoners," Carter revealed in one of his missives to the *Lancaster Ledger*. "But some fifty odd taken at other points were started to Richmond yesterday, and it is positively known they never reached the city—you can very easily guess what became of them." Carter

6 Caldwell, *The History of a Brigade of South Carolinians*, 230–232; Dunlop, *Lee's Sharpshooters*, 148–149; *OR* 42(1):688; "Army Correspondence of the Ledger," *Lancaster Ledger*, Aug. 30, 1864, 2. An account by Colonel Pond attributed the Confederate breakthrough to pressure on his left flank by Bratton's Brigade. His subordinate, Maj. Francis Kahler of the 62nd Ohio, stated that pressure from the right flank (McGowan's Brigade, and specifically the 12th South Carolina) was the impetus to his regiment's retreat. Cf. *OR* 42(1):694.

would also write ominously that that one USCT soldier "taken to the rear by a member of Company I, has mysteriously made his disappearance in the fog."[7]

Robert E. Lee had been on the battlefield that day. Tremendously pleased, he called the victory a brilliant success. It was also costly, and when the Federals before long requested a truce to bury their dead, the request was granted. As the Federals went about the grisly task, the men in McGowan's Brigade addressed their own casualties, tending to the wounded and burying their dead comrades. The brigade's casualty count attested to the battle's devastation: 13 killed, 93 wounded (including Lt. Col. Isaac Hunt and the brigade adjutant, J. F. J. Caldwell), and eight missing. The 12th sustained the second-highest count, behind only the 13th. Of the 150 or so men the regiment brought to the fight, three were killed and 16 wounded (including lieutenants A. S. Douglass and J. W. Hill). The missing/captured column listed eight men from the 12th—the brigade's entire number.[8]

Among the wounded was Joseph Templeton, who had been shot in the thigh and would be sent for care to Richmond on August 17. Why he was not on picket duty with his brother and the rest of Company B that day remains a mystery; it is possible he had transferred to another company by this point or was back in camp the day of the battle for an unknown reason. In Richmond, Templeton was admitted to General Hospital No. 9, a facility near the city's Virginia Central Railroad depot that served as the receiving hospital for Lee's army. The next day, he was transferred to the Jackson Hospital in the capital's western suburbs and would be granted a 30-day furlough on August 25. By August 29, he was home in South Carolina to recuperate. He would not return to the regiment until late November.[9]

An important soldier returned to the brigade two days after the victory at what would become known as the battle of Fussell's Mill: Brig. Gen. Samuel McGowan, sidelined since his wounding during the Spotsylvania Court House fighting. With McGowan reassuming command of his brigade, Lee handed the reins of Lane's Brigade to Conner on a temporary basis while General Lane continued to recover

7 D. J. Carter, "Army Correspondence of the Ledger," *Lancaster Ledger*, Aug. 30, 1864, 2. Despite Carter's boastful claims about the widescale slaughter of the USCT troops at Second Deep Bottom, casualty figures from Birney's brigade do not corroborate the assertion. In the Aug. 13–20 period, 13 USCT's were listed as "killed" and only four "missing," far less than the 50-plus Carter bragged in his exaggerated newspaper account. Regardless of the discrepancy, and whether it was one man or 50 slain, Carter's report on this shocking affair demonstrated the abhorrence many South Carolinians, and many Confederate soldiers in general, felt about Black troops now fighting in the U.S. Army. Carter, a former editor of the *Lancaster Ledger*, was well read and informed, and he was likely playing to the emotions of his audience back home, perhaps in a desire to sell more newspapers. Cf. *OR* 42(1):120.

8 Caldwell, *The History of a Brigade of South Carolinians*, 232.

9 William Templeton to Sarah Templeton, Aug. 29, 1864, and Sept. 3, 1864; Caldwell, *The History of a Brigade of South Carolinians*, 233.

from his groin wound at Cold Harbor. Lee felt it was important to keep Conner in the fold, a conviction the men clearly shared because of the stability and workmanlike competency he had brought to the brigade when McGowan and Colonel Brown (captured at North Anna) were lost within a two-week span during the May fighting.[10]

On August 20, the brigade was ordered back to Petersburg, where the two sides were already heavily entrenched. Interestingly, McGowan's men were initially posted near the site of the infamous Crater. One 12th South Carolina soldier noted that only about 150 yards separated the opposing lines at this section of the field and that small-arms and mortar fire never ceased, day and night. On August 22, though, the brigade moved to the Weldon Railroad, a principal artery supplying Lee's army from the south. This position was near the extreme right flank of Lee's entire army.[11]

Although he had done so at an incredible human cost, Grant had gradually put himself in position to dictate the broader, strategic picture in the Eastern Theater. He had succeeding in forcing Lee to wind his way south from Central Virginia in May and June, and although Lee had fought him to a draw or had defeated him outright at three major engagements, the Army of Northern Virginia was now pinned on a tenuous front between Richmond and Petersburg, its manpower at dangerously low levels. Lee's hallmark for more than two years had been his penchant to maneuver and strike quickly against a collection of overmatched Union generals. Those generals would usually lose the battle, retreat, and then try again perhaps a short term later with similar futility. Grant had eliminated that advantage. Lee had landed a few heavy punches as the two commanders jostled toward the Confederate capital, but his campaign strategy had been mostly one of reaction rather than action. Lee knew he did not have the numbers to resort to extended siege warfare, but he also accepted that he could not simply sacrifice Petersburg and somehow try to coerce Grant to fight on more favorable ground. If this critical railroad hub fell, inevitably so too would Richmond.

It is against this backdrop that the men of the 12th South Carolina and the other regiments in McGowan's Brigade reestablished their camps near the Weldon Railroad. Running north into the western reaches of Petersburg, the railroad was the Confederate army's lifeline—the main artery for both communication and the supply of materiel and men from the Deep South. As Grant continued to invest his hold on Petersburg, possession of the entire Weldon line became of the utmost importance. With the railroad in Union hands, Lee would be forced to unload

10 *OR* 42(2):1185.

11 Dunlop, *Lee's Sharpshooters*, 154–155.

supplies far south of Petersburg and transport them to his army by wagon. Precious men and time would be lost in the process. Holding onto as much of the Weldon line as possible was vital to Lee's ability to continue to hold the Cockade City.

On August 18, Gouverneur Warren's V Corps occupied a section of the railroad roughly six miles south of Petersburg, near Globe Tavern. The following day, General Mahone's Division launched an attack that broke through a small gap between Warren's right flank and portions of Parke's IX Corps that had arrived as reinforcements overnight. Mahone's assault netted scores of prisoners from Samual Crawford's division and put the Union position in considerable danger. A subsequent attack by Henry Heth's Division would be turned back, and Parke launched a counterattack before dark that kept the battle essentially deadlocked.

The Federals blunted separate attacks by Heth and Mahone on the morning of August 21 and Lee finally pulled his men back. The impact of the four-day battle of Globe Tavern was mixed. Total Union casualties topped 7,000 men to only 1,620 on the Confederate side, but technically it was a Union victory because a key stretch of the railroad was now in Union possession. Not satisfied, Grant wanted to keep the pressure on Lee and recalled Hancock's II Corps, as well as Gregg's cavalry division, from Deep Bottom. Their destination was Ream's Station, 10 miles south of Petersburg; Hancock was ordered to destroy as much of the railroad as possible, which Brig. Gen. Nelson Miles's division accomplished. Hancock's other division, commanded by John Gibbon, took control of Ream's Station itself on August 23, compelling Lee to order an attack there by his new Cavalry Corps commander, Lt. Gen. Wade Hampton. When Hampton's clash with Gibbon ended indecisively, Lee turned to A. P. Hill's Third Corps to reclaim this vital section of the disrupted line.[12]

On August 24, Wilcox and the Light Division began moving toward Ream's Station, accompanied by Heth's Division and Pegram's artillery battalion. The men of the 12th South Carolina were in the middle of enhancing their breastworks on their front when the order came to move out about 2:00 p.m. Kerr and the regiment quickly joined their brigade's advance, positioned behind Scales's Brigade. The men would bivouac that evening at Armstrong's Mill, about three miles from Ream's Station.[13]

The march resumed the next day at 8:00 a.m. Later that morning, with the column less than a mile from Ream's Station, Wilcox ordered Scales to form a line of battle from left to right. Sharpshooters from both brigades moved forward first and quickly engaged. Scales and McGowan had been directed to follow the

12 *SHSP* 19:113–114.

13 Dunlop, *Lee's Sharpshooters*, 189–190; Caldwell, *The History of a Brigade of South Carolinians*, 234.

sharpshooters to determine whether the enemy position was fortified. If not, they were to attack; if so, the commanders were to report back to Wilcox.[14]

After clearing the woods, the brigades drew to a halt on an open plain. Before them was the Weldon Railroad and a formidable line of Federals from the II Corps. Hancock's Yankees were also heavily fortified. "The enemy were posted just at the railroad, in a position of great strength, and defended by considerable quantity," recalled one veteran, and another would note that they had "entrenched themselves strongly on the west side of the railroad."[15]

McGowan led his brigade a short distance up a steep, wooded incline and halted. Dunlop's sharpshooters had driven enemy skirmishers from their rifle pits in the field and had pursued them roughly 400 yards to the Federal works before falling back. After reporting to Wilcox that the position was indeed fortified, McGowan was directed to make his primary attack on the left as the sharpshooters created a diversion on the right.

The sharpshooters dutifully complied. Using the brow of the hill as a shield, they stepped to the crest, fired a series of volleys, and retired to reload before returning to the crest to reengage. Dunlop, however, recalled that his men soon ran out of ammunition, necessitating "a relay of active couriers played between the front and main line [that] replenished our cartridge boxes from the brigade from time to time as the battle progressed." Pegram's artillery also moved up in support, unlimbering just behind the sharpshooters. McGowan then sent the 13th South Carolina and Orr's Rifles forward to assist both the sharpshooters and the batteries, while the 1st, 12th, and 14th remained shielded below the crest, waiting for orders to attack the Federal right.[16]

Captain Langdon Haskell, McGowan's assistant adjutant general, had command of the contingent creating the diversion. When he heard the other three regiments' advance on the left, Haskell was to lead his two regiments and the sharpshooters against the enemy works. As McGowan recalled in his after-action report:

> They scaled the works near the angle, which they made with the railroad embankment, and captured four pieces of artillery and one stand of colors, twelve horses, many small arms, and about 400 prisoners. The prisoners were not counted—there was no time for that. [As] soon as captured they were pushed over the fortifications and the work continued, but all the officers agree that the number could not have been

14 *Supplement to OR* 7(1):506–510.

15 Caldwell, *The History of a Brigade of South Carolinians*, 234–235; *SHSP* 19:114.

16 *Supplement to OR* 7(1):506–510; Dunlop, *Lee's Sharpshooters*, 193.

> less than that stated. When this small force of two regiments first got into the works they were alone, none of the column on the left coming up for fifteen minutes. Three of the guns taken were in the angle made by the railroad embankment and the fortifications, and one was near the railroad embankment above this angle.

Dunlop admitted after the war that the sharpshooters were not supposed to advance with the 13th and Orr's Rifles, but "when the Confederate battle cry was raised and the lines went sweeping across the field amid the roar of artillery and the clash of arms, the sharpshooters could not be held [back]; so they were turned loose, and the whole force—sharpshooters and all—like a 'rushing mighty wind' stormed down upon the Federal lines and over the breastworks, completely routing the whole force, which fled through the woods in the wildest confusion." As testament to their bravery, McGowan would refer to the battle of Ream's Station as "the sharpshooters fight."

With these favorable results, McGowan decided to press the advantage and ordered the 1st, 12th, and 14th forward to the right of the breakthrough. Upon their arrival, however, one of Hill's staff officers ordered McGowan to move his entire brigade to the left, including the 13th South Carolina and Orr's Rifles. It was nearly dark by the time McGowan halted the men at a dirt-road intersection adjacent to a house (the owner or resident of this house was never identified). With the 13th and Orr's Rifles still trailing the main column, the general ordered a bivouac and threw out pickets in all directions.

As the men prepared for the evening by their fires, McGowan consulted with Kerr, informing him that the 12th had been chosen to march nearly 2,000 prisoners captured that day to Petersburg. It was not recorded why McGowan selected the 12th for this—perhaps because it was one of the brigade's smallest regiments and the commander wanted to be sure he had as many soldiers on hand as possible should more fighting break out. It was also not recorded how long the assignment lasted, though correspondence from members of the regiment dated August 29 still had them in Petersburg proper.[17]

The rest of the brigade marched back to their original position near the Weldon Railroad the next day. Morale in the 12th South Carolina soared after the battle of Ream's Station, although the regiment actually had not truly fought there. In one of his most descriptive letters during the war, William Templeton

17 *Supplement to OR* 7(1):506–510; William Templeton to Sarah Templeton, Aug. 29, 1864; Dunlop, *Lee's Sharpshooters,* 196, 200. A review of the "Confederate Inspection Reports" dated September 1, 1864, show the brigade's regimental strengths as: 1st South Carolina, 189; Orr's Rifles, 263; 12th South Carolina, 242; 13th South Carolina, 266; and 14th South Carolina, 279. [See "Confederate Inspection Reports," 24: 17—McGowan's Brigade, September 1, 1864.].

proudly recalled that, "we had a fight since we came here down on the railroad. We gave the Yanks a good thrashing. We did not lose many. They were fortified on the railroad. Scales' and Anderson's brigades charged them and were repulsed. Cook's and Lane's brigades charged them then the tarheels raised the shout and went strait forward. They took the works and 7 stand of colors and 9 pieces of artillery and 2500 prisoners. They made a very poor resistance in our front of our brigade and just fired one volley and then gave up . . . we did not lose any in our company."[18]

Sometime between August 29 and September 12, the 12th returned to the brigade's position in the line of breastworks near the Weldon Railroad, what several accounts indicated was about three miles southwest of Petersburg. The men were allowed to rest for the first time in several weeks, but on September 13 they resumed their spot on the front line, assigned a "heap of fatigue" duty. One piece of good news for the 12th was the return of Lt. Col. Edwin Bookter, who had been out of action since his May 5 wounding at the Wilderness. This would be the first time since May that a field officer commanded the regiment.

Bookter, in his mid-20's, was vintage 12th South Carolina. A native of the state's Richland District, he had graduated from South Carolina College in 1858 and was working as a planter and a state representative when the war began three years later. Raising his own company, he joined the 12th South Carolina at Lightwood Knot Springs and served as one of the senior company commanders during the bloody campaigns of 1862. When Col. Cadwallader Jones was forced to resign because of health in the winter of 1862–63, Bookter was promoted to major and then lieutenant colonel in the fall of 1863 with Henry C. Davis's resignation. Bookter briefly assumed command of the regiment when Col. John Miller was mortally wounded at the Wilderness, only to be wounded in the same assault.

As a younger regimental officer, Bookter was a strict disciplinarian and precise in drill and troop management. Though stern on the field, he was amiable when not on duty and had the unqualified respect of the men under his command—a reverence gained during a dozen battles and three severe woundings. He would find his return to a regiment decimated by its past four months of marching, counter-marching, and fighting a bit of a shock. Indeed, the 12th was now a shell of the unit that had marched confidently down the Orange Plank Road to the Wilderness on May 4. At that time, the regiment numbered a very respectable 480 officers and men. As of September 1, only 242 were present for duty in the trenches and that number would only marginally increase by the end of the month to 248.[19]

18 William Templeton to Joseph Templeton, Sept. 3, 1864 (edited for clarity and punctuation).

19 Caldwell, *The History of a Brigade of South Carolinians*, 242; "Confederate Inspection Reports," 24: 17—McGowan's Brigade, September 1, 1864.

Out of necessity, Bookter made the improvement of the regiment's defenses one of his first priorities. The brigade's picket line lay about 600 yards in front of the main entrenchments, featuring a series of rifle pits that ran through both a cornfield and a dense forest. Stationed just beyond the picket line was a chain of videttes, and 400 yards beyond that was the main Federal line.

The men in the 12th preferred picket duty in the cornfield, which one soldier recalled was "in a full state of roasting ear, and being on neutral ground, both sides claimed the right to forage from it, at least to the center of the field. This foraging continued without objection until the field was stripped to a narrow belt running across the center."[20]

Throughout September, raids and sporadic firefights along the picket line were common, as the enemy troops continued testing each other. "The fighting was spasmodic," recalled William Miller of Company H. "At times the enemy would attack our line, to be driven off, then the sharpshooters would continue to worry us." According to Dunlop, the normally accepted "rules of engagement" for the armies' advanced lines were evolving, given the changing characteristics of the war:

> A period had now been reached in the progress of the great struggle where the extraordinary conditions which prevailed all along the lines seemed to demand some modification in the rules of official responsibility, which would justify the commanding general in distributing to his lieutenants, and through them to the different divisions and brigade commanders, such power and discretion in their respective commands as would authorize them to strike whenever in their judgment an effective blow could be delivered, without formal authority from their superiors in rank. And now that the enemy were constantly in our immediate presence, the importance of an active, vigilant and spirited picket line, largely free from the control of officers of the line, became more and more vital and indispensable to the safety of our lines. These exigencies of the service were fully appreciated by General Lee, and the liberty suggested, with proper limitations, henceforth became the rule in the Army of Northern Virginia.[21]

The 12th would be involved in one of the random skirmishes in mid-September, teaming with the brigade's sharpshooter battalion and pickets from Lane's Brigade in a charge on a Federal position that netted 93 prisoners (including one officer) with the loss of only one man wounded. William Templeton was proudly part of

20 Dunlop, *Lee's Sharpshooters*, 204.

21 Ibid., 155.

the effort, what he labeled a "littel skurmish with the yanks the other day" in a letter to his sister.[22]

* * *

In an attempt to disrupt the Army of Northern Virginia's communication and supply lines and hopefully force it to either abandon the two cities, surrender, or come out and take Grant on in the open field, Grant in late September launched offensives on both flanks of Lee's thin line running from Chaffin's Bluff near Richmond to the Weldon Railroad southwest of Petersburg. The Federal attack at Chaffin's Bluff would take place September 29-30, led by Ben Butler's Army of the James. Butler enjoyed some success at the outset of the dawn attack, overrunning New Market Heights and Fort Harrison (where McGowan's South Carolinians were first stationed in July).

About 9:00 a.m. on September 30, Lee sent Wilcox's Light Division north to support the embattled Confederates in that sector. The 12th assumed the left flank of McGowan's Brigade, which at this point was down to an estimated 1,287 men. After Wilcox's men began moving toward Fort Harrison, however, Grant delivered his second blow—this one on the extreme right of Lee's line, the Confederate-controlled section of the Weldon Railroad that McGowan's command had helped defend over the past month.

Warren's V Corps and Maj. Gen. John Parke's two-division IX Corps led the attack, advancing toward a cluster of roads just north of the Poplar Springs Church. If the Federals could secure a foothold on the railroad, Grant could extend his lines to the west and possibly secure possession of the Boydton Plank Road, another of Lee's vital supply routes. Wade Hampton's cavalry would intercept the Federal column along the Poplar Springs Road, however, and a sharp fight erupted. Suddenly forced to defend his endangered right flank, Lee wasted no time recalling Wilcox and his men from their foray north.[23]

McGowan's Brigade had advanced only a few miles when the order to countermarch came. The men grumbled as they headed back along the Boydton Plank Road and formed the left flank of a three-brigade force now tasked with stopping the Federal surge from the Church Road (Lane's Tar Heels were directly to McGowan's right, but Scales's Brigade continued marching toward Fort Harrison).

22 William Templeton to Sarah Templeton, Sept. 19, 1864; Caldwell, *The History of a Brigade of South Carolinians*, 236.

23 Dunlop, *Lee's Sharpshooters*, 209; *OR* 42(2):1307; Caldwell, *The History of a Brigade of South Carolinians*, 237. Caldwell referred to this as the "Church Road" in his account.

It was about 5:00 p.m.; from their position on the extreme left, the men of the 12th could vaguely make out the Federal line forming around the Jones House on a plateau roughly 600 yards ahead. A soldier in the regiment recalled that a heavy line of Federal sharpshooters "began to pepper us with scattering fire the instant our lines were formed."[24]

McGowan ordered a response by Dunlop's sharpshooters, who swiftly advanced up a hill toward the Jones House, driving back their Federal counterparts and reportedly capturing about two dozen prisoners. That produced a Federal counter: an advance by Brig. Gen. Robert B. Potter's 2nd Division in Parke's IX Corps. Bookter had the 12th assume a defensive posture, the men holding their fire as the blue wave moved in their direction. As the Yankees closed in, McGowan and Conner (commanding Lane's Brigade) were ordered to charge. The two brigades, as one observer would recall, advanced "in a style which elicited universal admiration."

His sword drawn, Bookter led the 12th forward, obliquing the regiment slightly to the right as it made contact with Potter's troops. Bookter, however, would be struck down as they swept forward, shot directly in the head during a series of close-range volleys by Federals in Brig. Gen. Simon Griffin's 2nd Brigade. William Templeton was nearby as it happened, writing in a letter home that the popular colonel died instantly, his brains "shot out."

Although staggered by the outburst of fire and Bookter's death, the 12th continued its advance. With Bookter gone and no other field officers on hand to take the reins, it is likely (though unconfirmed) that Captain Kerr reassumed command of the regiment. "The enemy were in such large force and so far overlapped my right, that I apprehended they would get on the road by which I had advanced and cut me off," Potter observed of the 12th's unshakable advance.

To meet the threat, Potter ordered Griffin to shift his brigade's front to the right, although it would be too late in the face of the 12th's swift surge. The 17th Vermont on Griffin's right, for instance, wheeled to face the South Carolina regiment directly, only to crumble and retreat in the "wildest disorder." As the men fired into the fleeing New Englanders, Potter and Griffin attempted to rally the stunned brigade with no success. Recalling the action, Griffin granted that his "whole line was carried away."

Both of Potter's brigades broke to the rear, driven to the southwest by the galvanized Confederates, who continued firing away at point-blank range, killing and wounding several of the fleeing Yankees. After securing the ground on the

24 Dunlop, *Lee's Sharpshooters*, 210.

Jones farm, the 12th joined the brigade's unchecked sweep across an open field to a line of pine trees where the Federals had halted to make a stand.[25]

McGowan's roused South Carolinians hammered and dislodged Potter's second Federal line, the panic-stricken Yankees soon stampeding toward their fortifications at the rear. But before long, confusion reigned across the brigade. In their pursuit, the men came upon a large swamp creating a fork in the Poplar Springs Road. The bulk of Potter's Federals had streamed right at the fork, so a congested majority of McGowan's Brigade followed in that direction, continuing about another mile toward the Pegram house. Because the 12th South Carolina was on the brigade's left, it likely used the left fork to bypass the swamp.

Regardless, all semblance of order had been lost in the joyous chase. "In this rapid advance," McGowan would admit, "the brigade became a good deal mixed up; but I thought it best not to dampen the ardor of the victorious pursuit by stopping to reform." The winded South Carolinians halted, however, as they neared the Pegram house, finding a strong line of Federals waiting.[26]

Neither McGowan nor Caldwell established in their accounts whether the 12th reunited with the rest of the brigade in front of the Pegram house after its diversion left. Nevertheless, the brigade's chase ended there. About 9:00 p.m., the five regiments were recalled to the Jones house, where they formed a battle line and bivouacked. The next day, the brigade remained in battle formation and advanced back down the Poplar Springs Road toward the Pegram house, staying to the left at the fork this time. The sharpshooter battalion leading the advance was engaged as it passed the swamp and would capture 240 Federals, as well as weapons, ammunition, and other plunder. That would be the extent of fighting that day.

Casualties for the brigade in what is generally known as the battle of Peebles' farm were 162 (26 killed, 129 wounded, and seven missing/captured). The 12th had 23 casualties, with two killed (including Colonel Bookter), 18 wounded, and three missing/captured). Bookter was the third—and fortunately final—commanding officer of the regiment killed in the war.[27]

Rain greeted the men on October 2 as they marched back to the Jones house and began building breastworks and digging rifle pits for the pickets. Lee now had a battle line extending west to Hatcher's Run.

Not only was the loss of Bookter felt in the 12th, but also the entire brigade. As one of the regiment's earliest company commanders, he had risen through

25 William Templeton to Sarah Templeton, Oct. 3, 1864; Caldwell, *The History of a Brigade of South Carolinians*, 239; *OR* 42(1):579; 587–588.

26 Caldwell, *The History of a Brigade of South Carolinians*, 240; *Supplement to OR* 7(1):506–510.

27 Caldwell, *The History of a Brigade of South Carolinians*, 240–241.

the ranks while directing some of the fiercest fighting of the war. "He is one of the best officers in Wilcox's Division, and is looked upon as far superior to any in this brigade," a soldier in Company I bragged prior to Bookter's death. His replacement, Captain Kerr, provided some stability at least.[28]

Little is known about the brigade's activities in the immediate aftermath of the clash near the Jones farm, other than the standard drilling, picket duty, and improving the works should Grant launch another offensive. Certain days of the week became known as "fasting" days when the men received no rations. "Next Wednesday is fast day," Templeton wrote his sister, "but I expect we will have fast before that if we do not get any more than Jeff [Davis] gives us."

Fighting would break out closer to Richmond in October, but three notable engagements all ended in frustration for the Federals. At Petersburg, a relatively quiet month would end on October 27 with an offensive by Hancock's II Corps and Gregg's cavalry against the Boydton Plank Road, one of Lee's critical supply routes from the south, and from there the South Side Railroad. The Federals enjoyed early success and seemed on the verge of a breakthrough. When A. P. Hill, commanding the army's defenses on this flank, became too ill to remain in the field, he handed command to Heth; however, he directed Heth to lead a response that would succeed in stemming the Federal momentum. Late in the day, Hancock had control of the Boydton Plank Road, but realizing his men were in a vulnerable position and without solid support, he decided to pull his II Corps back to the main Federal lines. It was Hancock's final decision as a field commander. Still burdened by the serious wounds he suffered at Gettysburg and the incredible duress of the fighting since May, Hancock handed Grant his resignation, as would Gregg for other reasons in January 1865.

On October 27, the 12th and the rest of McGowan's Brigade formed, preparing to step up in support of Mahone's Division, embroiled in fighting near Hatcher's Run, but they would not be engaged that day. In early- to mid-November, the entire brigade established winter quarters on Lee's flank near Hatcher's Run, just to the right of the position it held during the October fighting at the Boydton Plank Road.[29]

McGowan's men would be placed in the trenches between General Lane's Tar Heels on the right and Brig. Gen. William MacRae's Brigade, in Heth's Division, on the left. Directly behind the 12th South Carolina's portion of the line was a

28 Dunlop, *Lee's Sharpshooters*, 215; William Templeton to Sarah Templeton, Oct. 3, 1864; LOCAL, "For the Lancaster Ledger," *Lancaster Ledger*, June 7, 1864, 2.

29 William Templeton to Sarah Templeton, Nov. 9, 1864; Caldwell, *The History of a Brigade of South Carolinians*, 243.

white-framed, Tudor-style home owned by a Dr. Boisseau, which McGowan used as brigade headquarters.

The weather turned colder, and the men of the 12th in particular spent the rest of November building cabins and huts with dirt floors and dabbed chimneys, similar to the ones they occupied near Orange Court House the previous two winters. Some of the cabins had canvas roofs; others plank or log roofing.

In a letter written November 24, William Templeton informed his sister: "I have been busy working at my house. I have not got it done yet. I have it to cover and the chimney to build and to dab before it is done." William Miller in Company H would recall: "[We] built houses of pine poles about ten by twelve feet square, with a mud chimney. Occasionally a Yankee bomb shell would come along and demolish a few of the huts, and the chaplains and servants would have a race for a place of safety. It was great sport for the soldiers to see them running."[30]

As they settled into their new quarters, the men took stock of the losses incurred during the horrific campaigns of 1864. Six months earlier, the regiment had marched out of its camp at Orange Court House with approximately 480 men under the command of Colonel John Miller (450 enlisted men and non-commissioned officers, 25 commissioned officers, and a field staff of approximately five). By mid-November, the regiment was in Captain Robert Kerr's hands and, as shown in the chart here, had suffered approximately 341 casualties:

Company	Killed	Wounded	Wounded & Missing	Missing	Total
A	5	11	0	7	23
B	4	23	0	8	35
C	6	18	2	8	34
D	9	24	2	11	46
E	9	20	1	7	37
F	7	7	1	11	26
G	7	18	1	7	28
H	5	20	0	17	42
I	9	32	0	11	42
K	4	12	0	6	22
Field and Staff	2	4	0	0	6
Total	67	189[31]	7	93	341

30 Caldwell, *The History of a Brigade of South Carolinians*, 243; William Templeton to Sarah Templeton, Nov. 24, 1864; Miller, "My Experience," 222–223.

31 LOCAL, "Army Correspondence of the Ledger," *Lancaster Ledger*, Nov. 8, 1864, 2. This figure is incorrectly listed as 174 in the source.

Despite the high number of casualties, some accounts indicate that the regiment benefited in those six or so months with the return of men from furloughs and the addition of soldiers through conscription. Some of the wounded men represented in the chart above no doubt returned to the regiment before the end of the Petersburg campaign as well.

Although some regiments in the brigade possibly increased their numbers to 300–350 men by this time, it is unlikely the 12th was that fortunate, given the casualties it sustained in 1864. Likely the regiment's strength remained in the range of 200–300 men by the start of winter. That low aggregate probably accounts for Lee's decision to keep Kerr, a captain, in command after Bookter's death.[32]

As had been the case in previous winters, families back home and the faithful "Central Association" continued to donate goods to the front to keep the men supplied. Many pleaded with their loved ones to take advantage of the lull in operations to get them needed items such as clothing and blankets, as well as food. It typically took 10 days to transport goods from Columbia to the Petersburg lines, and trains would leave Columbia every Wednesday. Ironically, many of the care packages arrived via the Weldon Railroad, the line the regiment had defended most of the summer and fall against Yankee attacks and sabotage.

As the fighting began to subside at the start of November, the men of the 12th also made sure to cast their absentee ballots for state and local elections back home. They also finally received a replacement for the battle flag that was destroyed during the Mule Shoe Salient fighting on May 12. Women in York County began a fundraising campaign to raise money for a new "suitable Banner" for the regiment and urged women from other counties to pitch in to raise the thousand dollars necessary for materials and construction. They would not be disappointed, as \$280—nearly a third of the amount needed—was raised within a few weeks. "These are gratifying evidences of the patriotic spirit of the ladies of Lancaster," wrote one newspaper editor.[33]

Improvements to the entrenchments along Lee's lines continued to be made as fall turned to winter. At some points, the opposing armies' entrenchments were about a mile apart, their picket lines separated by only about 250 yards. The 12th furnished a daily detail of about 40 soldiers to man the picket line on its front,

32 "Confederate Inspection Reports," 24: 17—McGowan's Brigade, September 27, 1864. According to the Inspection Reports, the 12th South Carolina numbered 248 officers and men present for duty; however, as winter set in, there were the obvious influxes of conscripts and reductions for illnesses.

33 William Templeton to Sarah Templeton, Nov. 24, 1864; *OR* 42(3):726–727; LOCAL, "Army Correspondence of the Ledger," *Lancaster Ledger*, Nov. 8, 1864, 2; *Lancaster Ledger*, Nov. 1, 1864, 2; *Lancaster Ledger*, Nov. 29, 1864, 2; *Lancaster Ledger*, Oct. 18, 1864, 2; "Central Association," *Edgefield Advertiser*, Nov. 9, 1864, 1.

as did the brigade's other four regiments. While on picket duty, the men were required to remain in the pits and keep their accoutrements on and stay in place.

Picket duty returned to a more informal and civilized state than it had been in September when quick and rash raids and firefights were routine between the lines. Soldiers in the 1st and 12th left recollections stating that there generally was no firing between the picket lines and that, though fraternization and trading was technically forbidden, it did not stop the soldiers in these regiments from making acquaintances with their counterparts on the picket line. William Miller recalled after the war, "[W]hen quiet we would swap newspapers, tobacco for coffee, with the enemy. It was a very simple process. A Yankee out on the picket line would shake a paper or bundle of coffee and holler at us as to what he had to exchange with us. And he would place it on a stump or some elevated place, and go off; then we would go and get it and leave our package for the party to come for. I never knew or heard of either party cheating."

Soldiers in the trenches apparently were also not prohibited to visit their comrades on the picket line, as men would occasionally bring rations to their hungry pards suffering in the cold and windy conditions in the rifle pits. The line was spread so thin in the trenches that when the 12th formed it resembled a strong, single rank-skirmish line rather than a two-rank battle line. William Miller remembered that when his entire company was on the trench line, about eight feet separated each man. Men struggled to keep an adequate fuel supply for their huts, which meant that before long every sapling and tree was cut down and carried away. Details were even sent far to the rear to attain longer logs they could carry back on their shoulders, and in some instances men used the opportunity cut down trees close to the Federal picket lines, risking capture or death. Things became so bad that McGowan permitted the men to use the brigade's supply wagons to haul the wood, but those endeavors tended to be in vain because of the typical length of the trip, the rough roads, and the generally poor health of the horses.[34]

Many officers who had their own private cabins decided to invite their wives to the front for the winter. As for enlisted men, on average, about five men were quartered in each hut, and as a general rule, these men were considered "mess mates." These informal groupings shared their rations and the daily cooking workload. In William Templeton's mess were his brother Joseph (now back from South Carolina), J. D. Stuart, and William Wallace. Rations would decrease significantly as winter progressed. In February, William Miller wrote home that the entire regiment had gone without meat rations for two weeks. Coffee was issued

34 William Templeton to Sarah Templeton, Nov. 9, 1864; Caldwell, *The History of a Brigade of South Carolinians*, 252–255; Miller, "My Experience," 222–223.

sporadically and low-grade tobacco was handed out once a month. To supplement the meager rations, select soldiers in the regiment were detailed to North Carolina on an extensive foraging mission that took three weeks. One highlight occurred after the New Year when each man in the brigade received a half-gill of whiskey (roughly two ounces).[35]

The weather was rainy in December and January, and temperatures plummeted, adding to the men's struggles. Their spirits were lifted around Christmas, though, when a rumor circulated in camp that the ladies of Richmond and Petersburg were preparing meals to be sent to the men. Although done with commendable intent, it proved a little underwhelming, at least for the men of the 12th. "The conception was generous and lofty, the sentiment patriotic and tender," recalled a soldier in Company B. "Of these we all received our share. But when it came to the grub itself, we received only an intimation of the generous donation."[36]

Clothing shortages remained an issue, especially uniforms. "What we received was coarse and flimsy," Caldwell recalled. New overcoats and blankets were nonexistent, as were shoes. Some of the troops were completely barefoot, according to one deserter who reported the shortages to Federal authorities. The lack of basic necessities combined with the decrease in rations had worn the men out "in mind and in body, and every effort had become painfully irksome," Caldwell noted, although not all of the soldiers shared that opinion. William Templeton claimed in one of his letters in February that "the health of the army is very good at this time."[37]

Desertion became an increasing problem for Lee's entire army, and McGowan's Brigade was no exception. That said, the 12th and the 1st South Carolina were exemplary in keeping their men from abandoning their service commitments, with only two deserters each. Orr's Rifles had nine, the 14th four, and the 13th a shocking 26. The desertion of those 26 men was particularly embarrassing and egregious, taking place while all were on picket duty. Surprisingly, the desertions occurred in broad daylight, as those men scrambled across to the Federal picket line all at once, unharmed despite receiving fire from their unsuspecting comrades who stayed put. Many of the deserters were conscripts who had only recently joined the army.[38]

35 William Templeton to Sister, Dec. 22, 1864, and Joseph Templeton to Sarah Templeton, Feb. 8, 1864; Caldwell, *The History of a Brigade of South Carolinians*, 254–255, Welch, *A Confederate Surgeon's Letters to His Wife*, 116.

36 Dunlop, *Lee's Sharpshooters*, 228–229.

37 Caldwell, *The History of a Brigade of South Carolinians*, 255; Joseph Templeton to Sarah Templeton, Feb. 10, 1864; *OR* 42(3):1008.

38 Caldwell, *The History of a Brigade of South Carolinians*, 256.

One of the 12th's two deserters would provide intelligence on the identities and positions of Wilcox's three brigades. Union intelligence officer Jonathan Babcock informed General Meade: "The following deserters received to-day; First Tennessee, Archer's brigade, Heth's division; Twelfth South Carolina, McGowan's brigade, Wilcox's division. . . . Deserter from McGowan reports no changes in Wilcox's division, which is posted from right to left as follows: McGowan, Lane, Scales."[39]

In an otherwise gloomy winter with no fighting, the brigade would enjoy one military highlight on December 31. Dunlop's sharpshooter battalion and its counterpart in Scales's Brigade received permission from Wilcox to "requisition" camp equipment, overcoats, shoes, and blankets from the enemy picket lines. The raid took place a couple hours before dawn.

Dunlop targeted the raid for a gap that had opened between the 1st and 3rd brigades in Brig. Gen. Frank Wheaton's 1st Division in Horatio Wright's VI Corps. Behind a handpicked 16-man band of guards, the two battalions advanced in parallel single-rank columns. "Silently and stealthily," Dunlop recalled, "as a tiger would skirt a jungle, this double traverse line with spike head in front, slipped through the darkness on the unsuspecting enemy."

As the lines advanced, however, one of Dunlop's men tripped in a ditch and accidentally discharged his weapon. Although the enemy pickets in the rifle pits had been aroused, the battalions surged ahead in the face of heavy gunfire, quickly breaching the picket line. Having advanced halfway through the gap, the two columns swept left and right, respectively, and overran a series of about 20 rifle pits with flank fire, capturing scores of prisoners and, as hoped, plenty of needed supplies.

The entire raid lasted only a few minutes. Dunlop reported that he lost only one man and inflicted nearly 300 casualties, though the Federals claimed a significantly smaller number. "We secured all the supplies necessary to our comfort for the winter and returned to camp about sunrise, a happy command" Dunlop triumphantly recalled.[40]

Despite this small victory for the men of the brigade, the overall picture as 1865 dawned was bleak. "We looked our condition in the face, and we saw that the war was rapidly drawing to an issue more or less disastrous to us," one soldier recalled. "The conviction everywhere prevailed that we could sustain but one more campaign."[41]

39 *OR* 42(3):820–821.

40 Dunlop, *Lee's Sharpshooters*, 224–228; *OR* 42(3):1106–1107; 1111–1112.

41 Caldwell, *The History of a Brigade of South Carolinians*, 256.

Chapter Thirteen

Final Resistance

SHORTLY INTO THE new year, in an effort to procure desperately needed supplies, an unknown number of soldiers in the 12th South Carolina left the front lines at Petersburg to join the army's commissary department. William Templeton was in that lot, and in March he wrote home that in two months he and his comrades had combed for bounty in five nearby counties: Dinwiddie, Lynchburg, Nottaway, Mecklenburg, and Brunswick. The soldiers from either the 12th or the brigade's other regiments who accompanied Templeton on the mission were apparently never recorded, but it is highly unlikely the entire regiment left the trenches, given the Army of Northern Virginia's ever-shrinking numbers. As the war's final year began, McGowan's Brigade numbered 1,398 men, with about 125 of those assigned to William Dunlop's sharpshooter battalion. The 12th was the second-smallest of the five regiments, behind only the 1st. Captain Kerr's command likely was down to fewer than 200 men.[1]

Regular drilling and troop reviews resumed in February and early March at the behest of General Lee, who somewhat wishfully ordered that the drills take place eight times a day. The leaders in McGowan's Brigade would do their best to comply but were usually content to conduct 2–4 drills per day with regiments routinely conducting battalion drill behind the lines. It was not as though the men didn't need the work, as many of the veterans had grown "careless and inaccurate," according to one soldier, and new recruits and conscripts had no experience on

1 William Templeton to Sarah Templeton, March 15, 1865; Caldwell, *The History of a Brigade of South Carolinians*, 260.

which to fall back. That said, McGowan's Brigade upheld its reputation as one of the army's best-drilled and disciplined units. In a letter to his sister after his mid-March return from commissary detail, Templeton mentioned that a full regimental review was held near the camp.[2]

Despite the earnest commitment by Lee and his commanders to sustain the Confederate war effort, the Army of Northern Virginia continued to hemorrhage men because of desertion, and the men became increasingly unsettled as spring approached by incessant whispers that the army was about to abandon Petersburg. Eventually, rations would be issued on a two-day basis, a telling sign that the army needed to be prepared to move without delay. Henry Heth, for instance, received orders in late March to have the men in his division cook their rations in anticipation of an immediate evacuation, and Generals Mahone and Wilcox were directed to keep their divisions ready to follow at a moment's notice. One prominent commander greatly disturbed by this talk of abandoning the Cockade City was Lt. Gen. A. P. Hill, who during a meeting with several prominent citizens in Richmond declared that he did not wish to survive the fall of the Confederate capital. That, he knew, was inevitable without control of Petersburg.[3]

While encamped near Dr. Boisseau's home on the southwestern fringes of Petersburg, McGowan was encouraged by an uptick in his brigade's numbers in March, which now hovered at about 1,500 men and officers. Official returns for the 12th South Carolina have been lost, but it is likely the regiment still had only about 200 men in the ranks. As the start of spring neared, and with it the resumption of active campaigning, the brigade's regimental picket line was strengthened. This included the return of Dunlop's sharpshooters to regular picket duty, a particular relief to the various regiments' overworked guard details.

With the fighting on hold and little else to do in camp in early 1865, the men's religious proclivities remained strong, many of them worshiping collectively throughout the week, not just on Sunday. In his postwar book *Lee's Sharpshooters*, Dunlop noted the effect one of those salient Sundays had on him personally, recalling that the sight of the camp's various pastors administering sacraments to their flocks that day was "a touchingly solemn scene in which many joined for the last time." He and so many of his comrades had come to terms with the hard reality that a return to arms would begin any day now.[4]

2 Caldwell, *The History of a Brigade of South Carolinians*, 262–263; William Templeton to Sarah Templeton, March 15, 1865.

3 *OR* 46(2):676; *SHSP* 19:185.

4 *OR* 46(2):901; Dunlop, *Lee's Sharpshooters*, 240–242.

* * *

In late March, the Confederate lines around Petersburg were at their literal breaking point. Lieutenant General James Longstreet, still not completely recovered from his serious wounding at the Wilderness the previous May, had returned to command the First Corps and was responsible for covering the left of Lee's defenses between Petersburg and Richmond. Major General John B. Gordon, who had replaced Jubal Early as the Second Corps' commander in the wake of the October 1864 Cedar Creek Campaign, occupied Petersburg in the center, and Hill's Third Corps defended the line west of Petersburg to Hatcher's Run. In all, Lee had 50,000–60,000 men defending a line about 40 miles long.

With the arrival of spring, Lee began to look for a way to extricate himself from Petersburg and move south to join Joe Johnston's Army of the South in North Carolina, which was barely holding on against William Sherman's army near Goldsboro. Hoping to divert Grant's focus before the Union commander had a chance to make the first move of the coming campaign, Lee assumed a characteristically offensive mindset and consulted directly with Gordon.[5]

Gordon had determined that the Federals' Fort Stedman was the surest target for an offensive and received the green light from Lee to lead that attack with his Second Corps. According to the plan Gordon devised, the Confederates would use deception to overrun the Federal picket line in front of Stedman and then the dirt bastion itself. That, he hoped, would punch a hole in the Union line and force Grant to transfer men from his left to defend the broken line. If the opening attack and a series of follow-up strikes were indeed successful, Meade Station—a critical supply depot a mile to the rear on the U.S. Military Railroad—would be in the path of Gordon's onslaught, and from there Grant's headquarters at City Point stood just 10 miles away. The prospect of capturing Grant at City Point was too alluring for Gordon and Lee to ignore. Little did they know that Abraham Lincoln had already planned a meeting with Grant there that morning.

The abduction of both Grant and Lincoln would have proved a remarkable feat had Gordon's attack progressed in ideal fashion. But even if that last scenario never evolved, the offensive offered a lucrative outcome if Grant were to respond to the loss of Fort Stedman with a troop shift, as that might create an opening on the Federal left that Lee could march through and ultimately unite with Johnston's

5 Dunlop, *Lee's Sharpshooters*, 244–245. For Gordon's postwar account of the meeting with Lee, see John B. Gordon, Reminiscences of the Civil War (New York, 1903), 393–394. For Gordon's postwar account of the meeting with Lee, see John B. Gordon, *Reminiscences of the Civil War* (New York, 1903), 393–394.

forces in North Carolina. Although a long shot, this was Lee's only real option short of surrender or allowing Grant to make the first move. Until the end, Lee was going to try to make the enemy dance to his song.

Gordon launched his attack well before dawn on March 25 and was initially successful, leading to the capture of the fort itself and nearby Batteries X and XI (500 total prisoners and nine pieces of artillery). His success, though, was short-lived. With the Second Corps operating in the dark, and without the arrival of sufficient support yet, Gordon's assault stalled out well short of Meade Station. A fierce counterattack by Brig. Gen. John Hartranft's 3rd Division in Parke's IX Corps quickly turned the tide. Gordon received permission from Lee to call off the attack, but it would cost him Fort Stedman and nearly 2,000 men as prisoners.[6]

The night before Gordon's attack, Hill had ordered McGowan to prepare his brigade for a possible Federal counterattack. The weary South Carolinians rose about 3:00 a.m. As some in the 12th were cooking their breakfasts on small fires at the rear of their works, artillery fire sounded to the right, followed by skirmish fire along their front.

Pickets noticed Federal troops in Wright's VI Corps moving toward the brigade and sounded the alarm that an attack was imminent. The South Carolinians in all five regiments moved forward in the trenches and anxiously waited for the drama to play out. As a large line of blue swarmed the Confederate picket lines, some men in the 12th climbed atop the works to view the spectacle and others unleashed a boisterous round of Rebel yells, hoping to stiffen their comrades in the face of the ominous Federal surge.

Wright's cheering mass of troops captured many of the 1st, 12th, and 13th South Carolina pickets in the rifle pits, while many of those who fled in desperation toward the main works were mowed down at point-blank range. The pickets in the 14th South Carolina and Orr's Rifles on the left held strong momentarily before breaking, tasting the same result. Only a few of the pickets managed to make it back to the trenches.

In less than an hour, the Federals controlled the area to the brigade's immediate front. McGowan turned to his sharpshooters, whom Dunlop led emphatically into the breach about 2:00 p.m. The major had his men in skirmish formation and engaged the Federals at approximately 200 yards, prompting a robust response from Federal artillery. Several huts in the works that soldiers in the 12th had used were destroyed during the bombardment, and an explosion from a shell striking an ammunition chest killed two men and wounded a few others. For protection, McGowan kept his men in the works as the Union attack unfolded. At one

6 Ibid., 246–247; Caldwell, *The History of a Brigade of South Carolinians*, 263.

point, Lee rode along the line inspecting the works and briefly decided that it was paramount for the South Carolinians to reclaim the rifle pits with a charge, only to change his mind and concede that sort of risk was unnecessary. Finally that evening, the brigade established a new picket line closer to the main line.[7]

Of the brigade's 49 casualties on March 25—most of these wounded or captured—the 12th reported one killed and five missing. The next day, some normalcy returned and the men were allowed some rest. That evening, however, they were put back on alert and rushed to the front of the works as support for a planned March 27 attack on the Federal line near McIlwaine Hill. That attack would involve Dunlop's sharpshooter battalion and their counterparts in three other brigades, and though the sharpshooters succeeded in taking the hill, they quickly returned to the lines. There would be no further action until March 29.

The hours that followed the March 27 attack were anxious ones for the men in the 12th. William Templeton found time to write his sister Sarah and report on affairs. "Wee had some fighting, but the yankies did not make any thing of us," he wrote. "They tried to charg our works but got whipped every time. . . . we are looking for a big fight every day." It would be the last letter either Templeton brother would write during the war.[8]

Late in the afternoon of March 29, McGowan would be ordered to move his brigade at 10:00 p.m. Any man currently on picket duty, however, was required to remain in place. The advance was in response to news that Maj. Gen. George Pickett's Division was headed toward Hatcher's Run to the right. Nevertheless, as Pickett's Virginians filed by, many of McGowan's men believed their planned march would be canceled. Any hope of that was dashed rather quickly, however, with reports of gunfire in the vicinity of Hatcher's Run. Before long, a courier delivered orders to McGowan that he was to move at once. Within minutes, the South Carolinians were on their way, marching in Pickett's wake down the familiar, muddy Boydton Plank Road. In the darkness and torrential rain, the march was an incredible struggle. Little did the men know they would never return to their camp.

After a slog of three or so miles, the brigade halted on the banks of Hatcher's Run. Falling out of ranks, the men quickly used whatever brush they could find for fires and would spend the rest of a miserable night huddled around those fires, enduring the continuing rain without cover.

* * *

7 Caldwell, *The History of a Brigade of South Carolinians*, 264–266; Dunlop, *Lee's Sharpshooters*, 248.

8 Caldwell, *The History of a Brigade of South Carolinians*, 266; Joseph Templeton to Sarah Templeton, March 28, 1865.

The next morning, the South Carolinians crossed Hatcher's Run at Burgess Mill and halted with their left flank resting on a small redoubt. Lee had planned an attack that day on the Federals' White Oak Road position, but after pickets were sent forward and the brigade shifted slightly to the right, the attack was called off. The men were in for another unpleasant, rain-drenched night.[9]

On March 31, McGowan's Brigade advanced with Brig. Gen. Young M. Moody's Alabama Brigade to the extreme right of the Confederate line, putting them directly opposite of Romeyn Ayres's 2nd Division in Warren's V Corps. Fielding an estimated 1,000 rifles, the brigade had difficulty preserving its lines as it moved through the woods, the respective regiments struggling across the difficult ground. The subsequent strike on Ayres's lines, though, sent the Federals fleeing quickly. The 1st and 12th South Carolina on the right led the way, changing front and slamming into the left flank of the retreating masses.

The fleeing Federals attempted several stands but were unable to turn back the fervent Confederate pursuit. The energized South Carolinians spewed forward, sweeping everything before them and somehow remaining aligned with the other regiments of the brigade. For more than a mile through pine thickets, open fields, and marshes, the rout continued. "I have no idea that the brigade ever killed more men than it did this day," Caldwell recalled.

At Gravelly Run, the two brigades halted near a ravine to rest and replenish ammunition. Reinforcements were supposed to aid them in a final assault against Ayres' command, but those never came. Instead, it would be the Federals who received reinforcements. Slowly the disgruntled Confederates were driven almost to where the attack began that morning.

Despite the brilliant success earlier in the day, lack of support doomed the effort. Losses were heavy: The brigade lost 71 men, with the 12th losing one killed and 16 wounded. Lee, watching the entire engagement, was impressed by the South Carolinians' work and was heard to say to McGowan, "I congratulate you on the gallant conduct of your brigade." Although the margin for error was growing increasingly narrow, the Army of Northern Virginia had shown it could still land a blow. It was, however, the brigade's last offensive operation and last tactical success of the war.[10]

* * *

9 Caldwell, *The History of a Brigade of South Carolinians*, 269–270; Dunlop, *Lee's Sharpshooters*, 258.

10 Caldwell, *The History of a Brigade of South Carolinians*, 272–274.

In reestablishing the position it held that morning, McGowan's Brigade was now the army's right flank. That, of course, put added pressure on the 12th, as it held McGowan's extreme right. At some point, McGowan visited the regiment's lines to confer with Capt. J. C. B. Smith, just as his men began to stand down from the morning's exploits. Smith had previously served as the regimental adjutant and was now in command of Company K. McGowan quickly informed Smith the reason for his visit. To protect the brigade's flank should the Federals attack its right rear, the general needed a force to move 300–400 yards in that direction and occupy an elevated ridge. With little time to spare, McGowan ordered Smith to take three companies to the ridge, demanding that he hold the position at all hazards.

Smith ordered the right three companies, including his own Company K, to break off to the rear, march by the right flank, and double-quick toward the ridge through a thick pine thicket. As the drained troops approached the elevated ground, however, Smith turned around to find a large Federal force making its way between his small command and the 12th's right flank—threatening to overlap the regiment and, with it, the brigade. Quickly countermarching the three companies, Smith formed them in a line facing the Yankees, who, as he feared, had begun to envelop the regiment's right flank.

Smith had roughly 50 men on hand, but he was not one to back down from a fight. Ordering his little band to "give it to them boys, and fall back slowly," the Confederates opened fire on the unsuspecting Federals, then slowly withdrew toward the brigade's main lines. As they gradually gave ground, drawing the Federals in their direction, the small Confederate force found itself spread out in the thicket and in potential danger.

Approaching a small farmhouse, Smith spotted an unidentified mounted Confederate officer trotting along the road near a ridge. "My men fought like good fellows, passing around the farm house, and through the garden, where they soon reached the ridge," Smith recalled in a letter after the war, "and I proceeded down the slope through a forest of heavy timber to regain my regiment which was done after some tramping." As Smith and his band passed through the garden, the mounted officer asked one of the weary soldiers who commanded the detachment. Amid the echoes of musketry against the walls of the outbuildings came the reply: "Captain Smith, of the Twelfth Regiment, South Carolina."

After the firefight sputtered to an end and Smith returned with the three companies to the 12th's main lines, McGowan found the captain sitting on a pine log in the regiment's bivouac. "Smith, my dear fellow, you have covered yourself with glory," McGowan proclaimed. "I have just returned from General Lee's quarters, to whom Colonel [Charles] Venable of his staff had reported your conduct and gallantry in the evening's engagement." Lee, McGowan continued, had spared no praise for the young captain that evening, calling Smith "one of the best men in the army," and even requested that McGowan bring him to Confederate headquarters so they could be introduced. Unfortunately for Smith, "the downfall of Petersburg and Richmond prevented the introduction" to the illustrious commander.[11]

Later that evening, details from each regiment were sent forward about 300 yards to post pickets as the exhausted men slept. The next morning, April 1, the 1st South Carolina conducted a reconnaissance to the front but apparently found little to report. As that occurred, the other four regiments—with the 12th in the lead—were rushed toward Dinwiddie Court House, only to be quickly recalled to their original positions. It was approximately noon.

That afternoon, however, McGowan ordered the 12th, the 1st, and Dunlop's sharpshooter battalion to establish a strong picket line to the front. Sporadic skirmishing with their Federal counterparts broke out, and at one point, the men of the 12th heard distant firing to their left, near Petersburg, and to their right near Dinwiddie Court House. These sudden barrages portended disaster.[12]

In what he hoped would be a last, great push to end the war, Grant had ordered probes against several key points in the Confederate lines, steadily tightening the noose around Lee's army. As the men of the 12th helplessly stood picket that evening, the rattle of musketry continued to increase toward beleaguered Petersburg. At sunrise on April 2, the pickets were called in and the brigade moved several hundred yards to the right, forming a line of battle along a set of previously built breastworks. They had no sooner arrived at their new position than the Federals attacked—what proved to be a rather short assault that was beaten back decisively.

The brigade was then ordered forward out of the works in column and hurried in the direction of Sutherland's Station along the Southside Railroad, about three miles away. McGowan's command was now part of a Confederate force consisting of several brigades, approximately 4,000 men in size, that would deploy along the Cox Road near the summit of a ridge about 100 yards beyond the railroad.

Reaching the destination, the men dug in, using rails from nearby fences to construct their works. McGowan's South Carolinians were to assume the extreme left of the four-brigade force, with the regiments ordered from right to left: 13th, 1st, 14th, 12th, and Orr's Rifles. As was standard, Dunlop's sharpshooters took position several hundred yards to the front as skirmishers.

11 J. C. B. Smith to Samuel McGowan, July 6, 1895, in "Miscellaneous Reading," *Yorkville Enquirer*, March 13, 1896, 1.

12 Caldwell, *The History of a Brigade of South Carolinians*, 275; 277–278.

Before long, a parade of bluecoats in Maj. Gen. Andrew Humphreys's II Corps appeared on open ground to their front, advancing against the Confederate right. When that assault was repulsed, the Federals attempted a second attack on the left flank: McGowan's Brigade. In an instant, Dunlop's sharpshooters were thrown back along the main line and a sharp firefight erupted. "We opened upon them at three or four hundred yards," recalled one South Carolinian. "Tore fearful rents in their line, covered the ground with dead and dying, and sent forth, above all the roar of artillery and musketry, ringing peals of cheers."

Close to the epicenter of this second assault, Kerr and the 12th South Carolina obliqued their fire past their comrades in Orr's Rifles to the left—with terrible effect. Dunlop's command followed the desperately retreating bluecoats, inflicting additional casualties and reestablishing the picket line.[13]

As the Federals re-formed their lines, McGowan shifted Orr's Rifles from his brigade's extreme left to the rear, placing it in reserve should the Federals attempt another attack on the left flank, now occupied by the 12th. In case of such an attack, he decided, Orr's Rifles could sweep in, catch the enemy in reverse flank, and drive them away.

That attack took place mid-morning; the sharpshooters held their own but were eventually driven back into the main lines. As Kerr readied the 12th for the onslaught, clearly angled against the regiment's right flank, a major Federal push broke out simultaneously along the brigade's front.

The skirmishers quickly gave way, and Bvt. Brig. Gen. John Ramsey's 4th Brigade—part of Nelson Miles's 1st Division in the II Corps—slammed into the 12th's left flank. Ramsey's 53rd Pennsylvania, under the command of Col. William M. Mintzer, went so far to the right it overlapped Orr's Rifles waiting in reserve 100 or so yards to the rear. Without hesitating, and with hearty cheers, Ramsey's 66th New York, 116th Pennsylvania, and 148th Pennsylvania rushed forward. The 12th and Orr's Rifles fought with trademark stubbornness for several minutes, but the sheer weight of the assault and the Yankees' favorable position overpowered the two small regiments, both soon cut off from the rest of the brigade and caught in a vicious crossfire as additional II Corps troops surged through the lines in other sectors.

To no avail, Kerr attempted to rally the remnants of the 12th. Converging on the Confederates from more than one angle, Ramsey's brigade swept down the line in what became a rout. Dozens would be captured, including Kerr, Dunlop, and Col. George M. Miller, the commander of Orr's Rifles. Major Edward D. Brailsford of the 1st South Carolina was among the wounded.

13 Ibid., 282–284.

The Confederate dam had broken. "A perfect bedlam ensued," recalled one soldier. "Officers and men mixed together in wildest confusion, fled before the withering blasts of consuming fire which swept the hill." As another South Carolinian described it: "Some were resisting to the last, some advised immediate flight, some gave up the cause, and counselled unconditional surrender. . . . On came the Federal lines, like converging currents of a storm, cheering, firing, sweeping over the whole field."

With the regiments falling like dominoes against the onslaught, Colonel Hunt of the 13th South Carolina, holding the brigade's right flank, attempted a last stand. He, too, would be compelled to retire.

"Now was the most disorderly movement I ever saw among Confederate troops," recalled one officer. "We had to pass over two to three hundred yards of clear field, under fire of infantry on our flank and in rear and under shelling of their artillery." As the men fled west toward the Appomattox River, the various regiments meshed together, with command and control hopelessly lost. Despite the loss of three of its five regimental commanders, a good portion of the brigade remained close enough together to reach the Appomattox in a consolidated, albeit disorganized, group.

Thankfully McGowan had been spared capture and tried to rally and organize the survivors in what became a fruitless effort. Some of the men drowned in the swift currents while attempting to cross the river; others simply clung to the south bank and worked their way west, hoping to find a safer spot to cross. The mass of men was strung out for miles, intermingled with commands from other brigades and divisions. Groups of exhausted men kept together as best they could and camped that night along the river, unsure what the next day would bring.[14]

For Lee's army, April 2 was an unmitigated disaster. While McGowan's Brigade fought for its life near the Southside Railroad, Grant ordered a general assault on the rest of Lee's lines at Petersburg with devastating success. In the wake of the desperate evacuation of Petersburg and Richmond, Lee's army had no choice but to retreat west in the general direction of Amelia Court House. The casualty count would be monumental, as many men surrendered or were taken prisoner while others simply scattered to the wind.

How many casualties the 12th—and McGowan's Brigade as a whole—suffered during its fight at Sutherland's Station is unknown, perhaps never recorded. The regiment, however, suffered severe losses in its officers' corps: Kerr, Lt. W. H. Rives, Capt. William J. Stover, Capt. John R. Thomas, Lt. J. B. White, Lt. J. M. Hencken,

14 Ibid., 283–287; Dunlop, *Lee's Sharpshooters*, 277; *OR* 46(1):711, 746, 749, 751, 753, 755.

Lt. J. W. Watson, and Lt. J. C. Rallings were all captured. Nearly the entirety of the regiment's command structure had been eliminated.[15]

One casualty was especially distressing to McGowan's men: Lt. Gen. A. P. Hill, who was shot and killed that morning several miles to the east as he rode out to rally his men being driven from the trenches. Hill had been at Lee's headquarters that morning when the Federal assault began. As he rode toward the fighting, he found himself between the lines and was shot by a Union infantryman near the Boydton Plank Road. Although Hill, like others, was not flawless while fighting for the Army of Northern Virginia, he had served Lee faithfully for nearly three years and had been a true friend to the South Carolinians since the glory days of 1862 when the brigade was an integral part of the Light Division's success. Hearing of Hill's demise, Robert E. Lee accurately and ominously declared, "He is at rest now, and we who are left are the ones to suffer.[16]

With their regimental leadership in shambles and the Petersburg–Richmond lines broken, the survivors of the 12th South Carolina took stock of their losses on the morning of April 3. Companies were now commanded by lieutenants, sergeants, and corporals. Lee had ordered his shattered forces toward Amelia Court House, and despite the attrition, the remnants of the 12th continued to move together in small groups, although unfortunately strung out along the road. The men remained quiet and sullen as they trudged along. News that Amelia Court House, roughly 39 miles from Petersburg, was occupied by Phil Sheridan's Federal cavalry did nothing to raise their spirits.

When the column paused the march that afternoon, having traversed several miles, orders went out for the men to scatter into the woods and fields to forage. At some point during the tedious march, Capt. John H. Kinsler, commanding what was left of Company D, brought his men into camp from Petersburg. Kept behind on picket duty when the brigade moved out on March 29, Kinsler's company had finally caught up to the regiment. Kinsler, however, had only two men with him. The company had been virtually destroyed, first on the picket line and then on the intervening marches toward the 12th's present location.

That evening, the column began moving again, veering away from the Appomattox River, and on the morning of April 4, McGowan made a concerted effort to organize his brigade. Dozens of men, not only from the 12th but also the other four regiments who had crossed to the north side of the Appomattox over the previous two days, recrossed the river and joined the command. The entire brigade

15 Caldwell, *The History of a Brigade of South Carolinians*, 289.

16 *SHSP* 12: 184; *Confederate Veteran* 27: 342.

Captain John Kinsler, Company D. *South Carolina Confederate Relic Room and Military Museum, Columbia, SC*

numbered about 700–800 men, and with the addition of Kinsler's three-man Company D, the 12th now had in its ranks about 150-175 men. Captain J. C. Bell of Company F, the senior captain, assumed command of the regiment.

That afternoon, the brigade reached Amelia Court House, where the men received a scant yet welcome ration of meat and bread. As skirmishing began in the distance, Bell ordered the men to construct field works, and with most of the army in the vicinity, spirits and morale rose for the first time in several days. All day and night the men of the regiment waited in the hastily constructed works for an assault that never came.[17]

Early on April 5, the brigade resumed its march, heading first to the north in the direction of the Appomattox. The column was soon diverted back south and away from the river. Throughout the afternoon firing could be heard to the front. The column halted in an open meadow just before dark, though the men were not dismissed. As the men waited to break ranks, Bell surprised them instead with orders to tie down their canteens and other personal items known to make noise while marching. Strict silence was ordered down the line. The men waited impatiently in formation, and when darkness arrived, they were quickly and quietly moved around a deep valley in which flickering Federal campfires could be prominently seen. During the detour, many in the ranks believed that a rare night attack was in store against an unsuspecting enemy, but it was not to be. The column continued west until just before dawn on April 6, when it halted roughly 10 miles from Farmville to rest for a few hours.

The weary column resumed marching just after sunrise but was now headed to the northwest. Enemy attacks on the left that morning necessitated the brigade

17 Ibid., 291–292.

to form a battle line in that direction and be prepared to advance. Nothing evolved from those attacks, however, and the column continued unmolested. About noon, the column halted near Farmville and again formed a battle line within sight of the enemy. Shelling commenced against the line but resulted in no casualties in either the regiment or brigade. Ordered to construct breastworks, the men of the 12th quickly scoured the area for logs and debris. McGowan threw out what was left of the sharpshooter battalion (perhaps a company) as skirmishers against what had the makings of a Federal push on the South Carolinians, but nothing materialized.

Calamity, however, had befallen another element of Lee's army, as a reserve force commanded by General Ewell (officially known as the Department of Richmond) was surrounded and forced to surrender at Sailor's Creek. Ewell's command was one of three Confederate forces engaged in the battle there that day, along with John Gordon's Second Corps and Richard Anderson's Fourth Corps. Total casualties for all three were approximately 8,000, opposed to just less than 1,200 for the Federals.[18]

After midnight on April 7, the 12th was hastily thrown into line again and began moving with the rest of the brigade toward Farmville. Disrupted by frequent starts and stops, however, the pressing march bogged down miserably. Later that morning, the South Carolinians finally crossed the Bush River and entered Farmville, an otherwise cozy village in the heart of a small valley. With the Federals not too far behind, familiar faces in Scales's North Carolina Brigade formed as the division's rear guard.

As they settled in the village, the men of the 12th and others in the brigade could see the Light Division's wagon train across the nearby Appomattox, as well as plumes of campfire smoke—a pleasing sign that rations were likely forthcoming. While the men waited in loose ranks for those rations, however, McGowan ordered the brigade back to the rear to support Scales's Brigade, now threatened by intense enemy pressure.

Understandably, the famished cluster of men grumbled as they formed on a road to countermarch toward the fighting. Smelling food being cooked as they did so, William Miller and a friend, Lt. James Ferguson, glanced quickly to the side of the road. With a wistful glance, the duo made out an old man cooking corn cakes on a pot-bellied stove. Since the regiment was already on its way, the hungry duo reluctantly kept their place in the ranks.

Once the brigade exited Farmville, it was ordered to about-face and return to the village at the double-quick. The South Carolinians would find complete confusion. Two columns of infantry jammed the streets, and cavalry intermingled

18 Ibid., 292–293.

with frantic citizens—the amalgamation headed as quickly as possible toward the nearby High Bridge; with enemy troops again on their heels, the sturdy wooden bridge was the only safe pathway left for a Confederate escape to the north bank of the Appomattox and relative safety. As they passed the old man's house again, Miller and Ferguson jumped out of the ranks and made a dash for the coveted corn cakes. "We got some and left and when we got to the bridge over the river, it was afire," Miller recalled. To destroy the bridge before the trailing Yankees could use it, Confederate engineers had prematurely set it on fire before all of the brigades had crossed.

This meant that infantry and cavalry still south of the river had to make their way down a steep descent to ford the river at another point.[19] It became every regiment for itself. The 12th crossed the Appomattox at one of these other sites in fairly stable condition and luckily avoided a melee, thanks to Bell's quick thinking and stirring leadership. Seeing the bridge ablaze, the captain did not hesitate to order his men to ford the river. As Bell and his excited troops ascended the north bank, however, Federal cavalry on the opposite shore demanded that the retreating South Carolinians surrender, shooting at them when the surrender ultimatum was ignored.

Miller and his comrades remained committed to their escape. "We concluded that we were not ready to give up," he recalled, "so we started up the hill and they commenced to shoot at us, and continued until we were not too far off. I think the thing that saved us was that we were running up a steep hill and the balls were striking the ground near our feet. Apparently, they did not think of our rising up, all the time and moving briskly. Anyway, we did not surrender as others were doing."

"We got over and then followed the river for about a quarter of a mile or more," he added, "but not before the enemy's cavalry captured and killed many as they attempted to cross."

That night, Miller could count only three men in his company. The rest, he noted, were either strung out along the road, killed, captured or "completely worn out." The brigade's march resumed at midnight, traversing narrow country roads, open fields, and plenty of wet terrain. Little time for rest was granted, the men implored to continue marching at a brisk pace whenever possible.

At 8:00 a.m. on April 8, the column filed off the road and into a pasture. McGowan directed each regiment to form a battle line and close the column. Ordering his men to go into line on the first company, Bell had the 12th quickly drawn up alongside the others in the field, then ordered the regiment to stack

19 Ibid., 293–295; Miller, "My Experience," 223.

arms and rest. The opportunity to relax would not last long. As the men began to build fires, ready to cook what rations they had, McGowan abruptly ordered the brigade to fall in. The troops, understandably irked, were soon back on the road marching toward Lynchburg. It would be a daylong march, with the exhausted men finally bivouacking that evening about four miles east of the small village of Appomattox Court House.[20]

Despite the disorganized retreat from Petersburg, the disaster at Sutherland's Station, and the near-disaster at High Bridge, McGowan's five regiments by and large had stayed relatively intact through a series of demanding marches. Even those units that initially became separated did what they could to stay together in clusters and somehow preserve their esprit de corps under harsh circumstances. Certainly, there had been straggling, and some men fell out never to rejoin their respective regiments, but a postwar account by former sharpshooter Berry Benson of the 1st South Carolina provided a fitting portrayal of the brigade's extraordinary discipline and ability to adapt to setbacks:

> Being now pretty well rested, we made as good time as possible amongst the straggling troops that now thronged the road. I do not remember seeing any organized body. Each man seemed to be for himself, getting along as fast or as slow as he was able. Amidst this helter-skelter, dejected crowd, we marched in order, with arms at the 'right shoulder.' As we passed the weary, exhausted groups, they stared in amazement to see our little band of sixteen, still preserving discipline and still better, cheerfulness. And it was more than one compliment that we received from the old, ragged, weather-beaten, war-worn soldiers that had followed Longstreet in many a battle to victory, as they now followed him in defeat. And a compliment from such tongues was indeed a compliment, sweeter today to remember than would be the most glowing praise from smoother tongues.[21]

Just before dawn on April 9, the regiment was roused, fell into line, and was soon on its way with the rest of the brigade toward Appomattox Court House. A long train of artillery and wagons preceded the South Carolinians' advance, so McGowan guided his men around the train, recognizing the urgency in getting them to the front of Lee's army. After roughly a three-mile march, the general filed the brigade off the road and again formed a column of regiments. With that,

20 Caldwell, *The History of a Brigade of South Carolinians*, 295–297; Miller, "My Experience," 223.

21 Benson, *Berry Benson's Civil War Book*, 194.

Bell ordered the men of the 12th to stack arms and rest. Many simply fell to the ground in exhaustion.

According to one witness, a subdued chaos surrounded the South Carolinians that "exceeded anything I have ever witnessed in the army": straggling cavalry and infantry, groups of men wandering about without commanders, commanders without troops, and wagons and artillery crowded together on both sides of the road. The men found themselves in an extensive basin surrounded by undulating hills. "A horrible calm brooded over us," J. F. J. Caldwell recalled.

Troops from the rear slowly arrived and filed off into the same field. One unit containing about 250 men halted just to the rear of the brigade. When asked what regiment it was, a soldier replied that it was Joseph Kershaw's *entire* division. Ahead of the gathering troops, the sound of battle was unmistakable. Apparently, troops in Gordon's Second Corps were making a determined push to open a line of retreat toward Lynchburg, convincing many in McGowan's Brigade that the sudden massing of troops in the meadow was a preamble to a final decisive charge by the Army of Northern Virginia to break out and race toward North Carolina.

About 10:00 a.m., the brigade formed again and continued to move toward Appomattox Court House. "The way was rugged, and beset with stragglers of all arms of the service," recalled one soldier. Coming upon a full Federal battery as they approached the town, the men assumed it had been captured that morning. Shortly, the men of the 12th caught a glimpse of Maj. Gen. George Armstrong Custer, the famed Union cavalry commander, "riding at full speed and accompanied by several Confederate officers," recalled one witness to this bizarre scenario. Although there were those who believed Custer was a prisoner, others were not so sure. After all, Custer was riding in an unusually cocky manner—more like the conqueror than the conquered—and he carried a white handkerchief. The mystery would soon be answered.

After proceeding just south of Appomattox Court House, the brigade halted and filed off the road. Turned around by a staff officer, the South Carolinians returned to the road and again halted. As this occurred, the firing to the front ceased. Officers gathered in the road to determine the cause of the holdup, but the realization began to set in that the army was being surrendered. That would be confirmed by a mounted Confederate staff officer, who approached the column, bowed his head, and acknowledged in a hushed tone that the war in the Eastern Theater was indeed over. Lee would meet with Grant that afternoon at Wilmer McLean's residence in Appomattox to discuss terms for the formal surrender of the Army of Northern Virginia.[22]

22 Caldwell, *The History of a Brigade of South Carolinians*, 299–302.

As word filtered down through the column, the news reached the 12th South Carolina. "I saw strong men shed tears," Miller recalled. After Bell countermarched the regiment to the rear, the men gloomily stacked arms; some fell helplessly to the ground while others stared aimlessly into space. "It is impossible to describe the anguish of the troops when it became known that the Army of Northern Virginia had been surrendered," recalled a Company B soldier.

Dunlop recalled how the men of the 12th responded when Lee emerged about 3:00 p.m. from his meeting with Grant at the McLean House, accompanied by Lt. Col. Charles Marshall, his aide de camp. "[A] shout of welcome instinctively ran through," Dunlop wrote after the war. "But instantly recollecting the sad occasion that brought him before them, their shouts sank into silence, every hat was raised and the bronzed faces of the thousands of grim warriors were bathed in tears. As [Lee] rode slowly along the lines, hundreds of his devoted veterans pressed around their noble chief, eager to take his hand, touch his person, or even lay their hands upon his horse; thus exhibiting their great affection." There was no joy in William Miller's blunt memory of the watershed moment. "[S]oon the enemy had us surrounded," he bluntly recalled. "Their cavalry was in front and the infantry pressing us closely. Then Genl. Lee surrendered us all."[23]

The army was quickly consolidated and tightly camped in the small valley near Appomattox Court House. For the next three rainy days, the men wandered about without shelter, officers took rolls of their companies, and men waited for the inevitable moment when they would lay down their arms. Stragglers caught up to the army as well. As he had done at Farmville a few days earlier, William Miller decided to take matters into his own hands and secure some rations from the Federal camps, this time with his friend McCoy. Sneaking off through a thicket without authority, Miller and McCoy ran across a Yankee picket who agreed to let them through on the condition they not tell anyone. Miller and McCoy gave the picket their assurance and were soon in a bountiful camp full of generous Yankees. "They gave us all we wished of crackers and pickled pork, and then made for us around the fire to boil our meat and eat our fill," Miller recalled.

To gain some quick spending money for the trip home, the duo even began to sell off their Confederate money to their newfound friends as souvenirs. Arriving back at camp with full pockets and stomachs, Miller and McCoy gloated about their experience with the charitable Yankee hosts, prompting others in the regiment to follow their lead and sneak over to the Federal camps.[24]

23 Dunlop, *Lee's Sharpshooters*, 280–281; Miller, "My Experience," 224.

24 Miller, "My Experience," 224.

On April 9, 1865, Robert E. Lee surrendered the Army of Northern Virginia to Ulysses S. Grant in the home of Wilmer McLean. *Library of Congress*

According to the terms of surrender, the Confederates were required to lay down their arms and flags in a formal ceremony in the presence of the Federal army. For the 12th South Carolina, McGowan's Brigade, and others in Lee's army, that bitter day came on April 12, a cold and rainy Wednesday. That morning, Pvt. Enoch Blackmon, the regiment's stubborn color-bearer, decided that the 12th's battle flag would not be surrendered. Blackmon swore that the Yankees would never have possession of a standard under which the regiment had fought for so long, a sentiment with which his pards in Company H wholeheartedly agreed. He and Thomas Roach, a loyal friend, removed the flag from the staff and sewed it inside the lining of Blackmon's jacket, which would allow the color-bearer to secret it home to South Carolina.[25]

That same morning, Captain Bell formed the 12th South Carolina for the last time, its final march into history. As the various companies came together in formation, the stark reality of the losses the regiment had sustained over the last four years drew into sharp focus. The final roll call revealed 158 men present: 145 enlisted men, 3 noncommissioned officers serving on regimental staff, and 10 officers. The company aggregates at Appomattox were as follows:

25 *Recollections and Reminiscences* 6:222; 8:275; "The Recent Battles," *Yorkville Enquirer*, April 26, 1865, 2; "12th Regiment, S. C. V.," *Yorkville Enquirer*, April 26, 1865, 2.

The last battle flag of the 12th South Carolina. *South Carolina Confederate Relic Room and Military Museum, Columbia, SC*

Company A, commanded by Capt. J. T. Parker—15 privates;

Company B, commanded by 1st Lt. M. V. Darwin—1 sergeant, 2 corporals, 12 privates;

Company C, commanded by Corp. J. H. Cooper—1 corporal, 13 privates;

Company D, commanded by Capt. John H. Kinsler—3 privates;

Company E, commanded by Corp. J. F. Fale—1 corporal, 13 privates;

Company F, commanded by 1st Lt. D. L. Glenn—1 sergeant, 2 corporals, 8 privates;

Company G, no commanding officer or noncommissioned officer—7 privates;

Company H, commanded by 2nd Lt. A. M. Black—2 sergeants, 3 corporals, 26 privates;

Company I, commanded by 2nd Lt. J. S. Williamson—3 sergeants, 3 corporals, 1 musician, 22 privates;

Company K, commanded by Capt. Jno. Blunt—1 corporal, 6 privates.

Several of the soldiers quoted in this book were present at Appomattox, including both Joseph and William Templeton of Company B and William Miller of Company H. Benjamin Powell, one of the finest sharpshooters of the entire war, was paroled with Company I, as was D. J. Carter. Regimental surgeon W. H. Bailey, who negligently amputated Lt. J. R. Boyles's leg at Gettysburg, was among those who surrendered as well. Nearly all of the men left had been wounded at least once during the conflict; some as many as three times.

By comparison, the brigade's other regiments paroled the following aggregates: 1st South Carolina (115); 13th South Carolina (196); 14th South Carolina (264); and Orr's Rifles (155). The total number of men in McGowan's Brigade on April 12, 1865, was just short of 900 men, including brigade staff. McGowan posited after the war that his command was the second largest brigade to surrender in the army behind only Brig. Gen. John Bratton's South Carolina Brigade in Longstreet's combined First/Third Corps, which according to the National Park Service had 1,547 in the ranks during the campaign.[26]

Casualties in the 12th South Carolina throughout the conflict tell the story of a regiment decimated in battle. Unlike most Civil War regiments, more men in the regiment died from wounds sustained in battle than disease. A total of 414 men in the regiment died during the war: 230 killed in battle or resulting from wounds sustained in battle and 184 of disease. An astounding 678 men were wounded and survived, although many of them, such as J. R. Boyles of Company C, were crippled forever. Interestingly, 882 men of the 12th were killed or wounded in battle, the lowest raw figure of any regiment in the brigade. That relative number to the other regiments speaks to two primary overarching themes. First, the 12th was often the smallest regiment within the brigade, which typically equated to lower casualties. This was especially true in the last, bloody year of fighting, from the Wilderness to Appomattox. With fewer men in the line, there were fewer men for

26 *SHSP* 15:368, 371–373; "Reunion of Old Comrades," *Yorkville Enquirer*, Aug. 26, 1880, 1. Aggregate parole numbers such as these usually vary according to the source. According to the National Park Service (nps.gov/apco/order-of-battle.htm), three other brigades besides Bratton's had higher numbers than McGowan's during the campaign: William Perry's (Law's) Alabama Brigade and G. T. Anderson's Georgia Brigade in Charles Field's Division (996 and 987, respectively) and William Forney's Brigade in Mahone's Division (950). Forney's command fielded six regiments, however. At the other end of the scale was Joseph R. Davis's Brigade in Heth's Division, with only 66 men in five regiments.

the enemy to shoot. Second, the 12th's offensive minded commanders, aggressive approach, and superior fighting capabilities in battle meant that it did not suffer as many casualties because it often was the one inflicting those casualties on its foe.

As Walter Taylor, Robert E. Lee's assistant adjutant general, stated on Lee's behalf in General Orders No. 63 in May 1863: "The loss sustained by a brigade or regiment is by no means an indication of the magnitude of the service performed or perils encountered, as experience shows that those who attack most rapidly, vigorously, and effectually generally suffer least." By this way of thinking, the 12th may well stake the claim of being the most efficient regiment in the brigade during battle.[27]

The brigade of five small but proud regiments marched solemnly toward the village of Appomattox Court House on the morning of April 12, led by an emotional Samuel McGowan. Prior to the ceremony, a soldier found the brigadier in the woods weeping as he changed from his dirty field attire into his clean, dress uniform. As the brigade approached the village on the Richmond-Lynchburg Stage Road, Caldwell noted that "a line of Federal soldiers was drawn up on each side of the road between us and Appomattox Court House." Coming abreast of those troops, the brigade halted, fronted, and stacked arms. One soldier described it as a "humiliating task," and Miller conceded: "It was a bitter pill to give our guns to the enemy."

From there, the men fell out to receive their individual paroles near a tavern in the village, although some purportedly had their paroles already issued on April 10. Then, in small groups of friends and comrades, the men quietly returned to their camp to gather their personal belongings and make plans to return home.

By nature a paternal leader, McGowan desired to bring the entire brigade back to the Palmetto State unified and intact, such as it was. That afternoon, in fact, Cadmus Wilcox's entire Light Division passed through the Federal lines in this fashion after it departed the camp. Following that impressive spectacle, Wilcox gave his brigade commanders free rein from there, and McGowan began to march his men south. It was soon clear, however, that marching 900 or so men several hundred miles without rations or money would be impossible. At the first stop, McGowan attempted to secure food for the men from a farm, only to return with a single ear of corn. Recognizing the handwriting on the wall, the general accepted that his desire to have the brigade return as one unit was simply not feasible. The men began to disperse on their own, heading south mostly in small groups from the same companies. McGowan formally bade farewell to the men still with him somewhere in southern Virginia.

27 Brown, *A Colonel at Gettysburg and Spotsylvania*, 142.

"Then it was for us to get home," recalled William, who joined a dozen or so comrades from Company H, each pledging to stick together until they got home. His story is representative of many in the army who headed home that spring, many of whom likewise struggled for food and provisions along the way; many with only the clothes on their backs as possessions. On one occasion, the Company H contingent strong-armed a local man into giving them a bushel-and-a-half of cornmeal. They also shot and killed a hog in a field and stole a chicken. While camping that evening, one of the men visited a nearby home to borrow a pot. The group then used that pot not only to create corn dodgers from the cornmeal but also to cook the hog and the chicken—a tasty smorgasbord that would last until they arrived in Greensboro, North Carolina.

In Greensboro, Miller and McCoy used the last of their Yankee dollars to buy flour. That was enough to get them to Charlotte, where they visited Miller's aunt and enjoyed a hearty meal. From Charlotte, Miller and his comrades took a train to the Catawba River, crossing into South Carolina. Men started to disband as they reached their communities and neighborhoods. When several men departed the procession in the Neeley's Creek area, only Miller, Ferguson, A. M. Black, and J. G. Noland remained for the final trek toward Rock Hill. They would arrive there on April 20–21.

At Ebenezer, Miller bade farewell to comrades with whom he had served and fought for more than four years. "Then I left them, coming up through Ebenezer to the dear old home," he recalled. "Mother was looking for me. I stayed at home the balance of the year, but was busy all the time. The next year, 1866, I found one of the prettiest and best girls in York County and married her."[28]

By May 1, nearly every member of the 12th South Carolina who had surrendered at Appomattox was home.

28 Caldwell, *The History of a Brigade of South Carolinians*, 308–310; Benson, *Berry Benson's Civil War Book*, 201; Miller, "My Experience," 224–225.

Chapter Fourteen

Reunion and Remembrance

From August 30, 1861, to April 12, 1865, approximately 1,400 soldiers served in the 12th South Carolina. Some fought from the regiment's first meaningful engagement at Bay Point and Hilton Head until its last devasting clash at Sutherland's Station, while others, conscripted late in the conflict, served for only a few months. As primary accounts by those who fought either in the 12th or McGowan's Brigade are unfortunately few, it is not easy to calculate what motivated many to enlist in the first place and what kept them going for so long despite interminable and often-unspeakable hardships. Indeed, relatively few men left narratives of their years of service, and those who did rarely divulged a rationale for joining and fighting for the Confederacy. Private William H. Miller, for example, admitted enlisting in June 1861—when he was merely 15 years old—because fellow students in his parochial school began boasting they intended to do just that once summer recess arrived. "This, I suppose, is the reason that I thought I ought to follow their example," Miller recalled after the war. For many, the desire for seeming adventure trumped enlistment for broader causes such as states' rights, slavery, or singular defense of the Palmetto State.[1]

On February 9, 1864, with the 12th South Carolina encamped near Orange Court House, soldiers in the regiment were part of an extraordinary meeting that sheds perhaps the greatest light on the motivations of many who served. At the time, several brigades in Lee's army that had committed to two- or three-year

1 Miller, "My Experience," 216.

Lancaster veterans gather for a photograph at the court house. *Claude Sinclair*

enlistments began to reenlist en masse "for the war." The 12th, however, was already a so-called "war regiment," as it had initially committed to fight regardless of whether hostilities lasted for five months or five years. As such, its troops were not obligated to participate in the reenlistment process. Nevertheless, inspired to show support for their brother regiments, they met to deliberate details of a resolution to express their personal feelings about the war and their rationale for fighting.

"We have met today, not to re-enlist, but as a war regiment, to show to our brave comrades in arms that we are with them heart and hand in this noble work," Col. John L. Miller told the regiment. "It is simply intended to reiterate our determination to remain in service until our independence is established."

A committee composed of both regular soldiers and noncommissioned officers drafted the document that day, the language of which can be found verbatim in Chapter 9. The document addressed the regiment's fear of "subjugation," "confiscation," and "utter ruin" should the Confederacy lose its bid for independence and justified its service as an uncompromising struggle against the "cruel persecution" and "dangers, hardships and privations to which we have been subjected," as well as a threat of "deserted homes and desolate fields" in their hometowns and across the south. With citations of liberty, sovereignty, and independence, the resolution comes the closest of any known account to confirming that the men in the 12th South Carolina believed in a limited form of government and were convinced that their way of life would end if the United States prevailed in the war. A separate resolution by McGowan's full brigade, published in February 1865, would echo these sentiments.[2]

The way of life the men favored, however, did include the institution of slavery and its ramifications. Although slavery as a justification for war is absent in any of the available first-person accounts, those in the regiment—from officers down to privates—clearly had a vested interest in "the peculiar institution." Whether a particular soldier owned slaves or not, notions of racial superiority were pervasive: the bulk of the men in the 12th—if not all—considered African Americans inferior. For evidence of this, one need only examine how several soldiers reacted in the aftermath of the August 1864 fighting at Second Deep Bottom after facing USCT troops for the first time.

Notably, multiple accounts reveal that this level of contempt rarely extended to White counterparts in the Federal army. The regiment's treatment of Irish soldiers captured on the Virginia Peninsula in 1862 and the German Federals they marched to Richmond after Chancellorsville are indelible examples of the wide respect shown to enemy soldiers as long as they were of the same race. The fear the men expressed about "subjugation" and "confiscation" in both the February 1864 and February 1865 resolutions, combined with their harsh treatment of USCTs at Second Deep Bottom, substantiate their motivations for fighting and their thoughts regarding race.

Among rationales for fighting such as liberty, defense of their homes, and notions of limited government, the men of the 12th also abhorred the thought of being conquered and having their social and racial class system interrupted.

One can only wonder if the pointed language of the regiment's resolution in 1864 would have been written in less severe and finite terms had it been drafted in August 1861. Three years of death, destruction, and sacrifice clearly had jaded the soldiers to the point at which they understood the conflict as one of complete conquest—the struggle of one way of life versus another. In this vein, the resolution by the regiment is telling evidence of the men's motivations not only to fight, but also to continue braving seemingly endless horror.

As a fourth year of fighting neared in April 1864, the conflict had become a "do or die" proposition for many. If, as William Miller suggested, many had joined

2 "The 12th Regiment," *Yorkville Enquirer*, Feb. 24, 1864, 2; "McGowan's Brigade," *Yorkville Enquirer*, Feb. 15, 1865, 1. The brigade's resolution was four paragraphs long, encapsulating themes of self-defense, self-government, a belief that the United States intended to subjugate and enslave the Confederate people, and assurance that continuation of the struggle rightly honored the sacrifices and losses of the men who fought.

the army in 1861 for inconsequential reasons such as boredom or because others were enlisting, those still in uniform by the start of the Overland campaign had reached the stark realization that the stakes were much higher and that nothing but victory or death would suffice.

* * *

Regardless of why they had fought, the men of the 12th always felt immense pride in their service, and rather than simply forget, they strove to keep the memories alive well after the war. They also felt it was crucial to highlight the regiment's achievements as a whole and not focus on individual success. J. R. Boyles of Company C, who was seriously wounded at Gettysburg, was among those lamenting how easily the younger generation in the south tended to overlook the monumental sacrifice Confederate soldiers had made from 1861 to 1865. "There are a great many boys and young men, whose fathers belonged to the army, that are unable to say what command they were in," Boyles mourned. "I hate to see this."

The horrific wound Boyles received at Gettysburg nearly cost him his life. Left at a field hospital, he was captured a few days later during the Army of Northern Virginia's retreat from Pennsylvania and would persevere through a lengthy stay in a Union prison camp. Eventually paroled, he made it home to South Carolina but struggled for years with the after-effects of the botched amputation of his leg by unqualified regimental surgeon W. H. Bailey, who had been indisputably drunk at the time. Boyles would die in August 1896 at the age of 59; because of Bailey's transgression, he was unable to wear a proper prosthetic limb for the remaining 33 years of his life.

Despite Boyles's anger about the circumstances behind his amputation, the wound was a constant reminder of his hard-fought service in the 12th and remained a driving force in his quest to memorialize the regiment's many accomplishments. By the 1870s, he and cohorts from the regiment created company-specific "survivors' associations" in the counties from which the various companies were originally recruited. These would be among the earliest Confederate veteran organizations created in the south.[3]

On June 28, 1879, Company F and Boyles's own Company C teamed to reorganize their survivors' associations as a single entity at a meeting in Winnsboro, South Carolina. A formal governing committee would be established at this meeting, consisting of a president, two vice presidents, a treasurer, and both a

3 Boyles, *Reminiscences*, 3.

recording secretary and a corresponding secretary. The association was named "The Reunion of Companies C and F, 12th Regiment, S. C. V."

Henry C. Davis, Company C's respected lieutenant colonel early in the war, assumed the reins as the coalition's first president and stated on the record that it was his desire to see a reorganization of the entire 12th in the future. Davis, in fact, invited the regiment's other associations to a full reunion in August 1880, marking the 19th anniversary of the regiment's muster at Lightwood Knot Springs.[4]

Reunions of other survivors' associations took place in the late 1870s and were usually grand affairs with speakers, dinners, and considerable reminiscence. At the Companies C and F reunion on August 20, 1879, so many veterans from other companies in the 12th attended, however, that this gathering became a de facto full regimental reunion. In addition to Davis, former officers Cadwallader Jones and John Kinsler delivered memorable speeches, and Davis moved that Jones be instituted as president of the full survivors' association and that a committee consisting of two men from each representative county would meet to draft a constitution.

The new entity's official name was the "Survivors Reunion Association of the 12th Regiment, first Gregg's, afterwards McGowan's Brigade" and its primary objective would be "to gather and preserve all facts connected with and illustrative of the history of the Regiment, to preserve and perfect its records, and to keep alive the memories and friendships formed in the camps and field." For these aging veterans, preservation of the 12th's history and its legacy was of utmost importance.

During the August 1879 meeting, the committee nominated and unanimously adopted the association's first board. Joining Jones as president were Davis as first vice president, Frank Clyburn as second vice president, Kinsler as third vice president, C. B. Smith as fourth vice president, and R. G. Whitesides as fifth vice president. Boyles would be elected both secretary and treasurer, and attendees roundly thanked him for his selfless efforts in "pushing forward the organization."[5]

The committee moved quickly to secure a keynote speaker for the planned 1880 reunion, deciding it should be Samuel McGowan, the brigade's longest-serving commander. McGowan graciously responded to the invitation from his home in Abbeville, stating in a letter dated November 4, 1879, that he was excited to address the regiment. "I have long entertained the hope that we could have a re-union of all the regiments of the old brigade," he emphasized, "but if we are not to have that now, I know of no more fitting place to commence the movement

4 "The Twelfth Regiment," *Yorkville Enquirer*, July 10, 1879, 2.

5 "The Twelfth Regiment," *The News and Herald* (Winnsboro, SC), Aug. 23, 1879, 2.

than in the glorious 'Old Twelfth' which was always in the habit of leading." It is safe to surmise that had another regiment in the brigade already considered or implemented a reunion, McGowan would have been apprised.[6]

* * *

On August 19, 1880, a crowd numbering between 2,500 and 3,000 people gathered in Yorkville for this first "official" reunion of the 12th South Carolina. Many of the veterans were already in town and had begun celebrating the day before, and scores more arrived the morning of August 19 by special train. Clouds and rain threatened the gathering, but the sun broke through as the morning progressed, providing a fitting backdrop to the festivities. As the old acquaintances reconnected and reminisced, at least two bands regaled the crowds with music.

About 11:00 a.m., the veterans assembled in the town square, joined by cadets from the local King's Mountain Military School. With the Yorkville Cornet Band in the lead, the cadets escorted the procession of veterans from the square to the grounds of the nearby Yorkville Female Institute. A grandstand, colorfully decorated by some of the town's ladies, had been built at the institute to host various speakers.

Arriving at the grandstand, the congregation was happy to see association president Cadwallader Jones, members of the association's executive committee, and assorted dignitaries, politicians, and clergy assembled. An honored guest from another war was on the platform, too: Samuel Smith, a War of 1812 veteran and local celebrity in his own right.

After a prayer service, Jones introduced keynote speaker McGowan, who in an exciting and sweeping address paid tribute to the regiment's exploits and the elevated reputation it had earned on the battlefield. He also honored officers who had been killed in combat and added a few intriguing vignettes from the war while furnishing a short but pleasant history of the brigade itself. In praising the regiment's efforts to bring the veterans together like this, McGowan rejoiced that "the battle scarred veterans of the glorious old Twelfth . . . were among the first to lead the way in having a reunion of all survivors, as it was the foremost in the charge in many a well fought field."

The accomplished brigadier also shed light on why an endeavor of this magnitude had yet to be undertaken:

6 "Twelfth Regiment Survivors," *Yorkville Enquirer*, Nov. 20, 1879, 2.

> For some time after the war, from the peculiar condition of the country, it was not considered prudent for the failing party to have reunions of the surviving soldiers of the war. It might have had a tendency to keep alive the passions engendered by the strife, which no good citizen desired. It might have been supposed to be the beginning of a new rebellion. But that condition of things has happily passed away. I hope the time has come when we can have re-unions of old Confederate soldiers in peace, and without creating the least suspicion of want of fidelity or loyalty to the government.[7]

McGowan was effusive in his praise for the 12th, professing: "We can only state in general terms the exact truth that the Twelfth regiment was one of the finest of that immortal army commanded by the peerless Lee, distinguished alike by its good conduct in camp and gallant in the field." He had been fortunate to observe the regiment at close quarters throughout the war, first as colonel of the 14th South Carolina and then as the brigade's commander. In McGowan's view, much of the credit for the regiment's gallant conduct in the field could be attributed to the leadership examples of its field officers and staff. That leadership, he would also emphasize, had come at a steep price, as three of the regiment's commanders—Dixon Barnes, John L. Miller, and Edwin Bookter—were killed leading the regiment in battle. Other than R. G. M. Dunovant, who led the way for a relatively short period, the only full colonel to survive the war was Cadwallader Jones, who had been forced to resign a few months after assuming command because of his health.

Unfortunately, the qualities that made the 12th stand out as it had in combat—aggressiveness, recklessness, impetuosity, and bravery—also became factors in the paucity of available primary source material to help document the regiment's story. After all, many who could have written recollections and reminiscences died during the war, as only about 150 men remained in the ranks at Appomattox. Had they survived, field officers certainly would have taken time to recount their Civil War experiences, likely joining the growing market for such reminiscences as the 19th century drew to a close.

Dunovant, the 12th's first colonel, served for only eight months, and his association with the regiment thereafter is somewhat of an anomaly. Although he survived the war, Dunovant never made a genuine effort to identify as a member of the 12th, and it does not appear that those in charge of the regimental reunion committees made any attempt to bring him into the fold either. There is no evidence he followed the regiment's activities once he left command or ever planned

7 "Reunion of Old Comrades," *Yorkville Enquirer*, Aug. 26, 1880, 1.

to participate in a reunion. Although he was the 12th's first colonel, Dunovant's name is conspicuously absent from much of the material the soldiers wrote, and he failed to leave any known postwar accounts of his time in the regiment. Unfortunately, his after-action reports, which were detailed at least, touched on only a limited timetable—the most valuable being the battle of Port Royal Sound in November 1861.

Even though Dixon Barnes, Dunovant's successor, commanded the regiment for only six months, he led it during the dreadful battles of the Seven Days' campaign and then at Second Manassas and Sharpsburg, the period in which the 12th established its reputation as a sterling combat regiment. Barnes, however, left only one after-action report of those operations (i.e., the Seven Days'). Mortally wounded at Sharpsburg, he never authored reports of the 12th's efforts in that battle—which had been truly remarkable despite a strategic loss—or the resounding victory at Second Manassas a few weeks earlier. His untimely death meant that he would not survive to recount any of these engagements or offer reminiscences of any kind.

Cadwallader Jones, like Dunovant, survived the war, although he commanded the regiment in only one battle: Fredericksburg. A report of that action was either lost to time or never written, and there is no record he attempted to author a significant postwar account of his service. As a colonel, lieutenant colonel, and major commanding in 1861–62, he would have been in a position to provide an insightful recollection of the regiment's actions up to his resignation in early 1863. Interestingly, although Jones had resigned command because of his health, he outlived most of his fellow officers—finally dying on December 1, 1899, just shy of the start of the 20th century. That meant he had an astounding 34 years of postwar life to pick up a pen and write something significant, but apparently never did.

Another commander who eschewed the written word before his death, it seems, was John Miller, who led the regiment for more than a year after serving as a company commander from the beginning of the conflict in 1861. He was mortally wounded during the fighting at the Wilderness in May 1864, and no after-action reports or firsthand accounts that he might have written before then have survived or been located. Had he indeed lived, personal information about his time as a company commander, the 1863 battle of Chancellorsville, the invasion into Pennsylvania and the subsequent battle of Gettysburg, and perhaps even the Overland campaign would have been welcome treasures in supplementing the regiment's history.

Edwin F. Bookter, meanwhile, served as a company and regimental officer until late in the war, fighting in nearly every major engagement. He was struck down by a bullet in the fall of 1864 at Petersburg—just as he assumed command of the 12th. He is not known to have authored any reports or personal accounts. His death—and the inability of his successors R. M. Kerr and J. C. Bell to contribute any after-action reports or other postwar documentation, whether intentional or not—means no detailed analysis or description of the regiment's actions by a commanding officer from 1863 to 1865 exists.

As it stands, there are only a few official after-action reports from commanding officers of the 12th: Dunovant's report on the action at Forts Walker and Beauregard in 1861; Barnes's reports on the fight near Pocataligo in January 1862 as well as the Seven Days' campaign; and Maj. William H. McCorkle's brief reports documenting the battles of Second Manassas and Sharpsburg.

Unequivocally, the deaths of Barnes, Miller, and Bookter and the lack of postwar recollections by surviving company officers—combined with A. P. Hill's death in the final days of the war—have been considerations in the damning absence of recognition for the regiment in the Army of Northern Virginia's historiography. No doubt Hill would have been responsible in some manner for a comprehensive history of both the Light Division and the Third Corps, which surely would have highlighted the myriad contributions of McGowan's Brigade and the 12th in particular, had he survived the war.

Hill's Light Division successor, Dorsey Pender, was mortally wounded at Gettysburg, and thereby left no reports or subsequent writings of the division. And Pender's successor, Cadmus Wilcox, provided no history or significant accounts of his command tenure—quite unfortunate given that he commanded the Light Division longer than even A. P. Hill.

* * *

The 12th South Carolina was indisputably one of the hardest-hitting and aggressive regiments in the entire Army of Northern Virginia, and McGowan's Brigade could be counted among the best in this famed fraternity. Again, the absence of Third Corps and Light Division accounts and histories adds to the reasons the 12th and McGowan's command are underrepresented in Confederate histories—compared, for instance, to such famed units as the Texas Brigade or Stonewall Brigade, which served, respectively, in the First and Second Corps under James Longstreet and Stonewall Jackson. That Longstreet survived the war, combined with the postwar controversy surrounding his alleged shortcomings at Gettysburg, have long driven interest in his First Corps, with countless first-person accounts appearing in "Battles and Leaders of the Civil War" and other such volumes.

Jackson and the Second Corps had generated their fame and prominence well before the end of the war. If anything, Jackson's death after the fighting at

Chancellorsville only magnified his fame, and many of his surrogates did all they could during the war and after to ensure that the Second Corps received a rightful place in the history of the army. Regrettably, Hill's Corps, which included not only the Light Division but also Henry Heth's and Richard Anderson's divisions, have never achieved that level of appeal. As the daughter of Col. Joseph Brown of the 14th South Carolina aptly explained in a biography of her father, Hill's "men were men of action only—vigorous, impetuous action—but not writers. . . . they wrote fewer reports than officers of other corps[;] therefore their part was less definitely known to historians."[8]

Even during the war, the men of the 12th were aware that the regiment's success was often marginalized. Writing about the prevalence of the Richmond newspapers to diminish the actions of non-Virginia regiments in favor of those from the Old Dominion, a soldier in Company I lamented in an 1862 letter: "It is a notable fact . . . that these papers represent Virginians as accomplishing more than all the balance of the troops from the other states. It seems strange indeed that they know of nothing any other Regiment or brigade [has] done. . . . We do not object to giving praise where it is due, and there is no doubt [that] Virginians fought as bravely as any other State troops, but then, they did not do all the work themselves."

The following year, a soldier wrote to the *Lancaster Ledger* that the officers of McGowan's Brigade were "gallant, patriotic and intelligent gentlemen" and "none who have done harder fighting . . . yet, there has been less said about them." The obvious favoritism did not escape the scrutiny of the officers either. Writing in June 1864 after taking command of McGowan's Brigade, newly minted Brig. Gen. James Conner took issue with the Virginia-centric phenomenon in the press while describing in a letter home a minor skirmish near Richmond: "In about two hundred yards we struck the enemy, and forced him steadily back, for a mile, retaking all the ground and occupying the key points, and threw up breastworks. I see by the papers that [Virginian Brig. Gen. William] Mahone took part in it. He is a Virginian and that accounts for it. The only two Brigades engaged were mine and [Alfred] Scales and was nothing more than a skirmish."

Colonel Jones touched on this inequality at the August 1879 Companies C & F reunion, stating emphatically after assuming the chairmanship: "I address men who composed a regiment that has never been known to turn its back on

8 Brown, *A Colonel at Gettysburg and Spotsylvania*, 188.

the enemy—a regiment, it is true of which not much has been said in history, but which has a bright record in the Army of Northern Virginia."[9]

The men who did write about their experiences, such as J. R. Boyles, William Dunlop, Cadwallader Jones Jr., and William Miller, endeavored to fill in as many gaps as possible. Their accounts, however, often lacked detail or were incomplete due to circumstances beyond their control. Boyles's wonderful 1890 account, *Reminiscences of the Civil War*, was exceptionally well-written and detailed. Nevertheless, his wounding at Gettysburg and subsequent loss of a leg prevented him from serving in the field after July 1, 1863, which meant that the ensuing parts of his work focused not on warfare but his hospitalization, his time in captivity, and his return home.

Dunlop was also an exceptional and prolific writer; however, his account, *Lee's Sharpshooters*, begins in 1864 after he was assigned command of McGowan's sharpshooter battalion and concentrates more on the details and actions of that body rather than the 12th as a whole. Captain Cadwallader Jones Jr., Colonel Jones's wonderfully erudite son, rose to command of Company H and penned the best cache of postwar letters of any soldier in the regiment. His letters to his brother in the early 1920s are replete with rich detail about various battles as well as vignettes and stories about life in the regiment. His analysis of the regiment's actions after Gettysburg, the Wilderness, Spotsylvania Court House, and the Petersburg campaign are especially valuable. If only there had been more.

William Miller of Company H fought the entire war and wrote about it, but his work lacks important details and there are extensive narrative gaps that frustrate well-intentioned attempts to piece together the hectic final year of the war. And though brothers Joseph and William Templeton of Company B wrote dozens of letters home during the conflict, those letters were more often than not short, formulaic, and lacking in critical detail of battles or campaigns. Limited usually to observations about rations, health, and such minutiae, these dutiful missives were eventually published in the 1994 album *The Civil War Letters of Joseph and William Templeton*, but as the introduction to that work correctly points out: "The Templeton Letters cannot be said to belong to the body of vivid first-person accounts such as those of Samuel Watkins or Elisha Hunt Rhodes."[10]

* * *

9 LOCAL, "Army Correspondence." *Lancaster Ledger*, July 23, 1862, 2; LOCAL, "For the Lancaster Ledger." *Lancaster Ledger*, May 13, 1863, 1; "Survivor's Reunion," *Yorkville Enquirer*, Aug. 7, 1879, 2; J. C. to My Dear Mother, June 15, 1864, in Moffett, *Letters of James Conner*, 133.

10 Templeton Letters Introduction, 1.

The 12th South Carolina was a multifaceted organization both on and off the battlefield. Some of the activities in the latter category varied from the formation of "Christian Associations," to the construction of chapels in camp to help spread the gospel, to the creation of committees to issue proclamations or endorse candidates for political office. Those sorts of enterprises clearly indicated that the soldiers were fully committed to society at large and to their families, friends, and communities hundreds of miles away in South Carolina, not just what was asked of them in preparing for combat or actually fighting, often against daunting odds. Whether they were volunteer warriors, career officers, gentlemen of standing, or barely literate farmers, fealty to this task never wavered.

The 12th's exploits and record in battle and on the march were arguably unmatched by any regiment in the Army of Northern Virginia. Routinely placed on the flank of the Brigade on contested terrain such as Gaines's Mill, Gettysburg, the Wilderness, and Spotsylvania Court House, the regiment was known to attack with swift and violent recklessness, invariably driving the enemy whenever and wherever it encountered it. This penchant for offensive-minded warfare was instilled in the regiment early in the war by Col. Dixon Barnes, who despised what he called "long taw firing" and favored closing in with the enemy and charging with the bayonet. The swift attacks he led at Gaines's Mill, Second Manassas, and Sharpsburg best illustrated his aggressive mind frame, one that endeared him to his superiors and gained the regiment a sterling reputation within the army.

Colonel James Armstrong of the 1st South Carolina recalled the 12th's trademark impetuosity during its 1883 reunion:

> How shall I describe your bold bearing and unflinching heroism during the struggle at Spotsylvania?—where, paradoxical as it may sound, the Twelfth was the first—I mean the first to reach the "Bloody Bend." This was by no means an uncommon occurrence. It seemed to me that the Twelfth was always in front, except when we were retiring, then they were fond of lagging behind so they would have the last shot at the enemy. . . . I have always regarded the charge of the Twelfth at Spotsylvania as one of the most striking scenes in the dread drama of war and well worthy of remembrance.[11]

Another prime example of the respect the 12th received from other regiments was a conversation Capt. John Kinsler had with the 1st South Carolina's colonel during the war. Kinsler recalled that while conversing in camp he told the unidentified colonel that the men in his regiment had high regard for the 1st and

11 "Twelfth Regiment Survivors," *Yorkville Enquirer*, Aug. 30, 1883, 1.

considered the 1st the brigade's best regiment. Taken aback, the colonel indicated that his men felt the 12th deserved that distinction. Recalled Kinsler: "[He] told me that when called into battle along with your Regiment, his men would say, 'It's all right today boys, we've got the Twelfth on our right.'"[12] And, in what can only be described as one of the, if not the highest compliment the regiment ever received from the most qualified and observant soldier in the brigade, J. F. J. Caldwell, the brigade's historian, stated frankly that the 12th was "the most rapid and resolute command in a charge I ever saw."

Cadwallader Jones Jr. was another surrogate eager to boast about the 12th's affinity for offense, writing after the war:

> We went into many a battle without knowing what was ahead of us. We were marched along, and carried into the very jaws of death, in all those greatest battles, without knowing any danger ahead. We had no time to know fear—we had no thought of it—we were in the midst of bullets & death and had but one feeling, and that was to charge, and we always did charge and were never stopped till we had driven back the enemy. As I have before told you, so far as I was individually concerned, it was only one time in all our great battles, that I fought behind works—and that was at Spotsylvania Court House. . . . We had works of course, and sometimes staid in them, but whenever it came to a fight, we went over them and charged out in the open.[13]

And though the regiment may have suffered a rare setback or was forced on occasion to retreat in battle, it almost never tasted outright defeat. Indeed, many of the men viewed only the mass retreat on the second day of the Wilderness as a tactical defeat and Gettysburg as the army's lone strategic defeat. As Jones recollected in one of his letters in 1922: "In my whole experience of four years in the war, I can't recall anytime when we were forced back except the time at the Wilderness and the only time that I know of when we retreated was after the battle of Gettysburg, and then we fell back leisurely across the river in pontoons."

In that same letter, however, he would rein in that assessment by acknowledging: "Of course, I suppose we were whipped in that battle, but along our line we thought at the time, that the Yankees could no more have driven us from our position than we could have driven them from theirs. . . . In all the battles we had in Virginia, our lines were never broken nor driven back." (It must be noted

12 "The Twelfth Regiment." *The News and Herald* (Winnsboro, SC), Aug. 23, 1879, 2; Caldwell, "McGowan's Brigade at the Battle of the Wilderness," August 17, 1882, 1.

13 Cadwallader Jones Jr. to My Dear Brother, Oct. 3, 1922, UNC.

that the captain happened to be on furlough during the regiment's hectic retreat from Petersburg and did not participate in any action during the subsequent Appomattox campaign.)[14]

The discipline instilled in the men through fastidious training and drill in the war's early months by commanders such as Barnes and the elder Cadwallader Jones was a major reason for the regiment's effectiveness and success throughout the war. The calming, mature personalities of Barnes and Jones—and subsequently men like Miller and, at the brigade level, McGowan—created a paternalistic relationship between officer and soldier that did not necessarily exist in counterpart regiments. That the regiment and brigade both survived intact to surrender at Appomattox speaks volumes to the leadership of those in command and the dedication of those who followed.

Few brigades, let alone divisions, could boast 900 men by the end of the war. With about 150 men in the ranks at Appomattox, the regiment still fielded all 10 companies, each intact with a leadership structure. While other regiments, brigades, and divisions disintegrated to some degree during the march west in April 1865, the 12th and McGowan's Brigade continued to operate as independent military entities. The regiment's rapid reorganization on April 4 after it was ravaged by a flank attack at Sutherland's Station and its ability to ford the Appomattox River near Farmville so proficiently on April 7 exemplified a well-led and disciplined command until the end.

In addition, the inclination of the men of the 12th to preserve the bonds they had made with fellow soldiers in camp and combat remained conspicuously strong well after the war. "I wish I could command words to express the gratification I feel to see my friends of the Twelfth once more," Kinsler said at the storied 1879 reunion. "I am proud to have been connected with that command—it is an honor that I would not part with for all other honors upon earth. There was not a better Regiment in the Confederate service."

The men of the 12th also never forgot that the tight-knit communities from which they hailed in northern South Carolina were all part of a much-broader community invested in the long-term survival of the Confederacy. Keeping contact through letters and correspondence to local newspapers not only kept families, friends, and the public informed of the regiment's progress, but it also nurtured a steady fellowship with the home front that helped invigorate the soldiers, reassuring them that their immense sacrifice was not being overlooked.

There is no question that the regiment's proximity to South Carolina also benefited and facilitated its success. Mail to and from the regiment was consistent

14 Ibid.

and allowed the expedient transfer of letters, supplies, foodstuffs, and clothing. The dependable contact with loved ones at home no doubt stiffened and reassured the men in their resolve. And as battle casualties took their toll, especially after 1863, it also helped that new volunteers and conscripts could be transferred swiftly the relatively short distance to Virginia to replenish the ranks.

A further benefit was that the communities from which the companies came were not subject to Federal occupation until relatively late in the war. In addition to resupplying the regiment with men and materiel, it was important in allowing the men to serve without the added pressure of knowing their hometowns were behind Union lines and cut off from communication. That only a few desertions in the 12th South Carolina occurred the last winter of the war shows that the men were not overly concerned about the safety of their families at a time even when Confederate fortunes overall were at a breaking point.

No other factor played a larger role in the regiment's social fabric and success, however, than religion. Testament to that could be found, for example, in the collaborative peacetime efforts several companies made to build altars for worship in their respective camp streets or when large parties traveled to hear sermons in nearby regimental camps. Religion brought the men together for a common purpose, whether they were officers of wealth and standing or common soldiers without means. It was an equalizer, like war itself, that bonded the men in a manner only they could fully comprehend. Living in such harsh conditions and facing constant bodily harm or death, the men of the 12th required something greater than patriotism and a $11 monthly payment to get them through the war's devastation and trauma—an outlet that provided a moral compass despite inevitable lapses of one's beliefs in moments of excessive passion, violence, or even unconscionable moral breaks as occurred against USCT troops at Second Deep Bottom in August 1864.

* * *

Annual 12th South Carolina reunions would take place at sites across the state until 1886. After the 1879 Companies C & F reunion and the 1880 regimental gathering, Lancaster Court House hosted the third such event on August 18, 1881, with Captain Kinsler delivering the keynote address. The fourth took place in Rock Hill on August 17, 1882, with the Rev. C. B. Betts—the regiment's much-admired former chaplain—providing the address. It was during the business meeting following Bett's speech that Henry Davis, then president of the survivors' association, expressed the desire to have a full, written regimental history of the 12th published. Davis would be handed the authority to "procure data" from the various company commanders still living to prepare such a history. Whatever became of this effort, however, remains unknown.[15]

For the fifth reunion, held in Columbia on August 16, 1883, Brig. Gen. James Conner—who briefly commanded McGowan's Brigade in the summer of 1864—had been asked to give the keynote address. Conner, his health failing, declined the invitation, and by the time of the reunion, he had indeed died. Stepping in was Col. James Armstrong of the 1st South Carolina, who in his remarks warmly praised the regiment's valor in battle.

Lieutenant Colonel Edward McCrady, also of the 1st South Carolina, delivered the address at the following year's reunion, August 21, 1884, in Wallhalla. McCrady regaled the veterans with an in-depth history of the 12th's performance at Second Manassas. His keynote address, in fact, would be published in the *Southern Historical Society Papers*, the premier postwar outlet for officers and men to share stories, vignettes, honors, and spirited debates.[16]

Although a seventh reunion was planned for 1885, it was canceled when the 6th South Carolina Regiment Survivors' Association extended an invitation for veterans of the 12th to attend a battlefield tour of Gaines's Mill, the site of momentous battles in both 1862 (Seven Days') and 1864 (Overland campaign). Discounted roundtrip train tickets for the trek to Richmond were sold for $5.75 and good for one week. With so many men taking the opportunity to travel north to view the ground marking the regiment's first standup fight in Virginia, the 12th's reunion was postponed until October and was eventually canceled. And because of the popularity of the Gaines's Mill battlefield tour, the survivors' association leaders decided to hold the 1886 reunion in Fredericksburg.[17]

No reunions for the entire regiment would take place after 1886, although Companies C and F held one in Winnsboro on October 1, 1887. Soldiers from other companies likely attended, but the event was not promoted as an entire regimental effort. That fall, a reunion of all five of McGowan's regiments was scheduled for December 13 in Columbia, but it was canceled and never rescheduled. In November 1888, William S. Dunlop organized a gathering of 12 or so sharpshooters from his battalion, but that was likely the only reunion of its kind.

15 "Reunion of Old Comrades," *Yorkville Enquirer*, Aug. 26, 1880, 1; "Reunion of the Twelfth Regiment," *Yorkville Enquirer*, Sept. 1, 1881, 4; "Survivor's Association," *Yorkville Enquirer*, Aug. 24, 1882, 3.

16 "Twelfth Regiment Survivors," *Yorkville Enquirer*, Aug. 30, 1883, 1.

17 "Twelfth Regiment Survivors," *Yorkville Enquirer*, July 23, 1885, 1; "Twelfth Regiment Survivors," *Yorkville Enquirer*, Aug. 27, 1885, p. 2; "Twelfth Regiment Reunion," *Yorkville Enquirer*, Sept. 10, 1885, 2; "Twelfth Regiment Survivors," *Yorkville Enquirer*, Sept. 24, 1885, 2.

The record is devoid of "official" reunions of any scale for the regiment or brigade after 1888, though about 65 men representing Companies A, B, H, D, G, and K participated in a York County reunion for Confederate veterans on August 6, 1891, which included veterans from other Palmetto State regiments as well as some from other states. Attending that event were Maj. William McCorkle and Thomas J. Roach, the man who had assisted Pvt. Enoch Blackmon of Company H in preventing the regiment's colors from being surrendered at Appomattox.

In 1895, York County hosted another reunion encompassing several regiments, with nearly 60 men from the 12th participating, including the aging Cadwallader Jones. This occasion was likely the last time a significant number of men from the regiment gathered in one place. By this time, many veterans of the 12th had joined the "Micah Jenkins Camp of Confederate Veterans," a postwar association and forerunner of the Sons of Confederate Veterans that became a melting pot of the various regimental associations.

Two years later, David Moore and I. W. Ruff traveled to Nashville with the 12th's "old and tattered" battle flag to take part in a reunion of Confederate veterans from across the south. And in what can only be described as an amazing accomplishment for those that attended, an obscure account from 1913 indicates that a few veterans from Company I's "Lancaster Hornets"—including the famed sharpshooter, Ben Powell—attended the 50th reunion/anniversary of the battle of Gettysburg.[18]

The story of what became of the 12th's final battle flag is fascinating. After removing it from the staff in the field at Appomattox prior to the surrender ceremony so it would not fall into Yankee hands, Blackmon sewed the banner into the lining of his jacket and carried it home to Rock Hill. The flag was special to him, and he retained possession of it for some time after the war. Inscribed with the names of 31 engagements, which were stenciled to its folds, the flag was a symbol of the heroism and sacrifice of his comrades and was no doubt one of his most prized possessions.

With the advent of the regimental reunions in the 1880s, it appears pressure was placed on Blackmon to part with the banner and donate it to the regimental survivors' association, which he "reluctantly" agreed to do at the 1882 reunion.

18 N. C. Robertson, "Twelfth Regiment Meeting," *Yorkville Enquirer*, Oct. 19, 1887, 4; "Reunion Postponed," *Yorkville Enquirer*, Dec. 14, 1887, 2; "McGowan's Brigade," *Yorkville Enquirer*, Nov. 21, 1888, 2; "Confederate Veterans," *Yorkville Enquirer*, Aug. 12, 1891, 1. One 12th South Carolina veteran attendee at this reunion, Dan Witherspoon, was listed and described as "colored"; "Survivor's Re-union," *Yorkville Enquirer*, Oct. 17, 1896, 2; "Scraps and Facts," *Yorkville Enquirer*, June 16, 1897, 2; "York County Survivors," *Yorkville Enquirer*, Aug. 30, 1895, 1. One 12th South Carolina veteran attendee at this reunion, Jim Harris, was listed and described as "Catawba Indian"; "Went to Gettysburg," *Yorkville Enquirer*, July 8, 1913, 2.

Who retained possession of the flag thereafter is unrecorded; on October 30, 1907, however, the flag was presented to South Carolina Gov. Martin Ansel "for preservation in the relic room at the capitol." Teaming to make the presentation were Pvt. Allen Jones (Cadwallader Jones's son), Sgt. David Moore of Company D, Thomas Sligh of Company D, James Martin of Company D, W. A. Marshall of Company I, and W. B. Bruce of Company I. To this day, the flag resides at the Confederate Relic Room in Columbia, unsurrendered and still in southern hands. Somewhere, Col. Dixon Barnes is smiling.[19]

* * *

With the golden era of reunion and reconciliation over in the late 1880s and early 1890s, the memory of the war began to fade from the collective minds of the country. Notwithstanding an occasional article featuring a recollection or reminiscence, the newspapers in the communities where the regiment was formed usually reported veteran obituaries more than other stories of the war. As America approached the turn of the century, the war was omnipresent in the collective consciousness of South Carolinians, but it also became a secondary focus as the generation who fought the war began to expire. With each passing year, fewer and fewer men were around to divulge the story of their exploits and deeds on the battlefield. With their deaths, the opportunity to record a more complete story of the regiment expired as well.

"It would be impossible on an occasion of this kind, to give anything like a history of the Twelfth Regiment, or tell half of its gallant deeds," McGowan conceded in his address at the 1880 reunion. "That would require a volume. If we were to undertake it, we could not escape the innumerable sins of both commission and omission. It is to be hoped that the Survivors' Association will collect the facts for some future historian. It would be a rich subject for pen or pencil. Surely, there will arise some descendant of the actors to record their achievements."[20]

McGowan perhaps said more than he knew at that 1880 reunion, but he was right. The history of "The Invincible Twelfth" and the soldiers who fought and perished for this unwavering regiment, is truly a rich subject—wrought with heroism, tragedy, emotion, success, failure, and inspiration. It is a story long overdue in the Army of Northern Virginia's historiography and one that deserves to be read and remembered.

19 "Battle-Scarred Flag of the Gallant 12th Regiment Presented to the State," *Lancaster News*, Nov. 2, 1907, 1.

20 "Reunion of Old Comrades," *Yorkville Enquirer*, Aug. 26, 1880, 1.

Bibliography

Primary Sources

Books

Allan, William. *Stonewall Jackson, Robert E. Lee, and the Army of Northern Virginia, 1862.* New York: Da Capo Press, 1995.

Benson, Susan Williams, ed. *Berry Benson's Civil War Book*. Athens, GA: The University of Georgia Press, 2007.

Boyles, J.R. *Reminiscences of the Civil War.* Columbia, SC: The Bryan Printing Company, 1892.

Caldwell, James Fitz James. *The History of a Brigade of South Carolinians.* Dayton, OH: Morningside Press, 1992.

Cozzens, Peter. *General John Pope: A Life for the Nation*. Urbana, IL: The University of Illinois Press, 2000.

Cutrer, Thomas, ed. *Longstreet's Aide: The Civil War Letters of Major Thomas J. Goree.* Charlottesville, VA: The University Press of Virginia, 1995.

Daly, Louise Haskell. *Alexander Cheves Haskell: The Portrait of a Man.* Norwood, MA: Plimpton Press, 1934.

Dickert, D. Agustus. *History of Kershaw's Brigade*. Dayton, OH: Morningside Bookshop, 1873.

Dunlop, William S. *Lee's Sharpshooters; or The Forefront of Battle*. Little Rock, AR: Tunnah & Pittard, 1899.

Freeman, Douglas S., ed. *Lee's Dispatches: Unpublished Letters of General Robert E. Lee, C.S.A., to Jefferson Davis and the War Department of the Confederate States of America, 1862–1865.* Baton Rouge, LA, The Louisiana State University Press, 1994.

Fremantle, Arthur Lyon. *Three Months in the Southern States: April*–June 1863. New York: John Bradburn, 1864.

Gallagher, Gary W., ed. *Fighting for the Confederacy: The Personal Recollections of General Edward Porter Alexander*. Chapel Hill, NC: University of North Carolina Press, 1989.

Gordon, John B. *Reminiscences of the Civil War*. New York: Charles Scribner's Sons, 1903.

Griffith, Harrison Patillo. *Variosa—A Collection of Sketches, Essays and Verses.* India: Skilled Books, 1911.

Long, Armistead. *Memoirs of Robert E. Lee.* Secaucus, NJ: The Blue and Grey Press, 1983.

Mackowski, Chris. *A Tempest of Iron and Lead: Spotsylvania Court House, May 8–21, 1864.* El Dorado Hills, CA: Savas Beatie, 2024.

Mackowski, Chris & White, Kristopher. *A Season of Slaughter: The Battle of Spotsylvania Court House, May 8–21, 1864.* El Dorado Hills, CA: Savas Beatie, 2013.

Jones, John B. *A Rebel War Clerk's Diary.* 2 Vols. Philadelphia, PA: Lippencott & Co., 1866.

Laborde, M. *Central Association for the Relief of the Soldiers of South Carolina: The Plan, and Address, Adopted by the Citizens of Columbia, October 20, 1862.* Charleston, SC: Steam-Power Press of Evans and Cogswell, 1862.

Lee, Robert E., Jr. *My Father, General Lee.* Garden City, NY: Doubleday & Company, Inc., 1960.

Littlejohn, Thomas A. "Recollections of a Confederate Soldier." Manassas National Battlefield Park Collection, copy, Vertical File V7-SC1, Gettysburg National Military Park Library.

McSwain, Eleanor, ed. *Crumbling Defenses or Memoirs and Reminiscences of John Logan Black, Colonel C.S.A.,* Macon, GA: The J.W. Burke Company, 1960.

Moffett, Mary Conner. *Letters of General James Conner, C.S.A.* Charleston, SC: The R. L. Bryan Co., 1950.

Morrison, James L., Jr., ed. *The Memoirs of Henry Heth.* Westport, CT: Greenwood Press, 1974.

Rhea, Gordon. *The Battle of Cold Harbor.* Fort Washington, PA: Eastern National Press, 2001.

_____. *The Battles for Spotsylvania Court House and the Road to Yellow Tavern, May 7–12, 1864.* Baton Rouge, LA: The Louisiana State University Press, 1997.

_____. *To the North Anna River: Grant and Lee, May 13–25, 1864.* Baton Rouge, LA: The Louisiana State University Press, 2000.

Rossino, Alexander B. *Calamity at Frederick: Robert E. Lee, Special Orders No. 191, and Confederate Misfortune on the Road to Antietam.* El Dorado Hills, CA: Savas Beatie, 2023.

Sorrel, Gilbert Moxley. *Recollections of a Confederate Staff Officer.* New York: The Neale Publishing Company, 1905.

Templeton, Joseph & Templeton, William. *The Civil War Letters of Joseph and William Templeton.* Columbia, SC: The South Caroliniana Library, 1994.

Welch, Spencer. *A Confederate Surgeon's Letters to His Wife.* New York: The Neale Publishing Company, 1911.

Official Publications

The War of the Rebellion: A Compilation of the Official Records of the Union and Confederate Armies, 128 Volumes. Washington, D.C.: Government Printing Office, 1880–1901.

Supplement to the War of the Rebellion: A Compilation of the Official Records of the Union and Confederate Armies. Wilmington, NC: Broadfoot Publishing Company, 1998.

Periodicals and Periodical Collections

Blummer, Thomas. "Record of Catawba Indians' Confederate Service." *The South Carolina Historical Magazine,* 96(3). July 1995.

Brock, Robert Alonzo, ed. *Southern Historical Society Papers.* 52 Vols. Richmond, VA: Virginia Historical Society, 1876–1959.

Brown, B. F. "A. P. Hill's Light Division," in *Confederate Veteran.* 40 Vols. Nashville, TN: National Historical Society, 1893–1932.

Capers, Ellison. "South Carolina," in *Confederate Military History,* edited by Clement Evans. 12 Vols. Atlanta, GA: Confederate Publishing Company, 1899.

Dunlop, William S. "The Confederate War: Company B, Twelfth S.C.V. in Bivouac and Battles," in the *Yorkville Enquirer* [Parts 1 through 6, October 23, 1889–November 27, 1889].

Field, Ron. "Clothing the Confederate Soldiers of South Carolina, 1861–1865," *The Military Collector & Historian*, 70(1):4-5 (2018).

Jones, Cadwallader Jr. *Cadwallader Jones Papers, 1847–1925*. Chapel Hill, NC. Southern Historical Collection/University of North Carolina, 2009. [Collection ID: 02487].

Leach, John. "John Leach to John Bachelder," in *The Bachelder Papers*, transcribed and edited by David L. and Audrey J. Ladd. 3 Vols. Dayton, OH: Morningside Books, 1994.

Miller, William Joseph. "My Experience as a Soldier in the Confederate Army," in UDC *Recollections and Reminiscences*. 11 Vols. Columbia, SC, 1992. pp. 216–225.

Perrin, Abner. *Abner Perrin to Governor Pickens*, July 29, 1863, in Milledge L. Bonham Jr., ed., "A Little More Light on Gettysburg." *Mississippi Valley Historical Review*, Vol. 24 (1937–38). p. 519.

Powell, Benjamin Medicus. "Benjamin Powell to Wife, November 21, 1907." Letter published in "The Westchester Civil War Round Table Newsletter." Croton Falls, NY, 1980.

United Daughters of the Confederacy/Georgia Division, *Confederate Reminiscences and Letters 1861-1865*. Vol. XIV. Atlanta, 2000.

United Daughters of the Confederacy/South Carolina Division, *Recollections and Reminiscences, 1861–1865 Through World War I*. 11 Vols. Columbia, SC, 1992. [LOC Catalog No. 90–62317]

_____. *South Carolina Women in the Confederacy* (Columbia, SC, 1907).

Wilcox, Cadmus, "Lee and Grant in the Wilderness," in *The Annals of the Civil War, Written by Leading Participants North and South* [originally published in the *Philadelphia Weekly Times*]. Dayton, OH: Morningside Books, 1988.

Online Sites

Campi, Jim. "A Roar From the Portals of Hell." American Battlefield Trust, https://www.battlefields.org/learn/articles/roar-portals-hell, accessed Jan. 29, 2025.

"Appomattox Court House: Order of Battle." [nps.gov/apco/order-of-battle.htm]

Newspapers

Abbeville [SC] *Press and Banner*
Augusta [GA] *Chronicle*
Camden [SC] *Confederate*
Carolina Spartan [Spartanburg, SC]
Charleston [SC] *Daily Courier*
Charleston [SC] *Mercury*
Daily Journal [Wilmington, NC]
Edgefield [SC] *Advertiser*
Keowee [SC] *Courier*
Lancaster [SC] *Ledger*
Lightwood Knot [SC] *Herald and Daily Expositor*
National Tribune [Washington, D.C.]
Newberry Herald [SC]
The News and Herald [Winnsboro, SC]
Richmond [VA] *Dispatch*
Richmond Enquirer [VA]
The State [Columbia, SC]
Twin City [NC] *Daily Sentinel*

Wilmington [NC] *Morning Star*
Yorkville [SC] *Enquirer*

Unpublished

Flowerday, Benjamin. "Painting a Picture of a South Carolina Regiment Marching into Pennsylvania: An Analysis of Clothing Requisitions of the 12th South Carolina During the Second Quarter of 1863." Unpublished paper in author's possession, 2024.

Helsel, Bob. Personal interview by author, August 27, 1994.

Keith, Willis. Wilkinson-Keith Papers, Charleston, SC: College of Charleston.

Mackowski, Chris. Conversation with author, January 29, 2025.

Maxcy Gregg Papers. University of South Carolina, Columbia, SC.

Wardlaw, Andrew B., Diary entry, Sept. 17, 1862. Copy in the collection of Robert K. Krick, Fredericksburg, VA.

Secondary Sources

Books

Allardice, Bruce. *More Generals in Gray*. Baton Rouge, LA, 1995.

Brown, Kent Masterson. *Retreat From Gettysburg*. Chapel Hill, NC: University of North Carolina Press, 2005.

Brown, Varina. *A Colonel at Gettysburg and Spotsylvania*. Columbia, SC: The State Company, 1931.

Crute, Joseph. *Units of the Confederate Army*. Gaithersburg, MD: Olde Soldier Books, Inc., 1987.

Freeman, Douglas S. *Lee's Lieutenants: A Study in Command*. 3 Vols. New York: Charles Scribner's Sons, 1942-1944.

Hardy, Michael C. *General Lee's Immortals—The Battles and Campaigns of the Branch–Lane Brigade in the Army of Northern Virginia, 1861–1865*. El Dorado Hills, CA: Savas Beatie, LLC, 2018.

Hennessy, John J. *Return to Bull Run: The Campaign and Battle of Second Manassas*. New York: Simon & Schuster, 1993.

Pierro, Joseph, ed. *The Maryland Campaign of September 1862—Ezra A. Carman's Definitive Study of the Union and Confederate Armies at Antietam*. New York: Taylor & Francis Group, LLC, 2008.

Reardon, Carol & Vossler, Tom. *A Field Guide to Antietam*. Chapel Hill, NC: The University of North Carolina Press, 2016.

Roberston, James. *General A. P. Hill, The Story of a Confederate Warrior*. New York: Random House, 1987.

_____. *Stonewall Jackson*. New York: Macmillian Publishing USA, 1997.

Tedards, Rosalind Todd. *Orr's Rifles*. Wilmington, NC: Broadfoot Publishing, 2017.

Periodicals and Periodical Collections

Jones, Willie. "Roll of Company H, 12th South Carolina Regiment," in UDC *Recollections and Reminiscences,* 6:456. 11 Vols. Columbia, SC, 1992.

McCrady, Edward Jr. "Heroes of the Old Camden District, South Carolina, 1776–1861," in Robert Alonzo Brock, ed., *Southern Historical Society Papers,* 16:3-14. 52 Vols. (Richmond, VA, 1888).

Government Documents

Bachelder, Jno. *Gettysburg Battlefield* [Map]. New York: Endicott & Co. Lithograph.

U.S. Government Printing Office. *Inspection Reports and Related Records Received by the Inspection Branch in the Confederate Adjutant and Inspector General's Office* [National Archives Microfilm Publication M935, Roll 10: Inspection Reports, No. 24, PP.12–39]. Washington, D.C.: War Department Collection of Confederate Records, Record Group 109; National Archives Building.

Index

Entries in *italics* denote images

About the Author

Benjamin L. Cwayna is an attorney in private practice and a prominent leader in the Civil War reenacting and living history community. For many years, Ben commanded the 12th South Carolina/4th Michigan Volunteer Infantry, Inc., a nationally recognized reenacting organization. He has been featured on the "Addressing Gettysburg Podcast" with Matt Callery and has dedicated his life to preserving the memory of the Civil War through living history demonstrations, presentations, and tours on numerous battlefields. A graduate of Michigan State University and Michigan State University College of Law, Benjamin resides with his son, Grant, in Grand Ledge, Michigan. An active member of the community, Cwayna is a member and past president of the Grand Ledge Rotary Club, volunteer coach, and participant in numerous other civic organizations.